NATURAL LANGUAGE GENERATION IN ARTIFICIAL INTELLIGENCE AND COMPUTATIONAL LINGUISTICS

THE KLUWER INTERNATIONAL SERIES IN ENGINEERING AND COMPUTER SCIENCE

NATURAL LANGUAGE PROCESSING AND MACHINE TRANSLATION

Consulting Editor

Jaime Carbonell

Other books in the series:

EFFICIENT PARSING FOR NATURAL LANGUAGE: A FAST ALGORITHM FOR PRACTICAL SYSTEMS, M. Tomita
    ISBN 0-89838-202-5

A NATURAL LANGUAGE INTERFACE FOR COMPUTER AIDED DESIGN, T. Samad
    ISBN 0-89838-222-X

INTEGRATED NATURAL LANGUAGE DIALOGUE: A COMPUTATIONAL MODEL, R.E. Frederking
    ISBN 0-89838-255-6

NAIVE SEMANTICS FOR NATURAL LANGUAGE UNDERSTANDING, K. Dahlgren
    ISBN 0-89838-287-4

UNDERSTANDING EDITORIAL TEXT: A Computer Model of Argument Comprehension, S.J. Alvarado
    ISBN: 0-7923-9123-3

NATURAL LANGUAGE GENERATION IN ARTIFICIAL INTELLIGENCE AND COMPUTATIONAL LINGUISTICS

Editors

Cécile L. Paris

William R. Swartout

William C. Mann

University of Southern California

Information Sciences Institute

KLUWER ACADEMIC PUBLISHERS

Boston/Dordrecht/London

Distributors for North America:
Kluwer Academic Publishers
101 Philip Drive
Assinippi Park
Norwell, Massachusetts 02061 USA

Distributors for all other countries:
Kluwer Academic Publishers Group
Distribution Centre
Post Office Box 322
3300 AH Dordrecht, THE NETHERLANDS

Library of Congress Cataloging-in-Publication Data

Natural language generation in artificial intelligence and
  computational linguistics / by editors, Cécile L. Paris, William R.
  Swartout, William C. Mann.
      p.   cm. — (The Kluwer international series in engineering and
  computer science ; SECS 119)
    Includes index.
    ISBN 978-1-4419-5125-0
    1. Natural language processing (Computer science)   2. Artificial
  intelligence.   3. Computational linguistics.   I. Paris, Cécile L.
  II. Swartout, William R.   III. Mann, William C.   IV. Series.
  QA76.9.N38N38   1991
  006.3 ′5—dc20   90–48885
                                                                     CIP

Copyright © 1991 by Kluwer Academic Publishers
Softcover reprint of the hardcover 1st edition 1991

Printed on acid-free paper.

Contents

Preface

One of the aims of Natural Language Processing is to facilitate the use of computers by allowing their users to communicate in natural language. There are two important aspects to person-machine communication: understanding and generating. While natural language understanding has been a major focus of research, natural language generation is a relatively new and increasingly active field of research. This book presents an overview of the state of the art in natural language generation, describing both new results and directions for new research.

The principal emphasis of natural language generation is not only to facilitate the use of computers but also to develop a computational theory of human language ability. In doing so, it is a tool for extending, clarifying and verifying theories that have been put forth in linguistics, psychology and sociology about how people communicate.

A natural language generator will typically have access to a large body of knowledge from which to select information to present to users as well as numerous ways of expressing it. Generating a text can thus be seen as a problem of decision-making under multiple constraints: constraints from the propositional knowledge at hand, from the linguistic tools available, from the communicative goals and intentions to be achieved, from the audience the text is aimed at and from the situation and past discourse. Researchers in generation try to identify the factors involved in this process and determine how best to represent the factors and their dependencies.

To generate text, a system must choose some information from its knowledge base (or determine which information is to be disregarded), decide how to organize it, and determine how to realize the text in natural language, which includes both deciding on lexical items and syntactic structures. While these tasks are related, there are two general classes of decisions to be made in generation: one type involves determining the content and organization of the text, while the other is concerned with choosing the lexical items and syntactic constructions which present the information most effectively. This has led to a common division of the generation process into a *text planning* component, and a *realization* component, which can in turn be divided into two tasks, that of choosing lexical items and that of making grammatical choices. All these components are concerned with making the appropriate choices in order to best express the 'meaning' at hand. Research in generation is concerned about all these aspects of the generation process, determining what factors are involved, and how the various tasks affect each other.

The papers in this volume were selected, based on peer review, from papers presented at the *Fourth International Workshop on Natural Language Generation*, which was attended by most of the leading researchers in the field of Natural Language Generation. This book brings together papers by internationally reknowned researchers describing the most current research in natural language generation, in all aspects of the generation process, with an emphasis on text planning and lexical choice, as much research has been done in these areas recently. This book is comprised of three sections: one on text planning, one on lexical choice, and one on grammar. Each is described briefly below.

Text planning

Recently, there have been significant advances in the area of text planning. These include: building flexible text planners that tailor their answers to users and allow systems to participate in a dialog with their users; identifying constraints that affect the text planning process; understanding the task of a text planning system, not only in terms of constructing texts but also in terms of being able to drive a realization component; and, finally, understanding the constraints that incremental generation imposes on the architecture of a generation system and the interaction of a text planner and the realization component. This section presents results of new research concerning these aspects of generation. The section ends with a discussion of the potential problems with user models in text generation, an issue very pertinent at this point, as many generation systems in the past have emphasized user modelling.

In their papers, Moore and Swartout as well as Paris present an approach to text planning in which a system plans a text in a top-down fashion, being responsive to some communicative goal a speaker has in mind, and rules of coherence. Information is selected from the knowledge base and organized into coherent text during the planning process. The tasks addressed in these works is that of generating texts for complex systems such as expert systems that interact with a wide variety of users. This imposes further constraints upon the generation process, such as the ability to participate in a dialogue with a user and the flexibility to tailor answers to users.

Because of the top-down approach adopted by these systems, however, the planning process is somewhat restricted, in that it cannot achieve opportunistic planning, that is the ability to somehow work into a text some information that the speaker considers to be relevant. In his approach Hovy adopts a paradigm in which both top-down and bottom-up planning is possible, thus enabling a system to do some opportunistic generation. Because of the bottom-up approach increases flexibility, constraints become even more important. McCoy and Cheng present constraints that can be used to control this process.

Uncovering and understanding the constraints on the generation process is an important concern in generation research. In his paper, Bateman shows how the methodology provided by systemic-functional grammars can be applied to uncover and organize the constraints and decision points in the generation of Japanese texts. Taking a different approach, Meteer examined the differences between original texts and revised versions of the texts produced by professional editors. Based on these differences, she was able to identify classes of revisions that can help in determining the decision points that control the variation between the original and revised texts.

Many generation systems perform all of their text planning in one stage and then pass the complete text plan to a realization component that can turn the plan into text. Reithinger's paper describes POPEL, which can plan text incrementally and thereby integrate more tightly the "what-to-say" concerns of the text planner with the "how-to-say-it" concerns of the realization component. Incremental generation is particularly important in supporting dialogue.

In the final paper in this section, Sparck-Jones discusses user modelling in generation. Her paper raises important questions concerning the feasibility of user modelling.

Lexical Choice

Lexical choice is an area of generation that has been given very little attention until recently. Many generation systems in the past simply associated one lexical item with a concept in a knowledge base and the lexical choice problem was not addressed. With the increase in sophistication of generation systems and the recognition that a concept can be realized in a English in a variety of ways, researchers have started looking at the problem of lexical choice in depth, from both linguistic and computational points of view. In doing so, they have pointed out the difficulty of the problem, how it needs to be addressed within a theoretical framework, and how it cannot just be studied by looking at the surface level in language.

In his paper, McDonald argues against the traditionally held view that lexical choice is a surface-level concern of the generator. In McDonald's view, lexical choice should not be viewed as a concern of the generator, but is a deep issue which is more appropriately addressed at the level of the underlying conceptual representation upon which the generator operates. McDonald shows how this view can result in a simpler processing architecture.

Taking a linguistic point of view, Matthiessen argues that lexical choice should not be considered in isolation, but instead should be viewed as part of the problem of lexicogrammatical choice. Iordanskaja, Kittredge and Polguère present an implementation of a generator based on the Meaning-Text Theory. In this system the lexicon plays a central role, influencing the realization process in several ways.

Grammatical resources

The grammar used in a text generation system is an important component of the system, as it makes decisions on how to syntactically express the desired information. In this section, Sigurd presents a grammar that takes into account discourse referents, and shows how this grammar makes it easier to keep track of both the sentence and discourse referents. De Smedt and Kempen present a grammar especially designed to handle the needs of incremental sentence generation. The section ends with a paper by McKeown and Elhadad which attempts to evaluate several grammar formalisms that have been used in generation.

To summarize, Natural Language Generation is still a relatively new field, which is receiving increasing research attention. Generators are now capable of participating in dialogues and producing texts using large, linguistically-motivated grammars, which are capabilities that were only hopes a few years ago. Significant progress has been made in the last five years of generation research. With increased interest in the field, we look forward to even more progress in the next five.

We would like to thank the following persons and institutions:

- Jeanine Yamazaki, Cindy Kagawa, and the administrative staff of the USC Marine Center for their help in organizing the workshop.

- The administrative staff of the Information Sciences Institute of the University of Southern California for efficient organizational backing in organizing the workshop.

- The participants of the workshop who all contributed to a successful workshop and who reviewed the papers for this book.

- David Benjamin for his help in formatting the papers.

- Kary Lau for her secretarial assistance during the book preparation.

- The American Association of Artificial Intelligence (AAAI), the Special Interest Group on Artificial Intelligence (SIGART) of the ACM, and the Association for Computational Linguistics (ACL) for their financial contributions towards the workshop.

- The Defense Advanced Research Projects Agency (DARPA) for their continuous financial support during the editing of this book, through a DSS-W contract (DSS-W Contract MDA903-87-C-0641) and a NASA Ames cooperative agreement (number NCC 2-520).

Cécile Paris
William Swartout
William Mann

Authors

John A. Bateman
USC/Information Sciences Institute
4676 Admiralty Way
Marina del Rey, CA 90292-6695
USA
bateman@isi.edu

Jeannette Cheng
University of Delaware
Newark
Delaware 19716
USA

Koenraad De Smedt
Nijmegen Institute for
Cognition Research and
Information Technology (NICI)
University of Nijmegen
6525 HR Nijmegen
THE NETHERLANDS
desmedt@hnykun53.bitnet

Michael Elhadad
Department of Computer Science
450 Computer Science Building
Columbia University
New York, N.Y. 10027
USA
elhadad@cs.columbia.edu

Eduard Hovy
USC/Information Sciences Institute
4676 Admiralty Way
Marina del Rey, CA 90292-6695
USA
hovy@isi.edu

Lidija Iordanskaja
Odyssey Research Associates
1290 Van Horne
Montreal QC H2V1K6
CANADA

Gerard Kempen
Nijmegen Institute for
Cognition Research and
Information Technology (NICI)
University of Nijmegen
6525 HR Nijmegen
THE NETHERLANDS
kempen@hnykun52.bitnet

Richard Kittredge
Departement de Linguistique
Universite de Montreal
C.P. 6128, succ. A
Montreal H3C 3J7 Quebec
CANADA
kittredg@iro.udem.ca

Christian Matthiessen
University of Sydney
Sydney
NSW 2006
AUSTRALIA
jafta@psych44.psych.su.oz.au

Kathleen F. McCoy
University of Delaware
Newark, Delaware 19716
USA
mccoy@udel.edu

David D. McDonald
Content Technologies. Inc.
14 Brantwood Road
Arlington
Massachussetts 02174
USA

Kathleen R. McKeown
Department of Computer Science
450 Computer Science Building
Columbia University
New York, N.Y. 10027, USA
mckeown@cs.columbia.edu

Marie W. Meteer
BBN Systems and Technologies
Corporation
10 Moulton Street
Cambridge, MA 02238
USA
mmeteer@bbn.com

Johanna D. Moore
Computer Science Department
and Learning Research and
Development Center
University of Pittsburgh
Pittsburg, PA 15260, USA
jmoore@cs.pitt.edu

Cécile L. Paris
USC/Information Sciences Institute
4676 Admiralty Way
Marina del Rey, CA 90292-6695
USA
paris@isi.edu

Alain Polguere
Odyssey Research Associates
1290 Van Horne, Montreal
QC H2V1K6, CANADA
polguere@IRO.UMontreal.CA

Norbert Reithinger
SFB 314: Artificial Intelligence – Knowledge-Based
Systems; FB 10 – Informatik IV
University of Saarbrucken, Im Stadtwald 15
D-6600 Saarbrucken 11, WEST GERMANY
bert@fb10vax.informatik.uni-saarland.dbp.de
bert%sbsvax@unido.uucp

Bengt Sigurd
Dept of Linguistics and Phonetics
Helgonabacken 12
S-223 69 LUND
SWEDEN
linglund@gemini.ldc.lu.se

Karen Sparck Jones
Computer Laboratory
University of Cambridge
Pembroke Street
Cambridge CB2 3QG
ENGLAND
ksj%computer-lab.cambridge.ac.uk

William R. Swartout
USC/Information Sciences Institute
4676 Admiralty Way
Marina del Rey
CA 90292-6695
USA
swartout@isi.edu

Part I

TEXT PLANNING

Chapter 1

A Reactive Approach to Explanation: Taking the User's Feedback into Account

Johanna D. Moore and William R. Swartout

Abstract: Explanation is an interactive process, requiring a dialogue between advice-giver and advice-seeker. Yet current expert systems cannot participate in a dialogue with users. In particular these systems cannot clarify misunderstood explanations, elaborate on previous explanations, or respond to follow-up questions in the context of the on-going dialogue. In this paper, we describe a reactive approach to explanation – one that can participate in an on-going dialogue and employs feedback from the user to guide subsequent explanations. Our system plans explanations from a rich set of explanation strategies, recording the system's discourse goals, the plans used to achieve them, and any assumptions made while planning a response. This record provides the dialogue context the system needs to respond appropriately to the user's feedback. We illustrate our approach with examples of disambiguating a follow-up question and producing a clarifying elaboration in response to a misunderstood explanation.

1.1   INTRODUCTION

Explanation is an interactive process, requiring a dialogue between advice-giver and advice-seeker. Yet current expert systems cannot participate in a dialogue with users. In particular these systems cannot clarify misunderstood explanations, elaborate on previous explanations, or respond to follow-up questions in the context of the on-going dialogue. In part, the explanation components of current expert systems are limited because they are quite simple. However, even the more sophisticated generation techniques employed in computational linguistics are inadequate for responding to follow-up questions. The problem is that both expert system explanation and natural language generation systems view generating responses as a *one-shot process*. That is, a system is assumed to have one opportunity to produce a response that the user will find satisfactory.

But is the one-shot model of explanation *appropriate*? The answer to this question is most certainly no. If it were appropriate, one would expect interactions to proceed from one topic to another, with listeners always understanding the speaker's statements. However, this is inconsistent with analyses of naturally occurring advisory dialogues. In a study of a "naturally occurring" expert system, Pollack *et al.* (1982) found that user-expert dialogues are best viewed as a negotiation process in which the user and expert negotiate the statement of the problem to be solved as well as a solution the user can understand and accept. In our own study of office-hour interactions between students and teaching assistants, we observed that students frequently did not fully understand the instructor's response. They frequently asked follow-up questions requesting clarification, elaboration, or re-explanation. In some cases follow-up questions took the form of a well-articulated query; in other cases, the follow-up was a vaguely articulated mumble or sentence fragment. Often the instructor did not have much to go on, but still had to provide an appropriate response.

Evidence from psycho- and sociolinguistics indicates that dialogue is a highly reactive process in which feedback plays an important role. Ringle and Bruce (1981) have noted the existence of *checking moves* in conversation whose primary purpose is to elicit information about the level of comprehension of the dialogue participants. In addition, there is evidence that speakers monitor the effect of their utterances. In a study of the direction of eye gaze during conversation, Kendon (1967) found that speakers tend to look away from their listeners as they begin a long utterance, and then look up at the listener towards the end of the utterance, usually during the last phrase, and continue to look at the listener thereafter. Kendon's interpretation of these results is that by looking away at the beginning of a long utterance, the speaker is shutting out one important source of input from his listener so that he can concentrate on planning what to say. But as the speaker approaches the end of the utterance, he reaches a "choice point" in the interaction where what he does next will depend largely on how the listener reacts. At this point, the speaker seeks information about the listener and therefore looks at him, i.e., the speaker is monitoring the effect of the execution of his plan.

The one-shot view of explanation is clearly inconsistent with analyses of naturally occurring advisory interactions. Moreover, if a system has only one opportunity to produce a text that achieves the speaker's goals without over- or under-informing, boring or confusing the listener, then that system must have an enormous amount of detailed knowledge about the listener. The one-shot view of explanation has led to the over-emphasis of *user modeling* as a source of leverage for better text production while other sources have been ignored. Much recent research has been devoted to demonstrating how the quality of responses generated can be improved given a detailed model of the user – including what the user knows about the domain, how information should be presented to that user, and so forth (Appelt, 1985; McCoy, 1989; Paris, 1988; Kass and Finin, 1988). However, approaches that require a detailed model of the user are suspect since it is unlikely that we will be able to build complete and correct user models. Sparck Jones (1984) has questioned not only the feasibility of acquiring a detailed user model, but also of verifying its correctness, and the tractability of utilizing such a model to affect an expert system's reasoning and generation of responses. Further, by focusing on user models, researchers have ignored the rich source of guidance that people use in producing explanations, namely feedback from the listener. By abandoning the one-shot assumption, we can make use of that guidance.

We believe that a more *reactive* approach to explanation is required – one that accepts feedback from the user about the understandability of its explanations and alters its plans if necessary. We believe an expert system explanation facility should include the ability to:

- monitor the effects of its utterances on the hearer

- recover if feedback indicates the listener is not satisfied with the response

- answer follow-up questions taking into account previous explanations – *not* as independent questions,

- offer further explanations even if the user does not ask a well-formulated follow-up question.

- construct responses taking into account information in the user model if it is available, but not require it.

In this paper, we claim that the reactive capabilities we desire can be provided by a system that explicitly represents and reasons about the "design" of the explanations it produces. We describe a model that treats explanation generation as a planning problem and show how the reasoning about the design of an explanation can be captured and used to endow a system with the ability to elaborate on previous explanations, provide clarifications, and answer follow-up questions in the context of previous explanations.

In the sections that follow, we first discuss the limitations of current explanation systems in more detail. We also describe approaches to producing multi-sentential text taken in natural language generation and identify the reasons why those approaches could not immediately be adopted to provide the reactive capabilities we desire. We then present an overview of the reactive approach, followed by a more extensive description of the architecture of our explanation system. Two detailed examples are given. The first shows how the system disambiguates a follow-up why-question and the second demonstrates the system's ability to offer an elaboration in response to the user's feedback indicating that an explanation was not understood. Elsewhere, we have shown how our approach can be used to select perspective when describing or comparing objects (Moore, 1989), and to avoid repeating information that has already been communicated (Moore and Paris, 1989). We have also been able to exploit the information about the design of an explanation that our system records in order to build a hypertext-like interface that allows users to point to the portion of the system's explanation they would like clarified (Moore and Swartout, 1990).

1.2   LIMITATIONS OF CONVENTIONAL EXPLANATION SYSTEMS

Much of the early research on explanation was done in the context of MYCIN, a rule-based expert system for providing diagnostic and therapeutic advice about a patient with an infection (Davis, 1976). Experience with the MYCIN system showed that it often gave responses that users found unsatisfactory. To understand the reasons for this, MYCIN's builders studied several examples of situations where the system produced an inadequate response to a user's query (Buchanan and Shortliffe, 1984). They identified three problems which caused the inadequate responses:

1. lack of support knowledge, in particular the underlying knowledge explaining why the conclusion of a rule follows logically from its premises.

2. misinterpretation of user's intent in asking a question. They identified examples of simple questions that had four or five possible meanings depending on what the user knows, the current diagnostic context, and the content of previous dialogue.

3. failure to deal with context in which a question was asked, i.e., follow-up questions are not answered in context.

The first of these problems has to do with the kinds of domain knowledge represented in the system and the way that knowledge is structured. In

MYCIN, much of the knowledge needed for explanation was represented implicitly or not at all – see (Clancey, 1983; Swartout, 1983) for a good discussion of this topic. The problem of enhancing the knowledge bases of expert systems to include the kinds of knowledge needed to support explanation has been dealt with extensively elsewhere (Swartout, 1981; Clancey, 1981; Swartout and Smoliar, 1987) and will not be discussed further here. However, the second two problems cannot be alleviated by improvements in the knowledge bases and domain reasoning strategies of systems alone. These problems stem from the fact that a *dialogue* is occurring between the system and the user. To solve them requires building mechanisms into the system for dialogue support.

We believe there are three main reasons why current systems cannot participate in a dialogue with their users. First, to be able to clarify a misunderstood explanation or respond to a follow-up question in context, a speaker must understand the explanation he has produced. Unfortunately, current expert systems produce explanations by filling in templates or using canned text and thus have little or no "understanding" of their own explanations. They do not represent the goal of the explanation, what rhetorical purposes are served by individual clauses in the text, or what assumptions about the listeners knowledge may have been made. Lacking this knowledge, they cannot engage in a dialogue.

Second, current systems always interpret questions in the same way. For example, in the MYCIN system when a user types "why?" after the system has asked a question or produced an explanation, MYCIN assumes that the user is asking what higher-level domain goal gave rise to the current one. Subsequent "whys" retrieve information about still higher-level domain goals that posted the ones just described. As we discuss later, this single interpretation fails to take into account the dialogue context and can be unnatural.

The third problem with current systems is that they typically have only a single response strategy associated with each question type. Making oneself understood often requires the ability to present the same information in multiple ways or to provide different information to illustrate the same point. Without multiple strategies for responding to a question, a system cannot offer an alternative response even if it understands why a previous explanation was not satisfactory.

1.3 RELATED WORK IN NATURAL LANGUAGE GENERATION

Computational models of text generation put forth to date fall into two extremes. In one approach, language is viewed as action that is planned with the intention of achieving the speaker's goals (Cohen and Perrault, 1979; Appelt, 1985). In this view, text is planned by reasoning about the beliefs of the hearer and speaker and the effects of surface speech acts (e.g., REQUEST, INFORM) on these beliefs. Thus far, implementations of this approach have been successfully employed to produce short, one- or two-sentence utterances, see for example (Appelt, 1985). As currently proposed, this approach offers no explicit theory of coherence, i.e., there is no knowledge about how to combine clausal units into larger bodies of coherent text to achieve a speaker's goals. The approach assumes that appropriate axioms could be added to generate larger bodies of text and the text produced will be coherent as a by-product of the planning process. However, this has not been demonstrated.

Generating explanations from expert or advice-giving systems requires the ability to define terms, compare and contrast alternative methods for achieving a goal, explain a causal model, or justify a result. Texts of this nature are often paragraph-size and thus this approach, in its current form, cannot be directly applied to the tasks required for explaining the knowledge and behavior of an expert system.

To produce the larger bodies of text required by these more complex responses, other researchers have turned to an approach that makes use of script-like structures (schemata) to generate coherent multi-sentential texts achieving a given discourse goal. Schemata have been successfully employed in several systems to perform tasks such as describing and comparing entities in a database (McKeown, 1985), providing corrective responses to a user's object-related misconceptions (McCoy, 1989), and describing complex physical objects (Paris, 1988).

Schemata encode standard patterns of discourse structure, but do not include knowledge of how the various parts of the schema relate to one another or what their intended effect on the hearer is. For example, McKeown (1985) noted that speakers frequently define or describe objects in terms of their constituent parts in the following way:

1. identify the object as a member of some generic class or give attributive information about it;

2. introduce constituents of the object being defined;

3. provide characteristic information about each constituent in turn;

4. provide attributive or analogical information about the object being defined.

This patterns is embodied in the *constituency schema* shown in Figure 1.1.

Note that this pattern says *what* to do when, e.g., introduce constituents of the object, give attributive information about a constituent, but does not say

---

[1]The "{}" indicate optionality, "/" indicates alternative, "+" indicates that the item may appear 1 or more times, and "*" indicates that the item is optional and may appear 0 or more times.

Identification/Attributive
Constituency
Cause-effect*/Attributive*/
    {Depth-identification/Depth-attributive
      {Particular-illustration/Evidence}
      {Comparison; Analogy/Renaming} }+
  {Amplification/Explanation/Attributive/Analogy}

Figure 1.1: TEXT Constituency Schema[1]

---

why this information is being presented. The schema does not make explicit what effects these portions of text are intended to achieve on the hearer, nor does it indicate how later clauses are (rhetorically) related to the first clause. From a schema such as this, a system only knows what to say and in what order it may be said. Except for the highest level goal, in this case *describe object*, the system does not understand the reasons for the utterances it produces.

A schema can be viewed as the result of a "compilation" process where the *rationale* for all of the steps in the process has been compiled out. What remains is the top-level goal and the sequence of primitive acts that can achieve that goal. All of the intermediate structure, i.e., subgoals expressing the desired effects of portions of the text on the hearer, rhetorical strategies used to achieve these goals, has been lost. Because of this compilation, a schema is computationally efficient. However, if the hearer does not understand the utterance produced, it is very difficult to recover. Without the information that has been compiled out, the system cannot know which part of the schema failed to achieve its effect on the hearer and which rhetorical strategy failed to achieve this effect. If a system knows only the *top-level* discourse goal that was being achieved by the text (e.g., describe entity, persuade the hearer to perform an action), and not what effects the individual parts of the text were intended to have on the hearer and how they fit together to achieve this top-level goal, its only recourse is to use a different strategy to achieve the top-level goal. It is not able to re-explain or clarify any *part* of the explanation. This will severely limit the system's ability to recover from failures.

1.4 SYSTEM OVERVIEW

In an attempt to alleviate some of these problems, we have built an explanation component for an expert system. To provide the capabilities we described above, we have found the need to incorporate the following in our system design:

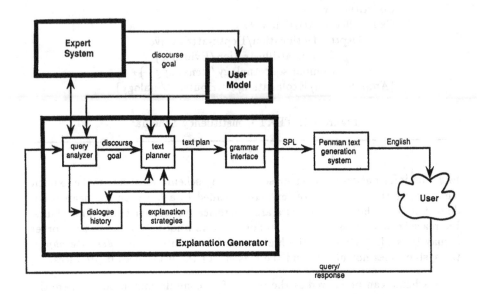

Figure 1.2: Architecture of Explanation System

- to plan responses such that the intentional and rhetorical structure of the responses is explicit and can be reasoned about,

- to keep track of conversational context by remembering not only what the user asks, but also the planning process that led to an explanation,

- to taxonomize the types of (follow-up) questions that are asked and understand their relationship to the current context, and

- to provide flexible explanation strategies with many and varied plans for achieving a given discourse goal.

In order for the system to understand what it has said and be able to reason about its utterances in responding to follow-up questions, we must capture the knowledge that has been compiled out of script-like schemata. Our planner reasons about the intended effects of speech acts on the hearer's beliefs and the rhetorical relations between speech acts when they are used to achieve these effects.

Our explanation generation facility, which is the topic of this paper, is part of the Explainable Expert Systems (EES) framework (Neches *et al.*, 1985). When an expert system is built in EES, an extensive development history is created that records the goal structure and design decisions behind the expert system. This structure is available for use by the explanation facility.

We have used EES to construct a prototype expert system, called the Program Enhancement Advisor (PEA) (Neches *et al.*, 1985), which we are using as a testbed for our work on explanation generation. PEA is an advice-giving system intended to aid users in improving their Common Lisp programs by recommending transformations that enhance the user's code.[2] The user supplies PEA with the program to be enhanced. PEA begins the dialogue by asking what characteristics of the program the user would like to improve. The user may choose to enhance any combination of readability, maintainability, and efficiency. PEA then recommends transformations that would enhance the program along the chosen dimensions. After each recommendation is made, the user is free to ask questions about this recommendation.

An overview of the explanation generation facility (and its relation to the PEA expert system) is shown in Figure 1.2. To interact with the user, the expert system posts a discourse goal (e.g., persuade the hearer to do an act, describe an entity) to the text planner. A discourse goal may be posted as a result of reasoning in the expert system or as a result of a query from the user (see Figure 1.2). User queries must first be interpreted by the *query analyzer*. Even though we assume the user poses queries in a stylized notation,[3] ambiguities may still arise. It is the responsibility of the query analyzer to disambiguate the query and form the appropriate discourse goal. An example of an ambiguous follow-up question and the process we use to disambiguate it appears in Section 1.5.2.

In the plan language, discourse goals are represented in terms of the effects that the speaker intends his utterance to have on the hearer. The speaker may intend that the hearer believe some proposition, know about some concept, have some goal, or perform a certain action. Details of the representational primitives used in our system are beyond the scope of this paper. Interested readers are referred to (Moore, 1989). For clarity, we provide English paraphrases of the terminology in our examples.

Suppose that the user has indicated that one of the characteristics of the program he would like to enhance is readability. The expert system might wish to recommend that the user replace the function CAR with the function FIRST. To do so, the expert system would post the following discourse goal to the text planner:

(GOAL USER (DO USER REPLACE-1))

where

---

[2] PEA recommends transformations that improve the "style" of the user's code. It does not attempt to understand the content of the user's program.

[3] To avoid the myriad problems of parsing unrestricted natural language input, we require that the user's questions be posed in a stylized language.

```
REPLACE-1 = (REPLACE (actor USER)
                     (object CAR-FUNCTION)
                     (generalized-means FIRST-FUNCTION))
```

This goal says that the speaker wishes to achieve the state in which the hearer (i.e., the user) has adopted the goal of doing the replacement. The PEA system recommends transformations to the user. In many instances the system is capable of performing the transformation. In such cases, while the actual replacement is done by the system, the user's approval is required.

Using a top-down hierarchical expansion planning mechanism (Sacerdoti, 1975), the *text planner* constructs utterances to achieve discourse goals. When a discourse goal is posted, the text planner searches its library of explanation strategies looking for those that can achieve the goal. A strategy is selected and may in turn post subgoals for the planner to refine. As the system plans explanations to achieve its discourse goals, it keeps track of any assumptions it makes about what the user knows as well as alternative strategies that could have been used to achieve discourse goals. Planning continues in this fashion until all subgoals have been refined into primitive operators, i.e., speech acts such as INFORM, RECOMMEND. The planning process will be discussed in detail in Section 1.4.3 once we have discussed the planning language in more detail.

The result of the planning process is a *text plan* for achieving the original discourse goal. This text plan is recorded in the *dialogue history* and passed to the *grammar interface* which transforms the text plan into a sequence of specifications in Sentence Plan Language (SPL) (Kasper, 1989). These SPL specifications are passed, a sentence at a time, to the Penman text generation system (Mann and Matthiessen, 1983; Matthiessen, 1984) for translation into English. The dialogue history contains the completed text plans for responses previously generated by the system.

After a response has been generated, the system awaits feedback from the user. This feedback may be a follow-up question (e.g., "Why?", "What's the difference between CAR and FIRST?"), an indication that the user does not understand the system's response ("Huh?"), an indication that the user understands and has no follow-up question ("Go Ahead"), or a response to a question posed by the system. The query analyzer interprets this feedback and either returns control to the expert system, or formulates the appropriate discourse goal and passes it on to the text planner to produce a response.

In our system, a completed text plan provides an explicit representation of the explanation produced by the system indicating how parts of the plan are related and including what purposes different parts of the generated explanation serve. It also contains information about assumptions made and alternative strategies that could have been selected at various points during the planning process. This structure provides a context from which focus of attention can be derived. In addition, this context provides information that is essential to handling the user's feedback. If the user asks a follow-up question or indicates that he does not understand an explanation, the system examines the dialogue history. The text plans recorded there tell the system what it was trying to explain, how it explained it, what alternative ways could have been used to explain the same thing, and what, if any, assumptions were made in constructing the explanation. In Section 1.5, we show how this context is used to disambiguate a follow-up question and to provide a further explanation even when the user does not ask a well-formulated follow-up question.

1.4.1 The Plan Language

One of our goals is to produce coherent multi-sentential texts. In our plan language, we make use of the rhetorical relations defined in Rhetorical Structure Theory (RST) (Mann and Thompson, 1987). RST is a descriptive theory of the organization of natural language texts. Based on a study of hundreds of paragraphs from a wide variety of English texts, Mann and Thompson proposed approximately 25 relations that normally occur between portions of a coherent English text. An RST description of a text is a hierarchical structure that characterizes the text in terms of the relations that hold between parts of the text, clauses at the lowest level, portions of paragraphs at higher levels.

Each RST relation has two parts: a *nucleus (N)* and a *satellite (S)*.[4] The nucleus of the relation is that item in the pair that is most essential to the writer's purpose. The nucleus could stand on its own, but the satellite would be considered a non-sequitur without its corresponding nucleus. For example, without the claim in the nucleus, an EVIDENCE satellite is a non-sequitur. Moreover, the satellite portion of a text may be more easily replaced than the nucleus. An EVIDENCE satellite can be replaced with different evidence without greatly changing the function of the text as a whole. However, replacing the claim made in the nucleus of an EVIDENCE relation is considered more drastic.

The definition of each RST relation includes constraints on the two entities being related as well as constraints on the combination, and a specification of the effect which the speaker is attempting to achieve on the hearer's beliefs. A sample RST relation is shown in Figure 1.3.

RST has been used primarily as a tool for analyzing texts in order to investigate linguistic issues. When analyzing a text, the analyst breaks the text down into parts and then tries to find an RST relation that connects each pair of parts until all pairs are accounted for. To determine whether or not a relation holds between two parts of a text, the analyst checks to see whether the constraints on the nucleus and satellite hold and whether it is plausible that the writer desires the condition specified in the Effect field. All of the text is given. One need only determine whether or not the constraints are satisfied.

---

[4]This is not strictly true. For example, the SEQUENCE relation is *multinuclear* and can relate more than two pieces of text.

relation name: MOTIVATION
constraints on N: presents an action in which Hearer is the actor
(including accepting an offer), unrealized with
respect to the context of N.
constraints on S: none
constraints on N + S combination:
Comprehending S increases Hearer's desire to perform
action presented in N.
effect: Hearer's desire to perform action presented in N is increased.

Figure 1.3: RST Relation – Motivation

Using RST in a constructive process such as generating a response to a question is a very different task from analysis. When generating a text, none of the information to be included in the final answer is given. Instead the system is given a discourse goal that represents an abstract specification of the response to the query and the system must *choose* the information to include in the response. The constraints of the RST relations as described by Mann and Thompson are too loosely defined to be applied directly to this task. For example, in the MOTIVATION relation shown in Figure 1.3, the constraint on the nucleus/satellite combination requires that comprehending the satellite increases the hearer's desire to perform the action presented in the nucleus. This tells us nothing about how to search a knowledge base to find such information to include in the satellite. To use RST in a constructive process, we had to "tighten" the constraints to guide the search required to choose information to include in a response. That is, we had to define constraints which characterize the kinds of knowledge that can be used to achieve discourse goals such as increase the hearer's desire to perform an act.

In our plan language, each operator consists of:

- *an effect:* a characterization of what goal(s) this operator can be used to achieve. An effect may be an *intentional goal*, such as achieve the state where the hearer is persuaded to do act or a *rhetorical relation* to be achieved, such as provide motivation for an act.

- *a constraint list:* a list of conditions that must be true before the operator can be applied. Constraints may refer to facts in the system's knowledge base or in the user model.

- *a nucleus:* the main topic to be expressed. All operators must contain a nucleus.

- *satellites:* additional information needed to achieve the effect of the operator. When present, satellites may be required or optional.

Note from Figure 1.3 that RST relations consist of a relation name as well and an effect. The effect describes the intent that the speaker wishes to achieve on the hearer when using this relation. Therefore, we may view the effect as the goal to be achieved and the relation as the rhetorical strategy for achieving that goal. For example, a plan operator that embodies the knowledge contained in the RST relation **MOTIVATION** shown in Figure 1.3 is the operator shown in Figure 1.4.

When checking to determine whether this plan operator may be applied, the planner must check the operator's constraints. This causes the planner to search the knowledge base for acceptable bindings for the variable ?goal. The constraints of this operator thus indicate that in order to achieve the effect that the the hearer is persuaded to do an act, the system should look for domain goals that are shared by the hearer and that the act is a step in achieving. If any such goals are found, the planner will post one or more **MOTIVATION** subgoals. There are several operators for achieving a **MOTIVATION** goal. One of these, shown in Figure 1.5, motivates the hearer to perform the act by achieving the state where the hearer believes that the act is a step in achieving the shared domain goal. Another operator for achieving a **MOTIVATION** goal will be seen in Section 1.5.1.[5] Thus we see that the two operators shown in Figure 1.4 and 1.5 together provide one operationalization of the RST relation shown in Figure 1.3.

Comparison With Hovy's Structurer

The notion that RST could be used in a constructive process originates with Mann and Thompson. However, the first implementation that employed RST to control the construction of texts was developed by Hovy (1988a) who formalized some of the RST relations so that they could be used in a system that produces a coherent text when given a set of input propositions to express. Hovy's text structurer employs an opportunistic planning approach that orders the inputs according to the constraints on the RST relations, i.e., it looks for some coherent way to organize the text so that all of the information in the input is included.

There are two main limitations to the approach taken by Hovy. First, this type of strategy only works if there is some process which can identify the inputs in advance. We believe that any process which could identify all and only the information to be included in a response would have to do much of the work of a structurer anyway. We believe that the tasks of choosing what to say and choosing a strategy for saying it cannot be divided. They are intertwined and influence one another in many ways. What knowledge is included in a response greatly depends on the discourse goal being achieved and the strategy

---

[5]There are other ways to motivate a hearer to do an act. For example, the speaker could intimidate the hearer by threatening, or by citing the advice of experts. There are other plan operators which embody these strategies.

In Formal Notation:

    EFFECT: (PERSUADED ?hearer (GOAL ?hearer (DO ?hearer ?act)))
    CONSTRAINTS: (AND (GOAL ?speaker ?goal)
                      (STEP ?act ?goal)
                      (GOAL ?hearer ?goal))
    NUCLEUS: (FORALL ?goal
                     (MOTIVATION ?act ?goal))
    SATELLITES: nil

English Translation:

    To achieve the state in which the hearer is persuaded to do an *act*,
    IF the *act* is a step in achieving some *goal(s)*,
       that the hearer shares,
    THEN motivate the *act* in terms of those *goal(s)*

      Figure 1.4: Plan Operator for Persuading User to Do An Act

---

In Formal Notation:

    EFFECT: (MOTIVATION ?act ?goal)
    CONSTRAINTS: (AND (GOAL ?speaker ?goal)
                      (STEP ?act ?goal)
                      (GOAL ?hearer ?goal))
    NUCLEUS: (BEL ?hearer (STEP ?act ?goal))
    SATELLITES: none

English Translation:

    To motivate an *act* in terms of a *goal*,
    IF the *act* is a step in achieving the *goal*,
       and the hearer shares the *goal*,
    THEN make the hearer believe that the *act* is a step
             in achieving the *goal*

          Figure 1.5: Plan Operator for Motivation

---

chosen to achieve that goal. Likewise, what strategy is chosen to achieve a discourse goal will depend in part on what knowledge is available. For example, the information included when achieving the goal of describing an object by drawing an analogy with a similar object will be quite different from the information included in a text that describes the object by discussing its component parts. Moreover, whether the system chooses to draw an analogy will depend on whether there is an analogous concept that is familiar to the hearer available in the system's knowledge base.

In our plan language, we too have formalized the RST relations in order to construct coherent natural language utterances (Moore and Paris, 1988; Moore and Paris, 1989). However, we do not assume that all of the topics to be discussed are given to our planner as input. Our planner is given a discourse (or intentional) goal, such as *persuade the hearer to do an act*, the knowledge base of the expert system, the execution trace of the expert system's reasoning, the user model, and the dialogue history containing past utterances. Our planner must then plan an utterance to achieve this goal, choosing what to say from the knowledge base *and* organizing it into a coherent structure.

The second problem with Hovy's approach is that his "RST plans" indicate only what relation can be used to relate two pieces of text and in what order they may appear. For example, consider the RST plan from Hovy's structurer shown in Figure 1.6. This plan says that the structurer can relate two pieces of text, ?PART and ?NEXT, with the SEQUENCE relation whenever there is a NEXT-ACTION relation between these two items in the knowledge base. The result of using this operator will be that the speaker and hearer mutually believe that the SEQUENCE relation holds between ?PART and ?NEXT. The operator includes Nucleus growth points and Satellite growth points. These growth points post additional subgoals to be satisfied in the order they appear in the plan.[6] So, for example, when expressing the Nucleus ?PART, the planner may also express CIRCUMSTANCES-OF, ATTRIBUTES-OF, PURPOSE-OF, or DETAILS-OF ?PART. In each case, the goal to be achieved is represented simply as the hearer and speaker mutually believing that the rhetorical relation, e.g., PURPOSE-OF, holds. What is missing are the higher-level goals that these rhetorical relations satisfy. For example, why include information about the purpose of ?PART at this point. A higher-level goal might be to make the hearer understand why ?PART is necessary in the sequence of actions being described. But goals such as this are not represented in Hovy's language.

From this perspective, Hovy's RST plans look much like the schemata of McKeown's TEXT system as described in Section 1.3. They include a description of *what* can be said when, but do not include information about *why* this information can or should be included at a particular point, i.e., what *in-*

---

[6]Hovy is currently extending this use of growth points to be more flexible. The growth points will not be limited to saying what is in the input set but may look in the knowledge base for additional topics to be discussed based on a set of criteria such as how verbose the text should be, and so forth (Hovy, 1990).

tentional goal(s) the relations in the growth points satisfy or what effect the speaker is hoping to have on the hearer. Hovy's approach conflates intentional and rhetorical structure, and therefore, a system using his approach could not later reason about which rhetorical strategies were used to achieve intentional goals.

In our own work on responding to follow-up questions and recovering when the hearer does not understand the response produced, we have found the need to incorporate the intentional goals omitted in Hovy's scheme. Thus, although our text planner also makes use of RST relations in order to construct coherent natural language utterances, we had to devise a new text planner that explicitly represents both the intended effects of each portion of text on the hearer, and the strategy used to achieve that effect. In this way, our system knows not only what relation each portion of the text plays a role in, but it knows *why* that portion of text appears in the response, i.e., what that portion of text is trying to make the hearer believe.

Contrast Hovy's RST plan with our plan operator shown in Figure 1.7. This is a plan operator for achieving the state where the hearer has adopted the goal of performing the specified act. This operator has a nucleus of recommending the act and two optional satellites. The first satellite corresponds to telling the hearer the information he needs to know in order to be competent to do the act, e.g., enablement information. The second is a subgoal to achieve the state where the hearer is persuaded to adopt the goal of performing the recommended act. An operator for achieving this persuade subgoal was shown in Figure 1.4. When this operator is applied, it will post one or more MOTIVATION subgoals. One operator for achieving a MOTIVATION goal was shown in Figure 1.5.

The high-level plan operator shown in Figure 1.7 is a type of "schema" in our planning language, the *recommend-enable-motivate* schema. However, note that each portion of the schema is either a primitive, i.e., a speech act such as RECOMMEND, or a goal describing intended effects on the hearer, e.g., (PERSUADED ?hearer (GOAL ?hearer (DO ?hearer ?act)). When the text planner constructs a text plan (as will be described in the next section) all satellite subgoals must eventually be satisfied by RST operators such as the MOTIVATION operator shown in Figure 1.5. Thus a completed text plan will consist of a nucleus and one or more satellites related to the nucleus by one of the RST relations.

In such a text plan, the system understands what discourse goal(s) it was trying to achieve, what rhetorical strategies were selected to achieve those goals and what role each speech act plays in achieving those goals. In this way, the system can recover from failures. For example, if the system knows that a portion of text is intended to persuade the hearer to do an act and that piece of text is not understood or accepted, it can try an alternative strategy for persuading the hearer to do the act. However, if the system does not know what effect(s) it is trying to achieve in the hearer's knowledge state, what strategies achieve what effects, or what strategies have been tried in attempting

---

SEQUENCE

Results
((BMB SPEAKER HEARER (SEQUENCE-OF ?PART ?NEXT)))

Nucleus requirements
((BMB SPEAKER HEARER (MAINTOPIC ?PART))
 (BMB SPEAKER HEARER (NEXT-ACTION ?PART ?NEXT)))

Nucleus growth points
((BMB SPEAKER HEARER (CIRCUMSTANCE-OF ?PART ?CIR))
 (BMB SPEAKER HEARER (ATTRIBUTE-OF ?PART ?VAL))
 (BMB SPEAKER HEARER (PURPOSE-OF ?PART ?PURP))
 (BMB SPEAKER HEARER (DETAILS-OF ?PART ?DETS)))

Satellite requirements
((BMB SPEAKER HEARER (MAINTOPIC ?NEXT)))

Satellite growth points
((BMB SPEAKER HEARER (ATTRIBUTE-OF ?NEXT ?VAL))
 (BMB SPEAKER HEARER (DETAILS-OF ?NEXT ?DETS))
 (BMB SPEAKER HEARER (SEQUENCE-OF ?NEXT ?FOLL))
 (BMB SPEAKER HEARER (PURPOSE-OF ?NEXT ?PURP)))

Order (NUCLEUS SATELLITE)

Activation question
"Could A be presented as start-point, mid-point, or end-point
of some succession of items along some dimension? – that is,
should the hearer know that A is part of a sequence?"

Relation phrases ("" "then" "next")

Figure 1.6: Hovy's RST Plan for Sequence

---

to achieve a given effect, the system cannot recover in this way. Examples of
how the structure built by our text planner is used in responding to follow-up
questions appear in Section 1.5 and a discussion of how our approach may be
used in execution monitoring appears in (Moore, 1989).

1.4.2 The Plan Operator Space

As we have already seen, there are two types of plan operators in our system.
One type are operators that achieve an intentional goal, such as the operator
shown in Figure 1.4 which can be used to persuade the hearer to perform an act.
The other type are operators that achieve a particular rhetorical relation, such
as the operator in Figure 1.5 which indicates one way to achieve a MOTIVATION
relation.

Plans that achieve intentional goals and those that achieve rhetorical rela-

---

NAME: **recommend-enable-motivate**
EFFECT: **(GOAL ?hearer (DO ?hearer ?act)))**
CONSTRAINTS: none
NUCLEUS: **(RECOMMEND ?speaker ?hearer ?act)**
SATELLITES:
    (((**COMPETENT ?hearer (DONE ?hearer ?act)) *optional***)
      (**PERSUADED ?hearer (GOAL ?hearer (DO ?hearer ?act))**
                optional))

Figure 1.7: High-level Plan Operator for Recommending an Act

---

tions are distinguished for two reasons. First, they are distinguished so that the completed plan structure will contain both the intentional goals of the speaker and the rhetorical means used to achieve them. Second, the distinction is useful because there are many different rhetorical strategies for achieving any given intentional goal. For example, the system has several plan operators for achieving the intentional goal of describing a concept. It may describe a concept by stating its class membership and describing its attributes and its parts, by drawing an analogy with a similar concept, or by giving examples of the concept. There may also be many different plan operators for achieving a particular rhetorical strategy. The planner has selection heuristics for choosing among applicable operators in a given situation. It is very important to be able to have several strategies for achieving the same goal and selection criteria to choose among them in order to increase the flexibility of the explanation component, and to be able to offer alternative explanations when the user is not satisfied with a given explanation.

Our plan language allows both general and specific explanation strategies to be represented. For example, the operator shown in Figure 1.8 can be used to achieve the hearer's belief of any proposition. This operator says that to achieve the state where the speaker believes a proposition, first inform the hearer of that proposition and then, optionally, post a subgoal to achieve the state where the hearer is persuaded that the proposition is true. Other operators are much more limited in their applicability. For example, the operator shown in Figure 1.9 may be applied only when the proposition that the speaker wishes the hearer to believe is of the form (STEP ?act ?goal). When this is the case, and when the constraints of the operator shown in Figure 1.9 are satisfied, an appropriate strategy is to use the rhetorical relation ELABORATION–GENERAL–SPECIFIC. This is a type of elaboration which gives additional information about a generic class by giving a specific instance of the class.

Because we allow very general operators as well as very specific ones, we can include both domain-independent as well as domain-dependent strategies. Thus we can handle the range of strategies necessary to handle any idiosyncrasies of the language used in a particular domain.

EFFECT: **(BEL ?hearer ?x)**
CONSTRAINTS: nil
NUCLEUS: **(INFORM ?speaker ?hearer ?x)**
SATELLITES: **(((PERSUADED ?hearer ?x) *optional*))**

Figure 1.8: Plan Operator for Achieving Hearer's Belief of a Proposition

---

EFFECT: **(BEL ?hearer (STEP ?act ?goal))**
CONSTRAINTS: **(AND (INDIVIDUAL-REFORMULATION ?goal2**
                                                             ?goal)
                           (IMMEDIATE-STEP ?act ?goal2))
NUCLEUS: **(ELABORATION-GENERAL-SPECIFIC ?goal ?goal2)**
SATELLITES: nil

Figure 1.9: Plan Operator for One Kind of Elaboration of Reasoning Chain

---

In the current implementation of the text planner, there are approximately 75 operators. Examples of some of these appear in Section 1.5 and a more complete list may be found in (Moore, 1989). The system currently makes use of the two speech acts INFORM and RECOMMEND.

1.4.3   The Planning Mechanism

The planning process begins when a discourse goal is posted. The planner identifies operators capable of satisfying a given discourse goal by finding all of the operators whose effect field matches the goal to be refined.[7] For each operator found, the planner then checks to see if its constraints are satisfied. Those operators whose constraints are satisfied become candidates for achieving the goal.

From the candidate plan operators, the planner selects an operator based on several factors including what the user knows (as indicated in the user model), the conversation that has occurred so far (as indicated in the dialogue history), the relative specificity of the candidate operators, and the assumption requirements of each operator (as indicated in the possible binding environments found when satisfying the constraints). The knowledge of preferences is encoded into a set of selection heuristics. Details of the selection process are beyond the scope of this paper and are discussed in (Moore, 1989).

As illustrated in Figure 1.4, constraints on plan operators often refer to the state of the hearer's goals or knowledge, in this case whether there is a goal that the speaker and hearer share. The user model contains information about the current user's goals and knowledge state, including information about what

---

[7]To make this search more efficient, plan operators in the plan library are stored in a discrimination network based on their effect field.

domain concepts and problem-solving knowledge, i.e., domain goals and plans, the system believes to be known to the user. However, in our approach, we do not assume that this model is either complete or correct.[8] Therefore, if a concept is not included in the user model, the concept may or may not be known to the user. The system simply does not know.

When the planner is checking constraints on an operator, it attempts to find variable bindings in the expert system's knowledge base and/or user model which satisfy all of the constraints in the constraint list. However, constraints that refer to the user's knowledge are not treated as rigid constraints, but instead are treated as a specification of what the user ideally should know in order to understand the text that will be produced if the operator is employed. Thus, the planner is permitted to make an assumption if the constraint is not satisfied by the user model. For example, in checking the constraints of the plan operator in Figure 1.4, the system first checks the constraints (GOAL SYSTEM ?goal) and (STEP ?act ?goal). This will result in several possible bindings for the variable ?goal. Some of these bindings will also satisfy the constraint (GOAL USER ?goal). Others will not. Those bindings which do not satisfy this third constraint will not be rejected immediately. Instead, they will be noted as possible bindings and each will be marked to indicate that if this binding is used, an assumption is being made that this goal is a goal of the user.

The text planner prefers choosing binding environments that require no assumptions to be made, but if no such binding environment exists, a binding that requires an assumption will be chosen. One of the selection heuristics controls how the planner treats operators that require assumptions to be made. This heuristic can be set to favor selecting operators that do not require assumptions to be made. However, the influence of other selection heuristics may outweigh this concern and an operator that requires making an assumption may ultimately be chosen. In that case, any assumptions that were made are recorded in the plan structure at the plan node where they occurred. In addition, the plan operator chosen is recorded in the plan node as the selected operator and all other candidate plan operators are recorded in the plan node as untried alternatives.

Once a plan operator has been selected, the planner instantiates that operator by posting its nucleus and required satellites as subgoals to be refined. RST does not strictly constrain ordering. However, Mann and Thompson (1987) have observed that for some relations one ordering is significantly more frequent than the other. In RST, these ordering observations are treated as "strong ten-

---

[8]Note that there are two senses in which a user model can be *correct*: 1. a user model is correct if it accurately reflects what the user believes, 2. a user model is correct if it does not contain any wrong information – i.e., it is a subset of the system's knowledge. When we say we do not assume that the user model is correct, we mean that we don't assume that it accurately records all of the things the user knows. The user may know things not in the user model and may not know some of the things in the user model. In this work, we do not attempt to detect inconsistencies between the user model and the system's knowledge, nor will we try to correct such errors.

dencies" rather than constraints. For example, in an EVIDENCE relation, the nuclear claim usually precedes the satellite providing evidence for the claim. In our system, since we are generating text, we must decide on ordering. We assume that the nucleus precedes the satellite except for those relations that have been identified as having a canonical order of satellite before nucleus. In our system, this ordering knowledge is part of the planning mechanism itself and is not represented explicitly in the plan operators.[9]

The planner then expands optional satellites based on information in the user model or the dialogue history. For example, there are two satellites of the high-level plan operator in Figure 1.7. The first satellite corresponds to making the hearer competent to perform the act by telling him anything that he needs to know to do so. The second satellite calls for persuading the hearer to perform the act. These satellites are both marked "optional," indicating that it would be sufficient to simply state the recommendation. The planner could choose not to expand any of the satellites and await feedback from the hearer. In this case, the system would simply recommend that the hearer perform the action. If, however, the user model indicates this listener is a novice or the dialogue history indicates the listener frequently asks "why?" after a recommendation has been presented, the planner may decide to expand the second optional satellite.[10] Planning is complete when all subgoals in the text plan have been refined into speech acts.

1.5 EXAMPLES

We begin this section with a detailed example showing how our system constructs a text plan for responding to a user's question. This discussion is followed by two examples illustrating how the system then uses the recorded text plans stored in its dialogue history to provide a context in which to interpret and respond to the user's follow-up questions. The first example shows how the system disambiguates a why-question following the system's explanation and the second example shows how the system reacts when the user asks the vaguely-articulated follow-up question, "Huh?".

1.5.1 Planning a Response

Consider the sample dialogue with our system shown in Figure 1.10. While enhancing readability, the system recommends that the user perform an act,

---

[9] This is not inherent to the planning process. We are currently modifying this to allow order to be specified in the plan operators.

[10] We are also looking into incorporating pragmatic or stylistic goals (Hovy, 1988b) into our text planner. Then stylistic goals such as "be verbose" will cause the planner to expand optional satellites.

SYSTEM	What characteristics of the program would you like to enhance?	[1]
USER	Readability and maintainability.	[2]

$$\vdots$$

SYSTEM	You should replace (CAR x) with (FIRST x).	[3]
USER	Why?	[4]
SYSTEM	I'm trying to enhance the readability of the program by applying transformations that enhance readability. CAR-to-FIRST is a transformation that enhances readability.	[5]
USER	Why?	[6]
SYSTEM	Transformations that enhance readability are transformations whose right-hand-side is more readable than their left-hand-side. One type of such transformations are transformations whose right-hand-side is a function whose function name is an English word and whose left-hand-side is a function whose function name is a technical word. CAR-to-FIRST is of this type.	[7]

Figure 1.10: Sample Dialogue 1

namely replace **CAR** with **FIRST**. To recommend this transformation to the user, the expert system posts the discourse goal:

```
(GOAL USER (DO USER REPLACE-1))
```

where

```
REPLACE-1 = (REPLACE (actor USER)
                     (object CAR-FUNCTION)
                     (generalized-means FIRST-FUNCTION))
```

The plan operator for achieving this goal was shown in Figure 1.7. When this plan operator is expanded the nucleus is posted as a subgoal. For the purpose of this example, assume that neither of the optional satellites are expanded. The planner now has one subgoal left to be refined, namely

```
(RECOMMEND PEA-SYSTEM USER REPLACE-1)
```

RECOMMEND is a speech act and is achieved by a primitive operator and so no further text planning is required. The completed text plan is shown in Figure 1.11. The explainer records this completed text plan in the dialogue history before passing it to the grammar interface to be transformed into a specification suitable as input to the Penman text generation system. The text generator produces the English utterance numbered [3] in the sample dialogue. The explainer then awaits feedback from the user.

In this example, the user then asks "Why?". To interpret this why-question, the query analyzer examines the dialogue history. At this point, the dialogue history contains only the text plan for recommending the act, **replace-1**.

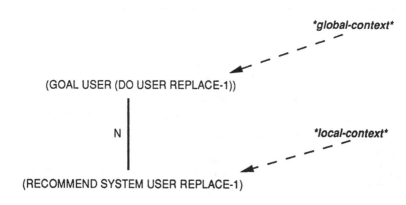

Figure 1.11: Completed Text Plan for Recommendation

When interpreting a query, the query analyzer first looks at the *local-context*. *Local-context* always points to the last clause that the system uttered. In this case, *local-context* is the speech act (RECOMMEND PEA-SYSTEM USER REPLACE -1). One of the heuristics used to interpret why-questions says that if the user asks "Why?" immediately after the system has recommended an act, then the user is asking why he should perform the recommended act. The query analyzer thus formulates a discourse goal to achieve the state where the user is persuaded to do the act and posts this goal to the text planner. In this case, the following discourse goal is posted:

(PERSUADED USER (GOAL USER (DO USER REPLACE-1)))

The text planner searches for plan operators capable of satisfying this discourse goal. One of the strategies for persuading the listener to perform an act is to find goals that this act is a step in achieving and to motivate the act in terms of these goals. The plan operator that embodies this strategy was shown in Figure 1.4 on page 16.

In the process of checking the constraints to see whether the plan operator in Figure 1.4 could be applied in this situation, the planner must find bindings for the variable ?goal. That is, the planner must search the expert system's knowledge base and the user model to find all ?goal such that: ?goal is a goal of the system, REPLACE-1 is a step in the method for achieving ?goal, and the speaker believes that ?goal is a goal of the hearer. In order to find such goals, the text planner examines the development history built by the EES program writer when the PEA expert system was automatically constructed. A portion of this structure is shown in Figure 1.12. By searching up the development history from the node where REPLACE-1 occurs, the system can find all of the goals that REPLACE-1 is a step in the method for achieving. These are:

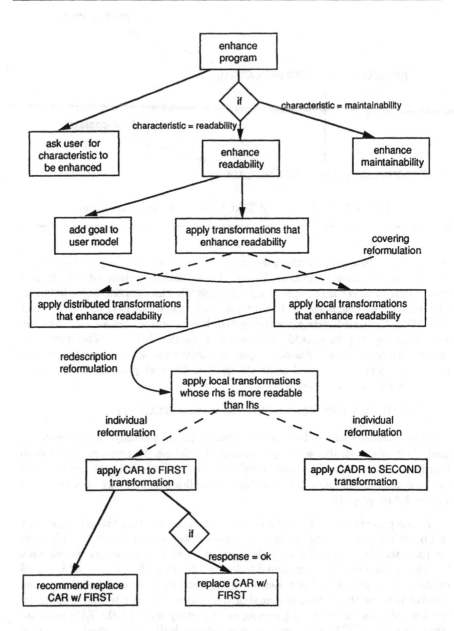

Figure 1.12: Portion of PEA Development History

NAME: **motivate-act-by-means**
EFFECT: (**MOTIVATION** ?act ?goal)
CONSTRAINTS: (**AND** (**GOAL** ?speaker ?goal)
(**GOAL** ?hearer ?goal)
(**STEP** ?act ?goal))
NUCLEUS: (**INFORM** ?speaker ?hearer ?goal)
SATELLITES: (((**MEANS** ?goal ?act) *required*))

Figure 1.13: A Plan Operator for Motivating an Act

```
APPLY-CAR-TO-FIRST-TRANSFORMATION
APPLY-LOCAL-TRANSFORMATIONS-WHOSE-RHS-IS-MORE-READABLE-THAN-LHS
APPLY-LOCAL-TRANSFORMATIONS-THAT-ENHANCE-READABILITY
APPLY-TRANSFORMATIONS-THAT-ENHANCE-READABILITY
ENHANCE-READABILITY
ENHANCE-PROGRAM
```

The third constraint on the operator in Figure 1.4 indicates that any acceptable binding for ?goal must be a goal that is shared by the user. The system assumes that the user shares its top-level goal, ENHANCE-PROGRAM, since he is using the system to perform that task. Furthermore, since the system asked what characteristics the user would like to enhance, the system can assume that the user shares the goal of enhancing those characteristics, in this case ENHANCE-READABILITY and ENHANCE-MAINTAINABILITY. The information that the user shares these two goals is included in the user model. Therefore, the two goals that satisfy the constraints of this operator are: ENHANCE-READABILITY and ENHANCE-PROGRAM. In order to avoid explaining parts of the reasoning chain that the user is familiar with, when one goal is a subgoal of another, the more specific goal is chosen. Once the constraints have been satisfied, the only possible binding for the variable ?goal is ENHANCE-READABILITY.

Note that this operator contains the special form FORALL. In general, FORALL causes the planner to create a subgoal for each of the possible bindings of the variable it ranges over. In this case, since there is only one such binding, the single subgoal

(MOTIVATION REPLACE-1 ENHANCE-READABILITY)

is posted.

One strategy for satisfying this type of motivation goal is to inform the hearer of the goal that the system is trying to achieve and then to establish that the act in question is part of the means for achieving the goal. The plan operator for this strategy is shown in Figure 1.13.

Assume that the planner chooses this operator to achieve the current goal. The planner can now expand the nucleus and satellites of this plan operator.

EFFECT: (MEANS ?goal ?act)
CONSTRAINTS: (AND (IMMEDIATE-STEP ?s1 ?goal)
                  (STEP ?act ?s1)
                  (NOT (AND (IMMEDIATE-STEP ?s2 ?goal)
                            (NOT (EQUAL ?s2 ?s1)))))
NUCLEUS: (INFORM ?speaker ?hearer ?s1)
SATELLITE: (((BEL ?hearer (STEP ?act ?s1))))

Figure 1.14: A Plan Operator for the Means Relation

Expanding the nucleus posts a subgoal to inform the hearer of the goal that the system is trying to achieve. INFORM is a primitive operator and so expansion of this branch of the plan will terminate here. Expanding the satellite posts a subgoal to establish that the means for achieving ?goal is the act, REPLACE-1. This subgoal requires further refinement.

One of the plan operators for achieving the goal of expressing a MEANS relation between a goal and an act is shown in Figure 1.14. The constraints of this operator bear some explanation. The first constraint looks for a subgoal ?s1 that is a step in the method for achieving the goal, in this case ENHANCE-READABILITY. The constraint (STEP ?act ?s1) guarantees that ?s1 is on the refinement path to the act in question (i.e., REPLACE-1). The last constraint checks to see that ?s1 is the only step in the method for achieving the goal ENHANCE-READABILITY. [11]

In this case, ?s1 will be bound to APPLY-TRANSFORMATIONS-THATENHANCE-READABILITY. Recall that this plan operator is intended to establish a MEANS relation between the goal mentioned in the previous plan operator and the recommended act. The nucleus of the plan operator informs the hearer of the method, ?s1, for achieving the goal, but has not yet related ?act to this method. To complete the strategy, the satellite of this operator posts a subgoal of making the hearer believe that ?act is a step in achieving the subgoal ?s1,[12] i.e.,

    (BEL USER
        (STEP REPLACE-1 APPLY-TRANSFORMATIONS-THAT-ENHANCE-READABILITY))

Goals of the form (BEL USER *proposition*) are treated specially.[13] If the user model indicates that the hearer already knows *proposition*, then the goal is trivially satisfied and no further planning need be done. In this way, the system avoids telling the listener information he already knows. In the current

---

[11] This plan operator is intended to generate text such as "I'm trying to achieve ?goal by doing ?s1." Another plan operator would be found if ?s1 were not the only step in the method for achieving the goal. That plan operator produces text of the form "I'm trying to achieve ?goal. One step in doing that is ?s1."

[12] If ?act were equal to ?s1 a different plan operator would be applicable.

[13] During normal operation, the variable ?hearer is typically bound to the individual concept USER.

EFFECT: (**BEL** ?hearer (**STEP** ?act ?goal))
CONSTRAINTS: (**AND** (**INDIVIDUAL-REFORMULATION** ?goal2
?goal)
(**IMMEDIATE-STEP** ?act ?goal2))
NUCLEUS: (**ELABORATION-GENERAL-SPECIFIC** ?goal ?goal2)
SATELLITES: **nil**

Figure 1.15: Plan Operator for One Kind of Elaboration of Reasoning Chain

---

example, if the hearer knows how the act relates to the method, i.e., if the user model contains the proposition
```
(STEP REPLACE-1 APPLY-TRANSFORMATIONS-THAT-ENHANCE-READABILITY)
```
the planner will not further expand this satellite node since the listener already knows this information.

However, assume that the user model does not contain this information. In that case, the planner must further refine this subgoal. One plan operator for satisfying such a goal was shown in Figure 1.9 and is repeated in Figure 1.15 for the reader's convenience. But the plan operator that was shown in Figure 1.8 (cf. page 21) is also applicable in this situation. Recall that the operator in Figure 1.8 is a very general plan operator that can be used to achieve the hearer's belief in any proposition and therefore could be used to achieve the current goal. One of the plan selection heuristics for choosing from a set of candidate plan operators is the specificity heuristic which can be set to favor choosing more specific plan operators over more general ones (other considerations being equal). Assuming such a setting has been made in this case, the plan operator shown in Figure 1.15 is preferred.

The planner must now refine the subgoal
```
(ELABORATION-GENERAL-SPECIFIC
           APPLY-TRANSFORMATIONS-THAT-ENHANCE-READABILITY
           APPLY-CAR-TO-FIRST)
```
There are several different types of reasoning that can relate a goal to an act in the EES system architecture. In this case, the act of replacing CAR with FIRST ultimately arises from an *individual reformulation*[14] of the subgoal APPLY-TRANSFORMATIONS-THAT-ENHANCE-READABILITY. When an individual reformulation has occurred, the appropriate rhetorical relation for elaborating this reasoning is ELABORATION-GENERAL-SPECIFIC, a subtype of ELABORATION in which a more general concept is elaborated by giving a specific instance

---

[14]The expert system architecture uses several forms of goal reformulation in its reasoning. When the expert system is trying to achieve a goal and it cannot find a plan for achieving the goal, the system tries to reformulate the goal into some other goal(s) that it may be able to satisfy. In this case, the system has a goal to apply a set of transformations. However, the system does not have a plan for applying a set of transformations. But it does have a plan for applying a single transformation. The reformulation knowledge allows the system to reformulate the goal of applying a set of transformations into several subgoals to apply each of the transformations in the set.

EFFECT: (**ELABORATION-GENERAL-SPECIFIC** ?goal1 ?goal2)
CONSTRAINTS: (**AND** (**INDIVIDUAL-REFORMULATION** ?goal2
                                              ?goal1)
                    (**INDIVIDUALIZED-ROLE** ?r1 ?goal1 ?goal2))
NUCLEUS: ((**SETQ** ?generic-concept (**FILLER-OF** ?r1 ?goal1))
         (**SETQ** ?individual-concept (**FILLER-OF** ?r1 ?goal2))
         (**BEL** ?hearer (**INSTANCE-OF** ?individual-concept
                                        ?generic-concept)))
SATELLITES: **nil**

Figure 1.16: Plan Operator for One Kind of Elaboration of Reasoning Chain

---

of the more general concept. The text plan for this type of elaboration is shown in Figure 1.16. This plan operator makes use of the special form SETQ which can be used in the nucleus or satellite to bind a variable to the value of an expression computed when the operator is expanded.

Expanding the nucleus of this operator posts the discourse goal

```
(BEL USER
      (INSTANCE-OF CAR-TO-FIRST
                    TRANSFORMATIONS-THAT-ENHANCE-READABILITY))
```

This goal says that the speaker wishes to achieve the state in which the hearer believes that the CAR-TO-FIRST transformation is an instance of the more general class of transformations, TRANSFORMATIONS-THAT-ENHANCE-READABILITY. The plan operator for achieving this goal was shown in Figure 1.8 and is the very general operator that can be used to make the hearer believe any proposition. This operator has a nucleus of informing the hearer of the proposition and an optional satellite to achieve the state in which the hearer is persuaded of the truth of the proposition. In this case, the planner posts only the nucleus and the nucleus subgoal can be satisfied by a primitive, i.e., the speech act INFORM, and thus text planning is complete. The completed text plan, shown in Figure 1.17, is added to the dialogue history and passed on to the grammar interface to produce the response on line [5] of the sample dialogue of Figure 1.10 on page 24.

1.5.2 Disambiguating Follow-up Why Questions

After the response on line [5] of Figure 1.10 is presented to the user, the user asks "Why?" a second time, line [6]. At this point, there are several possible interpretations of this question, including:

I1: Why are you trying to enhance the readability of the program?

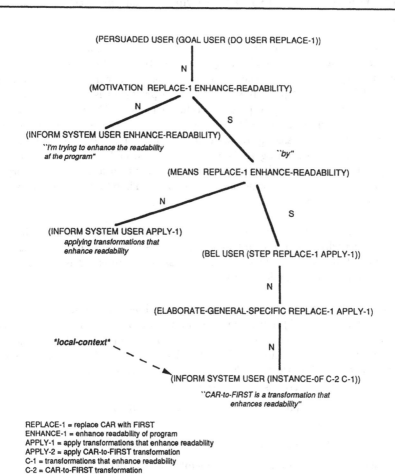

REPLACE-1 = replace CAR with FIRST
ENHANCE-1 = enhance readability of program
APPLY-1 = apply transformations that enhance readability
APPLY-2 = apply CAR-to-FIRST transformation
C-1 = transformations that enhance readability
C-2 = CAR-to-FIRST transformation

Figure 1.17: Completed Text Plan for Persuading the CAR-to-FIRST Transformation

I2:   Why are you trying to enhance the readability of the program by
       applying transformations that enhance readability? (as opposed to
       enhancing the program via some other method)

I3:   Why are you applying transformations that enhance readability?

I4:   Why is CAR-to-FIRST a transformation that enhances readability?

This example was constructed to parallel a problematic MYCIN example.
In cases such as this, MYCIN always assumes that "Why?" is asking why the
system is trying to achieve the higher-level goal. This corresponds to interpretation I1 in this example. However, this interpretation is often inappropriate.
The study of inadequate responses produced by MYCIN discussed earlier re-
vealed that when users asked "Why?" after an explanation had been produced,
they were frequently asking for justification of factual statements made in the
explanation, corresponding to I4 in this case. MYCIN cannot decide which
interpretation to choose because it does not maintain a dialogue history and
does not understand the responses it generates. Therefore, it cannot even use
a simple heuristic such as:

> "Why?" asked after the system has asked a question is probably
> asking why it is important to determine the information in the ques-
> tion, but "why?" asked after a rule has been presented is probably
> asking for justification of the rule.

How could a system choose between the possible interpretations? Resolving
ambiguity requires: (1) identifying candidate interpretations, and (2) choosing
among them. To recognize the possible interpretations of a why-question, the
system must have some notion of what "why?" can be asked about. From this
example, we see that we can ask why about (at least) the following:

Q1:   why a goal is being pursued

Q2:   why a particular method is being used to achieve that
       goal

Q3:   why a particular method is being applied

Q4:   why an individual is a member of a generic class

In our model, when the user asks "Why?", candidate interpretations are formed
by considering the text plan that generated the explanation that elicited the
user's why-question. Text plan trees contain two types of structures that can
lead to interpretations of why-questions: speech act nodes and RST nodes.
For each type of speech act and each type of RST relation currently employed
in our system, we have identified what why-question(s) can be asked about
that speech act or relation. A detailed discussion of the rules for generating
candidate interpretations is beyond the scope of this paper and may be found
in (Moore, 1989). However, the rules allow the system to generate the four
general classes of questions represented by Q1–Q4 above.

When several interpretations are possible, the system must be able to choose between them. Our system uses the following heuristics to identify and choose among multiple interpretations:

DH1: Follow immediate focus rules, i.e., continuing on the same topic is preferred over returning to a previously mentioned topic, (Sidner, 1979; McKeown, 1985).

DH2: Don't tell the user things he already knows.

DH3: Don't tell the user things you've already said.

The first heuristic, DH1, embodies the knowledge that focus of attention provides the strongest expectations about subsequent utterances. When the user simply asks "Why?", the question is probably referring to the last thing the speaker said. However, there are exceptions. What the hearer knows and what the hearer can reasonably expect the speaker to know that the hearer knows also affect what why-question is being asked. For example, if in the current situation the user model indicates that the user knows that CAR-to-FIRST is a transformation that enhances readability, then he is probably not asking question I4. Moreover, since the system began the dialogue by asking what characteristics of the program the user would like enhanced and the user chose readability, the user is very unlikely to ask the question in I1. Similarly, if the answer to the why-question under consideration has already been given in the previous dialogue, the user is probably not asking that question again. The knowledge of these exceptions is encoded in heuristics DH2 and DH3.

Although the tasks of identifying possible interpretations and selecting among them are distinct, it would be computationally inefficient to identify *all* interpretations and then choose among them, as there may be many possible interpretations. To increase efficiency, our system creates "likely" interpretations first, and then uses heuristics to rule them out. If an interpretation cannot be ruled out, it is chosen as the interpretation of the user's question and a response is generated. Of course, if the system's interpretation is incorrect, the user can still recover by asking a follow-up question.

We have found that focus of attention (DH1) is a powerful heuristic for ordering the generation of likely interpretations. In the current example when the user asks "Why?", the focus of attention (indicated by the *local-context*) is the statement "CAR-TO-FIRST is a transformation that enhances readability." The system thus infers that the question concerns the rationale behind this statement (I4), unless this interpretation can be ruled out by DH2 or DH3. For example, that interpretation could be ruled out by DH2 if the system inferred (based on the user model) that the user already knew why CAR-TO-FIRST enhances readability. Our system makes the assumption that if the user believes a fact, then he accepts it and is not asking why this fact is true. Thus, in this case, if the user model contains the assertion

A1: (BEL USER
        (INSTANCE-OF CAR-TO-FIRST
                     TRANSFORMATIONS-THAT-ENHANCE-READABILITY))
then the user is not asking why this is the case.

First, let us assume that our user model does *not* contain the assertion A1. Therefore interpretation I4 cannot be ruled out by heuristic DH2. Next, the system tries DH3. Since the dialogue history indicates that the system has not previously persuaded the user that CAR-TO-FIRST is a transformation that enhances readability, i.e., there is no completed text plan for the discourse goal

(PERSUADED USER
        (INSTANCE-OF CAR-TO-FIRST
                     TRANSFORMATIONS-THAT-ENHANCE-READABILITY))

DH3 also fails to rule out this interpretation and so the system interprets the user's question as asking "Why is CAR-TO-FIRST a transformation that enhances readability?" (interpretation I4).

To answer this question, the system must identify the features of the CAR-TO-FIRST transformation that allow it to be classified as a transformation that enhances readability. Figures 1.18 and 1.19 show some of the terminological knowledge that the PEA system has about transformations that enhance readability. In Figure 1.18, we see that a readability transformation is a transformation whose right-hand-side part is more readable than its left-hand-side part. Figure 1.19 shows that one type of readability transformation are those transformations whose rhs-part is a LISP function whose function name is an English word and whose lhs-part is a LISP function whose function name is a technical word. The CAR-to-FIRST transformation is of this type.

Explaining this terminological knowledge leads the system to generate the response on line [7] of Figure 1.10, repeated here for the reader's convenience.

> Transformations that enhance readability are transformations whose right-hand-side is more readable than their left-hand-side. One type of such transformations are transformations whose right-hand-side is a function whose function name is an English word and whose left-hand-side is a function whose function name is a technical word. CAR-to-FIRST is of this type.

To see how the remaining interpretations are identified, suppose now that the user model indicates that the user *does* know that CAR-TO-FIRST is a transformation that enhances readability and is therefore not asking why this fact is true. In this case, the first interpretation considered, I4, will be ruled out by DH2. When this occurs, the system uses the next most recent focus of attentionto form the next possible interpretation. The text plan records the order in which topics appear in the explanation. This information is used to derive foci of attention in order. The next most recent focus of attention in the text plan shown in Figure 1.17 is the node labeled 2. The interpretation of "Why?" formed from this ELABORATION-GENERAL-SPECIFIC RST node is

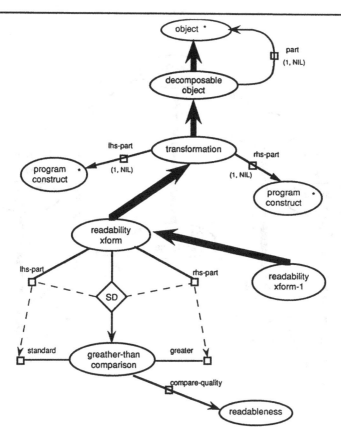

Figure 1.18: Terminological knowledge about CAR-to-FIRST Transformation - 1

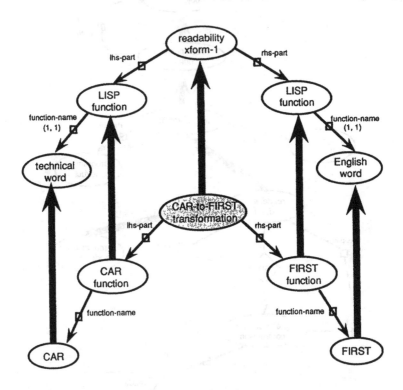

Figure 1.19: Terminological knowledge about CAR-to-FIRST Transformation - 2

> Why is applying CAR-TO-FIRST an instance of applying transformations that enhance readability?

However, this interpretation is subsumed by the interpretation formed from the **INFORM** in node 1, i.e., I4.[15] Thus if I4 were ruled out once, it will be ruled out again here. Therefore, the system considers the next most recently focused node, in this case, node 3.

Node 3 is an **INFORM** that states the method the system is applying to achieve a goal (i.e., **APPLY-TRANSFORMATIONS-THAT-ENHANCE-READABILITY**). This leads to interpretation I3, namely "Why are you applying transformations that enhance readability?". But note that the user would probably not wish to ask this question because it was already answered when the system said "I'm trying to enhance the readability of the program by applying transformations that enhance readability" (line [5], Figure 1.10). Our system can determine that this question has already been answered by examining the text plan that produced the system's previous utterance. To do this, the system uses the semantics of the rhetorical relation **MEANS**. The **MEANS** relation associates the statement of a goal with a statement of the method used to achieve that goal. Thus, since the act **APPLY-TRANSFORMATIONS-THAT-ENHANCE-READABILITY** appears in the second position of a **MEANS** relation, the system determines that it has just told the user why it is using this method, namely to achieve the goal **ENHANCE-READABILITY**. Therefore, heuristic DH3 rules out interpretation I3.

The next most recent focus is the **MEANS** relation itself, node 4. From this node, the system forms the interpretation that the user is asking why the system is using this particular method (**APPLY-TRANSFORMATIONS-THAT-ENHANCE-READA-BILITY**) to achieve the goal (**ENHANCE-READABILITY**). That is, the user is asking "Why are you trying to enhance the readability of the program by applying transformations that enhance readability?", interpretation I2. If this interpretation were also ruled out, the system would next consider the node labeled 5 in Figure 1.17. This node informs the user that the system is trying to achieve the goal **ENHANCE READABILITY OF THE PROGRAM**. This leads to interpretation I1, i.e., "Why are you trying to enhance the readability of the program?" But note that this interpretation will be ruled out by DH2 because the system knows that the user shares the goal of enhancing readability because of the exchange on lines [1] – [2] of the dialogue.

At this point, the system has run out of possible interpretations for the user's why-question since it has reached the top node in the text plan. When the system reaches top node in the text plan without finding an acceptable interpretation, it chooses the interpretation most favored by the focus heuristic, DH1. This will always correspond to the first interpretation considered. In this case, interpretation I4, "Why is CAR-to-FIRST a transformation that enhances readability?"

---

[15] See (Moore, 1989) for details.

SYSTEM	What characteristics of the program would you like to enhance?	[1]
USER	Readability and maintainability.	[2]
	⋮	
SYSTEM	You should replace (SETQ X 1) with (SETF X 1).	[3]
USER	What's the difference between SETF and SETQ?	[4]
SYSTEM	SETF can be used to assign a value to any generalized variable. SETQ can only be used to assign a value to a simple variable.	[5]
USER	What is a generalized-variable?	[6]
SYSTEM	Simple-variables are storage locations named by symbols. This concept can be generalized to a storage location that can be named by any accessor function. These storage locations are called generalized-variables.	[7]
USER	Huh?	[8]
SYSTEM	For example, the *car* and *cdr* of a cons are generalized-variables, named by the accessor functions CAR and CDR. Other examples are an element of an array or a component of a structure.	[9]

Figure 1.20: Sample Dialogue

Note that our system is able to come up with the four interpretations of the user's ambiguous why-question and intelligently choose among these interpretations precisely because it records and understands its own responses. It is important to note that in this example, context and focus information are derived from the *system's* statement, *not* the user's. The user simply types "Why?" in his first two queries in the dialogue; context comes from the response generated by the system. Until now, much work has concentrated on building discourse models that keep track of the user's goals and plans – both domain goals (Carberry, 1983; McKeown *et al.*, 1985) and discourse goals (Litman, 1985). Little work has been done on keeping track of the system's discourse goals and the plans it uses to achieve them.[16] As our example illustrates, conversational context must include the system's statements.

We intend that the disambiguation heuristics will identify the best interpretation of the question most of the time. However, there may be cases where, because the user model is incomplete or incorrect, the wrong interpretation is chosen and the wrong why-question is answered. In that case we rely on the user to indicate dissatisfaction in some way (possibly by re-asking the question in another form). The system must be prepared to recover later if the chosen interpretation is not the correct one. Because our system keeps track of what questions are asked and the planning process that led to its responses, it is able to do just that.

---

[16] Although in recent work on a theory of discourse structure, Grosz and Sidner (1986) show how recording the intentional, attentional, and linguistic structure of the entire discourse (i.e., of all participants) is needed in order to handle certain discourse phenomena such as interruptions, the use of certain types of referring expressions, and cue phrases. However, their model has not yet been implemented.

NAME: **describe-by-abstraction**
EFFECT: **(BEL ?hearer (CONCEPT ?concept))**
CONSTRAINTS: **(AND (SUBCLASS ?sub-concept ?concept)**
                     (BEL ?hearer (CONCEPT ?sub-concept))
                     (IMMEDIATE-SUBCLASS ?concept
                                ?super-concept))
NUCLEUS:
  ((SETQ ?diffs (FIND-ESSENTIAL-DIFFERENCES ?sub-concept
                                  ?super-concept))
   (SETQ ?subc-attrs
      (GET-ATTRS-OF-CONCEPT-FROM-DIFFS ?sub-concept
                                ?diffs))
   (SETQ ?concept-attrs
      (GET-ATTRS-OF-CONCEPT-FROM-DIFFS ?concept ?diffs))
   (INFORM ?speaker ?hearer
        (CLASS-ASCRIPTION ?sub-concept
                      (?super-concept ?subc-attrs))))
SATELLITES: **(((ABSTRACTION ?sub-concept ?concept**
                      ?super-concept ?concept-attrs)))

Figure 1.21: Plan Operator for Describing an Object by Abstraction

1.5.3 Answering a Vaguely-Articulated Follow-Up Question

Now consider the sample dialogue shown in Figure 1.20. In this example, the system uses the term "generalized variable" when explaining the difference between SETQ and SETF, see line [5]. The user is not familiar with this term and asks the question, "What is a generalized variable?" on line [6]. In this section, we illustrate how the system plans its response to this question and how the system then elaborates on that response after the user indicates that the response was not understood.

When the user asks the question, "What is a generalized-variable?" on line [6], the query analyzer interprets the question and posts the discourse goal (BEL USER (CONCEPT GENERALIZED-VARIABLE)) to the text planner. This goal may be paraphrased as saying the speaker wishes to achieve the state where the hearer knows about the concept GENERALIZED-VARIABLE. The system has several plan operators for achieving such a goal. For example, the system may describe a concept by describing its attributes and its parts, by drawing an analogy with a similar concept, by giving examples of the concept, or by generalizing a concept the user is familiar with. The plan operator for the latter is shown in Figure 1.21.

To choose from among these candidate plan operators, the planner has several selection heuristics, including:

SH1:   Prefer operators that require making no assumptions about the hearer's beliefs.

SH2:   Prefer operators that make use of a concept the hearer knows.

SH3:   Prefer operators that make use of a concept mentioned in the dialogue history.

In this case, suppose that the user model indicates that the hearer knows the concept SIMPLE-VARIABLE. Hence the operator in Figure 1.21 requires making no assumptions about the hearer's knowledge, makes use of a concept the hearer knows (SIMPLE-VARIABLE), and uses a concept previously mentioned in the dialogue (SIMPLE-VARIABLE). Thus it is ranked highest by the plan selection heuristics and is chosen. The final text plan for this example first describes SIMPLE-VARIABLE and then abstracts this concept to introduce GENERALIZED-VARIABLE. This produces the system's response on line [7] in the sample dialogue.

The user then indicates that he does not understand this explanation with the vaguely-articulated follow-up, "Huh?", line [8]. From our analysis of naturally occurring dialogues, we devised a set of *recovery heuristics* for responding when a user indicates misunderstanding, but does not ask a well-formulated question. These include:

RH1   If the discourse goal is to describe a concept, give example(s).

RH2   If the discourse goal is to describe a concept, and there is an analogous entity that the hearer knows, draw an analogy to the familiar concept.

RH3   Expand any unexpanded optional satellites in plan operators used in previous explanation.

RH4   If another plan exists for achieving the discourse goal, try it.

RH1 and RH2 apply in the context of a particular discourse goal, namely describing a concept, while the other heuristics are more general. The system tries to apply its most specific knowledge first. In this example, RH1 applies and the explainer recovers on line [9] by giving examples.

As illustrated in Figure 1.21, constraints on plan operators often refer to the state of the hearer's knowledge. The user model includes the domain concepts and problem-solving knowledge, i.e., goals and plans, assumed to be known to the current user. However, the system does not require that this model is be either complete or correct. Therefore, the user model may contain concepts the user does not actually know or omit concepts the user does know. To satisfy a constraint on an operator, the system may assume that a concept is known to the user even if it is not indicated in the user model. As described above, when such an assumption is made, the selection heuristics give the operator a lower rating. If the operator is selected, the fact that an assumption was made is recorded in the plan structure. The system must keep track of such assumptions because these are likely candidates if a misunderstanding occurs later. This leads to another recovery heuristic:

RH5   If any assumptions were made in planning the last explanation, plan responses to make these assumptions true.

For example, in producing the above response about the differences between SETF and SETQ, the system made the assumption that the user knew what generalized variables were and simply used this term in the explanation without describing it further. If, in the sample dialogue in Figure 1.20 the user had typed "Huh?" on line [6] instead of explicitly asking "What is a generalized variable?" the system would determine from the text plan for its previous response that it had made an assumption that the user knew the concept GENERALIZED-VARIABLE and would plan a response to make this assumption true by describing generalized variables.

1.6   STATUS AND FUTURE WORK

The expert system and explanation facility described are implemented in Common Lisp. There are approximately 75 plan operators, 5 plan selection heuristics, and 6 recovery heuristics. The system can participate in the dialogues shown and several others – see (Moore, 1989; Paris, 1990). The system can answer the following types of (follow-up) questions:

- Why?
- Why *conclusion*?
- Why are you trying to achieve *goal*?
- Why are you using *method* to achieve *goal*?
- Why are you doing *act*?
- How do you achieve *goal*?
- How did you achieve *goal* (in this case)?
- What is a *concept*?
- What is the difference between *concept1* and *concept2*?
- Huh?

The text planning system described in this paper is being incorporated into two additional expert systems currently under development. These systems will be installed and used in the field. This will give us an opportunity to evaluate the techniques described here.

1.6.1   More Sophisticated Management and Use of Dialogue History

One of the main areas for future work is in the management of the dialogue history. Currently the dialogue history is a simple stack. However, in some cases, it is apparent that a richer structure could easily be built. For example, consider the text plan produced for the recommendation shown in Figure 1.11 on page 25 and the subsequent text plan constructed in response to the user's why-question shown in Figure 1.17 on page 31. Rather than simply stacking these, we could build a larger structure relating the motivating information contained in Figure 1.17 to the recommendation. In fact, this structure is suggested by the "schema" *recommend-enable-motivate* embodied in the plan operator shown in Figure 1.7 on page 20. In this way, we could build a conceptual model of the dialogue as it progresses, relating subsequent utterances to the evolving model in appropriate ways.

Building such a structure may be useful in determining when topic shifts have occurred. For example, if a new utterance cannot be fit into the existing dialogue structure, this may signal that some type of subdialogue has been entered. Building such a structure may also aid in making effective use of the previous dialogue when producing new explanations. Using the completed text plans recorded in our dialogue history, we should be able to avoid repetitions as well as make more sophisticated use of previous explanations, such as drawing analogies to previous reasoning, and choosing examples from concepts that have previously been discussed.

Many questions about management and use of the dialogue history remain to be answered. It is not immediately obvious how all follow-up utterances are related to previous dialogue. For example, in the second sample dialogue on page 38, after the recommendation is made, the user asks how the two concepts mentioned in the recommendation differ. What is the relation between the text plan for contrasting the concepts and the recommendation that precedes it in dialogue history? Is it MOTIVATION, ELABORATION, or some other relation? How can the system determine the relationship in a systematic way? More work needs to be done in this area to determine what these relations are and how the explainer can recognize them to build a richer representation of the evolving conversation.

There are other interesting issues involved in managing the dialogue history. For example, how long should things be remembered? When can things be "forgotten"? Are some things more likely to be forgotten than others? What is the relationship between the dialogue history and the user model? When and what should migrate to user model? These are all interesting issues which we can investigate in the context of our current system.

1.6.2 Execution Monitoring

At the outset, we stated that a reactive explanation system should monitor the effects of its utterances on the listener and recover if feedback indicates the listener is not satisfied. With the current system, we have made preliminary progress towards these goals. Currently our system reacts to feedback initiated by the user after a complete response has been produced. There are two areas where future work is needed. First, the system should be capable of monitoring the effects of its utterances while they are being produced, and not only upon completion of an entire multi-sentential response. Second, the system should actively seek feedback from the listener by planning checking moves to determine if the listener is following and when enough has been said about a given topic.

More fine-grained execution monitoring would be desirable in our system, since if the hearer gets lost early on in an explanation, there may be little utility in completing it. Rather, the system should react and alter its strategy or provide elaboration so that the hearer is able to understand the rest of the explanation. In order to do this type of monitoring, the system must interleave the planning of a response with its realization. That is, the system must begin uttering the response before it has been completely planned. Some work in incremental sentence generation has been done (DeSmedt and Kempen, 1987, 1990), but little work has been done in the area of incremental generation of larger texts. In (Moore, 1989) we explore how we could interleave planning and realization in our current framework using the Penman system.

Once the system has the capability to interleave planning and realization, we can begin to consider when to seek feedback from the hearer and how to handle such feedback when it occurs. In (Moore, 1989), we discuss the requirements that the need to perform execution monitoring places on a planning system. There we argue that a rich representation of plan structure is essential to the tasks of execution monitoring and show how the text plan structures built by our text planner provide the information required. We also present preliminary ideas about how to decide what actions to monitor in a plan and to identify choice points during the planning process where feedback from the user would be helpful.

1.6.3 Incorporating Pragmatic Goals

In an attempt to alleviate some of the difficult problems of interleaving the tasks of text planning and realization, Hovy (1988b) has proposed an approach he calls *limited-commitment planning*. Such interleaving is difficult since the type of planning activated by the realization component is different from that of the text planner. To facilitate this interleaving, Hovy distinguishes two types planning needed for text generation. *Prescriptive goals* such as *persuade the hearer to perform an act* and *describe an object* act over and give shape to long ranges of text and are most naturally achieved in a top-down fashion. These are goals which activate prescriptive plans. *Restrictive goals* act over short ranges of text and usually aid the planner in selecting from a small number of alternatives presented to it by the realization component, e.g., choosing from a set of lexical items or acceptable syntactic structures. These are pragmatic and stylistic goals such as *impress the hearer* and *make the hearer feel socially subordinate*, and can never be totally achieved (Hovy, 1988b).

In our current work, we have only considered prescriptive goals in our planning model. We clearly need to incorporate pragmatic and stylistic goals into our system. In Hovy's model, there is currently no communication between prescriptive and restrictive goals, i.e., the choices made while satisfying prescriptive goals (e.g., persuade the hearer to perform an act) do not affect restrictive goals that are posted (e.g., be formal) or vice versa. We think there should be more interaction between these two types of goals since the discourse strategy chosen to achieve a prescriptive goal may affect the restrictive goals. For example, if we choose to persuade the hearer to do an act by citing the recommendations of experts, it may be appropriate to post pragmatic goals to make the hearer feel subordinate, impress the hearer, and be formal. However, if we choose to persuade the hearer by motivation (a strategy that enumerates all the goals an act will achieve), the pragmatic goals would be very different. Moreover, restrictive goals may affect prescriptive decisions. For example, if we have the goals to make the hearer feel subordinate and impress the hearer, it is more appropriate to persuade by invoking authority than to persuade by motivating. In addition, reacting to feedback or follow-up questions may cause changes in pragmatic goals, e.g., when asked to elaborate a previous response, the rhetorical goals of style such as detail and simplicity should become more important, while goals such as haste become less important.

1.6.4   Multi-Media Communication Planning

When people try to explain things to one another and feedback indicates that the listener is having trouble understanding, the speaker often finds it useful to draw a picture or diagram to make the explanation clearer. What do picture planning strategies look like? How can they be integrated with text planning strategies into a more general communication planning model? What are the primitive actions in planning diagrams? Are there any? What are the "rhetorical" relationships between parts of a diagram? How can a picture be elaborated, clarified? What kinds of follow-up activity makes sense after a picture is presented? Clearly there are many more questions than there are answers, but we would like to begin to explore some of these issues using our planner and see how our plan language and model of interaction will need to be extended to handle the demands of using a presentation medium other than text.

1.7   CONCLUSIONS

Current expert systems fail to support explanation as a dialogue. Their unnatural, one-shot approach to explanation depends critically on the quality of the user model and is seriously degraded if that model is incomplete or incorrect.

Given a query, one-shot systems respond with the best explanation they can produce. These systems do not keep a dialogue history, but even if they did, they do not have alternative strategies for producing responses or heuristics for deciding when different strategies are appropriate. Because they fail to support dialogue, these systems cannot clarify misunderstood explanations, elaborate on previous explanations, or respond to follow-up questions in the context of the on-going dialogue.

As an alternative, we proposed a reactive model of explanation – in which the system can employ feedback from the user and participate in a dialogue. Essential to our approach is the observation that the reactive capabilities we desire can be supported effectively by a system that explicitly represents and can reason about the "design" of its own explanations. Our explanation generation facility plans explanations from a rich set of strategies, keeping track of the system's discourse goals, the plans used to achieve them, and any assumptions made while planning a response. By maintaining a recorded history of the text plans used in producing responses, our system can later reason about its own responses when interpreting and determining how to respond to feedback from the listener. Our system can employ information in a user model when it is available, but is not critically dependent on that information.

ACKNOWLEDGMENTS

The research described in this paper was supported by the Defense Advanced Research Projects Agency (DARPA) under a NASA Ames cooperative agreement number NCC 2-520. The authors would like to thank Cécile Paris for her collaboration on the text planner, Eduard Hovy for useful discussions, the members of the Penman Project (Bob Kasper, John Bateman, Richard Whitney and Robert Albano) for their invaluable assistance, and all of the individuals mentioned above for their comments on earlier drafts of this paper.

BIBLIOGRAPHY

(Appelt, 1985) Appelt, Douglas E. 1985. *Planning English Sentences*. Cambridge University Press, Cambridge, England.

(Buchanan and Shortliffe, 1984) Buchanan, Bruce G. and Shortliffe, Edward H. 1984. *Rule-Based Expert Systems: The MYCIN Experiments of the Stanford Heuristic Programming Project*. Addison-Wesley Publishing Company.

(Carberry, 1983) Carberry, Sandra 1983. Tracking user goals in an information-seeking environment. In *Proceedings of the Third National Conference on Artificial Intelligence*, Washington, D.C. 59–63.

(Clancey and Letsinger, 1981) Clancey, William J. and Letsinger, Reed 1981. NEOMYCIN: Reconfiguring a rule-based expert system for application to teaching. In *Proceedings of the Seventh International Joint Conference on Artificial Intelligence*, Vancouver, B. C., Canada. 829–836.

(Clancey, 1983) Clancey, William J. 1983. The epistemology of a rule-based expert system: a framework for explanation. *Artificial Intelligence* 20(3):215–251.

(Cohen and Perrault, 1979) Cohen, Philip R. and Perrault, C. Raymond 1979. Elements of a plan-based theory of speech acts. *Cognitive Science* 3:177–212.

(Davis, 1976) Davis, Randall 1976. *Applications of Meta-level Knowledge to the Construction, Maintenance, and Use of Large Knowledge Bases*. Ph.D. Dissertation, Stanford University.

(De Smedt and Kempen, 1987) De Smedt, Koenraad and Kempen, Gerard 1987. Incremental sentence production, self-correction and coordination. In *Natural Language Generation: New Results in Artificial Intelligence*. Martinus Nijhoff Publishers.

(De Smedt and Kempen, 1990) De Smedt, Koenraad and Kempen, Gerard 1987. Segment Grammar: a Formalism for Incremental Sentence Generation In *Natural Language Generation in Artificial Intelligence and Computational Linguistics*, (this volume). Paris, Swartout, Mann (Eds). Kluwer Academic Publishers, Norwell, MA.

(Grosz and Sidner, 1986) Grosz, Barbara J. and Sidner, Candace L. 1986. Attention, intention, and the structure of discourse. *Computational Linguistics* 12(3):175–204.

(Hovy, 1988a) Hovy, Eduard H. 1988a. Planning coherent multisentential text. In *Proceedings of the Twenty-Sixth Annual Meeting of the Association for Computational Linguistics*, State University of New York, Buffalo, New York.

(Hovy, 1988b) Hovy, Eduard H. 1988b. Two types of planning in language generation. In *Proceedings of the Twenty-Sixth Annual Meeting of the Association for Computational Linguistics*, State University of New York, Buffalo, New York.

(Hovy, 1990) Hovy, Eduard H. 1990. Approaches to the planning of coherent text. In *Natural Language Generation in Artificial Intelligence and Computational Linguistics*, (this volume). Paris, Swartout, Mann (Eds). Kluwer Academic Publishers, Norwell, MA.

(Kasper, 1989) Kasper, Robert 1989. SPL: A sentence plan language for text generation. Technical Report forthcoming, USC/Information Sciences Institute.

(Kass and Finin, 1988) Kass, Robert and Finin, Tim 1988. Modeling the user in natural language systems. *Computational Linguistics* 14(3):5–22.

(Kendon, 1967) Kendon, Adam 1967. Some functions of gaze-direction in social interaction. *Acta Psychologica* 26:22–63.

(Litman, 1985) Litman, Diane 1985. *Plan Recognition and Discourse Analysis: An Integrated Approach for Understanding Dialogues.* Ph.D. Dissertation, University of Rochester. Published by University of Rochester as Technical Report TR 170.

(Mann and Matthiessen, 1983) Mann, William C. and Matthiessen, Christian 1983. Nigel: A systemic grammar for text generation. Technical Report RR-83-105, USC/Information Sciences Institute.

(Mann and Thompson, 1987) Mann, William C. and Thompson, Sandra A. 1987. Rhetorical Structure Theory: A theory of text organization. In Polanyi, Livia, editor 1987, *The Structure of Discourse.* Ablex Publishing Corporation, Norwood, N.J. Also available as USC/Information Sciences Institute Technical Report Number RS-87-190.

(Matthiessen, 1984) Matthiessen, Christian M. I. M. 1984. Systemic grammar in computation: the Nigel case. Technical Report RR-83-121, USC/Information Sciences Institute.

(McCoy, 1989) McCoy, Kathleen F. 1989. Generating context sensitive responses to object-related misconceptions. *Artificial Intelligence* 41(2):157–195.

(McKeown *et al.*, 1985) McKeown, Kathleen R.; Wish, Myron; and Matthews, Kevin 1985. Tailoring explanations for the user. In *Proceedings of the Ninth International Joint Conference on Artificial Intelligence*, Los Angeles, CA. 794–798.

(McKeown, 1985) McKeown, Kathleen R. 1985. *Text Generation: Using Discourse Strategies and Focus Constraints to Generate Natural Language Text.* Cambridge University Press, Cambridge, England.

(Moore and Paris, 1988) Moore, Johanna D. and Paris, Cécile L. 1988. Constructing coherent text using rhetorical relations. In *Proceedings of the Tenth Annual Conference of the Cognitive Science Society*, Montreal, Quebec.

(Moore and Paris, 1989) Moore, Johanna D. and Paris, Cécile L. 1989. Planning text for advisory dialogues. In *Proceedings of the Twenty-Seventh Annual Meeting of the Association for Computational Linguistics*, Vancouver, B.C., Canada.

(Moore and Swartout, 1990) Moore, Johanna D. and Swartout, William R. 1990. Pointing: A way toward explanation dialogue. In *Proceedings of the National Conference on Artificial Intelligence*, Boston, MA.

(Moore, 1989) Moore, Johanna D. 1989. *A Reactive Approach to Explanation in Expert and Advice-Giving Systems.* Ph.D. Dissertation, University of California, Los Angeles.

(Neches *et al.*, 1985) Neches, Robert, Swartout, William R. and Moore, Johanna D. 1985. Enhanced maintenance and explanation of expert systems through explicit models of their development. *IEEE Transactions on Software Engineering* SE-11(11).

(Paris, 1988) Paris, Cécile L. 1988. Tailoring object descriptions to the user's level of expertise. *Computational Linguistics* 14(3):64–78.

(Paris, 1990) Paris, Cécile L. 1990. Generation and explanation: Building an explanation facility for the explainable expert systems framework. In *Natural Language Generation in Artificial Intelligence and Computational Linguistics*, (this volume). Paris, Swartout, Mann (Eds). Kluwer Academic Publishers, Norwell, MA.

(Pollack *et al.*, 1982) Pollack, Martha E., Hirschberg, Julia and Webber, Bonnie Lynn 1982. User participation in the reasoning processes of expert systems. Technical Report CIS-82-10, University of Pennsylvania. A short version of this report appears in the Proceedings of the Second National Conference on Artificial Intelligence 1982.

(Ringle and Bruce, 1981) Ringle, Martin H. and Bruce, Bertram C. 1981. Conversation failure. In Lehnert, Wendy G. and Ringle, Martin H., editors 1981, *Knowledge Representation and Natural Language Processing*. Lawrence Erlbaum Associates, Hillsdale, New Jersey. 203–221.

(Sacerdoti, 1975) Sacerdoti, Earl D. 1975. A structure for plans and behavior. Technical Report TN-109, SRI.

(Sidner, 1979) Sidner, Candace L. 1979. *Toward a Computational Theory of Definite Anaphora Comprehension in English Discourse.* Ph.D. Dissertation, Massachusetts Institute of Technology, Cambridge, Mass.

(Sparck Jones, 1984) Sparck Jones, Karen 1984. User models and expert systems. Technical Report No. 61, University of Cambridge Computer Laboratory.

(Swartout and Smoliar, 1987) Swartout, William R. and Smoliar, Stephen W. 1987. On making expert systems more like experts. *Expert Systems* 4(3).

(Swartout, 1981) Swartout, William R. 1981. Explaining and justifying expert consulting programs. In *Proceedings of the Seventh International Joint Conference on Artificial Intelligence*, Vancouver, B. C., Canada. 815–823.

(Swartout, 1983) Swartout, William R. 1983. XPLAIN: A system for creating and explaining expert consulting systems. *Artificial Intelligence* 21(3):285–325. Also available as ISI/RS-83-4.

Chapter 2

Generation and Explanation: Building an Explanation Facility for the Explainable Expert Systems Framework

Cécile L. Paris

Abstract: Generating explanations for expert systems has not been seen as a sophisticated generation problem in the past, and researchers working on expert system explanations (mainly researchers working on expert systems themselves) have been largely separated from the natural language generation community. In this paper, we argue that explanation for expert systems can benefit from the more sophisticated generation techniques being developed in computational linguistics and that explanation for expert systems actually provides a rich domain in which to study natural language generation. We describe our efforts to build a generation facility for the Explainable Expert Systems (EES) framework, presenting the requirements for this generation task and the issues addressed. We initially tried to use known natural language generation techniques but were led to design a new text planner, as these techniques did not fit our needs. This paper thus presents an overview of the generation facility being built for EES, including an 'historical' perspective that explains the decisions we made. Finally, we briefly present directions for future research.

2.1   INTRODUCTION

Generating explanations for expert systems has not been seen as a sophisticated
generation problem in the past, and researchers working on expert system explanations (mainly researchers working on expert systems themselves) have been
largely separated from the natural language generation community. In this paper, we argue that explanation for expert systems can benefit from the more
sophisticated generation techniques being developed in computational linguistics and that explanation for expert systems actually provides a rich domain in
which to study natural language generation. This is the view that we are taking
in the Explainable Expert System (EES) project. We are currently building an
explanation facility for EES. In this paper, we start with an overview of the
EES project in terms of the generation task, identifying the problems involved
in producing an explanation. We then present the requirements we are imposing on our generation facility. We argue that it is not enough for a generation
facility to produce coherent text. In order to be really useful, a generation facility needs to have flexible discourse strategies, be able to tailor its answers to
various users, answer follow-up questions and tune itself based on experience.
We show how our initial attempt to construct our explanation routine has led
us to develop a new text planner to fit all our requirements. We also how we
were able to apply research done in previous work to tailor answers to users.
This paper ends with a brief discussion of new research being pursued.

2.2   NATURAL LANGUAGE GENERATION AND EXPLANATION FOR EXPERT SYSTEMS

2.2.1   Current Expert System Explanation Facilities

Generating explanations for an expert system is recognized as an important
problem as it is widely accepted that expert systems are most useful and trusted
when they can satisfactorily explain how they reached their conclusion or recommendation (Buchanan and Shortliffe, 1984; Swartout, 1983; Teach and Shortliffe, 1984). Much effort has been spent on trying to produce explanations of
the behavior of expert systems, e.g., (Wallis and Shortliffe, 1982; Clancey, 1981;
Clancey, 1983; Swartout, 1984). Yet, explanation routines of current expert systems do not provide entirely satisfactory results. The following are the main
reasons behind the inadequacy of current expert systems explanation capabilities:

- There is often a lack of underlying domain knowledge (Clancey, 1983;
  Swartout, 1985). An expert system typically has a lot of information

about problem solving techniques in a particular domain, but it does not have any information regarding why the problem solving rules it has can achieve their goals. This knowledge usually stays in the head of the experts who help build the system. As a result, it is impossible for a system to justify its behavior.

- Explanation has not been seen as a problem solving task separated from the expert system's problem solving activity. Explanation routines have been most often built in ad-hoc ways, with no linguistic knowledge about how texts should be constructed. As a result, explanations have for the most part been isomorphic to the problem solving structure. While the problem solving structure may be the most efficient way for an expert system to solve a problem, it is often not entirely coherent to users.

- While transcripts of interactions between expert and novices indicate that the explanation process should be highly interactive, explanation has usually been generated as a 'one-shot' response, that is one answer is generated and there are little dialogue capabilities. Typically, users cannot request an elaboration or clarification of a given answer.

2.2.2 Constructing an Appropriate Answer

The first point mentioned above has already been addressed by a number of researchers e.g., (Clancey, 1983; Swartout, 1983; Swartout, 1985) by augmenting an expert system's knowledge base with the underlying knowledge necessary to explain the problem solving techniques used by the system. While these efforts now allow a system to provide explanations, the resulting richer knowledge base renders the explanation process more complex, as there is now more information to choose from.

Anytime a knowledge base contains different kinds of knowledge, generating a coherent text from it in response to a question becomes a problem: a generation system has to choose the most appropriate facts from all the available knowledge and combine them into a coherent answer. Typically, there are no clear constraints indicating what should be included in a text. Furthermore, when a generation facility is to provide responses to several types of users, it becomes important to identify what type of answer is most appropriate for each.

In order to be effective and appropriate, a response should be:

- informative: it must contain information the user does not already know;

- coherent: it must be organized in some coherent manner;

- understandable: it must be stated in terms the user understands and contain information that the user will be able to grasp;

- relevant: it must provide information that will help users achieve their goals.

- of the correct interpersonal force: the tone of the response should be such as to not appear sharp or unpleasant.

Work in Natural Language Generation (NLG) has focused on developing sophisticated techniques to generate appropriate responses and coherent texts for various kinds of knowledge bases, specifically addressing the points mentioned above. In the past, expert systems have used very simple techniques to generate explanations of the system's behavior. As expert systems become more complex and the need for good explanation facility increase, it becomes important to consider expert system generation as a complex generation task, of the kind addressed by researchers in the field of text generation. Explanations have usually been generated using traces of the expert system's reasoning, and efforts were concentrated on finding heuristics to make the generated text 'more readable.' As more knowledge was added to expert system knowledge bases, expert system became very complex systems, containing different kinds of knowledge. One cannot expect appropriate explanations to be produced by merely paraphrasing the execution trace produced while solving a given problem. While an explanation facility needs to have access to the execution trace, it also needs to have linguistic knowledge about natural language. Furthermore, in explaining the system's behavior, it is sometimes necessary to include knowledge other than the execution trace, such as the terminology that underlies the system's method for solving a problem. Finally, explaining the expert system reasoning is not the only type of interaction that needs to be handled by a generation facility. For example, a user might want to know exactly when a method for solving a problem is applicable, or why would one method be preferred over another one.

The task of generating explanations for expert systems needs to be considered as a problem in text generation, a problem-solving task in its own right. It should be separated from the problem solving activity of the expert system and studied independently.[1]

In fact, expert system explanation is not just another application for natural language generation, for which all is needed is the straightforward application of known NLG techniques. Instead, it provides a rich domain in which to study language, as there are many kinds of questions that need be answered, different types of users that interact with the system, and many possibilities

---

[1] There have been some initial attempts at using discourse strategies to explain an expert system's behavior (Kukich, 1985) but they were not fully implemented. It is only recently that researchers in expert system explanations have started to step away from simply tracing the execution trace and that the range of possible questions to address has been broadened. This is illustrated in McKeown *et al.* (1985) and van Beek (1987) , as well as in the work that was presented at the AAAI-88 *Workshop on Explanation*, e.g., (Moore and Swartout, 1988a; Cheong and Zukerman, 1988; Maybury, 1988; Suthers, 1988; Rankin *et al.*, 1988).

for dialogues. Indeed, the complexity of the language generation requirements reflects the complexity of the functionality of the system and its interactions with users.

In the Explainable Expert System (EES) project, we are strongly advocating these points of view: we are studying natural language generation within the framework provided by expert system explanations, therefore addressing the task of producing explanations for an expert system taking a NLG perspective. This is also illustrated in (Moore and Swartout, 1990 – this volume).

2.3 THE EES ARCHITECTURE AND HOW IT AFFECTS EXPLANATION

As mentioned above, a major reason behind the inadequacy of conventional expert systems explanation capabilities is their lack of underlying domain knowledge. In the EES project, Swartout and Smoliar have been concerned with building an architecture for expert systems that would alleviate this problem by augmenting the expert system with additional knowledge beyond that used directly in the problem-solving activity of the system (Swartout and Smoliar, 1987a; Swartout and Smoliar, 1987b). The main concern of the architecture is to allow for explanation of the system reasoning *and* of its underlying knowledge. In this framework, the expert system is designed with explanation in mind from the outset.

The EES framework is based on the observation that an excellent source of explanation of a system's behavior is often the person who wrote the system in the first place. In this paradigm, system builders and domain experts collaborate to represent, in a high-level specification language, the various kinds of knowledge that comprise an expert system, i.e., the *support knowledge*. An interpreter then uses that structured knowledge base to solve a given problem by refinement from a high-level goal, recording all its steps and decisions in a rich execution trace. Alternatively, an automatic programmer *derives* the expert system *methods* from this support knowledge and records the derivation, which constitutes the *design knowledge* for the system. The execution trace, the derivation knowledge and the structured knowledge base provide the rationale behind the system's reasoning that is needed to provide justifications of the expert system's actions. All these sources of knowledge are available to the explanation facility. This is illustrated in Figure 2.1. In EES, knowledge which in conventional expert systems has been implicitly represented is now represented explicitly: thus the support knowledge for explanation is now provided.

In addition, there is a clear distinction between *descriptive* and *problem-solving* knowledge. The expert system can thus use the problem-solving knowledge to solve a problem efficiently, while the explanation routine can employ the support knowledge which underlies the problem-solving activity to explain the system's behavior. In order for an explanation to be trusted, however, it has to be correct and rooted in the problem-solving activity of the expert system. This is clearly the case in EES, since the expert system is derived from the support knowledge. Therefore, in EES, although the *task* of generating a text is decoupled from the problem-solving activity of the expert system, the *knowledge* used in producing a response is connected to the knowledge actually employed by the expert system in solving a problem in valid ways.[2]

An expert system using this improved knowledge representation can now make use of sophisticated generation techniques to answer questions. In fact, it *must* use more sophisticated techniques: while it becomes possible for a system to justify its conclusions more fully by providing background information and to answer other types of questions, the explanation routine must now choose among different kinds of knowledge in order to construct an explanation. Generating an explanation in a system built using this architecture is a challenging problem. Some of the types of knowledge now available for explanation are:

- *Terminology*: this corresponds to the *lexicon* of the terms used in a domain, together with their definitions. For example, in one of the current domains in which EES is applied, the Digital Circuit Domain, knowledge of terminology includes definitions for the terms `system`, `terminal` and `adder`. The definition for an `adder` is shown in Figure 2.2. The terminology provides the building blocks out of which other kinds of knowledge are built.

- *Domain model*: the domain model is a description of the world the program is intended to operate in. It includes generic implications such as causal and structural information (that apply in general rather than specific cases). In the Digital Circuit Domain, for example, the domain model includes a circuit schematic.

- *Problem-solving knowledge*: this is the 'how to' knowledge, that is, the *problem-solving techniques* that can be used in the domain. It includes *goals* that state what is to be achieved, and *methods*, or *plans*, that indicate a sequence of steps that need to be followed in order to achieve the goal. Terminology definitions, domain principles and the domain model are all provided by an expert and a knowledge engineer while building the system.

- *'Compiled' knowledge*: this body of knowledge is derived automatically by the automatic programmer from the domain principles, the domain model and the terminology. It is procedural problem-solving knowledge, that contains the actual methods that will be used by the expert system to solve a problem.

---

[2]This is in contrast to Wick and Thompson (1989), where the domain model used to provide explanations is totally separate from the domain model used in the problem-solving activity of the expert system.

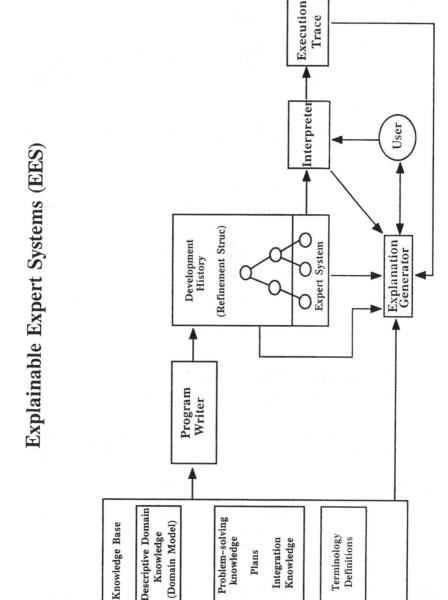

Figure 2.1: The Explainable Expert System Architecture

```
(define-type-attributes adder
    :specializes (primitive-system, binary-operator)
    :defining-conditions
        ((equal (expected-value (signal-part (output-part self)))
            (+ (expected-value (signal-part (first-binary-input self)))
                (expected-value (signal-part (second-binary-input self)))))))))
```

English paraphrase of this terminology definition:

An adder is a primitive system and binary operator. The expected value of its output terminal is equal to the sum of the expected values of its first binary input and its second binary input.

Figure 2.2: Example of Terminology Definition

- *A development history* or *refinement structure*: a trace of how the compiled knowledge, i.e., methods actually used by the expert system to solve a problem, have been derived, with a justification.

- *An execution trace*: a rich trace of the expert system problem-solving activity.

2.4   THE REQUIREMENTS FOR OUR EXPLANATION FACILITY

Given the complex knowledge base now at hand, an explanation facility has to be able to choose the appropriate facts to present to the user, and organize them in a coherent way. In this work, instead of simply tracing and augmenting the system execution trace, we decouple the generation task from the problem solving one and use *discourse strategies* to plan a text. Taking a natural language generation perspective, generating explanation for expert systems is a *text planning* issue and we will treat it as such. Our task is thus to design a *text planner* in which discourse strategies will become the plan operators. In designing this text planner, we want to make sure that the framework adopted will fit all the generation needs of EES (not just the short-term ones) as well as allow us to address all the issues that need to be considered. The requirements we are imposing on our generation facility are:

- *Ability to synthesize text directly from the underlying knowledge bases*: in order to be trusted, an explanation must reflect the system's reasoning and knowledge bases. To ensure this fidelity to the underlying knowledge sources, the explanation facility must construct explanations directly from these sources. It cannot rely on canned texts which are pre-written by a programmer. Indeed, as the system evolves and changes are made, it is impossible to ensure that the corresponding text has changed appropriately to reflect the change.

- *Ability to choose information to include and organize it into a coherent answer*: each different type of question to be considered requires a different type of answer, containing information from different sources, including, but not limited to, the execution trace. The information included in the answer should help users achieve their goal. The generation routine needs to be able to *decide* on the type of information needed and *extract* it from the knowledge base as well as *organize* it in a coherent way.

- *Extensibility to allow for breadth of coverage*: in order to be really useful, an expert system explanation facility needs to be able to handle many different types of questions, some of which are not necessarily foreseen at design time. When designing our text planner we must thus make sure that it will be possible to easily extend the explanation facility to respond to additional question types.

- *Tailoring answers to users*: given that an expert system can be used by different types of users, it will be most effective if it can customize its answers to each user, retrieving from its knowledge base the facts that are most appropriate and useful for that user. The explanation routine thus needs to construct responses taking into account information available in the user model (Cohen and Jones, 1987; van Beek, 1987; Paris, 1988b; McCoy, 1988). For example, information about a user's level of domain knowledge can guide the system in choosing information that the user does not already know but that he or she can understand.

- *Flexibility*: the effectiveness of an explanation routine is enhanced if it can produce multiple responses to one question, possibly using different perspectives. This is in fact required, in case an explanation is not understood the first time. The system must be able to offer a different explanation. Or, depending on the context, various explanations of the same aspect of the knowledge base might be required. We thus want to give our explanation routine the flexibility to use varied explanation strategies to present information to the users.

- *Dialogue capabilities*: studies have shown that, in naturally occurring situations (i.e., a person talking to an expert), the 'askers' frequently do not fully understand an expert's response. They often ask follow-up questions, which are requests for clarification, elaboration, or re-explanation of the expert's answer (Pollack *et al.*, 1982). We want our explanation facility to provide clarifying texts if an explanation is not understood.

- *Adaptive capabilities*: we would like to investigate the possibility to have the explanation facility automatically modify its existing strategies and learn new strategies based on experience and interactions with users.

An explanation will often require a multi-sentential text. In order to produce text that is coherent and most natural and understandable to the users, an explanation facility needs to have linguistic knowledge about how people use language to form coherent explanations, that is knowledge about how to structure a text to make it rhetorically coherent. We chose to express this knowledge using *discourse strategies*. Discourse strategies are designed by studying naturally occurring texts and interactions and thus characterize the kinds of explanations produced by humans. These strategies can guide our explanation facility in its decision process of deciding what to include in an answer and in organizing it. They have already been successfully used in generation systems, e.g., (Weiner, 1980; Mann, 1984; Kukich, 1985; McCoy, 1986; McKeown, 1985; Paris, 1987).

Before explaining how we built our explanation facility, we present the types of questions that we wish our system to be able to handle.

2.4.1 Identifying the Set of Questions to Answer

Many researchers have already studied the types of questions that need to be answered by an expert system in order to be useful (Swartout, 1985; Tanner and Josephson, 1988; Gilbert, 1988; Wexelblat, 1988). We are taking the following set as an initial set of questions to address:

1. Questions about methods: *how does the system do* action? *how shall I do what you ask me to do?*

2. Questions about events: *how did the system do* action?

3. Questions about the terminology: *what does* term *mean?*; *what is the difference between X and Y?*

4. Questions about the domain: *What does X cause?*

5. Justifications: *why is this question being asked? why is this action being recommended?*

6. Questions about preferences: *why is* method-a *preferred over* method-b?

7. Expectation failure: *why not* action *or* conclusion?

For each of these questions, we need to study how they should be answered and formalize the discourse strategies that will allow a generation facility to automatically produce answers to these questions. So far, we have addressed question 1 (describing a plan), part of question 3 (describing the terminology) and question 5 (justifying a conclusion or an action).

The next section presents our initial attempt to build the explanation facility for EES, together with an analysis of how well this attempt matched our requirements and how we were led to develop a new framework for the explanation routine. We then turn to one of our requirements, namely the tailoring of answers to the users. For a discussion of how the explanation facility is able to answer follow-up questions and participate in a dialogue, the reader is referred to (Moore and Swartout, 1990 – this volume).

2.5 DEVELOPING THE EXPLANATION FACILITY FOR EES

2.5.1 Initial Attempt: Use of Schemata

Based on our previous generation work (Paris, 1987), we first started to develop the explanation facility by developing *schemata* to answer several of the question types, namely for the terminology definitions and the behavior justifications. Using an already existing technique allowed us to start generating texts quickly as well as identify problems with the knowledge base and the design of the expert system.

Schemata are textual structures first posited by McKeown (1985) in her work on text generation. They were derived from linguistic analysis of texts having a common discourse goal. In such analysis, each sentence was classified as one of a set of rhetorical predicates.[3] Standard patterns of discourse emerged from these analyses. Schemata encode these standard patterns.

For the terminology definitions, we used the *identification* and the *constituency* schemata,[4] two of the schemata identified by McKeown. (In her work, McKeown had used these schemata to describe an object.) To justify a conclusion, we employed an adaptation of the *process trace*, a strategy identified in Paris (1987). (In Paris' system, this strategy was used to describe how an object performed its function.)

Both the identification schema and the constituency schema are *declarative strategies*, composed of rhetorical predicates, while the process trace is a *procedural strategy*, made up of *directives* on how to trace the knowledge base.[5] The three are script-like structures, which can be used in generation systems to generate coherent multi-sentential texts achieving a given discourse goal.

---

[3] Rhetorical predicates characterize the structural purpose of sentences.

[4] These schemata were simplified, as not all the information necessary to fulfill all the predicates contained in the schema is available in the knowledge base.

[5] The reader is referred to Paris and McKeown (1987) and Paris (1987, 1988b) for a fuller discussion on these two types of strategies.

2.5.2   Examples of How These Schemata Were Used to Produce Paragraph-Length Explanations

We will take terminology definitions as an illustration of how the schemata were used in the EES explanation facility. Two strategies could be used to explain the system terminology: the constituency schema and the identification schema. A strategy was chosen depending on the information contained in the knowledge base: if the object had parts, the constituency schema was applicable, otherwise, the identification schema was used. The constituency schema can be characterized by the four steps shown in Figure 2.3.[6]

Text is produced by 'filling the schema,' matching each rhetorical predicate against the knowledge base and retrieving the appropriate information. (Each predicate dictates the type of information to be retrieved from the knowledge base.) For example, the text generated using the constituency schema to produce a terminology definition of a `system` is shown in Figure 2.4. In the first sentence, the `system` is identified as a member of the generic class `physical object`. Then its parts are given, corresponding to the constituency predicate. Finally, the super-ordinate of some of the parts is presented when possible, corresponding to the depth-identification predicate.

Similarly, the identification schema is presented in Figure 2.5, and the text produced by filling this schema for an `adder` is given in Figure 2.6. (The internal definition of the `adder` was given earlier in the paper, in Figure 2.2.)

2.5.3   Do Schemata Fulfill Our Requirements?

Using this type of schemata for our generation facility allowed us to have a set of flexible discourse strategies that could be used to construct coherent texts, using patterns reflecting the ones used by humans. However, only five of our original requirements were fulfilled:

- *Ability to synthesize text directly from the underlying knowledge bases*: A function which retrieves the appropriate information from the knowledge base is associated with each predicate of the schema. As the schema is traversed, the appropriate information is thus obtained directly from the underlying knowledge sources.

- *Ability to choose information to include and organize it into a coherent answer*: the predicates used in a schema indicate the type of information to include in the answer, thus constraining the choice. When a schema

---

[6] This figure does not show the formal representation of the schema, including all the options and alternatives. A formal representation as well as a discussion about both the rhetorical predicates and the schemas have been presented at length elsewhere (McKeown, 1985; Paris, 1989).

Constituency Schema:

Identification	[Identify the object in terms of a generic class]
Constituency	[List the constituents (parts) of the object]
Depth-identification or *Depth-attributive*	
	[Provide some information about each part]
Attributive (opt)	[Provide additional information for the object]

Figure 2.3: The Constituency Schema

SYSTEM internal definition

```
(define-type-attributes system
    :new-relations ((input-part (specializes part)
                                (range input-terminal)
                                (inverse input-of))
                    (output-part (specializes part)
                                 (range output-terminal)
                                 (inverse output-of))
                    (component (specializes part)))
    :relation-restrictions ((input-part (min (necessary) 1))
                            (output-part (min (necessary) 1)))))
```

Description of a system using this schema:

A system is a physical object. *(identification)*
It has output-terminals, input-terminals and any number of components.
(constituency)
Output-terminals and input-terminals are terminals. *(depth-identification)*

Figure 2.4: Producing a definition of SYSTEM using the Constituency Schema

---

Identification Schema:

Identification   [Identify the object in terms of a generic class]
Analogy or *Attributive* [Analogy or Properties of the object]
Particular illustration or *Evidence* (opt)

Figure 2.5: The Identification Schema

An adder is a primitive system and a binary operator. *(identification)*
The expected value of its output terminal is equal to the sum of the expected
values of its first binary input and its second binary input. *(attributive)*

Figure 2.6: Producing a definition of adder using the Identification Schema

---

is filled, the information is extracted from the knowledge base. Furthermore, a schema constrains the order in which the information is to appear. Schemata can thus be employed to choose and organize information
to construct coherent multi-sentential texts. The examples given above
as well as previous work on generation illustrate this ability– e.g., see
(Weiner, 1980; Mann, 1984; Kukich, 1985; McCoy, 1986; McKeown, 1985;
Paris, 1987). As schemata are associated with discourse strategies for a
particular discourse goal, employing them enables a system to generate
answers providing information that will help users achieve their goals.

- *Extensibility*: adding new strategies is easy to do as we only need to add
  the corresponding schemata to the library of existing discourse strategies.

- *Flexibility*: flexibility is achieved by having several schemata for achieving
  the same discourse goal. For example, we had already built two schemata
  for the terminology definitions. While for some objects only one schema
  was applicable, it was still possible to use either schema for many of the
  domain concepts.

- *Tailoring*: the possibility to tailor answers to users using schemata has
  already been demonstrated in (Paris, 1987). A system can include different schemata representing the different discourse strategies employed for
  various users. Based on the information contained in a user model, the
  generation facility chooses the appropriate schema to traverse. It is also
  possible to combine schemata in one text for added flexibility in tailoring.

There were two capabilities that schemata could not provide: dialogue and
adaptive capabilities. In order to handle follow-up questions that may arise
in case the user does not fully understand a response given by the system,

the generation facility needs to know which part of the text failed to achieve its purpose. Using a schema as presented above, the system only knows the top-level discourse goal that was being achieved by the text (e.g., 'provide a terminology definition'). It does not know what effect the individual parts of the schema are intended to have on the hearer, or how they fit together to achieve the top-level goal. This information has been 'compiled out' into a 'script' that achieves a top-level goal, but the individual steps are no longer explainable. As a result, if the user did not understand a response, the only recovery possible is to use a different strategy to achieve the same top-level discourse goal. It is not possible to re-explain or clarify one part of the schema.[7]

Similarly, suppose the system notices that users always ask a particular question twice. This would probably be a good clue as to the inappropriateness of the first answer given. Using schemata of the type presented above, the only recourse the system would have is to stop using the discourse strategy employed in giving the answer the first time. It is more likely however that only part of the answer given was unclear and that it might just be necessary to modify only one step. This is not possible, as, again, there is no information that might allow the system to detect which part of the schema failed and why it failed.

To achieve these last two requirements, a text planner needs not only to have a set of flexible discourse strategies but it also needs to 'understand' the text plan it produces. The ability to produce coherent texts that might be tailored is not sufficient. An agent must understand the text it produces in terms of how each part of the text relates to the others, what effect each part is intended to have on the hearer and how the complete text achieves its goal. Once the text has been produced, a text planner must remember the discourse goals being achieved at any point and which rhetorical structures were being used. Otherwise, recovering from failure and learning (or self-tuning) is not possible. There is thus a need for a text plan to contain a *specification of the intended effect of individual parts of the text on the hearer and how the parts relate to one another.* The schemata employed in our initial attempt lacked such a specification (as it had been 'compiled out'), rendering our last two requirements impossible to fulfill.

2.5.4   Other Existing Generation Techniques

Besides schemata as used in our initial attempt to construct our generation facility, the other main computational model put forth to date is one in which text is planned by reasoning about the speaker and hearer's beliefs and the effects of utterances on these beliefs (Cohen and Perrault, 1979; Appelt, 1985). This approach has mainly been used to plan one- or two-sentence text containing *referring expressions* that are provably correct, i.e., it is possible to prove that

---

[7] Follow-up questions are discussed at length in (Moore and Swartout, 1990 – this volume).

the referent produced will be understood correctly, given the hearer's beliefs (Appelt, 1985). In this approach, plan operators include their effect on the hearer's beliefs (which was missing in the schema approach). However, there is no knowledge about how to combine individual speech acts into larger pieces of coherent text to achieve a high-level discourse goal. Furthermore, it appears that, because the system reasons about the hearer's beliefs at primitive speech act level and not at the level of high-level discourse goals, it is likely that this method would be quite computationally inefficient to plan paragraph-long sentences. Many of the questions that arise in a question answering system or an expert system explanation facility require generating text in response to a high-level discourse goal, such as 'provide a definition,' and 'justify a conclusion.' Answers to such questions are often paragraph-long and require combining several speech acts in a coherent manner. It is thus necessary to have the ability to combine individual speech acts into larger piece of texts as well as reason about the effects of various discourse goals on the hearer's beliefs.

At the time we started to develop our generation facility, Hovy had just started to employ rhetorical relations to structure multi-sentential texts. He had built a *text structurer*, addressing the task of taking a set of unordered input elements to be expressed and organizing them by means of rhetorical relations (Hovy, 1988b). In that work, he uses Rhetorical Structure Theory (RST), a theory of coherence developed by Mann and Thompson (1987).

Before Hovy's work, RST had been previously used mainly for text analysis (although it had been intended for use in generation). From an extensive text study, Mann and Thompson defined a set of relations that occur among pieces of texts (or among clauses). *Background* and *elaboration* are examples of such relations. The theory claims that a text is coherent if it can be hierarchically decomposed into segments (*text spans*) that can be linked using these relations. Each relation has a *nucleus* and zero or more *satellites*. The nucleus is the part of the text that is essential to the writer's purpose, while the satellites reinforce the effect of the nucleus. An RST decomposition of a text indicates how the text segments relate to one another, i.e., how they fit together. One decomposes a text using the schemata defined in (Mann and Thompson, 1987), in which each schema representing a relation specifies the requirement that must hold for the nucleus, the satellite and the combination of the two in order for this relation to hold. One can then draw a relation between the nucleus and a satellite. A nucleus may have more than one satellite. Figure 2.7 presents an example of a text decomposition, taken from (Mann and Thompson, 1987).

In this theory, any RST schema can be expanded into any other at any point. Furthermore, the RST schemata do not impose ordering constraints on a text. To use them in generation to construct a coherent text, one needs a way to dictate *which* relation to include *when* (Paris, 1987). Equally important, the constraints specified by Mann and Thompson for each relation are too loosely defined to allow a generation system to use them for actively constructing text, searching for appropriate information in the knowledge base.

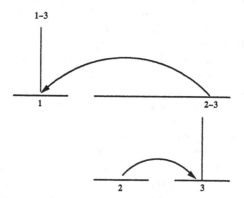

1. Concern that this material is harmful to health or the environment may be misplaced.

2. Although it is toxic to certain animals,

3. Evidence is lacking that it has any serious long-term effect on human beings.

Figure 2.7: Example of an RST text decomposition

In Hovy's structurer, the RST relations are represented as plans containing a nucleus and one or more satellites. Each plan indicates the relationship that must exist between the input element that is the nucleus and the input element that can satisfy the satellite requirement. For example, in order to construct a text containing the CIRCUMSTANCE relation between clauses describing X and Y, Y has to be the time of X or the location of X.[8]

In order to be able to construct *multi-sentential* text, Hovy included in each plan a set of *growth points*, which indicate other relations which might be appropriate at these particular points. Each plan is thus a group of rhetorical relations, indicating which relation is to appear when. A text is formed using a top-down planner which hierarchically expands the plans, looking for relations between input elements. This process is repeated until all the input elements have been used. (A more detailed presentation of this structurer is presented in (Hovy 1990 – this volume).)

Hovy also claims that it might be possible to consider expanding *any* of the RST relations at any point (which is more faithful to the RST theory as specified by Mann and Thompson), instead of the few specified in his plans at this time. In that case, however, there would be a need for some criteria for inclusion or exclusion of information as well as for the choice of the RST

---

[8] This is a loose paraphrase of the exact relations that are specified in Hovy (1988), namely *time* and *heading*.

to expand in order to constrain the process. Hovy mentions such criteria as the lack of space or the potential inability for the user to understand the extra information. These criteria alone, however, are not sufficient by themselves: for example, in order to include a fact in a text, it is not sufficient to know that it is understandable to the user. It must also be relevant to the discourse goal at hand. There is thus a need for some specification of a discourse goal to be achieved. Furthermore, these criteria have not yet been formalized. Currently, only the RST relations specified as growth points in the plan can be expanded, and, at each growth point, if the appropriate input is available, it is included in the text. The plans Hovy currently uses thus resemble McKeown's schemata (presented previously), except that the *rhetorical predicates* have been replaced by *rhetorical relations* so that a completed text plan includes the RST relations among the different pieces of text, indicating how they relate to each other. Like McKeown's schemata, these plans lack a specification of the effect of each text segment on the hearer's beliefs, i.e., what discourse goal was being achieved at each point while planning the text.

Finally, an implicit assumption of this approach is that choosing and organizing the information to be expressed are two unrelated tasks that can be decoupled. We do not believe this is a valid assumption in general, as we think that the two tasks often influence one another and are very dependent on each other. The choice of a rhetorical structure will affect the type of information to include in the text. Similarly, a particular piece of information that has to be included may require or at least favor the use of a particular predicate or relation for the subsequent proposition (Moore and Paris, 1988; Paris, 1988a). We want our generation facility to *both* choose the information and organize it into a coherent text. The lack of constraints that would allow a generation facility to choose the information to be expressed from the knowledge base is thus another drawback of Hovy's approach for our use.

2.5.5   From Schema to the New EES Text Plan Language

Because of the shortcomings of current generation techniques for our task, we found the need to develop a new plan language and a text planner that would incorporate both the discourse goals being achieved at any point and how the pieces of text relate to one another.[9]

Although we wanted to be able to reason about the speaker and hearer's beliefs, as in the plan-based approach, we also wanted to take advantage of the computational efficiency of the schema-based approach. Our system uses a top-down planning mechanism, in which plans are *either* representing a rhetorical relation or are plans that can be seen as small schemata *augmented* with the missing specifications of intended effects on the hearer. The steps of the schema

---

[9] This new plan language and text planner were developed jointly with Johanna Moore. It is also discussed in more detail in (Moore and Swartout, 1990 – this volume).

are either primitive speech acts or discourse goals specified in terms of their effects on the hearer. Our text planner reasons about both the intended effects of utterances on the hearer and the rhetorical means that were used to achieve these effects. Like Hovy, we are using RST as the theory of coherence necessary to indicate how the parts of a completed text plan relate to one another, as it provides us with a theory of text organization.

There are two types of plan operators in our system: operators whose effects are discourse goals, characterized in terms of their effect on the hearer's beliefs, and operators that achieve a particular rhetorical relation (an RST relation). Each plan operator consists of:

- **an effect:** a characterization of what goal(s) this operator can be used to achieve. An effect is either a discourse goal (such as *'convince the user that value1 is the result of achieving goal G'*) or a rhetorical relation (such as EVIDENCE), in which case the plan is used to achieve an RST relation.

- **a constraint list:** a list of conditions that must be true before the operator can be applied. Constraints may refer to facts or relations in the domain of discourse, states of the hearer's knowledge or other constraints on the user model. Some of the constraints correspond to the constraints on a nucleus and satellite as specified in RST. Additional constraints were introduced in order to extract information from the knowledge base.

- **a body:** one or more steps that, when executed, may achieve the effects of this operator. Each operator has at least one step, which we call the nucleus. In this language, the nucleus is the focus of the text produced by this operator and must be present. It can be a speech act or a desired state, which can later be expanded. There can be additional steps, called satellites. They may be required or optional.

Figure 2.8 shows a plan operator whose effect is the state where the hearer believes a given value is the result of accomplishing a goal.[10] This plan can be used to present the user with the result of achieving a goal given to the expert system problem-solving engine. In this plan, the nucleus is simply to INFORM the user of the result. This is a primitive speech act in our system. The satellite of the plan indicates that it is possible at this point to persuade the user that this is the case, thus justifying the result. This is a high-level discourse that needs to be expanded in turn. This satellite is optional, so that the text planner might choose not to expand it, and only produce the text that results from the nucleus. This would be the case, for example, for brevity, or because the system believes the user is knowledgeable and does not need a full explanation.

---

[10] To be exact, the effect should be: reach the state where *the speaker believes* that the hearer believes a given value is the result of accomplishing a goal. We chose not to express mutual beliefs for simplicity sake. Furthermore, since all the discourse goals posted to the text planner are from the system's point of view – the speaker in this case – we avoided repeating "the speaker believes..." for each goal. Also note that, in this figure, the constraint on the user model is not shown.

EFFECT:	(BEL H (RESULT ?G ?value))
CONSTRAINTS:	(AND (GOAL S ?G)
	(RESULT ?G ?value))
NUCLEUS:	(INFORM S H (RESULT ?G ?value))
SATELLITES:	((PERSUADED H (RESULT ?G ?value) *optional*)

Informally:

Effect: to get the hearer to believe that the result of
achieving goal ?G is ?value

Applicability Conditions: ?G is a goal of the system and
                          ?value is its result

Body of plan:
Inform the hearer that ?value is the result of achieving the goal
(primitive speech act) and post the discourse goal of justifying this result

Figure 2.8: Text plan for giving a conclusion

Suppose the system chooses to provide a full text and expand the satellite. The subgoal indicated in the satellite is posted. Satellite subgoals must eventually be achieved by an RST plan, indicating how the text generated from expanding the satellite is rhetorically connected to the text generated from the nucleus. The RST plan will post other discourse goals in turn, also resulting in text to be generated. A completed text plan built in that way thus indicates both the subgoals achieved at any point *and* the rhetorical relations among the various pieces of text. (Examples of such text plans as presented in Moore and Swartout (1990 – this volume).)

Figure 2.9 shows two more plans. The first one indicates that, in order to achieve the high-level goal of persuading the user of the result, the rhetorical relation EVIDENCE can be used. The second one is a text plan capable of achieving the rhetorical relation EVIDENCE, which provides evidence for the result given by providing the general method necessary to achieve the goal and then presenting the specific plan used in this case. This is only one of the plans that can be used to justify the result. Another plan might result in presenting to the user the whole sequence of events that happened during execution in order to arrive at this result.

In this plan, note that, as a result of instantiating the constraints against the knowledge base, the variable '?method' is bound to the method that was used in solving the problem. This illustrates how information is extracted from the knowledge base to be included in the text.

EFFECT:	(PERSUADED H (RESULT ?G ?value)
CONSTRAINTS:	(AND (GOAL S ?G)
	(RESULT ?G ?value))
NUCLEUS:	(EVIDENCE (RESULT ?G ?value))

Text plan to persuade the user of a conclusion

EFFECT:	(EVIDENCE (RESULT ?G ?value))
CONSTRAINTS:	(AND (GOAL S ?G)
	(METHOD-SELECTED ?method ?G)
	(RESULT ?G ?value))
NUCLEUS:	(INFORM S H (METHOD-SELECTED ?method ?G))
SATELLITE:	((ELABORATE-GENERAL-SPECIFIC
	(METHOD-SELECTED ?method ?G))
	required)

Text plan for providing an evidence

Figure 2.9: Two Text Plans

EFFECT:	(BEL H (?pred ?arg1 ?arg2))
CONSTRAINTS:	nil
NUCLEUS	(INFORM S H (?pred ?arg1 ?arg2))
SATELLITES	((PERSUADED H (?pred ?arg1 ?arg2)) *optional*))

Figure 2.10: A general plan

Plans can also be quite general. For example, Figure 2.10 presents a plan which, informally, states that to get the hearer to believe that a predicate holds between two arguments, one has to inform the hearer of that fact and optionally post the discourse subgoal of persuading the hearer of that fact. This plan is always applicable to achieve the specified effect as there are no constraints.

The planning mechanism we use is a conventional top-down hierarchical expansion planner (Sacerdoti, 1977). The planner begins with a high-level discourse goal of the speaker and successively refines it into other discourse subgoals or rhetorical means for achieving them. This process continues until the entire plan is refined into primitive operators, i.e., speech acts.

When a goal is posted, the planner finds all the plan operators whose effects match the goal. It then tries to satisfy the constraints of each operator, searching in the knowledge base for acceptable bindings if the constraints contain unbound variables, thereby obtaining from the knowledge base the information that will be expressed in the final text. Constraints referring to the user are checked against the user model. If the information is not contained in the user model, the planner might assume that the constraint is true nevertheless (i.e., the user model was incomplete) and record this assumption as part of the text plan. Or the planner might choose to plan text to make the assumption true before going further. The text planner then selects one such operator and posts the steps listed in the nucleus and satellites as subgoals to be satisfied. Finally, the completed text plan is passed through a grammar interface and given as input to the Penman sentence generation system.

It is important to note that we do not assume a correct and detailed user model (Moore and Swartout 1990, this volume). Our system is able to function even in the absence of a user model, and it is able to recover when assumptions about the user model were wrongly made. This is another reason why dialogue capabilities are crucial.

A text plan produced using our text planner provides a detailed representation of the text produced by the system, indicating how parts of the plan are related and which purposes different parts of the generated text serve. This text plan is recorded in a dialogue history and is later exploited to disambiguate follow-up questions, select perspective when describing or comparing objects, and provide further explanations.[11] In addition, the completed text plan can be used to update a user model upon receiving follow-up questions, as it is possible to examine the completed plan to determine whether information taken from the user model might have been inaccurate. Finally, we believe this complete and detailed plan will provide the information that will allow the system to modify its existing strategies and learn new strategies.

Besides these advantages, we believe that the approach proposed in this paper provides a computational model that unifies the schema-based and the

---

[11] For detailed examples of completed text plans using this mechanism as well as how our system can handle these tasks, see (Moore and Swartout, 1990 – this volume).

plan-based approaches, allowing to see them as two extremes of a continuum instead of two very different approaches. The plan structure proposed here can express the whole spectrum of plans: from primitive plans for speech acts to plans that achieve very high-level discourse goals and resemble schemata (Moore and Paris, 1988). Using this unified model, a schema can be viewed as a compiled version of a text plan, with all the non-terminal nodes pruned out and only the leaves remaining. It can produce the same behavior, but all of the rationale for the behavior has been compiled out. Because of this 'compilation,' a schema is computationally efficient. It may be necessary however to recover the information which has been compiled out in order to handle some discourse situations.[12] Note that, in our approach, the schema is being *built* during text planning, from small plan operators. From a library of plan operators, many varied schemata can result, improving the flexibility of the system.

2.6   TAILORING EXPLANATIONS

As an expert system is likely to be used by many users, its explanation facility would be more effective if it could customize its answers to each user, retrieving from its knowledge base the facts that are most appropriate and useful for that user. For example, in a medical diagnosis expert system, which is another domain EES is being applied to, various explanations to the same question 'how did you reach your conclusion?' are possible depending on its intended listener. A person developing the system is likely to be interested in different aspects of the problem solving than a doctor using the system. For a medical student using the system as a learning tool, providing the rationale behind the system's behavior might be more important than providing simply the problem solving techniques employed. It is important to realize that the explanation routine should be sensitive to these differences. In this section, we briefly show how we were able to incorporate previous work on tailoring answers to the users in our new framework. We also present new research in this area.

2.6.1   Tailoring the content and organization of the text

We started investigating the appropriateness of the different kinds of knowledge contained in an expert system using the EES framework for generating an explanation of the system's behavior to various types of users. We also studied how these different kinds of knowledge can be combined to provide an explanation of system behavior that is coherent and appropriate for different types of users, whether system developers or end-users.

---

[12] Note that this is similar to Swartout's argument in the XPLAIN system (Swartout, 1983), where Swartout points out that having implicit knowledge is usually not enough: one might need to recover the knowledge omitted in a compiled form.

In earlier work (Paris, 1985; Paris, 1987), we have argued that answers that are tailored according to a person's *domain knowledge* frequently occurs in human communication. We find evidence of this phenomenon in naturally occurring texts, where the information presented to readers varies with their assumed level of general knowledge. We believe the user's domain knowledge is an important factor if the answer provided is to be both informative and understandable. The answer should not provide information that is obvious to the user (Grice, 1975). However, if the answer assumes knowledge the user does not have, it may be very hard (if not impossible) for the user to understand the answer. In (Paris, 1987), we showed the feasibility of incorporating the user's domain knowledge, or *level of expertise*, into a generation system and addressed the issue of how this factor might affect an answer. Based on an analysis of texts describing complex physical objects aimed at audiences at the two ends of the knowledge spectrum (naive and expert), we found that the user's domain knowledge affected the *kind of information* and not just the *amount of detail* to include in a response. In the domain studied, the domain of complex physical objects, we found that texts aimed at naive readers contained a lot of process information while the texts aimed at more knowledgeable readers were mostly descriptive.

In (Paris, 1987), we had developed two distinct discourse strategies that could be used to generate texts aimed at naive and expert users. These strategies could be dynamically mixed to provide responses to users anywhere along the knowledge spectrum. We are now interested in applying these results to the generation of explanations in expert systems.

Based upon our previous study, we can expect that the different *kinds* and different *levels* of knowledge available in the system will be appropriate for different users and different contexts of use. Generating explanations for an expert system is particularly interesting because there are at least two dimensions along which users can be knowledgeable: the internals of the system and the application domain.

As a start, we are looking into tailoring terminology definitions and justifications of conclusions to two types of users: end-users (not necessarily expert in the domain to which the expert system is applied) who want to follow the system's reasoning and system developers who want to make sure the system is working correctly. As a test case, we are studying the kinds of explanations people in our research group wish to see. We are also looking at transcripts in order to get more data to extend our initial analysis.

We have found that terminology definitions and some background information are appropriate for end-users, while the actual trace of the execution trace is more useful to the system developers. We have developed strategies for both, and we plan to continue this work to cover more types of questions and users, allow for several possible responses for the same question and tailor to users anywhere along a spectrum instead of just extremes.

The plan language presented here allows us to tailor to users in a straight-forward way, as it is possible to express constraints on the user model in the plan. A particular plan thus gets applied only for the appropriate users. For example, Figure 2.11 shows a text for an end-user to present a result in the Digital Circuit Diagnosis domain. Because the explanation was tailored to an end-user, the plan chosen to justify a conclusion posted discourse subgoals to present the general method used by the system to achieve the problem solving goal at hand followed by the result of applying this method in the specific case at hand. Contrast this with the text tailored for a system developer presented in Figure 2.12.[13] In this case, because of a different constraint of the user model, the plan chosen to justify a conclusion posted discourse subgoals to present first the goal to be achieved, then all the methods that could have been used to achieve that goal, the method that was chosen, and, finally, the result.

In the examples above, a different strategy was chosen at the beginning of the planning process. This is not necessarily the case, however. Indeed, as in TAILOR (Paris, 1987), the planning mechanism allows us to 'switch' strategies easily: each time a new discourse goal gets posted as a subgoal, a new plan operator needs to be chosen: if the user knows a lot about the domain with respect to this particular discourse goal, the right plan operator gets chosen and, essentially, the strategy has 'switched'. The scope of each plan operator defines what was called the 'switching points' in TAILOR. Because the plans are finer grained, however, there are more 'switching points' allowed and thus more flexibility.

2.6.2 Tailoring the phrasing of the text

We have started to extend our tailoring to the *phrasing* of the text (i.e., the *lexical* and *syntactic* choice) as well as the content and organization. This is another important aspect of the tailoring process, or a text may be just as ineffective as texts which wrongly direct attention or which rely on knowledge that the hearer does not have. Indeed, a same propositional content can be phrased in various ways, depending on its expected reader.

Suppose, for example, that to answer the question "what is a faulty-system?" (in the Digital Circuit Diagnosis domain) the text planner decides to present only the conditions under which a system is faulty. This information (shown in Figure 2.6.2) is contained in one slot of the object frame. It is represented as predicate calculus and constitutes the basic propositional content that is to be expressed in the response. Given this propositional content, however, it is still possible to phrase this definition in several ways, each being appropriate for some different type of user, as illustrated in Figures 2.14, 2.15 and 2.16. Figure 2.14 presents a terminology definition which is appropriate for system

---

[13] The text was formatted in this figure for clarity. Our generation system does not yet format texts as shown here, although we will be addressing this issue in the future.

In order to determine whether a system is faulty, DIAGNOSER needs to determine
whether its actual outputs are equal to its expected outputs and its actual inputs
are equal to its expected inputs. In this case, DIAGNOSER has determined that
the actual output of A1 is not equal to its expected output and that its actual
inputs are equal to its expected inputs. (The actual output is 6 and the expected
output is 8). So, DIAGNOSER concluded that A1 is faulty.

Figure 2.11: Text for presenting a conclusion to an end-user

DIAGNOSER is trying to determine whether A1 is faulty. It found the following
applicable plans:

determine-whether-faulty-system,
determine-whether-isa?-constant,
determine-whether-isa?-expression
and *determine-whether-reformulate.*

determine-whether-faulty-system can be used to determine whether a system is
a faulty system.
determine-whether-isa?-constant can be used to determine whether some constant is of some type-instance.
determine-whether-isa?-expression can be used to determine whether some expression is of some type-instance.
determine-whether-reformulate can be used to determine whether some assertion is true. DIAGNOSER selected *determine-whether-faulty-system.* The result was T.

Figure 2.12: Text for presenting a conclusion to a system developer

developers: they wish to see terminology definitions in an English form as close as possible to the exact definition contained in the system, as they use the explanation facility for debugging purposes. It is not likely however that such a definition would be entirely understood by other end-users. Figure 2.15 shows the more appropriate text for these users. Finally, Figure 2.16 presents a terminology definition for a very naive user (or to be generated in a casual context).

We have started to construct a general phrasing control component that interfaces between the output of our text planner and the input to the grammar. A given user (or a class of users) and a situation, this component decides how to phrase the propositions that have already been chosen by the text planner (Bateman and Paris, 1989). The three text above were actually generated by our system.

2.7   DIRECTION FOR FUTURE WORK: ACQUIRING AND CHANGING PLAN OPERATORS

A generation facility for a large system that is to be used by many users, is unlikely to have a complete and correct library of discourse strategies, as it is very hard to foresee every situation that might occur and get transcripts of the exact type of interactions that will be taking place between the system and the users. It is thus desirable for a system to be able to learn new discourse strategies once it is actually being used. Furthermore, as people interact, they change their discourse strategies to reflect the feedback they obtained on their utterances, Likewise, a generation system should be able to learn from experience and respond to feedback from the users by modifying its existing strategies.

We are looking into the possibility for the system to learn new plan operators for achieving high-level discourse goals based on the information presented to the user and the follow-up questions asked. We would like our system to remember 'good plans', that is plans that were successful in presenting the information to the user without triggering a flock of follow-up questions, and learn plan operators that seem to be used often. We are investigating the feasibility of the following types of behavior for our generation system:

- *starting with a set of basic operators and grouping them to form larger schema*: we would like our generation system to start with a set of small 'basic' plan operators. Upon receiving a question, a text plan is formed from these basic plans. Once the text plan is completed, the leaves are abstracted ('compiled out') to form a schema that can be later efficiently employed to plan a text achieving the same top-level discourse goal without having to re-plan. However, as the rationale for the plan would be

```
(define-type-attributes faulty-system
    :property-restrictions ((faulty necessary sufficient))
    :defining-conditions
        ((and (E (o in (output-part self))
                (not (equal (expected-value (signal-part o))
                            (actual-value (signal-part o)))))
            (A (i in (input-part self))
                (equal (expected-value (signal-part i))
                        (actual-value (signal-part i)))))))
```

Figure 2.13: System definition of a faulty system

The system is faulty, if there exists a O in the set of the output terminals of the system such that the expected value of the signal part of O does not equal the actual value of the signal part of O and for all I in the set of the input terminals of the system, the expected value of the signal part of I equals the actual value of the signal part of I.

Figure 2.14: Terminology definitions for a system developer

The system is faulty, if all of the expected values of its input terminals equal their actual values and the expected value of one of its output terminals does not equal its actual value.

Figure 2.15: Terminology definitions for a user other than a system developer

The system is faulty, if the inputs are fine and the output is wrong.

Figure 2.16: Terminology definitions for a very naive user

A: Initially:
         System: I recommend act1
         User: why?
         System: Because it is a step towards achieving goal1

B: After learning a new schema:
   System: I recommend act1, because it is a step towards achieving goal1.

Figure 2.17: Learning a plan operator across several interactions

kept, it would still be possible to answer any follow-up questions that may arise.

- *changing a satellite from being optional to required*: based on the interaction with the user, the system might notice that anytime it chooses not to expand an optional satellite, that satellite is eventually expanded as a result of answering a follow-up question. In such a case, it might be adequate to make the satellite required.

- *adding a step to a plan operator*: Consider the scenario shown in Figure 2.17. In this scenario, the system learns a new plan operator across several interactions with the user by adding a step to its original basic plan. (Note that this is *not* an attempt to avoid follow-up questions, but possibly reduce their number.) It is clearly not always appropriate to group together the responses as shown in (B) in the figure, i.e., it is not always appropriate to learn a new plan. We need to study what factors are involved in deciding when the system should form a new plan operator. A similar scenario can be constructed using a non-basic plan, that is using a plan which already contains several steps. For example, in a plan that can be used to explain the terminology of the system, it might be necessary for a certain type of users to add an example.

- *replacing a step of a plan operator*: based on feedback from the user, the system might recognize that its discourse strategy is inadequate, i.e., that it might be necessary to replace a step by another one or delete a step (replace it with nothing), as it confuses the user.

- *adding or changing a constraint*: finally, the system might notice that the constraints on a plan operator are inadequate and need to be changed (e.g., the constraint on the user model is perhaps inappropriate). As in the previous case, we have only started to look at these issues and need to identify the factors involved in the various decisions.

2.8   CONCLUSIONS

In this paper, we presented our efforts to build an explanation facility for the Explainable Expert System, taking a Natural Language Generation perspective. We argued that providing explanations for expert systems is a very good domain in which to study natural language generation. We described the issues involved in building such an explanation facility for the EES system, and explained why we could not use existing NLG techniques. We briefly presented the new text planner, explaining how it fits our requirements.

ACKNOWLEDGMENTS

Many thanks to John Bateman, Eduard Hovy, Johanna Moore, and Bill Swartout for comments and discussions.

This work was supported in part by the Advanced Research Projects Agency (DARPA) under a NASA Ames cooperative agreement number NCC 2-520.

BIBLIOGRAPHY

(Appelt, 1985) Douglas E. Appelt. *Planning Natural Language Utterances.* Cambridge University Press, Cambridge, England, 1985.

(Bateman and Paris, 1989) John A. Bateman and Cécile L. Paris. Phrasing a text in terms the user can understand. In *Proceedings of the Eleventh International Joint Conference on Artificial Intelligence*, Detroit, Michigan, 1989.

(Buchanan and Shortliffe, 1984) Bruce G. Buchanan and E. H. Shortliffe. *Rule-Based Expert Systems: The MYCIN Experiments of the Stanford Heuristic Programming Project.* Addison-Wesley Publishing Company, Reading, Mass., 1984.

(Cheong and Zukerman, 1988) Yee Han Cheong and Ingrid Zukerman. Enhancing automatically generated explanations by means of rhetorical devices, 1988. Dept of Computer Science, Monash University, Clayton, Victoria 3168, Australia.

(Clancey, 1981) William Clancey. NEOMYCIN: Reconfiguring a rule-based expert system for application to teaching. Technical report, IJCAI, Vancouver, BC, August 1981.

(Clancey, 1983) William Clancey. The epistemology of a rule-based expert system: A framework for explanation. *Artificial Intelligence*, 20(3):215–251,

1983. Also in *Rule-Based Expert Systems: The MYCIN Experiments of the Stanford Heuristic Heuristic Programming Project*; Buchanan and Shortliffe (eds), Addison-Wesley, 1984.

(Cohen and Jones, 1987) Robin Cohen and Marlene Jones. Incorporating user models into expert systems for educational diagnosis. In Alfred Kobsa and Wolfgang Wahlster, editors, *User Models in Dialog Systems*. Springer Verlag, Symbolic Computation Series, Berlin Heidelberg New York Tokyo, 1987.

(Cohen and Perrault, 1979) P. R. Cohen and C. R. Perrault. Elements of a plan-based theory of speech acts. *Cognitive Science*, 3:pages 177 – 212, 1979.

(Gilbert, 1988) G. Nigel Gilbert. Forms of explanation, August 1988. Presented at the AAAI-88 Workshop on Explanations.

(Grice, 1975) H. P. Grice. Logic and conversation. In P. Cole and J. L. Morgan, editors, *Syntax and Semantics*. Academic Press, New York, 1975.

(Hovy, 1988a) Eduard H. Hovy. Approaches to the planning of coherent text, July 1988. To appear in selected papers from *The 4th International Workshop on text generation* Catalina, California. Edited by Paris, C., Swartout, W., and Mann, W.

(Hovy, 1988b) Eduard H. Hovy. Planning coherent multisentential texts. In *The Proceedings of the 26th. Annual Meeting of the Association of Computational Linguistics*, pages 163 – 169. Association for Computational Linguistics, June 1988.

(Kukich, 1985) Karen Kukich. Explanation structures in XSEL. In *Proceedings of the 23rd Annual Meeting of the Association for Computational Linguistics*, Chicago, Illinois, 1985. Association for Computational Linguistics.

(Mann and Thompson, 1987) William Mann and Sandra Thompson. Rhetorical structure theory: a theory of text organization. In Livia Polanyi, editor, *The Structure of Discourse*. Ablex Publishing Corporation, Norwood, New Jersey, 1987. Also available as USC/Information Sciences Institute Technical Report Number RS-87-190.

(Mann, 1984) William C. Mann. Discourse structure for text generation. Technical Report ISI/RR-84-127, Information Sciences Institute, February 1984. 4676 Admiralty Way, Marina del Rey, California 90292-6695.

(Maybury, 1988) Mark Maybury. Explanation rhetoric: The rhetorical progression of justifications, 1988. Rome Air Development Center, Griffiss AFB, Rome NY 13441-5700.

(McCoy, 1986) Kathleen F. McCoy. The ROMPER system: Responding to object-related misconceptions using perspective. In *Proceedings of the 24th Annual Meeting of the ACL*, New York City, New York, June 1986. Association of Computational Linguistics.

(McCoy, 1988) Kathleen F. McCoy. Reasoning on a dynamically highlighted user model to respond to misconceptions. *Computational Linguistics*, 14 (3), September 1988.

(McKeown *et al.*, 1985) Kathleen R. McKeown, Michael Wish, and Kevin Matthews. Tailoring explanations for the user. In *Proceedings of IJCAI-85*, Los Angeles, Ca., 1985. International Joint Conference on Artificial Intelligence.

(McKeown, 1985) Kathleen R. McKeown. *Text Generation: Using Discourse Strategies and Focus Constraints to Generate Natural Language Text*. Cambridge University Press, Cambridge, England, 1985.

(Moore and Paris, 1988) Johanna D. Moore and Cécile L. Paris. Constructing coherent texts using rhetorical relations. In *Proceedings of the Tenth Annual Conference of the Cognitive Science Society*. Cognitive Science Society, August 1988.

(Moore and Swartout, 1988a) Johanna D. Moore and William R. Swartout. A reactive approach to explanation, August 1988. Presented at the AAAI Workshop on Explanations.

(Moore and Swartout, 1988b) Johanna D. Moore and William R. Swartout. A reactive approach to explanation, July 1988. To appear in selected papers from *The 4th International Workshop on text generation* Catalina, California. Edited by Paris, C., Swartout, W., and Mann, W.

(Paris and McKeown, 1987) Cécile L. Paris and Kathleen R. McKeown. Discourse strategies for describing complex physical objects. In G. Kempen, editor, *Natural Language Generation: Recent Advances in Artificial Intelligence, Psychology, and Linguistics*. Kluwer Academic Publishers, Boston/Dordrecht, 1987. Paper presented at the Third International Workshop on Natural Language Generation, August 1986, Nijmegen, The Netherlands.

(Paris, 1985) Cécile L. Paris. Description strategies for naive and expert users. In *Proceedings of the 23rd Annual Meeting of the Association for Computational Linguistics*, Chicago, 1985.

(Paris, 1987) Cécile L. Paris. *The Use of Explicit User Models in Text Generation: Tailoring to a User's Level of Expertise*. PhD thesis, Columbia University Department of Computer Science, 1987. To be published in the "Communication in Artificial Intelligence" series, Steiner and Fawcett (eds), Frances Pinter, 1990.

(Paris, 1988a) Cécile L. Paris. Planning a text: can we and how should we modularize this process?, August 1988. Presented at the AAAI-88 Workshop on Text Planning and Realization.

(Paris, 1988b) Cécile L. Paris. Tailoring Object Descriptions to the User's Level of Expertise. *Computational Linguistics*, 14 (3):64–78, September 1988. Special Issue on User Modeling.

(Paris, 1989) Cécile L. Paris. The Use of Explicit User Models in a Generation System for Tailoring Answers to the User's Level of Expertise. In Alfred Kobsa and Wolfgang Wahlster, editors, *User Models in Dialog Systems*. Springer Verlag, Symbolic Computation Series, Berlin Heidelberg New York Tokyo, 1989.

(Pollack *et al.*, 1982) Martha Pollack, Julia Hirschberg, and Bonnie Webber. User participation in the reasoning processes of expert systems. In *Proceedings of the AAAI*, Pittsburgh, Pa, 1982. American Association of Artificial Intelligence.

(Rankin *et al.*, 1988) Ivan Rankin, Sture Hagglund, and Yvonne Waern. Generating user-centered explanations in a critiquing context, August 1988. Presented at the AAAI Workshop on Explanations.

(Sacerdoti, 1977) Earl Sacerdoti. *A Structure for Plans and Behavior*. American Elsevier North-Holland, New York, 1977.

(Suthers, 1988) Dan Suthers. Providing multiple views of reasoning for explanations, August 1988. Presented at the AAAI Workshop on Explanations.

(Swartout and Smoliar, 1987a) William Swartout and Steve W. Smoliar. Explaining the link between causal reasoning and expert behavior. In *Proceedings of the Symposium on Computer Applications in Medical Care*, Washington, D. C., November 1987. also to appear in "Topics in Medical Artificial Intelligence"; Miller, P.L. (ed), Springer-Verlag.

(Swartout and Smoliar, 1987b) William R. Swartout and Steve W. Smoliar. On making expert systems more like experts. *Expert Systems*, 4(3), August 1987.

(Swartout, 1983) William Swartout. XPLAIN: A System for Creating and Explaining Expert Consulting Systems. *Artificial Intelligence*, 21(3):285–325, September 1983. Also available as ISI/RS-83-4.

(Swartout, 1984) William R. Swartout. Explaining and justifying expert consulting programs. In *Readings in Medical Artificial Intelligence: The First Decade*. Addison-Wesley, 1984. Reprinted from Proceedings of the Seventh International Joint Conference on Artificial Intelligence, 1981.

(Swartout, 1985) William Swartout. Knowledge Needed for Expert System Explanation. In *AFIPS Conference Proceedings*, volume 54, pages 93–98. National Computer Conference, 1985.

(Tanner and Josephson, 1988) Michael C. Tanner and John R. Josephson. Justifying diagnostic conclusions, August 1988. Presented at the AAAI-88 Workshop on Explanations.

(Teach and Shortliffe, 1984) R. L. Teach and E. H. Shortliffe. An analysis of physicians' attitudes. In *Rule-Based Expert Systems: The MYCIN Experiments of the Stanford Heuristic Programming Project.* Addison-Wesley Publishing Company, Reading, Mass., 1984.

(van Beek, 1987) Peter van Beek. A model for generating better explanations. In *Proceedings of the 25th Annual Meeting of the ACL*, Palo Alto, California, 1987. Association of Computational Linguistics.

(Wallis and Shortliffe, 1982) J.W. Wallis and E.H. Shortliffe. Explanatory power for medical expert systems: Studies in the representation of causal relationships for clinical consultation. Technical Report STAN-CS-82-923, Stanford University, 1982. Heuristics Programming Project. Department of Medecine and Computer Science.

(Weiner, 1980) J. Weiner. Blah, a system that explains its reasoning. *Artificial Intelligence Journal*, 15:19 – 48, 1980.

(Wexelblat, 1988) R. L. Wexelblat. The confidence in their help, August 1988. Presented at the AAAI-88 Workshop on Explanations.

(Wick and Thompson, 1989) M.R. Wick and W.B. Thompson. Reconstructive Explanation: Explanation as Complex Problem Solving In *Proceedings of the Eleventh International Joint Conference on Artificial Intelligence*, Detroit, Michigan, 1989.

Chapter 3

Approaches to the Planning of Coherent Text

Eduard H. Hovy

Abstract: This paper discusses the planning of multisentential text by computer. In order to construct coherent paragraphs, we have been using relations from Rhetorical Structure Theory (RST) operationalized as plans. The paper first describes, in some detail, the current method of planning a paragraph using operationalized RST relation/plans. It then makes two points that illustrate why RST relation/plans are an ideal tool for planning paragraphs. First, these relation/plans can be shown to combine the best features of paragraph-sized schemas and clause-sized planning rules under a top-down planning regime in a way which affords much flexibility to the user. Second, RST relation/plans can support both standard top-down planning and open-ended conversation-like behavior; a small difference in treatment gives rise to either paradigm.

3.1   INTRODUCTION

In the past two years, the Penman project at ISI/USC has been investigating the planning of coherent multisentential paragraphs of text by computer. As our basic planning operators, we use RST relations from Rhetorical Structure Theory – (see Mann and Thompson, 1983; 1987), which posits that approximately 20 relations suffice to relate adjacent blocks of text (sentences and groups of sentences) in the ways that are coherent in English. We are operationalizing these relations and using them as plans in a top-down hierarchical expansion planning system – see (Hovy, 1988a) – to develop the dependency structure which underlies each coherent paragraph of text. This work, and an example, are described in the first section of this paper.

In the remainder of the paper, we describe the possibilities that operationalized RST relation/plans afford. The first point is prompted by the observation that two major approaches to planning paragraphs exist at present, but that the relationship between them has not yet been made clear. In one approach, structures called schemas – developed by McKeown (1982) are used as recipes for building paragraphs. In the other, rules about forming illocutionary acts, surface speech acts, and parts of sentences, are used to plan one- or two-sentence texts that achieve communicative goals – see (Appelt, 1981; 1985); this theory assumes that longer texts will also be coherent as a side-effect of proper planning. When these two theories are compared along the dimensions of data structure and planning process, it becomes apparent that each approach has a strength and a weakness, and can be made complementary when RST relation/plans are used instead of schemas in an appropriate way. With respect to the data structures involved:

- schemas straightforwardly provide the structure of paragraph-sized spans of text (a strength);

- planning rules provide only far more limited (i.e., clause-sized) structure, which must then be assembled somehow into paragraphs.

And with respect to the planning process,

- schema-based planning resembles script instantiation, affording relatively little dynamic variability;

- planning with rules is amenable to standard planning techniques and affords much flexibility (a strength).

While the two approaches make use of different planning methods and data structures, they are similar enough to suggest the existence of a generalized set of structures and planning method that subsume both. In our investigations, we have found that RST relation/plans can be used as such structures (being easily adaptable to act either as macro-level schemas or as micro-level planning rules), and our method of planning text structure with them can be used as the subsuming planning method.

The second point is the following: when being used to plan out larger spans of structure, RST relation/plans require that their growth points (explained later) be treated as mandatory planning rules. However, when the interpretation of growth points is relaxed to treat them as suggestions, more open-ended planning behavior ensues. Concomitantly, opportunities to apply additional criteria of control (such as focus and text balance) present themselves. The relation/plans' ability to simultaneously support differentially flexible growth points makes them a very useful vehicle with which to conduct text planning experiments.

3.2 STRUCTURING PARAGRAPHS USING RST

3.2.1 Background to the Planning

The text structuring planner we have developed operates antecedent to Penman, the systemic generator being built at ISI (Mann, 1983; Mann and Matthiessen, 1983; Matthiessen, 1984). The structurer[1] accepts inputs from the domain of discourse and rewrites the inputs into a common form (called here input units) which consist of collections of input characteristics. Using RST relation/plans to satisfy the communicative goals specified by the user, it assembles the input units into a tree that expresses the paragraph structure, in which branch nodes are instantiated RST relation/plans and leaves are input units. It then traverses the tree and dispatches its contents to be generated by Penman. An early version of the structurer is described in (Hovy, 1988a).

The structurer plans out coherent paragraphs to achieve communicative goals posted by the host system to affect the hearer's knowledge in some way. These goals are rhetorical; they pertain to the organization of the paragraph. Each goal is associated with one or more RST relation/plans.

The central data structure is the paragraph structure tree, which is composed primarily of instantiated RST relation/plans. All adjacent independent clauses in the text are linked by some RST relation/plan; adjacent pairs of RST relation/plans are themselves linked by another relation/plan, and so forth, until one relation/plan spans all (though not all relations need be binary, those implemented were made so for convenience). In the planning process, it is assumed that each relation/plan achieves some rhetorical goal, and hence acts as a plan or subplan in the plan tree. The understanding that a relation can be used as a plan (forming an operator of dual nature) is the principal insight that made this method of planning texts possible (see (Hovy 1988a); see also

---

[1] Since the task of text planning includes diverse subtasks, we will use the word *structurer* instead of *planner* for the task of organizing paragraphs of text from the given input.

(Moore and Paris, 1989), Moore and Swartout, and Paris, both in this volume, for work which developed out of that realization).

The structurer's plans are operationalizations of the rhetorical relations of RST. Each relation/plan has two parts, a *nucleus* and a *satellite*, and relates some unit(s) of the input (cast. as nucleus) to other unit(s) of the input (cast as satellite) in a unique way; the underlying theory is that when two or more units are successfully related, the resulting juxtaposition will help bring about coherent text. In order to admit only properly formed relations, nuclei and satellites contain requirements that must be matched by characteristics of the input units. (Thus, for example, the PURPOSE relation cannot be used to relate some input state or condition to some input action unless it can be proved (to the structurer's satisfaction, using the PURPOSE requirements) that the state was in fact the purpose of the action.) Thus the nucleus and satellite requirements are semantic in nature.

When studying relations between clauses, it can be seen that additional material is often included, its type depending on the type of relation. For example, when describing a problem and its solution, people often add background material to the problem to explain why it is a problem, and, to the solution, material explaining further results of the solution. For another example, in their study of salience in generation, Conklin and McDonald (1982) found that people always included an elaborating clause when introducing the main subject in a descriptive paragraph. In order to capture this capability, we built so-called *growth points* into RST relation/plans. Each growth point contains one or more goals to search for and include additional material of a type suitable to the relation. Thus growth points contain rhetorical information.

For this work, we assumed that the information to be generated had already been selected by some process. This assumption conforms to the typical relationship between text generators and host systems such as data base retrieval systems or report generation systems. However, as shown by the work of Moore and Swartout and of Paris (this volume), this assumption is unnecessarily strong, since a planning method of this type can also be used simultaneously to retrieve the information to be said from a collection of well-structured data, given powerful enough relation/plans.

3.2.2   An Example of the Planning Process

We initially tested the structurer in three domains of discourse (before Moore and Paris wrote their text planner, described in this book). In this paper, we present an example from the third domain, a Naval application in which the structurer and Penman are part of a larger system that presents data base information about U.S. Navy vessels to a user using maps, tables, and text (Arens *et al.*, 1988). Given its simplicity, this domain is ideal for preliminary experimentation. In this section, we describe the planning of the following text (where "C4" denotes a level of operational readiness):

```
((SHIP.EMPLOYMENT A105)
 (SHIP.R A105 KNOX)              (ENROUTE E105)
 (SHIP.COURSE.R A105 195)        (EBEG.R E105 870420)
 (CURRENT.POSITION.R A105 P102)  (EEND.R E105 870424)
 (POSITION P102)                 (DESTINATION.R E105 SASEBO)
 (LONGITUDE.R P102 79)           (LOAD E107)
 (LATITUDE.R P102 18)            (EBEG.R E107 870425)
 (READINESS.LEVEL.R A105 C4)     (EEND.R E107 870428))
 (NEXT.MAJOR.EMPLOYMENT.R A105 E107)
 (CURRENT.MAJOR.EMPLOYMENT.R A105 E105)
```

Figure 3.1: Unstructured data from the Navy domain.

```
Knox, which is C4, is en route to Sasebo.  It is at 18N
79E, heading SSW. It will arrive on 4/24.  It will load for
4 days.
```

The data base consists of lists of assertions about entities and actions that are defined in a property-inheritance network written in the language NIKL (Kaczmarek *et al.*, 1986). The network, which is accessible by Penman and the structurer, contains a full taxonomy of the entities found in the data base Navy world. A typical set of input elements, describing the ship Knox, appears in Figure 3.1. From this input the structurer builds six distinct units, each of which eventually becomes a clause, using a number of domain-specific rules; for example, the unit ARRIVE11400, representing the arrival of the Knox at Sasebo, is built according to a domain rule that an arrival occurs when a moving ship employment is followed by a stationary employment. Unit ARRIVE11400 is then linked to unit E105 by the addition of the term (NEXT-ACTION.R E105 ARRIVE11400) to the aspects of E105, this being the domain's way to represent temporal succession between events. The input units are shown in Figure 3.2.

Next follows the structure planning task. The structurer seeks to satisfy the following goal, posted by the host system:

(BMB SPEAKER HEARER (POSITION-OF E105 ?NEXT))

which can be glossed as: from the input units, tell the hearer the sequence of events of which E105 is a principal part (i.e., its temporal POSITION). More precisely, the goal is to be read as: achieve the state in which the hearer believes that it is the intention of the speaker that they mutually believe that the event E105 is followed by some other event.[2]

---

[2] This syntax, and the term BMB, are from the modal operator language developed by Cohen and Levesque, with which they tried to derive complex speech acts from a small set of primitive operators; see (Cohen and Levesque, 1985). Though they have subsequently retracted the conclusions of that paper, and hold instead that one requires also a notion of commitment when performing such derivations, the utility of this notation remains unaffected for our descriptive domains.

```
((ENROUTE E105)                           ((ARRIVE ARRIVE11400)
 (SHIP.R E105 KNOX)                         (SHIP.R ARRIVE11400 KNOX)
 (DESTINATION.R E105 SASEBO)                (TIME.R ARRIVE11400 870424)
 (HEADING.R E105 HEADING11416)              (NEXT-ACTION.R ARRIVE11400
                                                          E107))
 (READINESS.R E105 READINESS11408)
 (NEXT-ACTION.R E105 ARRIVE11400))        ((POSITION POSITION11410)
                                           (SHIP.R POSITION11410 KNOX)
((HEADING HEADING11416)                    (LONGITUDE.R POSITION11410 79)
 (SHIP.R HEADING11416 KNOX)                 (LATITUDE.R POSITION11410 18))
 (SHIP.COURSE.R HEADING11416 195)
 (POSITION.R HEADING11416 POSITION11410)) ((LOAD E107)
                                           (SHIP.R E107 KNOX)
((READINESS READINESS11408)                (EBEG.R E107 870425)
 (SHIP.R READINESS11408 KNOX)              (EEND.R E107 870428))
 (READINESS.LEVEL.R READINESS11408 C4))
```

Figure 3.2: Inputs to the structurer.

The structurer starts with this goal, which matches the *results* field of only one relation/plan, namely SEQUENCE (see Figure 3.3). In the match, ?PART is bound to E105. With this binding, the structurer begins searching for an appropriate nucleus. First it checks for an input unit whose contents match the combined nucleus and satellite requirements

((BMB SPEAKER HEARER (NEXT-ACTION.R E105 ?NEXT)))

The unit E105 can satisfy this requirement since its characteristics match when ?NEXT is bound to ARRIVE11400. With this binding for ?NEXT throughout the relation, the independent nucleus and satellite requirements become, respectively,

((BMB SPEAKER HEARER (TOPIC E105)))

and

((BMB SPEAKER HEARER (TOPIC ARRIVE11400)))

which can directly be fulfilled by simply saying E105 as the nucleus and ARRIVE 11400 as the satellite of the SEQUENCE relation/plan (the TOPIC terms are simply a programming convenience for binding variables). In this way the structurer relates E105 to ARRIVE11400, ensuring that the hearer will understand their sequentiality.

Notice that the growth points for both nucleus and satellite remain unfulfilled (had any of the input units' features matched them, they would have been satisfied and removed). Therefore, the growth points are posted on the structurer's agenda as extant goals to be achieved.

We continue this example one step further. The next goal on the agenda is the growth-point-turned-goal

```
Name: SEQUENCE

Results:
  ((BMB SPEAKER HEARER (POSITION-OF ?PART ?NEXT)))

Nucleus+Satellite requirements/subgoals:
  ((BMB SPEAKER HEARER (NEXT-ACTION.R ?PART ?NEXT)))

Nucleus requirements/subgoals:
  ((BMB SPEAKER HEARER (TOPIC ?PART)))

Nucleus growth points:
  ((BMB SPEAKER HEARER (CIRCUMSTANCE-OF ?PART ?CIR))
   (BMB SPEAKER HEARER (ATTRIBUTE-OF ?PART ?VAL))
   (BMB SPEAKER HEARER (PURPOSE-OF ?PART ?PURP)))

Satellite requirements/subgoals:
  ((BMB SPEAKER HEARER (TOPIC ?NEXT)))

Satellite growth points:
  ((BMB SPEAKER HEARER (ATTRIBUTE-OF ?NEXT ?VAL))
   (BMB SPEAKER HEARER (DETAILS-OF ?NEXT ?DETS))
   (BMB SPEAKER HEARER (POSITION-OF ?NEXT ?FOLL)))

Order: (NUCLEUS SATELLITE)
Relation-phrases: ("" "then" "next")
Activation-question:
  "Could ~A be presented as start-point, mid-point, or
   end-point of some succession of items along some
   dimension? -- that is, should the hearer know that
   ~A is part of a sequence?"
```

Figure 3.3: The RST relation/plan SEQUENCE

```
Name: CIRCUMSTANCE

Results:
  ((BMB SPEAKER HEARER (CIRCUMSTANCE-OF ?X ?CC))))

Nucleus+Satellite requirements/subgoals:
  ((OR (BMB SPEAKER HEARER (HEADING.R ?X ?CIRC))
       (BMB SPEAKER HEARER (TIME.R ?X ?CIRC))))

Nucleus requirements/subgoals:
  ((BMB SPEAKER HEARER (TOPIC ?X)))

Nucleus growth points:
  ((BMB SPEAKER HEARER (ATTRIBUTE-OF ?X ?ATT)))

Satellite requirements/subgoals:
  ((BMB SPEAKER HEARER (TOPIC ?CIRC)))

Satellite growth points:
  ((BMB SPEAKER HEARER (ATTRIBUTE-OF ?CIRC ?VAL)))

Order: (NUCLEUS SATELLITE)
Relation-phrases: ("")
Activation-question:
  "Could ~A be presented within some spatial, temporal,
   or situational framework? -- that is, should the hearer
   know to interpret ~A in some appropriate context?"
```

Figure 3.4: The RST relation/plan CIRCUMSTANCE

```
(BMB SPEAKER HEARER (CIRCUMSTANCE-OF E105 ?CIRC))
```

which matches the results field of only one relation/plan, CIRCUMSTANCE, given in Figure 3.4. (As can be seen from the nucleus requirements, this plan is tailored to the Navy domain. In a more sophisticated scheme, the terms for HEADING and TIME could be replaced by a single generalization such as SPATIO-TEMPORAL-LOCATION, and the matching process adapted accordingly.) After binding ?X to E105, the first requirement within the OR term matches the unit E105, since it contains the proposition

```
(BMB SPEAKER HEARER (HEADING.R E105 HEADING11416))
```

This match permits the structurer to form a new instantiation of the CIRCUM-STANCE relation to relate E105 to HEADING11416. The new relation fulfills one of the growth-points-turned-goals of the original SEQUENCE nucleus, and is therefore added into the paragraph tree as follows:

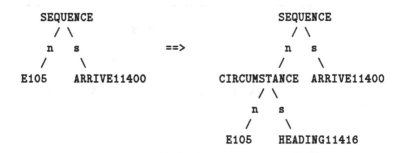

The nucleus **E105** is moved to become the nucleus of the newly-formed relation CIRCUMSTANCE, which replaces it in the paragraph tree. The remaining two unfulfilled nucleus growth points of the SEQUENCE relation are propagated along with it, and are joined by the unfulfilled nucleus growth point of the CIRCUMSTANCE relation. Together, these points potentially give rise to tree growth at the new position of **E105**. Similarly, the remaining growth point of the satellite **HEADING11416** is added to the agenda.

Planning proceeds as follows: one of the SEQUENCE nucleus growth points is fulfilled by an ELABORATION-ATTRIBUTE relation between **E105** and **READINESS 11400**, the unit that represents the operational status of the Knox. The remaining satellite growth point of the CIRCUMSTANCE gives rise to an ELABORATION-ATTRIBUTE relation between **HEADING11416** and **POSITION11410**, which represents the ship's latitude and longitude. Finally, the growth point term **POSITION -OF** in the **ARRIVE11400** satellite is fulfilled by a SEQUENCE relating that node to **E107**. Though at the end some growth points remain unsatisfied, all the input units have been related, and the structuring process stops with the paragraph structure in Figure 3.5.

As is clear, the planning cycle is the following: a new growth-point-turned-goal is taken from the agenda; zero or more relations are found to fulfill it; these relations (if any) furnish requirements for nucleus and satellite fillers; if any input units match, the relations are instantiated with the units and added to the tree. Unfulfilled growth points are added to the agenda of goals. When more than one relation/plan can be added, new trees are formed, identical except for the new relations, and the structurer proceeds to plan out all alternatives. (Not committing to any particular tree growth during planning is an experimentation strategy; since we have no hearer model or stylistic criteria on which to base a preference for one relation over another, and since the issue is clearly related to the hearer and the desired style of the text, we have chosen to plan out all options rather than commit to an option arbitrarily.)

When all input units have been used, or when no goals are left on the agenda, planning ceases. The structurer applies a simple evaluation metric to select the most comprehensive tree, if more than one have been built, as follows: the trees containing the most input units are collected, and of those the tree(s) with the fewest remaining unsatisfied growth point goals; in case of a resulting tie, one

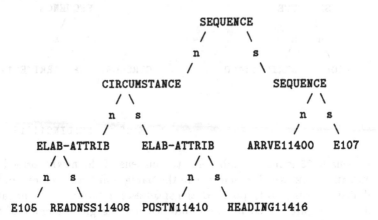

```
                          SEQUENCE
                          /     \
                         n       s
                        /         \
              CIRCUMSTANCE          SEQUENCE
                  / \                  / \
                 n   s                n   s
                /     \              /     \
        ELAB-ATTRIB    ELAB-ATTRIB  ARRVE11400   E107
          / \            / \
         n   s          n   s
        /     \        /     \
    E105  READNSS11408  POSTN11410   HEADING11416
```

Knox, which is C4, is en route to Sasebo. It is at 18N 79E,
heading SSW. It will arrive on 4/24. It will load for 4 days.

Figure 3.5: Paragraph structure and corresponding Navy text

tree is selected at random.

3.3 RELATION/PLANS, SCHEMAS, AND CLAUSE-LEVEL RULES

3.3.1 Relation/Plans and Schemas

Paragraphs of text can be planned and generated in various ways. The primary
method of planning paragraphs by computer (other than the method described
in this paper) makes use of data structures called schemas. Schemas capture
the stereotypical arrangement of clauses in common expository texts such as
descriptions of objects. First developed by McKeown (1982) and then extended
by the inclusion of the sophistication of the hearer's knowledge as decision
criterion (Paris, 1987), schemas are an extremely useful method of controlling
the collection and structuring of material from collections of data into lists of
clause-sized units that each support the production of a sentence.

Schemas have the advantage of being easy to build and use. For an application, a schema is defined for each type of paragraph to be generated. For
each clause typically appearing in the paragraph, a predicate is built into the
schema that represents the type of information it contains, as well as additional

information such as the number times it can occur in the paragraph. To use a schema, a schema traversal mechanism similar to a script instantiator evaluates the conditions of use on the predicates (taking into account focus, etc.), finds the appropriate material in the data base, and records what is eventually to be realized by the realization component.

One limitation on their use is the fact that schemas do not contain a description of the functional rhetorical role that each part of the paragraph plays with respect to the whole paragraph. This makes them unsuitable for systems requiring the ability to adapt dynamically (such as interactive systems that can be called upon to replan any particular piece of the paragraph at any time; see Moore and Swartout as well as Paris, both this volume). A second limitation is the inherent rigidity of schemas; however many optional and repeating predicates they contain, they still always mandate a paragraph of text.

The use of RST relation/plans instead of schemas overcomes some of these limitations: the paragraph trees contain a derivation history that shows the rhetorical relation between every two parts of the text, and they can control smaller spans of text than schemas — as small as two clauses in the limit. However, these advantages come at the cost of increased work, since it is more difficult to assemble an RST paragraph tree from a set of independent relations than it is to instantiate and traverse a schema, particularly under Mann and Thompson's original conception of RST, in which each relation has to be tested at every cycle of the growth of the paragraph for possible applicability – see (Mann and Thompson, 1987). Clearly, a melding of the two techniques that preserves their best aspects — the selectivity of schemas, the dependencies of relation/plans — would be very useful.

By developing the notion of growth points, we have managed to achieve a suitable melding. Rather than allowing all possible RST relations to enter at each cycle of the planning process, we allow growth of only those relations whose goals appear in the growth points fields, and we build in the growth points fields only those goals that support the texts commonly found in the domain of discourse. This is, of course, exactly the same approach taken in the development of schemas.

By the introduction of growth points we establish a functional equivalence between relation/plans and schemas. To see this, consider the following argument: in the SEQUENCE relation/plan of Figure 3.3, replace the CIRCUMS-TANCE-OF growth point goal by the nucleus and satellite growth point goals of the CIRCUMSTANCE relation, in order of appearance (see Figure 3.4), and add to the ends of the nucleus and satellite requirements an additional set of requirements for a second set of clauses, namely those from the CIRCUMSTANCE relation/plan's nucleus and satellite requirements respectively. Perform the same operation for each of the other nucleus and satellite growth point goals recursively. Though it may never end, this rewriting will produce a (possibly infinitely recursive) plan that prescribes saying the nucleus, then the bottommost satellite that fulfills the requirements, then the next bottom-most, etc., via the

CIRCUMSTANCE satellite, up to the initial SEQUENCE satellite, followed next by its associated relations. That is, one would compile a (possible infinitely recursive) single recipe for constructing the paragraph tree shown earlier. This recipe would contain, of course, the individual relations (such as CIRCUMSTANCE), as well as the rhetorical roles they play in the paragraph. Other than that, however, the recipe would resemble a (possible infinitely recursive) schema built for the purpose of producing paragraphs describing ships' employments, when given a finite collection of facts to be said.

Viewed this way, it is clear that a relation/plan without any growth point goals is simply a minimal two-place (if it has one nucleus and one satellite) schema. A relation/plan with growth point goals is a kind of generalized schema that builds a paragraph to achieve the communicative function of the relation/plan. Relation/plans can be combined into larger plans – see (Moore and Swartout and Paris, both papers in this volume), and even into schemas – see (Mann, 1988). Said differently, each RST relation/plan is simultaneously a basic rhetorical operator which can be incorporated into a schema as well as a generalized schema for building a specific type of paragraph.

3.3.2   Desirable Characteristics of Relation/Plans

RST relation/plans exhibit a number of desirable characteristics. First, growth point goals for expanding the tree reside in the relation/plans declaratively. No additional inclusion mechanism is required to suggest directions of growth. The simple procedure is: if the plan's growth points call for something, and it can be found in the material to be included, then say it.

Second, being stated declaratively, the growth point goals are ordered. No additional ordering criteria are required; and the procedure is: simply say things in the order given by growth points in the plan.

A third characteristic is the simplicity of this structure planning method. By representing the growth points declaratively in plans, the behavior of the structure planner, the kinds of trees it can build, and the ways in which relation/plans can be altered are perspicacious and easy to change. Making growth points explicit and separate contrasts with the approach of Moore and Paris (both in this volume), in which growth point injunctions are all incorporated into the satellite fields of the plans, with the result that the rhetorical relationship between the nucleus and its particular satellite is obscured. They overcome this problem to some degree by making their plans rather small (limiting the number of satellite entries per plan).

Another desirable characteristic pertains to the use of relation/plans. In planning the structure of a coherent paragraph, the planner constructs a tree that automatically records the rhetorical role played by each clause with respect to whole text. These roles can later be used to identify sections of the text that have been unsuccessful and can aid replanning or elaboration.

A fifth feature supports a type of planning that is still beyond our grasp. This involves representing growth point goals in a similar way to requirements. A structure planner more powerful than ones we can build today could try to make true any unsatisfied semantic requirements in the nucleus and satellite requirements fields in exactly the way it tries to achieve the goals in the growth point fields. It may thus be able to include material that violates nucleus and satellite requirements (that is, to "lie", or at least, to present material in a way not licensed by its features!) as long as the remaining unfulfilled requirements can be satisfied by the inclusion of additional material, in exactly the same way as growth point goals are fulfilled by new material. This approach was, in fact, part of the initial attempt at developing a text structure planner; in (Hovy, 1988a) no explicit growth point fields occur. The nucleus and satellite requirements ensured the relational compatibility of the nucleus and satellite entities while also containing what are now the growth point goals as ancillary "requirements" to produce an adequate paragraph.

The sixth characteristic, one of the central points of this paper, is the fact that the planning paradigm using relation/plans to plan multisentence paragraphs as described is exactly the same type of planning paradigm that has been followed in some approaches to plan out the contents of single sentences. This means that a single planning process can use, at the paragraph level, appropriate RST relation/plans, and, at the sentence level, clause-sized planning rules, in a homogeneous fashion. This point is discussed in the next section.

3.3.3   Relation/Plans and Clause-Level Rules

From the macro-sized planning of paragraphs, we turn next to the micro-sized planning of parts of individual sentences. Some of the most thorough work in this regard has been done by Appelt (1981; 1985), whose planner-generator KAMP achieved communicative goals by planning, via illocutionary acts and surface speech acts, so-called utterance acts which, being straightforwardly associated with syntactic knowledge, were used to build sentences.

In developing KAMP, Appelt's primary concern was with assembling the information that had to be built into a sentence in order to provably achieve the planner's communicative goals. The goals never called for more information than could be accommodated in one or two sentences, with the result that the issue of coherence did not arise. Thus KAMP's extensibility to paragraph-sized text was never illustrated in practice.

In order to extend Appelt's work into the multisentence range, the issue of coherence must be addressed. It is not sufficient simply to prove that the information provided in the clauses of the text individually suffice to support the desired informing result; it is also necessary to ensure that the development of the material and its interclausal linking supports the derivation of the desired interpretation.

The RST relation/plans and structure planner perform part of that function. Since both the structurer and KAMP are simplified versions of NOAH (Sacerdoti, 1977), the RST relation/plans can be used together with KAMP's intraclause-sized planning rules (so-called *concept activation actions*) in an appropriately general homogeneous system to plan paragraphs of text. Operating at the discourse level, relation/plans control the assembly of clause-sized units of representation into an appropriately linked tree structure, and operating at the clause level, concept activation action rules control the assembly of constituent-sized units of representation into an appropriately annotated pre-sentence structure which is then handed to a realization component.

The feasibility of such a smooth joining of discourse- and clause-level processing is enhanced by the fact that no clear boundary seems to exist between the structuring of paragraphs and the planning of clause parts such as preposition groups. That is to say, the leaves of a paragraph tree produced by the RST structurer need not always become separate clauses; very often, a number of leaves can be grouped together into a clause complex. For example, the last part of the SEQUENCE relation/plan in the tree in Figure 3.5 can be realized in at least two ways:

(a). `Knox, which is at 18N 79E, heads SSW, arriving on 4/24,`
`to load for 4 days.`

(b). `Knox, which is at 18N 79E, heads SSW. It arrives on`
`4/24. It loads for 4 days.`

Going further, a leaf of the paragraph tree need not even always be realized as a clause, but can sometimes give rise to a grammatically simpler constituent such as an adjective. The ELABORATION satellite is an example, as in "the man who is big..." vs "the big man...". This issue is even more pronounced in German and Swedish than in English (for example, the italicized clause in "the suspicion *which was confirmed by this discovery* is..." need not form a separate clause in German: "die *durch diese Entdeckung belegte* Vermutung ist..."). To handle this issue, we have had to arbitrarily stop RST structure planning at the clause level and use a number of default rules to control realization as dependent or independent clauses (for example, ELABORATION-ATTRIBUTE satellites become dependent clauses instead of separate sentences, as in Figure 3.5). Making use of clause-level planning rules such as those in KAMP would help resolve these problems.

RST relation/plans can thus be seen as an extension of Appelt's clause-level planning rules to handle paragraph-level structure planning. Though their formalization has not been carried out to a degree which would support proofs of communicative correctness, this has always been their intended use, and was also one of the reasons for the selection of Cohen and Levesque's (1985) belief-based modal notation with which to represent requirements and goals.

3.4 TOP-DOWN AND OPEN-ENDED PLANNING

3.4.1 A Different Treatment of Growth Points

The previous section described how RST relation/plans can be thought of as schemas which are susceptible to manipulation by a top-down planning algorithm. Though this approach has various desirable characteristics, such as explicitly representing the rhetorical role played by each clause in the paragraph structure tree, the inflexibility that can plague schemas is also present in relation/plans' growth points. In general, in order to overcome a difficulty of this nature, one requires criteria by which to make the decisions that afford the desired variation. This section shows how a slightly generalized treatment of relation/plans supports a far more flexible planning regime.

Consider again the nucleus growth points of the SEQUENCE relation in Figure 3.3:

```
Nucleus growth points:
   ((BMB SPEAKER HEARER (CIRCUMSTANCE-OF ?PART ?CIR))
    (BMB SPEAKER HEARER (ATTRIBUTE-OF ?PART ?VAL))
    (BMB SPEAKER HEARER (PURPOSE-OF ?PART ?PURP)))
```

These three requirements suggest material that respectively is circumstantial to, is an attribute of, and is a purpose for, the material in the nucleus.

As currently used, the growth points are treated as actual *injunctions* for further growth of the paragraph tree at this point, and in this order: whatever information is related to the nucleus material by any of these relations must be included, if it has been selected for inclusion by the application program. However, depending on the hearer's knowledge and expertise, the time available for the interaction, the detail and complexity of the material to be communicated, and so forth, it may very easily be the case that any elaboration of the topic as mandated by growth points is suboptimally ordered or even wholly inappropriate. What then are the ramifications of building a slightly more discriminating system? One could treat growth points merely as *suggestions* for growth, depending on additional criteria such as the amount of time or space available. In fact, in the limit, one could even altogether remove growth points from relation/plans and have the structurer attempt to grow the paragraph tree using *all* the relation/plans at its disposal in each expansion cycle (as mentioned earlier, this was Mann and Thompson's original conception of structure planning using RST), although one problem with the extreme approach is that one may lose some of the coherence afforded by limiting the growth appropriately to each relation/plan.

The essential difference between the two approaches is captured in the question "on what basis is the addition of a new block of text to the tree considered?". In the first case, the answer to this question is:

> (a) the impetus for finding a further block of text is the growth point injunction contained in the current relation/plan. No additions are considered unless they are suggested by the plan.

In the second case, the answer is:

> (b) some (or all) possible additions of further text are considered at each step in the planning cycle; the impetus for such consideration is either a suggestion in the plan or is built directly into the planning procedure itself.

Small though it may seem, this distinction gives rise to important differences in the structuring procedure. The first approach can be called the *strict top-down planning approach*. Here the RST relation/plans are plans in the traditional sense; the explicit injunctions for growth correspond to the steps, in proper order, necessary to achieve the goal. In contrast, the alternative approach just introduced can be called the *open-ended planning approach*. This approach is useful in many situations when top-down planning is inappropriate — whenever one needs less structured methods to adapt interactively to the environment and interlocutors, such as in conversations. Here the potential to grow any matched growth point goal relation at every point affords a flexibility to make opportunistic use of the best paragraph continuation under the changing circumstances. Of course, taking this approach, one has to abandon the strict pipeline model used so far, in which the structurer completes the text plan before allowing material to be realized. A model in which planner and realizer are interleaved, as suggested in (Hovy 1988b), is required. Regardless of the planning model, however, the point is that RST relation/plans support either paradigm, depending on the treatment accorded growth point goals.

However, there is no free lunch. With the enhanced opportunities to make more suitable text under the suggestion interpretation comes the responsibility of exercising choice. Criteria are required to control the inclusion and ordering of candidate growth point material. Work is in progress in developing such criteria. With respect to the inclusion of material, the following play a role:

Reasons for inclusion
1. Explicit goal to communicate the extra material
2. Rhetorical-stylistic considerations: balance/parallelism of text
3. Hearer's lack of knowledge
4. Hearer's inability to understand without extra information
5. Hearer asks for more information

Reasons for exclusion
1. Lack of time or space
2. Unpleasant/undesirable effects of extra material
3. Lack of known detail
4. Untrustworthiness of material

At present, some of these criteria seem more difficult to implement than others. Inclusion criteria 1 and 5 are simple: if the structurer is given or generates the explicit goal to include material of some kind, then such material must be searched for. Criterion 2 is more challenging, but still addressable: we can develop strategies for deciding based on an inspection of the content, balance, and parallel structure of the contents of the paragraph tree. Criteria 3 and 4 are harder, since they require a model of the hearer. The criteria for exclusion are all somewhat easier to address, since they mostly depend on the characteristics of the material itself.

A further criterion, relevant to both inclusion and ordering decisions, can be derived from the work on focus of McCoy and Cheng (this volume). At each point in the planning cycle, candidate growth point material that is neither in focus nor allowed by a legal focus move (according to McCoy and Cheng's algorithm) may not be included in the tree, and material which is initially not a legal focus move may be made so by appropriate reordering of nuclei and satellites in the RST paragraph tree. A preliminary description of the use of McCoy's focus theory to constrain RST tree structure growth appears in (Hovy and McCoy, 1989).

3.4.2 Hybridization

Though the top-down and open-ended planning paradigms seem very different, the fact that the difference hinges upon a simple change in the location and interpretation of the growth point goals means that RST relation/plans can be used in both planning paradigms, and hence serve a useful function in the investigation of the relative merits of each.

The correspondence is so close that it is quite possible to follow a hybrid paradigm, in which the optionality of each growth point goal is explicitly contained in the relation/plans. To the extent that one can provide criteria for deciding on the inclusion and order of relatable material, to that extent one can relax the injunctive nature of the growth point to perform open-ended planning, while the remaining goals can be left as ordered injunctions. In this way the degree of hybridization is easily altered.

An allied benefit is the variable level of constraint supported by such a hybrid scheme. Consider, for example, the genre of letters, in which the address, date, salutation, and closing are almost completely fixed. In addition, usually, the first and last paragraphs are somewhat fixed with respect to tone and content, while the body proper is usually much more free-form and open-ended. A hybrid schema/plan for a letter would contain fixed injunctions for the fixed parts, some less fixed addressee-related goals for the first and last paragraphs, and a number of optional growth goals for the body (in fact, it is not clear that one could build plans for a letter-planning structurer any differently). None of the optional goals need be followed, though doing so may give rise to a rather bizarre letter (to quote an example from Bill Mann: "Dear John, I hope all is well. I hate you and never want to see you again. Love, Mary").

3.5 CONCLUSION

In order to structure coherent paragraphs from given material, one requires plans. While it is possible, on the one hand, to build macro-level plans or schemas that describe whole paragraphs at a time, and, on the other, to build micro-level plans that determine the composition of individual parts of sentences, RST relation/plans (and plans of similar type) support the functionality of both. Relation/plans combine the best features of schemas (the definition of extended structures such as paragraphs; perspicuous representations) with the best features of hierarchical planning methods (power and flexibility). Thus relation/plans can be seen as generalizations of schemas that support hierarchical planning methods, and that are functional along the whole continuum from paragraphs to clause-internal constituents.

A second characteristic that makes relation/plans desirable is the ease with which they can be switched from the top-down structural planning regime required for optimally balanced, well-crafted text to the open-ended planning regime that supports the dynamic and flexible behavior required for interactive communication. By treating relation/plan growth points as injunctions, one can perform top-down planning; by treating them as suggestions and supplying criteria for their inclusion and ordering, one can perform open-ended planning.

This centrality and flexibility makes the RST relation/plans an extremely useful vehicle for investigating the planning of paragraph-length text. Opportunities for new work and unanswered questions abound; the use of plans to gather appropriate information from complex knowledge sources, and the criteria for including and excluding material are but two of the many avenues of text planning research that RST relation/plans open up.

ACKNOWLEDGMENTS

Many thanks to Johanna Moore, Cécile Paris, and Kathy McCoy for comments and discussions, and to John Bateman, Christian Matthiessen, Bill Mann, HaJo Novak, and Dietmar Rösner for comments.

This work was supported in part by the Advanced Research Projects Agency monitored by the Office of Naval Research under contract N00014-82-K-0149. It was also supported by AFOSR contract F49620-87-C-0005.

BIBLIOGRAPHY

Appelt, D.E., 1981. *Planning Natural Language Utterances to Satisfy Multiple Goals.* Ph.D. dissertation, Stanford University.

Appelt, D.E., 1985. *Planning English Sentences*. Cambridge: Cambridge University Press.

Arens, Y., Miller, L., Shapiro, S.C. and Sondheimer, N.K., 1988. Automatic Construction of User-Interface Displays. *Proceedings of the 7th AAAI Conference*, St. Paul (808-813).

Cohen, P.R. and Levesque, H.J., 1985. Speech Acts and Rationality. *Proceedings of the 23rd ACL Conference*, Chicago (49-59).

Conklin, E.J. and McDonald, D.D., 1982. Salience: The Key to the Selection Problem in Natural Language Generation. *Proceedings of the 20th ACL Conference*, Toronto (129-135).

Hovy, E.H., 1988a. Planning Coherent Multisentential Text. *Proceedings of the 26th ACL Conference*, Buffalo (163-169).

Hovy, E.H., 1988b. On the Study of Text Planning and Realization. *Proceedings of the AAAI Workshop on Text Planning and Realization*, St. Paul (17-29).

Hovy, E.H. and McCoy, K.F., 1989. Focusing your RST: A step toward generating coherent multisentential text. *Proceedings of the 11th Cognitive Science Society Conference*, Ann Arbor (667-674).

Kaczmarek, T.S., Bates, R. and Robins, G., 1986. Recent Developments in NIKL. *Proceedings of the 5th AAAI Conference*, Philadelphia (978-985).

Mann, W.C., 1983. An Overview of the Nigel Text Generation Grammar. USC/Information Sciences Institute Research Report RR-83-113.

Mann, W.C., 1988. Text Generation: The Problem of Text Structure. In McDonald, D.D. and Bolc, L. (eds), *Natural Language Generation Systems*, New York: Springer Verlag (47-68). Also USC/Information Sciences Institute Research Report RR-87-181.

Mann, W.C. and Matthiessen, C.M.I.M., 1983. Nigel: A Systemic Grammar for Text Generation. USC/Information Sciences Institute Research Report RR-83-105.

Mann, W.C. and Thompson, S.A., 1983. Relational Propositions in Discourse. USC/Information Sciences Institute Research Report RR-83-115.

Mann, W.C. and Thompson, S.A., 1987. Rhetorical Structure Theory: Description and Construction of Text Structures. In Kempen, G. (ed), *Natural Language Generation: New Results in Artificial Intelligence, Psychology, and Linguistics*, Dordrecht: Martinus Nijhoff Publishers (85-95). Also USC/Information Sciences Institute Research Report RR-86-174.

Matthiessen, C.M.I.M., 1984. Systemic Grammar in Computation: The Nigel Case. USC/Information Sciences Institute Research Report RR-84-121.

McCoy, K.F., 1985. *Correcting Object-Related Misconceptions*. Ph.D. dissertation, University of Pennsylvania.

McCoy, K.R. and Cheng, J., 1990. Focus of Attention: Constraining what can be said next. In *Natural Language Generation in Artificial Intelligence and Computational Linguistics*, (this volume). Paris, Swartout, Mann (Eds). Kluwer Academic Publishers, Norwell, MA.

McKeown, K.R., 1982. *Generating Natural Language Text in Response to Questions about Database Queries*. Ph.D. dissertation, University of Pennsylvania.

Moore, J.D. and Paris, C.L., 1989. Planning Text for Advisory Dialogues. *Proceedings of the 27th ACL Conference*, Vancouver (203-211).

Moore, J.D. and Swartout, W.R., 1990. A Reactive Approach to Explanation: Taking the User's Feedback into Account. In *Natural Language Generation in Artificial Intelligence and Computational Linguistics*, (this volume). Paris, Swartout, Mann (Eds). Kluwer Academic Publishers, Norwell, MA.

Paris, C.L., 1987. *The Use of Explicit User Models in Text Generation: Tailoring to a User's Level of Expertise*. Ph.D. dissertation, Columbia University. To be published by Frances Pinter Publishers in the "Communication in Artificial intelligence" series, Steiner and Fawcett (Eds)

Paris, C.L., 1990. Generation and Explanation: Building an Explanation Facility for the Explainable Expert Systems Framework. In *Natural Language Generation in Artificial Intelligence and Computational Linguistics*, (this volume). Paris, Swartout, Mann (Eds). Kluwer Academic Publishers, Norwell, MA.

Sacerdoti, E., 1977. *A Structure for Plans and Behavior*. Amsterdam: North-Holland Publishing Company.

Chapter 4

Focus of attention: Constraining what can be said next

Kathleen F. McCoy
and Jeannette Cheng

Abstract: During the course of a coherent conversation or discourse, the participants their attention on some subset of their knowledge. As the discourse goes on, this focused subset may change – it may grow to include more knowledge, narrow down to include just a subset of what it originally contained, or shift (either temporarily or permanently) to a new area of the participants' knowledge base. In this work we investigate the nature of this focusing during a discourse and its effect on a natural language generation system. Our research examines how the focused knowledge is tracked during human discourse and how changes in the focused set are marked by the human conversational partners. We hypothesize that there are several different kinds of focusing going on in discourse, and attempt to provide a unified account which can handle each. This resulting knowledge will be crucial for a generation system in deciding what to say next and in deciding how to appropriately mark unexpected changes in focus.

4.1   INTRODUCTION

During the course of a coherent conversation or discourse, the participants focus their attention on some subset of their knowledge. As the discourse goes on, this focused subset may change – it may grow to include more knowledge, narrow down to include just a subset of what it originally contained, or shift (either temporarily or permanently) to a new area of the participants' knowledge base. These changes, however, must occur in an orderly fashion. If a conversational partner is unable to track the changes in focus of attention, then the conversation will seem disjoint or incomprehensible.

In this work we investigate the nature of this focusing during a discourse and its effect on a natural language generation system. At any point in a discourse the focused knowledge represents the knowledge that a natural language generation system could reasonably be expected to include next in its interaction with the user. If the system has nothing to say about the currently focused knowledge, then it must explicitly indicate that the focused set of knowledge is shifting. Moreover, the shift in focus that it chooses cannot be random, but instead must be a shift that can be readily followed by the human conversational participant. Our research examines how this focused knowledge is tracked during human discourse and how changes in the focused set are marked by the human conversational partners. To this end it draws on research done by others in discourse structure and focus of attention – e.g., (Grosz and Sidner, 1985; Reichman, 1981; Reichman-Adar, 1984; Hobbs, 1979; Linde, 1979; Cohen, 1987; Carberry, 1983). It differs from this previous work in two major ways. First, the previous work has been mostly concerned with the interpretation of discourse. Hence they concentrate on problems such as determining the referent of a referring expression or understanding a text for a particular task. In contrast, this work is concerned with generation. It is an investigation into the way that focus of attention might be useful in the generation task. In particular, we want to investigate how focus of attention might be useful in narrowing down what might be included next in a text and how shifts in focus of attention should be marked by the generator so that the listener can follow.[1] Second, the previous work has, for the most part, been concerned with focusing phenomena found in particular kinds of discourses (e.g., task oriented dialogues or arguments). In this paper we attempt to provide a unified account which can handle shifts in focus of attention found in any kind of discourse. This requires handling several different types of focusing elements.

This paper, then, is a proposal for a type of machinery which we believe is necessary for generating coherent discourse. This machinery must necessarily be concerned with understanding as well as generation since it is necessary to

---

[1] We do not want to imply that focus of attention should be the only thing that should be taken into account in deciding what to include next in the text. Certainly some kind of text structuring device is also needed. For examples see (McKeown, 1985a; McCoy, 1985; Paris and McKeown, 1987; Mann and Thompson, 1987; Hovy, 1988a; Moore and Swartout, 1990) among others.

track focus of attention in order to coherently generate what comes next. The results of this research will allow us to build a natural language generation system that tracks and changes focused knowledge. This knowledge will be crucial in deciding what to say next and in deciding how to appropriately mark unexpected changes in focus.

4.2   DIFFERENT KINDS OF FOCUSING ITEMS

In any given conversation, there is some subset of the speaker's knowledge which is being focused on – that which has been primed by the conversation so far. It is something from this focused set of knowledge that is likely to be said next in the discourse. Thus we can think of the preceding dialogue as constraining what may be said next because it causes the knowledge base to be focused on in a particular way. One goal of this work is to determine what knowledge becomes primed due to the explicit mention of other items in a discourse. A claim of this work is that priming effects cannot be explained by the presence or absence of particular lexical items in isolation. Rather, the priming effect that a particular lexical item will induce is dependent on both the kind of information it is referring to in the discourse (e.g., object or event) and the focus of attention that has been set up by the dialogue preceding the mention of the lexical item.

Priming effects of preceding discourse have not gone unnoticed by previous researchers – e.g., (Schank and Abelson, 1977; Garrod and Sanford, 1983; Grosz, 1977; Carberry, 1983; Allen and Perrault, 1980; McCoy, 1985). In fact, several theories have been developed in an attempt to explain some of these priming effects. While we would claim that each of these researchers and each of their theories does in fact explain some kind of priming effect, it is unclear how they can be integrated into one framework. This work is an attempt to do just that. Here we attempt to give a unifying explanation to the different kinds of priming effects found by others. It will be one framework, yet the types of inferencing required to calculate the current priming will depend on the kind of information being used.

To understand the different priming effects previously noticed, consider the following set of examples each of which illustrates a different kind of focusing. The first example is taken from (Garrod and Sanford, 1983, p. 275-276). The first part of the example illustrates the oddness of certain discourses when what is said next has not been properly primed by the preceding dialogue.

(1)   Harry fell several times.
       ? **The snow** was cold and wet.

According to Garrod and Sanford (1983), the use of "the snow" in this example seems quite odd. The reader is left with questioning the relevance of snow to the previous discourse; it is difficult to integrate. Notice, however, that these same sentences embedded within a slightly longer context, seem quite reasonable:

(2)   *Learning to ski*
       Harry fell several times.
       (He didn't like skiing at all.)
       The snow was cold and wet.

Here the title "Learning to Ski" and the (optional) reference to skiing in the dialogue suddenly makes the reference to snow quite acceptable. They have caused an orientation to be taken on the domain knowledge in which snow holds a prominent position.

This type of priming has previously been explained using *scripts* (Schank and Abelson, 1977) or *scenarios* (Garrod and Sanford, 1983). These researchers argue that people have precompiled scripts which explain typical courses of action in various situations. When a particular script is recognized as being relevant to the current situation, its events and the objects needed in these events become primed by the discourse.

While we would not argue for or against the details of any particular knowledge representation theory, it seems clear that a priming effect was evident in (2) that was not evident in (1). In part this effect was generated by the setting established by the title given to the passage. This same setting priming effect can be found in discourses where its establishment is gained by more subtle means.

Other researchers have noticed a similar kind of priming effect in task oriented dialogues and have explained it in terms of a focusing mechanism gained from a planning formalism (Grosz, 1977; Carberry, 1983; Allen and Perrault, 1980). For instance:

(3)   Jane wanted to board the 9:10 train to Montreal.
       She waited on the platform for its arrival.

Jane's waiting on the platform seems like a reasonable next sentence because the action of waiting on the platform can be seen as a subpiece of the action of boarding the train. (E.g., In order to board the train you must find out the gate and time, go to the particular platform, and wait there for the train to arrive.) Thus, it is argued, plans may act as a mechanism for focusing attention on some subset of the knowledge. If, during a discourse, the goals of the participants can be deduced, then we may expect that the participants will attempt to achieve these goals by performing a sequence of actions. This planned sequence of actions can constrain what is talked about next to something that is related to the actions in the plan or to the objects involved in those actions. What we see in (3) is a definite reference to an object (the platform) which seems perfectly reasonable given the orientation to the domain established by the action introduced in the first sentence.

Yet another kind of focusing effect can be found in these example taken from (McKeown, 1982) in which a balloon is being described.

(4) ? The balloon was red and white striped. Because this balloon was designed to carry men, it had to be large. It had a silver circle at the top to reflect heat. In fact, it was larger than any balloon John had ever seen.

While the text might not be considered bad, it certainly is not smooth. The text can be greatly enhanced by reordering the sentences:

(5) The balloon was red and white striped. It had a silver circle at the top to reflect heat. Because this balloon was designed to carry men, it had to be large. In fact, it was larger than any balloon John had ever seen.

The difference in these two texts was explained by "layers of focusing" in (McKeown, 1982) and could be explained byobject perspective as described in (McCoy, 1985). The oddness of the first description, these researchers would argue, derives from the fact that the focusing going on in a sentence is going on at many levels. Even though the balloon is the focus of each of the sentences in the above passages, different perspectives on the balloon are being taken. Each perspective brings into focus different aspects of the balloon. For instance, we may take a perspective on the balloon in which color is important, or take another in which size is important. In a coherent discourse we do not, however, randomly jump from one perspective to another.

In these three examples we have seen how focusing affects the coherence of sentences in a discourse. In each case a different kind of focusing seemed to be in effect and a different proposal was made which seemed to explain the particular phenomenon seen. We would argue, however, that none of the three proposals would handle **all** of the focusing phenomena. Yet, we have given evidence which indicates that each seems to be found in discourse. What is needed is a theory of discourse focus which would allow all of the different kinds of focusing to be handled. This would allow a generation system to generate texts which establish and shift focus of attention in such a way that is understandable to the user. In this work we introduce the notion of a *discourse focus tree* which accounts for all of these different kinds of focusing in one unified approach. During a discourse, a focus tree is constructed and traversed, one node being visited at a time. The tree itself consists of several different types of nodes. The type of the currently visited node, along with its position in the tree, determines what entities from the knowledge base are highlighted (i.e., in focus).

As a result, the visited node in the discourse focus tree generates expectations about what may be said next in a discourse. What is said next should come either directly from the highlighted set of knowledge, or from the knowledge highlighted as the result of making one of a small number of moves in the discourse focus tree. If another focus move must be made, the generator must leave cues for the listener so that the listener will establish a focus of attention which is compatible with that of the speaker. These cues take on a variety of forms such as syntactic usage, tense, clue words, anaphora, voice inflections, pauses, and hand gestures. The more the speaker wishes to deviate from an orderly traversal of the tree, the stronger the cues s/he must leave for the listener. In addition, certain kinds of unexpected shifts in focus often leave the expectation that the original focus will be returned to.

4.3   DISCOURSE FOCUS TREES

We hypothesize the use of a *discourse focus tree* to track the focus of attention through a conversation. Each node in the tree is a "topic" of conversation – something which is talked about in the discourse – and points to an entity from the knowledge base. Thus, the nodes in the focus tree are of several different types (depending on the ontology of the domain). Each type of node may cause a different kind of highlighting to occur in the knowledge base. This, in turn, could account for the different kinds of focusing seen in the examples above.

We hypothesize that a discourse focus tree is being both built up and "traversed" by the participants of a discourse as the discourse progresses. New nodes are being added into the tree in order to integrate new information from the discourse into the focus tree established from the preceding discourse. At the same time, the current focus of attention of the participants in the discourse must be updated as the discourse proceeds. The focus of attention of a participant can be calculated from the node in the tree that the participant has marked as being visited at the current time. Thus a change in the focus of attention corresponds to changing the currently visited node.

The discourse focus tree and the currently visited node in the tree dictate how the knowledge base is highlighted at a particular point in the discourse. In terms of the (Grosz and Sidner, 1985) model of discourse, the discourse focus tree contains the information necessary to calculate the attentional state of the discourse. At first glance, it would seem that all knowledge related to the entity in the knowledge base corresponding to the currently visited node should be considered to be in focus. Thus the conversation may move, for example, to include any knowledge associated with that entity. However, in conversation this is not the case; mention of an item in one context may open avenues of conversation which are not opened by mention of the same item in another context. When people focus on, say, an object, they focus on it from a particular point of view. Thus some aspects of the object are more important than others and it is the important aspects which the conversation may move to. In order to capture this, we must calculate the focus of attention not based solely on the currently visited node, but based on the currently visited node in relation to its ancestors (and siblings) in the tree. A node ("child node") is subordinate to another node ("parent node") if, during the conversation, the child topic is viewed "in terms of" the parent topic. If a particular node is being visited in the tree, then the focused knowledge can be thought of as the knowledge related to information associated with that node intersected with the knowledge related to each of its parent nodes in the tree. Thus, the deeper we are in the discourse focus tree, the more restricted the focus space becomes. In this way, the parent nodes lend a perspective through which the currently visited node, and its children, are viewed. Consider the above figure which contains a

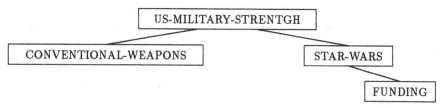

discourse focus tree for a hypothetical discourse. If the conversation dictates that the currently visited node is the root node, then all of the knowledge concerning US-MILITARY-STRENGTH is currently in focus and is thus legal to say next; the generation system may choose to say anything it wants about the subject. On the other hand, if FUNDING is the currently visited node, then the focused knowledge is a more constrained set. In particular, it consists of that knowledge concerned not only with FUNDING but also with STAR-WARS and US-MILITARY-STRENGTH. Put another way, we are focused on FUNDING viewed from the perspective of STAR-WARS which is viewed from the perspective of US-MILITARY-STRENGTH.

4.4   TRAVERSING AND BUILDING THE TREE

As a discourse progresses, each participant of the discourse is creating and traversing a discourse focus tree. Each participant has their own model of what the tree looks like at any given time. The models held by each participant are not necessarily the same. The closer the models are to each other, the more coherent the discourse seems.

It is the speaker's job to add to the tree and/or cause the currently visited node to change. The hearer, on the other hand, must try to make appropriate changes in his/her model of the tree based on what has been said.

In order to have a generation system take advantage of this model, we must further specify how a tree is being built by the participants (i.e., what inferencing can be used by the participants to put new nodes into the tree), what the expected traversal of the tree is and how this expectation can be deviated from, and what the different types of nodes in the tree are and what the expectations about the focus of the succeeding discourse they bring are.

The expectations about how the focus of attention is maintained (i.e., how the focus tree is built up) and the preferences concerning how the focus of attention is shifted (i.e., how the resulting tree is traversed), is dependent on the type of the currently visited node. That is, we do not have one kind of focusing mechanism. Rather, as a discourse progresses we have the opportunity to focus on many different kinds of things. For instance, I might have a conversation with you in which I am focusing on the *action* of renting an apartment. Thus "renting an apartment" might be a node in my discourse focus tree and everything in my knowledge base that I know about renting an apartment might be highlighted. From this point the conversation might move on to discuss an *object*: monthly payments. Here payments might be another node in the discourse focus tree that is subordinate to "renting an apartment". In this case, the focused knowledge about payments is constrained to be relevant to "renting an apartment".

The traversal of the discourse focus tree normally proceeds depth first. Thus what is most likely said next is either an expansion of the currently visited node, an expansion of one of its previously unexpanded children, or a new expansion of one of its ancestors.[2] Notice that this normal traversal of the tree is consistent with other works on focus of attention – cf. (Grosz and Sidner, 1985; Grosz, 1977; Sidner, 1979; McKeown, 1983). In these other works, when the focus of attention shifted to something newly introduced in the discourse (generated a child in the discourse focus tree), the old focus of attention was stacked. The next thing said could either continue with the same focus (not shift the visited node), go to something introduced (generate a child of the currently visited node), or return to something on the stack (return to an ancestor of the currently visited node). Thus in these previous works, a depth first traversal of the tree was the *only* available option.

In this work, while we claim that a depth first traversal of the tree is preferred, we allow other traversals of the tree to occur. If the speaker chooses to say something that is not consistent with a normal depth first traversal, then the speaker must mark that deviation so that the listener will update his/her tree accordingly – cf. (Weiner, 1980; Cohen, 1987). These clues may be both semantic and syntactic in nature. That is, either the placement of the new node in the tree will be clear based on the meaning of what was said, or a syntactic marker which directs the flow will have to be used. These syntactic markers may be necessary in some normal traversals of the tree as well (e.g., to tell the difference between an expansion of the current node and an expansion of one of its ancestors) and have been noted by previous researchers. They will be discussed further in Section 4.6.

---

[2] The expected expansions of a node depend on its type and will be discussed in the next section.

Not only is the discourse focus tree being traversed as the discourse progresses, it is also being built up. The building of the tree can happen in both a top-down and a bottom-up fashion. By top down we mean that each particular kind of node in the tree, when visited, gives rise to expectations as to where the focus may *progress* to. For instance, if the conversation is currently focusing on an action, it may next progress to talk about an object involved in that action or to a subaction or specialization of the action. This progression would cause a subordinate object node to be grown in the tree.

On the other hand, the discourse may call for a more bottom-up type of inferencing in order to construct the tree. For instance a discourse might at first seem somewhat disjoint because it mentions several different seemingly unrelated objects. Each object might give rise to an object node, yet it may be unclear how these disjoint object nodes can be fit into the tree. Once two or more of these nodes have been created, their commonality might be inferred and they can be fit into the tree by creating a parent object node which captures their commonality. Thus a bottom-up type of inference might be used to relate and put the proper perspective on individual nodes in the tree.

4.5   CATEGORIES OF FOCUS NODES

The nodes in the discourse focus tree point to elements in the knowledge base. Thus the nodes are of different types, depending on the ontology of the domain. In general, focus tree nodes belong to one of five types: object (property), attribute, setting, action, and event. Each category of node is treated differently in this theory. The most obvious difference is in the way the knowledge base is highlighted. Each type of node causes highlighting of a particular set of knowledge base entities, and in so doing, furnishes different candidates for what may next be coherently included in the text. Figure 4.1 gives a brief description of the expected shift for each of the node types. A fuller description is given below.

The node types also differ in the way they are inferred from the discourse and put in the tree, and in how and when they invite bottom-up inferencing to take place. For each type of node these various aspects will be discussed.

1. Object nodes cause an object to be focused on in terms of the different groups of properties that object may have. Object and attribute nodes most closely account for the kind of focusing previously discussed in McCoy (1985, 1987a) as object perspective. By object, we are referring to a physical entity or concept. An object node is usually directly given in the discourse in the sense that it is most often inferred because of the explicit noun mention of an object in the discourse.

    An object node raises expectations about where the discourse should progress. Under an object node in the tree we would expect to see at-

NODE TYPE	FOCUS SHIFT CANDIDATES
OBJECT:	attributes of the object, actions the object plays a prominent role in (e.g., is actor of)
ATTRIBUTE:	objects which have the attribute, more specific attribute
SETTING:	objects involved in the setting actions which typically occur in the setting
ACTION:	actor, object, etc., of the action – any participant role; see (Fillmore, 1977), purpose (goal) of action, next action in some sequence, subactions, specializations of the action
EVENT:	actions which can be grouped together into the event

Figure 4.1: Candidate Focus Shifts for Selected Node Types

tribute nodes or action nodes (where the object is a key participant in the action). Here both the underlying attribute and actions are viewed in terms of the mentioned object. Thus if the currently visited node is an object node, then we would expect that we may continue the conversation by talking about the object in terms of certain of its properties or in terms of actions in which it participates.

2. Attribute nodes may either be given directly in the dialogue or may be inferred from the discourse via bottom up inference. An attribute node usually occurs as a subordinate of an object node – although this relationship may be switched. It causes a property or group of properties to be focused.

The way that an object is being looked at can further be broken down into the sets of attributes that are being discussed. Each of these attributes would get an attribute node in the tree. The resulting sets of attribute nodes may be grouped to form a superclass attribute node which represents the type of all of the children attribute nodes – cf. (Schubert *et al.*, 1979). The expectation would be that the next attributes that are mentioned would probably be a "subclass" of this inferred attribute. Such inference also gives expectations as to what will not be discussed next. In particular, if a superclass attribute node has been inferred and the next attribute mentioned does not fit under this superclass (i.e., the focus has shifted away from the superclass attribute), then the expectation is that attributes that fit under the inferred superclass node will not be further discussed without marking a shift in focus.

For instance, suppose the conversation is centered on John and his brown hair and blue eyes. These attributes might be generalized to "physical attributes" with the expectation that another physical attribute might follow. Next, that John plays football and collects stamps might be mentioned. Since these attributes are not physical attributes, instead of being subordinates of "physical" they would be placed as siblings in the tree (as subordinates of John) indicating a focus shift away from physical. This second group of attributes might also be generalized as "interests attributes". The resulting tree is shown below. Assuming that "collects

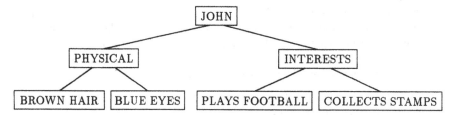

stamps" is the currently visited node, this tree brings with it the expectation that either "collects stamps" would be looked at further, or another interest would be mentioned, or some other non-physical attribute of John would next be mentioned. The introduction of another physical attribute of John would require that some clues be left for the listener.

3. Setting nodes cause a typical setting (course of events) to be focused on. The expected children of this type of node are usually objects (including times and places) but may also be actions. The object children are the things that usually occur in the setting.

   The setting node must usually be inferred via bottom-up inference from the presence of a number of (at first) seemingly unrelated objects. In the same way that unrelated attributes are grouped into clusters, so are unrelated objects. In the case of objects, their common thread is often that they are all a part of a setting. This type of node does not as often come up in a dialogue situation as it does in a narrative (book) type of situation. Once the setting has been inferred, it constrains what further objects may be introduced. Consider the following narrative:

   > The gun and knife were ready. The woods was dark and quiet.
   > A lone deer stood in the clearing. *He* aimed the gun.

   Many people agree that the *He* above refers to "a hunter". The presence of a hunter can be explained by the inference of a "hunting" setting node which accounts for the various objects mentioned in the passage. For instance the inferred discourse focus tree might be:

4. Action nodes cause a singular action to be focused on. Action nodes most closely capture the kind of focusing previously found in task oriented

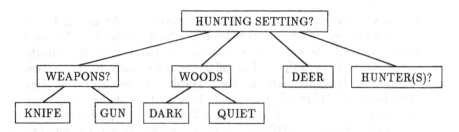

dialogues (Grosz, 1977; Carberry, 1983; Allen and Perrault, 1980). Under an action node we may find other actions (which can be viewed as sub-actions or specializations of this action) or objects (where the objects have something to do with the action – e.g., are actors or objects that are entailed by doing the action), or even attribute and setting nodes. Action nodes are most often given as verbs in a sentence. E.g.,

> Janet was going to board the train. She walked to the platform and waited for the train.

The following might be the resulting discourse focus tree:

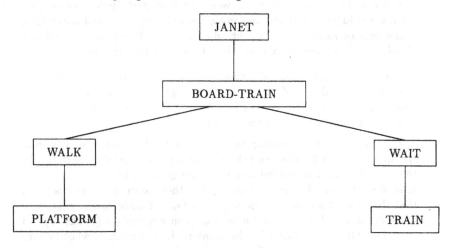

5. Event nodes cause a higher level "abstract" action to be focused on. Events and setting nodes correspond most closely with the script or scenario type focusing described in (Schank and Abelson, 1977; Garrod and Sanford, 1983). Event nodes are most often inferred rather than given explicitly. An event can be thought of as a "super action" in the sense that it is meant to capture something common about a group or sequence of actions sharing some common objects that have been mentioned. Yet, this commonality is not as tight as one would find in the typical planning formalism because the relationship between the actions and a goal is not quite as obvious. An example is:

The little boy carried the egg home with him. He placed the egg in the incubator so it would keep warm. Every day, the boy turned the egg over as gently as a mother duck. Finally, after 28 days of waiting and watching, the boy heard something peeping and pecking inside the egg.

This sequence of actions depicts an event perspective of a boy caring for the duck egg. Each subaction that occurred had something to do with caring for the egg until it was ready to hatch. The actor in each of these actions was the same: the boy.

The expectation derived from an event node is that further actions which can be seen as part of the event will be given next.

4.6 SYNTACTIC CLUES FOR TRAVERSING THE TREE

At any point in the discourse one node is currently being visited. Our expectation is that the next thing said will either fit under this node (and thus will be an expected child of the node type) or be a new expansion of one of its ancestors. In studying discourses, however, there are some situations in which neither of these is the case. In such situations, which we call perspective switches, the switch must be marked appropriately.[3] This marking may either be semantic in nature (i.e., it is clear where the node must be attached by virtue of its meaning), or syntactic in nature (i.e., a meaning independent clue is used to mark the appropriate placement). Our recent work has been investigating some of the syntactic clues that are available for movement within the discourse focus tree. Preliminary work suggests that some of the following are available for this use:

Clue words - Robin Cohen (1983) used a classification of clue words and showed their relevance in building the trees she used to represent argument structure. This same classification is useful in building discourse focus trees. What follows is not a comprehensive analysis, rather just some examples to see how the clue words might be used.

1. parallel : e.g., in addition. Causes the next node to be attached as a sibling of the currently visited node. E.g., in the context of a murder setting, if we were given, "John had a knife. In addition, he had a gun". Knife and gun would be made siblings of each other under the murder node.

2. detail : e.g., in particular. Causes the next node to be attached as a son. E.g., "John was going to help his brother. In particular he was

---

[3] It should be noted that a new expansion of an ancestor must often be marked as well.

going to bail him out of jail." In this case the root of this subtree would be John, it would have as a son the action node "help his brother". The "in particular" would cause "bail brother out of jail" to be placed under this action node.

3. inference : e.g., as a result. Causes the next node to be attached as a sibling. Consider the following continuation of the above example: "As a result, he would be free to defend himself". This sentence would cause an object node representing the brother (with an attribute of "free to defend himself" under it) to be placed under "bail brother out of jail" in the resulting tree.

4. summary : e.g., in sum. Causes the next node to be attached as a son of the node representing the actor along the path of current actions. E.g., "To sum it up, John was going to let his brother save himself" would be placed under John in our tree.

Tense - tense changes in the course of a discourse can indicate a perspective change. I.e., A switch from present to past tense may indicate an analogous event occurring at some other point in time.

Anaphor usage - indicates that the focus is still centered around an immediate object.

Pronoun Switching - the switching from pronoun usage back to explicit referencing of an object/action may indicate a change in focus, although this is not always the case. There are several different reasons for a pronoun switch and only some of these indicate a change in focus. There are four categories of reasons for changing to the explicit mention of a subject:

1. Summary/Conclusion - indicates the end of sequence/paragraph of a discourse. The use of a definite description rather than a pronoun for this reason will often indicate that this current sentence is the father of preceding discourse, and that this section of the focus tree is now finished being expanded. Thus focus is expected to shift away from the current topic.

2. Beginning - marks the beginning of an event or paragraph. In this case the switch back to a definite description indicates a focus change. Focus should be switched out of its current position back up the tree to the position of the particular topic (for which the definite description was used) with the expectation that a new child of this node will now be pursued.

3. Emphasis - to make an event/sentence stand out. Such a usage will not result in a focus switch.

4. Boredom - When a pronoun has been used too many times, the topic sometimes has to be reintroduced. This is simply to remind the listener of the current focused topic and does not indicate a focus change.

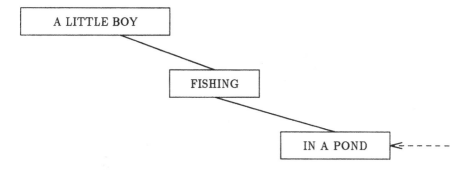

4.7 AN EXAMPLE

In this section an example will be given to illustrate how the discourse focus tree can be used. Suppose we are given the discourse focus tree below. The first node in the tree is an object node, under it is the action node fishing. The place of the fishing (a pond) is subordinate to the fishing node. At this point we may go on to talk about any of these three topics in more detail. However, what can be said about these things is constrained. For instance, if we decide to say more about the pond we should only bring up information about the pond that is related to the little boy fishing. If we do not keep this perspective on the pond, then we are opening up a new discourse focus space and we leave the expectation that we will return to the current space later.

This would be an example of an aside or interruption at this point – perhaps bringing a different perspective onto the action or object currently being visited. This is a legal thing to do, but raises the expectation that the original perspective will be returned to. This case corresponds with stacking the perspective trees. The conversation cannot be over until the stack is popped.

Suppose the next line is "again and again he threw in his line". Semantically we know that this is a subaction of fishing, and so becomes a child of the fishing node. The following tree results. Notice that this tree constrains what can be said next. We can easily say something that will make a child node to the current node (e.g., "it got stuck on a rock"), or that will make a new child for any of the ancestors of the current node (e.g., "finally he caught a fish"). We cannot, however, go back and add to a node that has already been "closed" (e.g., "it had a lot of fish in it"), unless we explicitly mark that we are doing so (e.g., "oh yea, the pond had a lot of fish in it").

4.8 CURRENT DIRECTIONS

There are several lines along which this research could be extended. Some have to do with further fleshing out this model of focusing in a discourse and

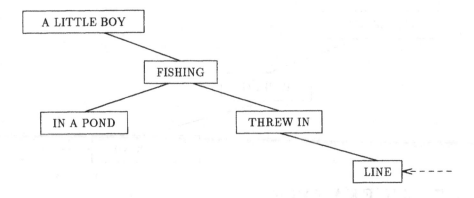

others have to do with further specifying how this model can be used for text generation in conjunction with a text structuring module. In this section we attempt to briefly examine some issues from each of these categories.

One major focus of future work involves making this focusing model more specific. This must be done along several lines. One of the first things that must be examined and refined is the types of the nodes in the discourse focus tree. The types settled on in this paper are a result of a limited text analysis and our intuitions about focusing. Eventually these types must be made to stand up to detailed scrutiny. We must have definitions for the node types so that the type of a particular element in a sentence can be determined unambiguously. In addition, since our claim is that the node type "names" some element in the knowledge base, there should be some evidence of these types being of conceptual nature. It is anticipated that work like that done by Jackendoff (Jackendoff, 1983) on conceptual categories will be useful.

A second line of refinement which is related to that above has to do with more clearly specifying exactly what is contained in a node. A clear case where this is a problem is in the action nodes. It is unclear where the actor of an action should be placed. Is it an object node which is superordinate or subordinate to the action, or should the actor of an action be placed *within* the action node itself? This question must be further investigated.

A third line along which the model must be further specified has to do with the relationship of the syntax of an individual sentence and the way the discourse focus tree is expanded when that sentence is encountered. What should the relationships between the various objects/actions in the sentence be? Should they all be given nodes in the tree? Are some more likely to be expanded than others? Can decisions about things like pronoun reference be determined based on the discourse focus tree alone or must we go to a more local level of focusing such as that described in (Sidner, 1979) or (Grosz *al.*, 1983).

A final line along which the focusing theory itself needs further specification has to do with the use of a tree structure to capture focus of attention. A tree is a potentially infinite data structure. Is there a limit on the amount of the tree that is available for returning to? As was mentioned earlier, some previous work on focus of attention uses a stack[4] to limit the focus spaces that can be returned to. We believe a stack does not accord the flexibility needed to account for some of the discourses we examined. On the other hand, there may be some other way of limiting the amount of the tree that must be available.

A second area of research has to do with fitting the model of focusing into a broader generation model. In particular, into a model which takes the structure of a discourse into account. McKeown (1985a) shows how focusing can be used in two ways during the generation process. She talks of a "global focus", which delineates a pool of knowledge which contains information to potentially be included in a response, and a "local focus", which can help choose between a number of propositions each of which would fulfill the structural needs of a text. The focus described here, may have usefulness in both of these roles. In some senses it can be thought of as a more dynamic and more refined notion of "global focus". More dynamic in the sense that what is relevant to say may not only depend on the question being responded to, but also on the part of the response generated so far. More refined in the sense that the elements of the global focus space will be highlighted differently depending on the amount of shift they would require in the focus tree. For instance, propositions which could be focus progressions from the currently visited node would be given greater highlighting than propositions which would require a focus shift. Finally, things which are no longer relevant because of the perspective the tree places on the knowledge base could be eliminated. The details of using the focus tree in this way must be worked out. It would also be interesting to investigate how this model of focusing could be used in conjunction with other models of the generation process – e.g., (Appelt, 1981; Hovy, 1988a; Mann and Thompson, 1987; Hovy, 1988b; Moore and Swartout, 1990).

4.9 RELATED RESEARCH

The work presented here draws on much work on focus of attention that has previously been reported on. As was mentioned earlier, the work described here can be thought of as a new look at the "attentional state" described in (Grosz and Sidner, 1985). In that model the "attentional state" is basically that part of the knowledge base that the dialogue participants are attending to at any moment in the discourse. The model changes as the discourse progresses – old states may be stacked and returned to later. The most obvious difference between this work and Grosz and Sidner's is our rejection of the stack and adoption of the tree. Notice, however, that we do not have a tree of attentional states; we have a tree from which the attentional states can be calculated. In this calculation the notion of a perspective or point of view taken on objects in

---

[4] Which, of course, is also a potentially infinite data structure.

the attentional state falls out (from intersecting the knowledge about the topics associated with the nodes from the visited node to the root node). It is unclear how the correct perspective is taken in Grosz and Sidner's model.

Another difference between our model and (Grosz and Sidner, 1985) has to do with where the discourse focus tree sits. In the Grosz and Sidner model, the attentional state is a function of the discourse itself. Presumably the discourse participants must each have a model of the discourse, but this point is never really discussed. In our model, we rely on the disparity in the models of the discourse focus tree held by the different participants to be an indicator of the perceived coherence of the discourse.

Finally, a major component of Grosz and Sidner's work discussed the interdependencies between attentional, intentional, and linguistic structures. We have not investigated how intentional structure affects the focus tree construction, and have only looked at the linguistic structure in a very limited way.

The work described here is also related to the work done by Reichman (1978, 1981) on context spaces. Reichman claims that a discourse is structured into hierarchically related *context spaces*. Each utterance in the discourse belongs to one of these spaces. One of her major focuses is on discourse moves which can take the conversation from one context space into another. The use of clue words is quite significant in identifying which context space a particular utterance belongs to.

Our work is similar to Reichman's in several ways besides the obvious use of clue words to determine how an utterance fits in with the model of the discourse so far. She also identifies the coherence of a discourse with the closeness of the models of the conversation being built up by the participants. In addition, like our different types of focus nodes, Reichman has (2) different types of focus spaces (Issues and Events). The different kinds of spaces affect the way the "focus level" is assigned to individual objects within a space. This is similar to the different kinds of expected expansions we associate with the different types of nodes in our discourse focus tree.

Other researchers have used a tree-like representation for particular kinds of discourses. In particular Cohen (1983, 1987) represented argument structure in a tree while Weiner (1980) used a tree structure to represent natural explanations. Both of these researchers talked in terms of generating the contents of the tree in such a way so that it could be reconstructed by the listener. In addition to "normal traversings" of these trees (by the generator) they point out how the use of clue words and phrases could be used in order to guide the hearer in attaching the next proposition to the correct place in the tree. While we would argue that our discourse focus trees are different in nature (in terms of what they represent), many of their ideas about traversing the trees and using clue words have been carried over to our model.

Another work on discourse structure which used a tree representation was that of Linde (1979). Linde focused on the structure of dialogues in which apartments were described. She analyzed these dialogues as basically being "traversals" through the apartment where the individual rooms were described as they were visited. Thus she represented the discourses as trees where each node represented a room in the apartment. Nodes were connected to each other in the tree based on the way they were introduced into the description. The currently visited node would define the focus of attention. Linde discussed pronoun choice within this model. While the use of a tree to represent the shifts of attention within a discourse is similar to our own, it is unclear exactly what Linde means by focus of attention, or what one could be expected to talk about when visiting one of these nodes.

4.10 CONCLUSIONS

A discourse focus tree has been introduced as a method to track the focus of attention in a discourse. The hypothesis is that a discourse focus tree is being built up and traversed as a discourse proceeds. At any point in the discourse, one node is said to be visited. The visited node, along with is relationship in the tree, dictates what parts of the knowledge base are in focus at a particular point in the discourse (and thus what the generation system can reasonably say next). The focused knowledge is the knowledge associated with the currently visited node intersected with the knowledge associated with each of its ancestors up the tree.

The discourse focus tree is composed of nodes of differing types each of which points to a type of information in the knowledge base. Each node-type gives rise to different expectations concerning what may be subordinate to it in the tree. What is said next should either be something which is an expectation generated by the current visited node, or a previously unexplored expectation of one of its ancestors. In this theory, however, other focus moves are possible (e.g., back to a previously "closed" topic) but such moves must be marked in the discourse.

Finally, some indication was given as to how the discourse focus tree is built up during the discourse. The tree is built by explicit mention of some elements and by inference of others. Speakers may use syntactic clues in the discourse to help the listener build up a tree which captures their intended effect.

The theory of discourse focus trees is important for a generation system in helping the system decide what should be said next. What is said next should be something which fit most easily into the discourse focus tree (i.e., an expansion of the currently visited node will be most preferred). If another move must be made, then it should be properly marked so that it can be followed by the conversational partner. The focus tree alone is not sufficient to ensure coherent text. The theory of discourse focus trees is meant to be used in text planning in conjunction with other text planning devices which worry about

the goals of the text and about rhetorical relations which hold between pieces
of the text.

BIBLIOGRAPHY

(Allen and Perrault, 1980) James F. Allen and C. Raymond Perrault. Analyzing intention in utterances. *Artificial Intelligence*, 15:143–178, 1980.

(Appelt, 1981) Doug E. Appelt. *Planning Natural-Language Utterances to Satisfy Multiple Goals*. PhD thesis, Stanford University, December 1981.
Also appears as: SRI International Technical Note 259, March 1982.

(Carberry, 1983) Sandra M. Carberry. Tracking user goals in an information-
seeking environment. In *Proceedings of The National Conference
on Artificial Intelligence*, pages 59–63, AAAI-83, Wathington, D.C.,
August 1983.

(Cohen, 1983) Robin Cohen. *A Computational Model for the Analysis of Arguments*. PhD thesis, University of Toronto, Dept of Computer Science,
1983. Also appears as: University of Toronto Computer Systems Research Group Technical Report No. 151.

(Cohen, 1987) Robin Cohen. Analyzing the structure of argumentative discourse. *Computational Linguistics Journal*, 13(1-2):11–24, 1987.

(Fillmore, 1977) C. J. Fillmore. The case for case reopened. In P. Cole and J. M.
Sadock, editors, *Syntax and Semantics VIII: Grammatical Relations*,
pages 59–81, Academic Press, New York, 1977.

(Grosz al., 1983) B. Grosz, A.K. Joshi, and S. Weinstein. Providing a unified
account of definite noun phrases in discourse. In *Proceedings of the
21st Annual Meeting*, pages 44–50, Association for Computational
Linguistics, Cambridge, Mass, June 1983.

(Grosz, 1977) Barbara Grosz. *The Representation and Use of Focus in Dialogue
Understanding*. Technical Report 151, SRI International, Menlo Park
Ca., 1977.

(Garrod and Sanford, 1983) Simon Garrod and Anthony Sanford. Topic dependent effects in language processing. In G.B. Flores d'Arcais
and R.J. Jarvella, editors, *The Process of Language Understanding*,
pages 271–296, John Wiley and Sons Ltd., 1983.

(Grosz and Sidner, 1985) Barbara Grosz and Candace Sidner. Discourse structure and the proper treatment of interruptions. In *Proceedings of the
1985 Joint Conference on Artificial Intelligence*, IJCAI85, Los Angeles, Ca., August 1985.

(Hobbs, 1979) Jerry Hobbs. Coherence and coreference. *Cognitive Science,* 3:67–90, 1979.

(Hovy, 1988a) Eduard H. Hovy. Planning coherent multisentential text. In *Proc. 26th Annual Meeting of the ACL,* pages 163–169, Assoc. Comp. Ling., Buffalo, New York, June 1988.

(Hovy, 1988b) Eduard H. Hovy. Two types of planning in language generation. In *Proc. 26th Annual Meeting of the ACL,* pages 179–186, Assoc. Comp. Ling., Buffalo, New York, June 1988.

(Jackendoff, 1983) Ray Jackendoff. *Current Studies in Linguistics Series: Semantics and Cognition.* MIT Press, Cambridge, Ma., 1983.

(Linde, 1979) Charlotte Linde. Focus of attention and the choice of pronouns in discourse. In T/. Givon, editor, *Syntax and Semantics, Vol. 12,* pages 337–354, Academic Press, New York, 1979.

(McCoy, 1985) Kathleen F. McCoy. *Correcting Object-Related Misconceptions.* PhD thesis, University of Pennsylvania, December 1985.

(McCoy, 1987) Kathleen F. McCoy. Contextual effects on responses to misconceptions. In G. Kempen, editor, *Natural Language Generation: New Results in Artificial Intelligence, Psychology, and Linguistics,* Martinus Nijhoff Publishers (Kluwer Academic Publishers), Dordrecht/Boston, 1987.

(McKeown, 1982) Kathleen R. McKeown. *Generating Natural Language Text in Response to Questions About Database Structure.* PhD thesis, University of Pennsylvania, May 1982.

(McKeown, 1983) Kathleen R. McKeown. Focus constraints on language generation. In *Proceedings of the 1983 International Joint Conference on Artificial Intelligence,* pages 582–587, IJCAI, Karlsruhe, Germany, August 1983.

(McKeown, 1985a) Kathleen R. McKeown. *Text generation: Using discourse strategies and focus constraints to generate natural language text.* Cambridge University Press, Cambridge UK, 1985.

(McKeown, 1985b) Kathleen R. McKeown. Discourse strategies for generating natural-language text. *Artificial Intelligence,* 27(1):1–41, 1985.

(Moore and Swartout, 1990) Johanna D. Moore and William R. Swartout. A Reactive Approach to Explanation: Taking the User's Feedback into Account. In *Natural Language Generation in Artificial Intelligence and Computational Linguistics,* (this volume). Paris, Swartout, Mann (Eds). Kluwer Academic Publishers, Norwell, MA, 1990.

(Mann and Thompson, 1987) William C. Mann and Sandra A. Thompson. Rhetorical structure theory: description and construction of text structures. In G. Kempen, editor, *Natural Language Generation: New Results in Artificial Intelligence, Psychology, and Linguistics*, Martinus Nijhoff Publishers (Kluwer Academic Publishers), Dordrecht/Boston, 1987.

(Paris and McKeown, 1987) Cécile L. Paris and Kathleen R. McKeown. Discourse strategies for descriptions of complex physical objects. In G. Kempen, editor, *Natural Language Generation: New Results in Artificial Intelligence, Psychology, and Linguistics*, Martinus Nijhoff Publishers (Kluwer Academic Publishers), Dordrecht/Boston, 1987.

(Reichman, 1981) Rachel Reichman. Conversational coherency. *Cognitive Science*, 2:283–327, December 1978.

(Reichman, 1981) Rachel Reichman. *Plain Speaking: A Theory and Grammar of Spontaneous Discourse*. PhD thesis, Harvard University, June 1981. BBN Report No. 4681.

(Reichman-Adar, 1984) Rachel Reichman-Adar. Extended person-machine interface. *Artificial Intelligence*, 22(2):157–218, 1984.

(Schank and Abelson, 1977) R. C. Schank and R. Abelson. *Scripts, Plans, Goals and Understanding: An Enquiry into Human Knowledge Structures*. Laurence Erlbaum Associates, Hillsdale, NJ, 1977.

(Schubert *et al.*, 1979) L. K. Schubert, R. G. Goebel, and N. J. Cercone. The structure and organization of a semantic network for comprehension and inference. In N. V. Findler, editor, *Associative Networks: Representation and Use of Knowledge by Computer*, Academic Press, N. Y., 1979.

(Sidner, 1979) Candace L. Sidner. *Towards a Computational Theory of Definite Anaphora Comprehension in English Discourse*. PhD thesis, MIT, June 1979.

(Weiner, 1980) J.L. Weiner. Blah, a system which explains its reasoning. *Artificial Intelligence*, 15:19–48, 1980.

Chapter 5

Uncovering textual meanings: a case study involving systemic-functional resources for the generation of Japanese texts

John A. Bateman

Abstract: A functional grammar of the systemic-functional variety decomposes the generation process in terms of sets of interrelated, functionally motivated grammatical alternatives. When such a grammar is used for generation, it has distinct informational needs: that is, if its supporting environment does not contain the information that the grammar requires in order to motivate the grammatical alternatives it offers, generation cannot proceed. The chooser and inquiry framework designed for the PENMAN system further decomposes grammatical alternatives into finer-grained semantic alternatives. These latter place specific constraints on the kinds of information that a generation system, and any underlying theory of semantics, must support and so can be used for determining what kinds of information are necessary. Significantly, the informational needs of a systemic-functional grammar are not restricted to 'propositional content'-related areas: textual and interpersonal areas are also entailed. The methodology of uncovering semantic distinctions based on the informational needs of a grammar should then be applicable in these areas also. In this paper, I investigate the area of *textual* meanings as required by a small, experimental systemic-functional grammar of Japanese. I conclude that the methodology is, indeed, appropriate for uncovering textual meanings and needs to be pursued on a larger scale.

5.1   INTRODUCTION

There is now a relatively long history of interaction between systemic-functional
linguistics (SFL) and computational approaches to English (cf.: Winograd,
1972; Davey, 1974; Mann, 1983, 1985; Patten, 1986; Fawcett and Tucker,
1989). Growing out of this, the context of the work described here is an experiment where the computational SFL techniques developed for English have
been applied to the development of systemic-functional grammatical resources
for Japanese (Bateman, 1985; Bateman, Kikui and Tabuchi, 1987; Bateman and
Li Hang, 1988). Japanese requires that we focus upon some types of meaning
whose importance is now increasingly being recognized in text generation (cf.:
Hovy, McDonald, Young and Appelt, 1988; and the other papers of this volume), and this has permitted us to explore further a methodology we are developing within computational SFL for uncovering the semantic/'pragmatic' distinctions necessary for text planning/generation. This methodology — termed
the 'grammar-as-filter' methodology — provides us with means both of incorporating existing theoretical results in pragmatics into the homogeneous control architecture of a computational systemic-functional text generator and of
discovering new results motivated by the functional organization of natural language grammars. The Japanese examples I will use provide clear-cut cases of
the types of distinctions at issue and so support particularly good illustrations
of how the methodology is to be applied. The function of the paper as a whole
should then be seen as providing one concrete illustration of a methodology for
text planning research that we feel promises substantial benefits.

5.1.1   The 'Grammar-as-Filter' Methodology

The grammatical resources that we have developed for Japanese follow general SFL practice in presenting grammar as a resource for expressing meanings;
meanings are realized by a network of interdependent options and particular
grammatical forms are arrived at by making choices of options from this network. The resources also follow the Nigel grammar of English in that they are
controlled by means of choice experts, called *choosers* (Mann, 1982), that collectively ensure that the choices made will be those appropriate for any particular
text need. Each choice point in the grammar network has associated with it a
chooser whose responsibility is to interrogate the text need in respect of just
those aspects of meaning necessary for determining the appropriate option to
take. These choosers are formalized as decision trees whose nodes consist of
basic semantically oriented interrogation primitives called *inquiries*.

Inquiries define semantic distinctions that need to be drawn in order for the
resources of a grammar to be used. Therefore it is possible to interpret them also
as *design constraints* for the processes that drive generation. *Those processes
must support the kinds of information that the inquiries require.* If they do
not, then choices in the grammar cannot be made and the resources available

may not be fully utilized. We make use of this relation between the grammar, its inquiries, and the processes that drive the grammar during generation, to construct a methodology for uncovering those higher-level distinctions that are necessary for text generation. The fine-detailed functional discriminations that make up a systemically-based grammar, when seen in terms of the inquiries that control those discriminations, motivate properties that must be possessed by the text planning processes and knowledge bases that support text generation if text generation is to be possible (cf.: Matthiessen, 1987). In a sense, we are using the grammar as a 'filter' through which one can examine the processes underlying its use and make visible the distinctions that need to be present for the grammar to operate. The general methodology is diagramed in Figure 5.1.

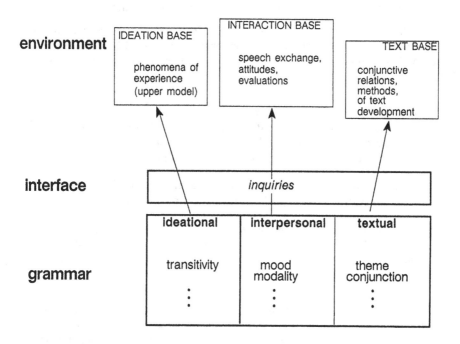

Figure 5.1: The three bases of the environment as seen from the grammar

This approach can be related to other current developments in linguistic theory where it is argued that the relationship between syntax and semantics is *not* arbitrary (cf.: Jackendoff 1983, 1987; Langacker, 1987; Partee, 1975).

Taking this seriously means that a well-developed account of grammar can provide important information concerning the organization of semantics. However, most of the theories beginning to work with this assumption base their view of grammar on syntactic structure, which is in sharp contrast to the *functional* orientation of systemically-based grammars. Moreover, SFL traditionally defines three distinct types of function, called *metafunctions*, to which any use of language is necessarily simultaneously responsive. In other theories of language, these metafunctions have not generally been granted equal status as grammatical resources: this means that a systemic-functional grammar will contain many distinctions that for other theories of language would be placed in a 'pragmatics' component and treated peripherally if at all. Accepting them within a grammar, however, considerably widens the range of evidence available for uncovering semantic distinctions since we can apply the 'grammar-as-filter' methodology to any grammatical distinction that is represented. We will be able to see this more concretely once the distinct types of metafunction present in a systemic-functional grammar have been introduced in more detail.

The three metafunctions are termed the *ideational*, the *interpersonal*, and the *textual*. They have been described extensively in the SFL literature (e.g., Halliday, 1978, 1985) and, for present purposes, may be simply glossed as follows.

- Ideational: the means we have of representing the world to ourselves; it largely corresponds to what has been termed 'propositional content'. Many accounts of syntax and semantics limit themselves exclusively to the range of variation controlled by this metafunction.

- Interpersonal: the range of meaning concerned with the expression of social relationships and speakers' attitudes and evaluations.

- Textual: the resources responsible for making a use of language appropriate to its particular context of use; the organizational resources that make the difference between connected and cohesive text and unrelated sentences.

Generally a systemic-functional grammar will be organized in terms of these three metafunctions; that is, the metafunctions define distinct functional regions within a grammar — such regions possess strong intra-region dependencies and weak inter-region dependencies. The distinctions that the grammar draws within each of the metafunctional regions, e.g., transitivity (case roles) in the ideational component, conjunction in the textual component, etc., all require inquiries by which they are controlled. These inquiries in turn require support from the grammar's 'environment' in the form of particular types of information and processes. This permits the 'grammar-as-filter' methodology to apply equally at the global scale of grammar organization: the overall organization of a systemic-functional grammar structures the overall organization that we can posit among the types of processes that must control the grammar. Furthermore, *each of the metafunctions gives rise to processes of a rather different nature:* the three metafunctions in the grammar give rise to three functionally distinct components in the environment corresponding to the distinct types of metafunctional meanings that the grammar covers. These components are termed, following Matthiessen (1987), the *ideation base*, the *interaction base*, and the *text base* and correspond to the ideational, interpersonal, and textual metafunctions of the grammar respectively. Figure 5.1 shows the interrelationships between these components.

The principal result of applying the 'filter' methodology so far has been in the development of the contents of the ideation base. By considering exclusively the Nigel grammar's *ideational* inquiries, it has been possible to construct a domain independent knowledge organization hierarchy, called the *upper model* (e.g., Bateman, Kasper, Moore and Whitney, 1989), which supports a substantial subset of the semantic distinctions necessary for driving the ideational distinctions drawn by the grammar. This is proving of value for both the control of the generation process and the transportability of the Nigel grammar.

The restriction to ideational distinctions makes the upper model rather similar to accounts of semantics such as those of Jackendoff (1983, 1987) and Langacker (1987) where the meanings investigated are usually restricted to the area of propositional content.[1] However, given the uniformity of treatment in a systemic-functional grammar across all three metafunctions, that is, all three metafunctions are represented in terms of grammatical options, choosers, and inquiries, it is in theory equally possible to apply the 'filter' methodology to the interpersonal and textual inquiries: this is the motivation for the inclusion of the text base and interaction base components of the grammar's environment depicted in Figure 5.1.

The success of the 'filter' methodology in the ideational component clearly motivates experiments that attempt to apply the methodology across the interpersonal and textual metafunctions also. Successful applications of the methodology for the interaction and text bases would permit us to obtain further information about distinctions in social relationships and processes of text orga-

---

[1]Or, as is the case with Langacker, syntactic differences are projected back onto some presumed differentiation in propositional content; e.g., Langacker distinguishes between *I sent a book to the library* and *I sent the library a book* on the basis that they "...embody different images: expressions of the form X VERB Y *to* Z highlight the path (with Z as goal) that Y traverses, whereas those of the form X VERB Z Y highlight instead the resulting state where Z possesses Y." (1987:51) Others might argue that this is a textual difference which should not be seen as altering the propositional content. Without a detailed theoretical account of where meanings are to be accounted for such as that provided by the metafunctional hypothesis, there are likely to be many such difficulties in determining an appropriate explanation. The 'filter' methodology ensures that the grammar can provide evidence as to where motivating distinctions are to be placed. If, for example, our grammar states that the variation in the example from Langacker is textual variation, then we should not attempt to model the distinction in the upper model. This provides a factorization of the description task that is not available when linguistic phenomena are unclassified according to metafunction.

nization. This information would not be directly available if we were to restrict ourselves to an ideationally centered view of grammar. Elsewhere I have been concerned with the appropriateness of the methodology when applied to the interpersonal metafunction (Bateman, 1988), and so the concern of the present paper will be to examine the *textual* metafunction inquiries in order to see what kinds of constraints may be placed on the internal details of the text base.

5.1.2 Pervasiveness of Non-Ideational Phenomena in Japanese

To carry out the experimental application of the 'grammar-as-filter' methodology to non-ideational components of the environment, it is necessary to have a set of non-ideational inquiries to consider. Our study of Japanese demanded a strong non-ideational bias that was ideal for revealing textual and grammatical distinctions without requiring a complex grammar. The work on Japanese therefore provides an ideal case study environment where we can see the 'filter' methodology at work in non-ideational components. It will become clear that one general theoretical benefit of considering Japanese at this time is that we are forced to come to terms with these non-ideational areas of meaning even in our basic treatments of grammar: Japanese therefore provides us with an opportunity to experiment with the application of the 'grammar-as-filter' methodology across the full range of meaning types hypothesized by SFL with a minimum of grammar development.

In this subsection, I motivate further the non-ideational bias that our treatment of Japanese exhibits with some examples from the interpersonal metafunction — the examples here are not contentious in that they are generally recognized as being interpersonal in nature. Some modern accounts of Japanese even attempt to build the distinctions at issue into the *grammar* itself (e.g., Gunji, 1987), showing just how central they are considered in Japanese. They serve to illustrate the 'grammaticization' of phenomena that in English would often be removed to a pragmatics component where they would not be available for inspection by means of the 'filter' methodology. In subsequent sections, I will turn to textual meanings and present analyses which claim these to be similiarly grammaticized, and hence available for application of the 'filter' methodology.

In Japanese, interpersonal meanings are 'grammaticized' to a far greater extent than in English. This makes them difficult to overlook and places them at the center of much current computational work on Japanese (e.g.: Sugimura, 1986; Kogure, 1988; Maeda, Kato, Kogure and Iida, 1988; Kume, Sato and Yoshimoto, 1989). For example, consider the following four Japanese clauses, all of which share the ideational meaning "It is a book".

(i)   *hon da*
(ii)   *hon desu*

(iii)   *hon degozaimasu*
(iv)   *hon deshou*

While the word *hon* ("book") remains invariant, the copula 'be' form necessarily inflects according to the social relationship between the speaker and the hearer. *It is not possible to express even the simple phrase "it is a book" without taking a stand on that social relationship.*

Another example of the grammaticization of interpersonal meaning is the following. If we wish to express a Japanese equivalent of "Thanks for your help", the following sentences are possibilities:

> *tetsudatte-kudasatte,*   *arigatoo-gozaimashita*
> helping-giving (respectful) thank you (formal)

> *tetsudatte-kurete,*   *arigatoo*
> helping-giving (familiar) thanks (familiar)

The following sentence, however, is *not* a possibility:

> * *tetsudatte,* *arigatoo-gozaimashita*
> helping   thank you (formal)

For fully acceptable Japanese it is insufficient that the speaker explicitly expresses the appropriate level of politeness – for example, the first of the acceptable sentences is quite formal and would be used between people whose social relationship is not close or where a superior is being addressed, while the latter is quite familiar and appropriate for family members, close friends, or inferiors. It is *in addition* necessary that the appropriate degree of gratitude is expressed — this is achieved by the inclusion of a morpheme of 'giving' such as *kudasatte* or *kurete*.

These distinctions prepare the ground for accepting in the grammar some types of meaning that would not traditionally be placed there; the realization of these interpersonal meanings needs to be as much a central part of a grammar of Japanese as does the realization of propositional content type information. Now we are ready to take this further and to explore the direct incorporation into the grammar of structures that realize textual meanings. I will argue that textual meanings in Japanese are often grammaticized in an entirely similar fashion and to a similar extent to the grammaticization of interpersonal meanings. This involves constructing components of grammar that are directly responsive to textual distinctions; that is, there will be subnetworks of grammatical options, with choosers and inquiries, that constrain grammatical structure and which are under the *direct control of textual distinctions in meaning*. This contrasts with previous approaches where it is assumed that the role of the grammar is to specify structural reconfigurations once some pragmatics orsemantics component has licensed base structures of certain kinds (e.g., Gunji, 1987); here, the organization of the grammar itself includes much of what would elsewhere be termed 'pragmatic'. The existence of inquiries then permits an immediate application of the 'grammar-as-filter' methodology to refine and constrain textual distinctions. This latter step is not available if responsibility for the selection of structures that differ textually is simply postponed to a pragmatics or semantics component. The application of the 'filter' methodology then provides for the construction of a view of the text base and its interaction with the grammar that integrates much former work on pragmatics in Japanese and some new areas of 'pragmatic' control — all within the standardly available representational resources of a computational systemic-functional grammar.

5.2 PARTICLE ASSIGNMENT IN JAPANESE

Although the accounts of Japanese we have been developing address a number of potentially relevant areas of Japanese grammar, in this paper I will restrict attention to the appropriate assignment and distribution of the Japanese nominal post-positions. This provides many good examples of the grammaticization of textual meanings and, further, has long been a source of difficulties and controversies in treatments of Japanese grammar (Kuno, 1973; Shibatani, 1977; Hinds, 1983b; Hinds, Maynard and Iwasaki, 1987; Gunji, 1987; and many others). In particular, I shall briefly present a systemic account of the principal uses of the Japanese postnominal particles, *wa*, *ga* and *wo*, and some of the uses of the 'indirect/oblique object' marker *ni*. This will begin to show the kinds of constraints that the computational SFL decomposition of the text generation task can bring to bear on necessary text planning processes when textual distinctions are admitted directly within the grammar.

I will not describe the linguistic data in any great depth; instead, some acceptable Japanese clauses will be presented, representing the range of particle assignments at issue. Although there appears to be a great deal of flexibility in particle assignment, the functional orientation of a systemic account requires that we consider this apparent flexibility in the light of the functionality that it provides. A fundamental assumption of SFL is that variation in language, until proved otherwise, carries functional loads that require description. The basic questions that we are led to ask are therefore:

1. why is any one assignment made over others in a particular context; i.e., what are the criteria for appropriate assignment? What functional load does the assignment carry?

2. precisely what are the limits of the flexibility of particle assignment; i.e., what assignments can and cannot be made?

I will first address the use of the so-called 'topic' particle *wa*, and then move on to discuss the 'case' particles *ga*, *wo*, and *ni*.

5.2.1 The 'Topic' Particle *wa*

The particle *wa* offers one of the most often cited examples of a linguistically realized textual distinction. Two principal meanings are typically assigned to its use:

- Topic introduction (e.g., Maynard, 1980; Hinds, 1983a). By means of the particle *wa* some general topic, or framework within which subsequent talk is to develop, is proposed. Examples of two common usages of this type are: (i) a topic is introduced, but taking up that topic and making a statement about it are left to subsequent contributions; this is a common way of asking questions, e.g.:

(1)   *ashita*   -*wa*
                       tomorrow-   TOPIC

                    "As for tomorrow...?"

and (ii), there is an identification of some topic and then a statement is made about that topic, e.g.:

(2) *ashita*   -*wa*   *eiga-*   *wo*   *mi-*   *ni*   *iku*
     tomorrow- TOPIC   movie-   OBJECT   see-   IN ORDER TO   go

     "As for tomorrow, I'll go to see a movie."

In both cases, the entity selected for topic status is typically taken to be already 'known' or 'predictable' in some sense. Thus, a conversation or text is held to have already established some range of possible topics, either explicitly or implicitly, and the selection of one such as the basis for future talk is achieved by marking with *wa*.

- Contrast (e.g., Kuno, 1973; Clancy and Downing, 1987). This may be either explicit or implicit in that the entity with respect to which a contrast is being made may either be expressed or not as is required. In these cases, the use of *wa* serves to mark *variations* in, or *restrictions* on, what is established. For example, if discussion is revolving around the comprehension of languages, variations in the applicability of the established predicate *wakaru* ('understand') might be expressed by:

(3) *eigo-wa   yoku   wakaru,*   *nihongo-wa zenzen   deki-nai*
     English   well   is understood, Japanese   at all   cannot

"English is understood well, but Japanese not at all."

In each case attention is focused upon the predicate being expressed, or rather in this case, upon the *polarity* of that predicate with respect to the particular language being addressed.

The part of the *grammar* responsible for the generation of structures of types (1) and (2) is set out in Figure 5.2.[2] Here the principal choice point is called the TOPIC LINKAGE system. This is responsible for the basic organization of a discourse contribution. The alternatives it presents are between relying upon a former establishment of topic, in which case no use of *wa* is required (grammatical feature *ImplicitTopic*), and expressing a topic explicitly (grammatical feature *ExplicitTopic*). The latter alternative admits of two further possibilities: either the contribution serves only as a discourse 'setter' which is content to establish the topic and not volunteer further development (example case 1), or that move itself offers further development (example case 2).

While the subnetwork describes the structural possibilities that Japanese provides, this is not sufficient. We also need to specify the conditions under which any of these structural possibilities is to be selected. This is handled by means of appropriate chooser and inquiries. The chooser and inquiry organization for controlling the network of Figure 5.2 is as follows. The two inquiries shown state the questions that need to be asked of the text plan for appropriate grammatical features to be selected.

TOPIC LINKAGE: Does the communicative intent propose a shift of topic?

    no: select *ImplicitTopic*
    yes: select *ExplicitTopic*
           Does the communicative intent involve
           a statement about that topic?

---

[2] In the networks shown in this paper, grammatical features are shown in upper and lower case letters and grammatical *functions* that determine constituency are shown in upper case. The *realization statements* that constrain structure are given in square brackets attached to their conditioning grammatical features; a variety of constraints may be imposed — for example, the constraining of constituents to bear particular grammatical features (by means of the *preselection* operator ':'), the *ordering* of constituents (by means of the realization operator '<'), the inclusion of particular constituents in the structure being generated (by means of the *insertion* operator '+'), and the 'unification' of specified constituents (by means of the *conflation* operator '/'). For more details on all aspects of the Nigel grammar from which these mechanisms are taken, see Mann (1985). The fragment from which all the networks shown in this paper are drawn currently has over 120 grammatical option points, or 'systems', and 'gates' (degenerate choice points with only one possible selection used for the convenient collecting together of realization statements) and a complete specification (to the level of detail supported in the grammar) of the choosers for clause and discourse move rank (consisting of around 60 choosers using over 90 inquiries).

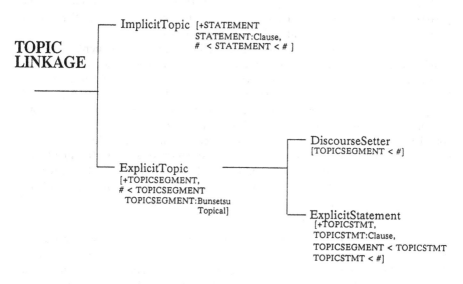

Figure 5.2: Systemic network for discourse moves

yes: select *ExplicitStatement*
no: select *DiscourseSetter*

Corresponding to the possible answers for these principal chooser inquiries, we get three sets of selected grammatical features: {ImplicitTopic}, {ExplicitTopic, DiscourseSetter}, and {ExplicitTopic, ExplicitStatement}. When the realization operations associated with these features, as shown in Figure 5.2, are applied, three possible structural results are motivated. For example, given a selection of features {ExplicitTopic, ExplicitStatement}, which are motivated by the textual semantic distinctions:

Does the communicative intent propose a shift of topic? : YES
Does the communicative intent involve a statement about that topic?
    : YES

the following realization statements are executed:

insert TOPICSEGMENT
order-at-left TOPICSEGMENT
preselect TOPICSEGMENT *to have features* {Bunsetsu, Topical}
insert TOPICSTMT
preselect TOPICSTMT *to have feature* {Clause}
order TOPICSEGMENT *before* TOPICSTMT
order-at-right TOPICSTMT

This is a structure of type (2), consisting of two components, a topic segment (marked by *wa*) followed by a topic statement (which is a clause). Structures of type (1) are generated similarly.[3] This illustrates the standard way in which structures are built up in a systemic-functional grammar: constituents are identified and manipulated in terms of their *functional labels*, e.g., in this case: TOPICSTMT and TOPICSEGMENT. Another useful property of the systemic-functional view of structure is that it is *layered*; that is, different functional components of the grammar often operate on sets of distinctively labeled constituents, which are subsequently combined into a single structure by *conflating* constituents whose labels originate from different functional regions. A simple example of this would be to observe that the SUBJECT of a clause (a label taken from an interpersonal layer) can simultaneously be the ACTOR of the clause (a label taken from the 'transitivity', or 'case roles', layer) and the THEME of the clause (a label taken from a textual layer). We will see examples of the use of this layering of structure below.

The grammar segment of Figure 5.3 contains the choice points for contrastive *wa* insertion (example case 3). This system is reached by a path in the grammar that considers how to construct clause *complexes*; i.e., sequences of more than one clause related grammatically – the particular inter-clause relation at issue here is accordingly that of *contrast*. If there is some contrast to be drawn, the grammar sets up a clause which possesses the feature *Contrasting*; this is eventually responsible for the insertion of the particle *wa* as the marker of the 'topic/theme' of the contrast being made. All that we need to say about the chooser relevant here, therefore, is that it needs to be able to ask the environment whether a contrast is being drawn or not; it may be noted that contrast is a common rhetorical relationship that text planners already typically support (e.g., Mann and Thompson, 1987; Hovy, 1988).

Following the definition of the two grammar fragments shown in Figures 5.2 and 5.3 and their corresponding choosers and inquiries, we have identified two types of textual meanings that must be supported in the text base: topicality and contrast. In addition, we know that it must be possible for the text plan to determine whether the text requires an explicit statement about a topic to be made or not. These meanings of *wa* have been proposed formerly in a large number of disparate frameworks, or as informal statements of when *wa* may be used. In their present form of expression as textual distinctions present in the text base, however, we have begun to form a pool of textual distinctions that the subsequent section will supplement — the natural question which then arises is to what extent these textual distinctions can be integrated or generalized from, as has been achieved with the upper model in the ideation base, to provide a more comprehensive and theoretically acceptable account of textual distinctions *per se*. Moreover, the participation of these textual distinctions in

---

[3] The third possibility is when no *wa*-marked constituent appears: *ImplicitTopic*. Further *wa*-marked consituents might be admitted by allowing a recursive, looping re-entry of the TOPIC LINKAGE system; I will not discuss this possibility further here — see Bateman (1989) for a discussion of some of the problems inherent with using networks with loops.

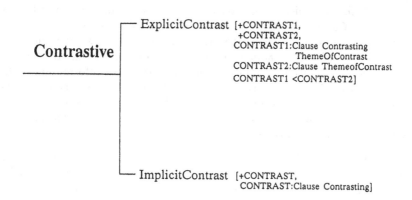

Figure 5.3: Contrastive clauses network

the interaction between the text base and the grammar ensures that, once the textual distinctions have been made, appropriate linguistic realizations of those distinctions may be generated automatically. This is one sense in which we can state that we have an account which shows the textual distinctions at issue to be 'grammaticized' in Japanese.

5.2.2 The 'Case' Particles *ga, wo,* and *ni*

The Japanese postnominal particles *ga, wo,* and *ni* are often referred to as 'case' particles, although there is often debate concerning whether this is to be interpreted as grammatical case (e.g., 'Nominative', 'Accusative', etc.: cf. Shibatani, 1977), grammatical relations (e.g., 'Subject', 'Object', etc.: cf. Gunji, 1987; Johnson, 1988), or semantic case (e.g., 'actor', 'goal', etc.). For example, *ga* is usually considered to mark the constituent which, in traditional terms, is appropriately the grammatical *subject* of its clause, *wo* marks either the direct object or the semantic 'goal', and *ni* marks less primary grammatical relations such as that of the 'demoted' subject in passive constructions and, as we shall see below, occasionally the actor of a process.[4] In this section, however, I will focus on some *textual* conditions for these particles' deployment; I will suggest that in main clauses this plays a decisive role in particle selection and so they should not be analysed as primarily marking either surface case or semantic role.

To begin, we can note that the use of the particle *ga* is typically said to pick out an entity that has not yet been 'established' in the discourse. Candidates for marking with *ga* are new discourse entities, entities whose appearance is

---

[4] *ni* also has a reading as a locational preposition that is not of concern here.

not predictable or known. Kuno (1976:23) further considers *ga* able to serve both as an "exhaustive listing" marker in which 'X-*ga* Predicate' claims that it is X *and only X* of which the predicate is true, and as a "neutral description" marker which does not entail exhaustivity, merely new, and possibly incomplete, information. All of these readings are essentially textual in that they signal aspects of the presentation of information rather than the information itself. Marking of an entity by *ga* must therefore at least be made sensitive to its status as either established or unknown, in addition to any simple consideration in terms of the permissible grammatical relationships for a clause (which, in fact, can also be textually conditioned).

Although this provides an initial set of chooser questions for controlling *ga* and for beginning to set out the conditions under which each reading may be considered appropriate — essentially choosers need to be able to ask the text base about the participant roles of a constituent and about that constituent's information status — the situation is complicated by the distributions of particle deployment shown in Figure 5.4. Here it becomes difficult to maintain the commitment to *ga* functioning as a subject marker: for example, clauses (2c), (3c), and (4b) all contain two *ga*-marked constituents which cannot both be subject in any traditional sense.[5] It is also not sufficient for selection of *ga* for the information status of a participant to be new: acceptable clause (3c) and unacceptable clause (a) need not differ with respect to the straightforward information statuses of their participants and yet, in the latter case, it is not possible to have both participants marked by *ga*. Furthermore, as was the case with the examples of interpersonal grammaticization shown previously, many of the acceptable clauses shown in Figure 5.4 appear to largely share their ideational meaning — e.g., (2b) and (2c), (3b) and (3c), (3b) and (3d), and (4b) and (4c). It is also necessary to tease out how these clauses differ so that the different forms that occur can be functionally motivated; otherwise groups of clause-types such as these remain in free variation with the possible danger that selections will prove inappropriate in particular contexts of use. Speakers do, in fact, deploy these clause-types differently, and it is the role of the analysis to uncover what their distinctive properties are: it is necessary to be more explicit about the conditions that govern the appropriateness, or otherwise, of *ga* selection.

Rather than presenting here a more complete analysis drawing upon the situated use of these clauses in texts, for the purposes of this paper I will instead move directly to the conclusions that have been drawn and their systemic representation. I will show how the basic meanings for *ga* given above can be straightforwardly extended to cover, functionally motivate, and control the distribution patterns shown in Figure 5.4 in terms of the interaction of two layers of functional organization in the clause: the *information* layer and the *agency* layer.

---

[5]Even though these constructions are occasionally referred to as 'double subject' constructions.

Some acceptable clauses

(1) a.   *taroo-ga*   *iku*
       Taroo   goes
    b.   *taroo-ga*   *mondai-wo*   *toku*
       Taroo   problem   solves

(2) a.   *biiru-ga*   *nomi-tai*
       beer   there is a wish to drink
    b.   *taroo-ga*   *biiru-wo*   *nomi-tai*
       Taroo   beer   wants to drink
    c.   *taroo-ga*   *biiru-ga*   *nomi-tai*
       Taroo   beer   wants to drink

(3) a.   *mondai-ga*   *tokeru*
       problem   there is the ability to solve
    b.   *taroo-ga*   *mondai-wo*   *tokeru*
       Taroo   problem   can solve
    c.   *taroo-ga*   *mondai-ga*   *tokeru*
       Taroo   problem   can solve
    d.   *taroo-ni*   *mondai-ga*   *tokeru*
       by Taroo   problem   there is the ability to solve

(4) a.   *hebi-ga*   *kowai*
       snake   is frightening
    b.   *taroo-ga*   *hebi-ga*   *kowai*
       Taroo   snakes   is frightened of
    c.   *taroo-ni (wa)*   *hebi-ga*   *kowai*
       Taroo   snakes   is frightened of

Some unacceptable clauses

a.   *taroo-ga*   *mondai-ga*   *toku*
      Taroo   problem   solve

b.   *taroo-ni*   *mondai-wo*   *tokeru*
      Taroo   problem   can solve

Figure 5.4: Contrasting acceptable and unacceptable particle deployments

---

Corresponding to previous analyses of *ga* as marking nonestablished status within a text, each use of *ga* is here taken to be compatible with the occurrence of a constituent functionally labeled as NEWS. Additionally, the use of *ga* as an exhaustive listing marker will be taken as a symptom of a constituent functionally labeled as the FOCUS of the news. Since there is no reason for presuming prior to analysis that these functions will necessarily be realized as a single constituent, cases where two constituents appear marked by *ga*, one marking the NEWS the other the FOCUS, are readily predictable; clauses (2c), (3c), and (4b) provide examples of this.

While Kuno (1973:68) discusses clauses where there are more than one *ga*-marked constituents and argues that the leftmost constituent can receive an exhaustive listing reading while the others can only be neutral, Gunji (1987) seems to consider neutral and exhaustive readings of *ga* to occur more freely, even allowing cases where multiple exhaustive *ga*-marked constituents occur with no neutral *ga*-marked constituents; as in, for example:

Ken-ga	*imooto-ga*	*kodomo-ga*	*namaikida*
Ken-EXH	sister-EXH	child-EXH	puppyish

literally: It's Ken who is such that it's his sister who is
such that it's her child that is puppyish.

(Gunji, 1987:204; footnote 25, example (i.d))

It is admitted by both Kuno and Gunji, however, that judgements about the relative focusing of these constituents are often difficult to elicit and so I will not discuss them further here; further extensive text studies will be necessary to uncover the precise conditions for these constructions' occurrences. For the present examples, it will suffice to state that in cases where two *ga*-marked constituents occur, the leftmost *ga*-constituent will be considered the FOCUS and the second will be simply NEWS. Given this view of *ga* deployment and evidence concerning the consequences for focusing that various selections of verb forms have – e.g., selection of passive, (as in English, although this is not so common in Japanese), and selection of 'desire' forms (the clauses under (2)) and forms that express ability (3) – we can motivate the deployments of *ga* on 'pragmatic' grounds directly without requiring complex particle assignment rules based on surface ordering, structural configurations, or grammatical relations. The network of Figure 5.5 contains the textually motivated grammatical distinctions that achieve this. I will present the inquiries relevant to these distinctions after a brief discussion of the particle *wo*.

Once the possibility of defining constituents in functional terms is accepted, as is fundamental to the systemic-functional view of structure, the use of the particle *wo* can also be summarized very simply. I have characterized the use of *ga* in terms of constituents labeled functionally in terms of NEWS and FOCUS; both of these labels are drawn from the set of labels manipulated by the functional region of the grammar concerned with information management and presentation. We can state, therefore, that the occurence of *ga* is a reflex of the *information* layer of structure. The use of *wo*, however, is not controlled from within this region. A further layer, called the *agency* layer, independently motivated within the grammar, provides much of the mechanism for controlling *wo*.[6] The principal grammatical functions, or functional labels, of the agency layer are AGENT and MEDIUM; the MEDIUM is taken as the entity that participates centrally in a process, while the AGENT function provides for possible external agency. This, following Halliday (1985:151), allows us to distinguish the following cases:

> The glass broke
> Someone broke the glass
> The glass was broken

In all three clauses the *glass* is the MEDIUM — this participant is crucially effected by the process. Furthermore, in the first clause there is no external agency; in the second, *someone* provides an external AGENT that brought the occurrence of the process about; and in the third, the passive form of the verb is responsive to the fact that there *was* some external agent, but that agent's identity is not being expressed.

With this level of analysis also available, we can state that the particle *wo* marks the MEDIUM of the clause unless that MEDIUM has been selected as NEWS.[7] This is related to the traditional analysis of the particle as a 'direct object' marker. However, the treatment in terms of MEDIUM focuses on the *semantic* contribution that selection as a 'direct object' makes. The AGENT-MEDIUM articulation of the clause provides a *grammatical* resource for presenting an event as one where some 'agent' actively operates upon some entity that serves as the 'end point' of the process undertaken. The following causative constructions offer a clear example of this supportive dependence of 'grammatical' and semantic relations: the former is far more easily interpreted in the sense of 'I let Taroo go to the movies', while the latter favors an interpretation such as 'I made Taroo go to the movies'.

taroo-ni	*eiga-e*	*ika-se-ta*

---

[6] The agency layer is, in fact, equally crucial for English: cf., Halliday (1985:144) – where the terms of the analysis adapted here for Japanese are defined; Jackendoff (1987); and many others. This layer is distinct from the *transitivity* layer of process and participants that one finds given central place in case-based accounts and theories of 'thematic relations' in, for example, the Government and Binding tradition (e.g., Chomsky, 1981) or Lexical-Functional Grammar (Bresnan, 1982). Halliday (1985) argues that both layers are necessary for an effective analysis.

[7] In fact, the particle *wo* should more accurately be seen as realizing the combination of functions MEDIUM (agency layer) and GOAL (transitivity layer). I will not add the complexity of the transitivity layer to the discussion here, however, as it does not contribute to the basic point being made.

	Taroo	movies-to	go-cause-past
	OBLIQUE	LOCATION	PROCESS

	taroo-o	*eiga-e*	*ika-se-ta*
	Taroo	movies-to	go-cause-past
	MEDIUM	LOCATION	PROCESS

(Shibatani, 1976:234-5)

While the use of the indirect object/oblique particle *ni* does not assign agent-like status to Taroo with respect to Taroo's responsibility for making the decision to go, the use of MEDIUM suggests additionally that the entity picked out is a direct 'end point' or affected entity of an active process of 'making go'. In both cases, regardless of the fact that logically (or, better, in terms of the *transitivity* relations of the participants) Taroo is also an actor of some kind in that he did the actual going, the perspectives that we are led to take on the event by the deployment of the grammatical particles can explicitly de-emphasize this.

These abstract *grammatical* meanings of the available particle selections more naturally cover the distinct cases that occur than do treatments that reduce the meaning involved to notions such as Shibatani's (1976) 'permissive' *vs.* 'forced coercion'. For example, Tonoike (1978) and Gunji (1987) note that there are circumstances in which the particle *wo* can be used with a permissive rather than forced coercion reading:

Susan-	*wa*	*imooto-wo*	*hutyuui-de*	*kegasa-sete-shimat-ta*
	-TOP	sister-ACC	carelessness-by	be injured-cause-perf-past

Susan carelessly caused her sister to be injured
(Gunji, 1987:57)

Here, Susan 'allowed' the injury to take place, due to her carelessness, rather than forcing her sister to undergo it. Note, however, that the sister is still quite definitely the 'end-point' of the process of being injured and so the occurrence of *wo* as a reflex of the grammatical function MEDIUM that I am proposing remains quite predictable. This MEDIUM aspect of the meaning needs to be maintained independently of semantic/pragmatic notions of permission and coercion.

Figure 5.5 also contains the grammatical options responsible for the use of the particle *wo*. This network is not, of course, complete in itself[8]; what it represents is the particular set of grammatical alternations discussed in this section and the choice points where choosers for appropriately selecting particles for particular communicative purposes may be attached.

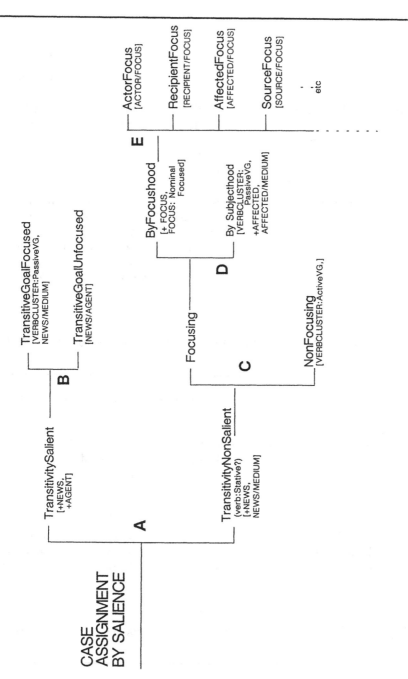

Figure 5.5: The case assignment by salience network

FEATURES	FUNCTION STRUCTURES AND EXAMPLES		
TransitivityNonSalient:	FOCUS	NEWS	VERB
Focusing:	AGENT	MEDIUM	Stative?
ByFocushood:			
ActorFocus:	(ACTOR)		
i.e.	X-*ga*	Y-*ga*	

e.g. (transitive)	*taroo-ga*	*mondai-ga*	*tokeru*
	'It is Taroo for whom the problem is solvable'		
or	*taroo-ga*	*biiru-ga*	*nomitai*
	'It is Taroo who wants to drink the beer'		
but not	*taroo-ga*	*biiru-ga*	*nomu*
	? 'It is Taroo for whom the beer drinks'		

Figure 5.6: Structures constrained by the case assignment by salience systems: 1

FEATURES	FUNCTION STRUCTURES AND EXAMPLES		
TransitivitySalient:			
TransitiveGoalUnfocused	NEWS		VERB
	AGENT	MEDIUM	
		(GOAL)	
i.e.	X-*ga*	Y-*wo*	VERB

e.g. 'X drinks Y'	X-*ga*	Y-*wo*	*nomu*
'X wants to drink Y'	X-*ga*	Y-*wo*	*nomi-tai*
'X is able to drink Y'	X-*ga*	Y-*wo*	*nomeru etc.*

Figure 5.7: Structures constrained by the case assignment by salience systems: 2

Figures 5.6 and 5.7 show examples of the kinds of structures that the network generates. Figure 5.6 shows the result of following the path: {TransitivityNonSalient, Focusing, ByFocushood, ActorFocus}; Figure 5.7 shows the result of the path {TransitivitySalient, TransitiveGoalUnfocused}. The structural results show the two layers of organization (and, additionally, where it is especially relevant, the placement of the transitivity functions ACTOR and GOAL) that combine to determine the particle selection. Simplifying the situation somewhat, we can state the presence of an information layer function NEWS or FOCUS is sufficient for marking with *ga*; otherwise MEDIUM will receive marking by *wo* and AGENT by *ni*.[9]

Although most of the possible combinations involving *ga* and *wo* are covered by the network as given, what is important in the context of text generation, is not so much covering the space of grammatical possibilities, but *controlling* those resources that are available. For this, we need to examine the choosers associated with the network. As we saw in the discussion of the 'topic' particle, each choice point in the grammar network has associated with it a decision based upon the kinds of textual distinctions that the grammatical distinction has been found to be helping to express; these may be set out as follows, respecting the labeling given in the figure.

A: Is it salient to express whether the event/state under consideration involves an actor actively acting upon a goal or not?

    yes: select *TransitivitySalient*

    no: select *TransitivityNonSalient*

B: Is the goal (medium) of the predicate to be particularly highlighted?

    yes: select *TransitiveGoalFocused*

    no: select *TransitiveGoalUnfocused*

C: Is there some element that is to be particularly highlighted?

    yes: select *Focusing*

    no: select *NonFocusing*

D: Does the pattern of 'thematic development' (cf.: Daneš, 1974; Fries, 1981; Bateman, 1986) decided upon favor highlighting some particular element that is *non-established*, or simply *proposed* as far as the current state of development of the discourse is concerned?

---

[8] In particular, there are some interesting interactions with available process types and configurations of participants that are not shown. For example, selection of certain forms of the process, such as 'desire' or ability (e.g.: *nomi-tai* - 'want to drink', *tokeru* - 'able to solve') co-occur with available patterns of news and salience.

[9] Again, this is primarily for main clauses where the full range of information status options are available; I will not discuss here the restricted options that are available in subordinate clauses and how the reduced role of textual considerations there can increase the role played by grammatical relations.

yes: select *ByFocushood*
no: select *BySubjecthood*

E: Does the element to be focused stand in an actor relationship with its
    predicate?

yes: select *ActorFocus*
no: Does the element to be focused stand in an affected
        relationship with its predicate?
        yes: select *AffectedFocus*
        no: Does the element to be focused...etc.

We can now contrast those clauses shown in Figure 5.4 that appeared to
share ideational meaning to see how they differ; the principal examples were
(2b,c), (3b,c,d), and (4b,c). The clauses may be grouped in terms of their
grammatical features as follows:

clauses	*grammatical features*
(2b), (3b)	{TransitivitySalient, TransitiveGoalUnfocused}
(2c), (3c), (4b)	{TransitivityNonSalient, Focusing, ByFocushood}
(3d), (4c)	{TransitivityNonSalient, NonFocusing}

This shows the commonalities and differences between the clauses in terms
of their feature selections. Clause (3c), for example, is similar to clauses (2c)
and (4b), while simultaneously differing from clause (3d), in that it selects to
single out one of its participants as focused and does not grant any particular
salience to the transitivity relationship of some agent actively acting upon some
medium or goal; clause (3d) also does not grant any salience to a transitivity
relationship but does not focus especially on any of its participants. Similarly,
clause (2b) differs from clause (2c) in that it grants the transitivity relationship
salience while clause (2c) does not. Each of the different clauses that appear to
share ideational meaning can now be functionally motivated in this way.

5.3   TOWARDS TEXT BASE
DISTINCTIONS

From the intended interpretation of the inquiries of these choosers, it is possible
to abstract out the textual distinctions that a text plan needs to maintain in
order to control these central regions of Japanese clause grammar and add
these to the pool of textual distinctions that it is necessary for the text base
to maintain and organize. Including the considerations from the part of the

grammar concerned with the deployment of the 'topic' particle *wa*, the principal textual distinctions that appear necessary so far are:

1. thematic development   proposed elements *vs.* established elements

2. transitivity   the relationship of some entity actively 'acting upon a goal', or an 'affected entity'

3. highlighting   the selection of elements as being of particular communicative importance

4. topicality   creating new (but necessarily already established) topics for the text

5. contrastiveness   comparison between already established entities referred to in the text

The account outlined here argues that these text organizational properties are directly realized in particle assignment. Thus, the pragmatic control of these particles is directly incorporated in the organization of the grammar and does not need to be postponed to a later stage of analysis. According to this view, treatments that attempt to restrict their account to clause-internal phenomena, such as grammatical relations or structural position (cf., Kuno, 1973), will be unlikely to be able to *functionally motivate* the full range of particle deployments that can be seen in Japanese and so will not be able to generate *under control* the linguistic variation that different contexts of use require.

In addition, the few functional attempts to motivate particle assignment do not have the benefit of a framework of functional organization such as inquiry semantics and this limits their possibilities for expressing functional generalizations. The theoretical link that is established between linguistic structures, inquiries, and components of the text base provides a natural framework within which previously disparate, or undiscovered, facts concerning the textual control of linguistic constructions can be integrated and generalizations sought.

Given a text plan specification which includes the sources of information of the text base the grammar network can fully control its deployment of particles. Conversely, given that the grammar, choosers, and inquiries that deal with this area of Japanese require these types of distinctions in order to operate, a text planner that does not plan in terms of these features will be unable to control the grammar and inappropriate or unconstrained choices are likely to result. The textual distinctions uncovered here should therefore be accepted as initial, working hypotheses for the contents of the text base. It is clear that some of these areas already form the basis for work on text planning — e.g., work on focus such as Grosz and Sidner (1986), Hovy and McCoy (1989), etc. It is not, therefore, unreasonable to expect a text planner to provide this information and, again, this provides further sources of information for what is to be included in the text base and for what kind of control processes might be necessary for its manipulation. Such work now needs to be augmented further to incorporate other areas of textual meaning that can be uncovered in investigations such as the one reported on here.

5.4   PRINCIPAL CONCLUSIONS OF THE EXPLORATION

Although fast changing, it is clear that most of the effort in computational approaches to language has been placed upon the ideational resources of language. In fact, the sheer pervasiveness of textually and interpersonally conditioned phenomena has still not been sufficiently appreciated within the generation paradigm. The simple examples given in this paper have shown that

- it is possible to use the grammar-as-filter methodology for *textual* meanings as well as for ideational and interpersonal meanings and in languages other than English.

A systemically-based grammar can, therefore, be used to place constraints on the kinds of reasoning that a text planner should perform and the kinds of information that it needs to maintain. This provides us with a systematic methodology for incorporating the control of textually conditioned phenomena directly in our accounts of grammar and text planning.

In addition, the general framework shown here can serve as a medium for integrating linguistic insights from a variety of sources: we have seen contributions to the present analysis from many of those who have studied particle deployment in Japanese. The framework provides a functionally-motivated metalanguage for representing linguistic analyses and for shaping those analyses more effectively in the context of the linguistic system as a whole.

Finally, the more complete and extensive a grammar becomes, the more detailed are the constraints that can be placed upon the processes that drive that grammar. As a grammar grows in 'delicacy', it places finer demands of discrimination on its support information. Thus, while the distinctions drawn by the grammar of Japanese are as yet not so finely developed, the Nigel grammar of English makes very fine functional discriminations across all three metafunctions — the textual included. The positive results of the exploratory research reported here therefore suggest that a detailed exploration of the constraints that Nigel might bring to bear on the processes of text planning would be a valuable research effort and an investigation of this type is now underway (Bateman and Matthiessen, in preparation).

ACKNOWLEDGMENTS

Particular thanks are due to Cécile Paris for improving the organization and clarity of this paper, also to Bill Swartout and the anonymous reviewers of the Catalina workshop, and to Johanna Moore, Bob Kasper, Bill Mann, and Ed Hovy for improving the talk it was based upon, to Mayumi Masuko for additional comments on some of the paper's forerunners, and to Professors Makoto Nagao, Jun-ichi Tsujii, Jun-ichi Nakamura, and the students of the Nagao Laboratory, Kyoto University, for making the doing of the research a pleasure. I remain responsible for the misunderstandings and misinterpretations of Japanese¡ that I have no doubt still succeeded in perpetrating. Financial support in Japan was provided by a post-doctoral research fellowship from the Japan Society for the Promotion of Science (Tokyo) and the Royal Society (London).

BIBLIOGRAPHY

[1] Bateman, John A. (1985) 'An initial fragment of a computational systemic grammar for Japanese'. Dept. of Electrical Engineering, Kyoto University, Kyoto.

[2] Bateman, John A. (1986) 'Text planning for a systemic-functional grammar of Japanese'. Dept. of Electrical Engineering, Kyoto University.

[3] Bateman, John A. (1988) 'Aspects of clause politeness in Japanese: an extended inquiry semantics treatment'. *Proceedings of the 26th International Conference on Computational Linguistics*, Buffalo, New York, pp147-154. Also available as ISI Reprint Series report RS-88-211, USC/Information Sciences Institute, Marina del Rey, California.

[4] Bateman, John A. (1989) 'Dynamic systemic-functional grammar: a new frontier'. *Word*, **40**.1-2, 263-286. Also available as ISI Reprint Series report RS-89-217, USC/Information Sciences Institute, Marina del Rey, California.

[5] Bateman, John A., Kasper, Robert T., Moore, Johanna D., and Whitney, Richard A. (1989) 'The Penman Upper Model – 1989'. Technical Report, USC/Information Sciences Institute, Marina del Rey, California.

[6] Bateman, John A., Kikui, Gen-ichiro, and Tabuchi, Atsushi. (1987) 'Designing a computational systemic grammar of Japanese for text generation: a progress report'. Kyoto University, Dept. of Electrical Engineering.

[7] Bateman, John A. and Li Hang (1988) 'The application of systemic-functional grammar to Japanese and Chinese for use in text generation'.

Proceedings of the 1988 International Conference on Computer Process-ing of Chinese and Oriental Languages, Toronto, Canada, August 29 - September 1, 1988, pp443-447.

[8] Bateman, John A. and Matthiessen, Christian M.I.M. (in preparation) 'Uncovering the text base'. Paper presented at the 1st. International Con-ference on Text and Language Research, Xi'an Jiaotong University, Xi'an, P.R. China, March 1989. USC/Information Sciences Institute and Sydney University/Linguistics Department.

[9] Bresnan, Joan (ed.)(1982) *The Mental Representation of Grammatical Re-lations.* Cambridge: MIT Press.

[10] Chomsky, Noam (1981) *Lectures on Government and Binding.* Cinnamin-son, N.J.: Foris.

[11] Clancy, Patricia M. and Downing, Pamela (1987) 'The use of *wa* as a cohesion marker in Japanese oral narratives'. In Hinds, J. *et al.* (eds.)*op. cit.*, pp3-56.

[12] Daneš, František (1974) 'Functional sentence perspective and the organiza-tion of the text'. In Daneš, František (ed.) *Papers on Functional Sentence Perspective*, Academia, Prague, pp106-128.

[13] Davey, Anthony (1974) *Discourse Production.* Ph.D. thesis, University of Edinburgh; published by Edinburgh University Press, 1979.

[14] Fawcett, Robin P. and Tucker, Gordon H. (1989) 'Prototype Generators 1 and 2'. Communal Project, Report 10. Computational Linguistics Unit, University of Wales College of Cardiff, Wales.

[15] Fries, Peter (1981) 'On the status of theme in English: arguments from discourse'. *Forum Linguisticum*, 6.1, 1-38.

[16] Grosz, Barbara J. and Sidner, Candace L. (1986) 'Attention, Intentions and the Structure of Discourse'. *Computational Linguistics Journal*, 12.3, 175-204.

[17] Gunji, Takao (1987) *Japanese Phrase Structure Grammar.* Dordrecht: Rei-del Publishing Company.

[18] Halliday, Michael A.K. (1978) *Language as social semiotic.* Edward Arnold, London.

[19] Halliday, Michael A.K. (1985) *Introduction to functional grammar.* Edward Arnold, London.

[20] Hinds, John (1983a) 'Topic continuity in Japanese'. In Givón, T. (ed.) *Topic continuity in discourse: a quantitative cross-language study.* Ams-terdam: John Benjamins Publishing Company.

[21] Hinds, John (1983b) 'Case marking in Japanese'. *Linguistics*, **20**, 541-557.

[22] Hinds, John, Maynard, Senko K., and Iwasaki, Shoichi (eds.)(1987) *Perspectives on Topicalization: the case of Japanese 'wa'*. Amsterdam: John Benjamins.

[23] Hovy, Eduard H. (1988) 'Planning coherent multi-sentential text'. *Proceedings of the 26th. Annual Meeting of the Association for Computational Linguistics*, Buffalo, New York, pp163-167.

[24] Hovy, Eduard H., McDonald, David D., Young, Sheryl, and Appelt, Doug (eds.)(1988) *Proceedings of the 1st AAAI Workshop on Text Planning and Realization*, AAAI-88, Minnesota: St. Paul.

[25] Hovy, Eduard H. and McCoy, Kathy F. (1989) 'Focusing your RST: A step towards generating coherent multisentential text'. *Proceedings of the 11th. Annual Conference of the Cognitive Science Society*, August 16-19, 1989, University of Michigan, Ann Arbor, Michigan. Hillsdale, New Jersey: Lawrence Erlbaum Associates, p667-674.

[26] Jackendoff, Ray (1983) *Semantics and Cognition*; The MIT Press.

[27] Jackendoff, Ray (1987) 'The status of thematic relations in linguistic theory'. *Linguistic Inquiry*, **18**.3, 369-411.

[28] Johnson, David E. (1988) 'JETS: A Japanese-English Translation system based on Relational Grammar'. IBM Research Report, Tokyo Scientific Center, Tokyo, Japan.

[29] Kogure, Kiyoshi (1988) 'A method of analyzing Japanese Speech Act types'. ATR Technical Report, TR-I-0026. Advanced Telecommunications Research Institute International, Kyoto, Japan.

[30] Kume, Masako, Sato, Gayle K., Yoshimoto, Kei (1989) 'A descriptive framework for translating speaker's meaning: towards a dialogue translation system between Japanese and English'. In *Proceedings of the 4th. Annual Meeting of the European Chapter of the Association for Computational Linguistics*, pp264-271, UMIST, Manchester, England.

[31] Kuno, Susumo (1972) 'Functional sentence perspective'. *Linguistic Inquiry*, **3**, pp269-320.

[32] Kuno, Susumo (1973) *The structures of the Japanese language*. MIT Press.

[33] Kuno, Susumo (1976) 'Subject, Theme and the Speaker's Empathy'. In Li, C., (ed.) *Subject and Topic*, Academic Press.

[34] Langacker, Ronald W. (1987) *Foundations of Cognitive Grammar: Volume 1, Theoretical Prerequisites*. Stanford University Press, Stanford, California.

[35] Maeda, H., Kato, S., Kogure, K., Iida, H. (1988) 'Parsing Japanese Honorifics in Unification-based Grammar'. *Proceedings of the 26th. Annual Meeting of the Association for Computational Linguistics*, pp139-146.

[36] Mann, William C. (1982) 'The Anatomy of a Systemic Choice', University of Southern California/Information Sciences Institute ISI/RR-82-104.

[37] Mann, William C. (1983) 'Systemic encounters with computation'. *Network*, 5, 27-32.

[38] Mann, William C. (1985) 'An introduction to the Nigel text generation grammar'. In Benson, James D. and Greaves, William S. (eds.) *Systemic Perspectives on Discourse: Selected Theoretical Papers from the 9th. International Systemic Workshop*, Norwood, N.J.: Ablex Pub. Corp., pp84-95.

[39] Mann, William C. and Thompson, Sandra A. (1987) 'Rhetorical structure theory: description and construction of text structures'. In Kempen, Gerard (ed.)*Natural Language Generation: Recent Advances in Artificial Intelligence, Psychology, and Linguistics*, Boston/Dordrecht: Kluwer Academic Publishers, pp85-96.

[40] Matthiessen, Christian M.I.M. (1987) 'Notes on the Organization of the environment of a text generation grammar'. In G. Kempen (ed.) *Natural Language Generation: Recent Advances in Artificial Intelligence, Psychology, and Linguistics*, Boston/Dordrecht: Kluwer Academic Publishers.

[41] Matthiessen, Christian M.I.M. (1988) 'Representational Issues in Systemic-functional grammar'. In Benson, James D. and Greaves, William S. (eds.) *Systemic-functional approaches to discourse*, Norwood, N.J.: Ablex.

[42] Maynard, Senko K. (1980) 'Discourse functions of the Japanese theme marker *wa*'. Ph.D. dissertation, Northwestern University, Illinois.

[43] Partee, Barbara (1975) 'Montague Grammar and Transformational Grammar'. *Linguistic Inquiry*, 6, 203-300.

[44] Patten, Terry (1986) *Interpreting Systemic Grammar as a Computational Representation: A Problem Solving Approach to Text Generation*. Ph.D. dissertation, Department of Artificial Intelligence, Edinburgh University, Scotland.

[45] Shibatani, Masoyoshi (1976) 'Causativization'. In Shibatani, M. (ed.) *Syntax and Semantics 5: Japanese Generative Grammar*, New York: Academic Press, pp239-294.

[46] Shibatani, Masoyoshi (1977) 'Grammatical relations and surface cases'. *Language*, 53.4, 789-809.

[47] Sugimura, R. (1986) 'Japanese Honorifics and Situation Semantics'. In *Coling-86*, pp507-510.

[48] Tonoike, S. (1978) 'On the Causative Construction in Japanese'. In Hinds, J. and Howard, I. (eds.) *Problems in Japanese Syntax and Semantics*, Tokyo: Kaitakusha, pp3-29.

[49] Winograd, Terry (1972) *Understanding Natural Language*, Edinburgh University Press.

Chapter 6

The Implications of Revisions for Natural Language Generation

Marie W. Meteer

Abstract: Analysis of naturally occurring data is essential for developing computational models of language processes. In this paper, I describe the results of my analysis of revised texts and show how generalizations of the data can contribute to the development of an architecture for natural language generation. In particular, I look at how identifying classes of revisions can help in the design of intermediate levels of representation by determining the decision points necessary to permit the variations between the original and revised versions of the same passage to be generated. The work presented here summarizes the analysis of over 500 instances of revisions of technical papers made by professional editors.

6.1   INTRODUCTION

Analysis of naturally occurring data is important in understanding a process one
is trying to model. In the work presented here, I use the analysis of revised text
to aid in developing an architecture for Natural Language Generation. Careful
analysis of revisions can not only provide a descriptive account of well written
text, but can also provide a framework in which to develop an explanatory
account of the generation and revision processes themselves. Analysis can help
determine what decisions were made originally and how those decisions were
changed to improve the text. Work in generation to date has focused primarily
on simply producing grammatical sentences with the appropriate content. This
work focuses on a much subtler kind of decision making, that which improves
the style and readability of the text. I have limited the data to texts written by
competent writers and edited by professional editors in order to filter, on the
one hand, errors, and on the other, changes to content. The analysis presented
here contributes to our understanding of natural language generation in three
ways:

1. discovering what kinds of changes are made by an editor whose goal it is
   to "improve" the text while leaving the content the same;

2. looking at variation of expression: the original and revised versions provide two ways of saying the same thing in the same context;

3. determining the implications of the data on the architecture of a generation system.

The first phase of the analysis, described in Section 6.2, was to simply item-
ize the changes and look at how they functioned to improve the text. The goal
of the next phase was to look for "classes" of revisions which have the same general description for both the original and revised versions. Identifying classes
allows you to develop criteria for representational levels and decisions within
the generator so that both the original and revised texts may be generated
(i.e., are within the competence of the generator) and to develop strategies for
recognizing and revising new instances of the class when they are found in subsequent texts. In Section 6.3, I address issues in generalizing over instances from
the data and in Section 6.4, I sketch a level of representation which attempts
to capture those generalizations. The final phase, described in Section 6.5, is
to look at the implications of the analysis for the architecture of a generation
system.

6.2   DESCRIPTION OF THE DATA

The first phase of the work was to simply collect samples of revised texts and
look at the kinds of changes that were made. In the data I have analyzed so

far, there were approximately 500 instances of revisions. Nearly all the text samples were technical papers revised by a professional editor who was not the author. Since the original authors were all competent writers, there were few actual "errors" (such as grammatical or spelling mistakes) and since a goal of the editors was to improve the style without altering the original meaning of the text, there was minimal change to the content.[1] Therefore, this sample allowed me to focus on changes made to improve the style of the text. More than half the instances were from one particular document.[2]

6.2.1 Survey of the Data

In this section, I present a survey of the most common kinds of revisions I found. I have grouped them for descriptive purposes; the categories are not meant to be exclusive nor is the order reflective of the frequency of each type.[3]

Ellipsis: This category contains deletions of an identical word (or pro-form of the word) in a corresponding syntactic position in a conjoined phrase. In the following example, the subjects of conjoined clauses are elided in the revised version.

1. A: Definitions are made more systematic and explicit, they introduce a new functional element, and incidentally they also reflect more expertise in text analysis.

    B: Definitions are made more systematic and explicit, introduce a new functional element, and incidentally reflect more expertise in text analysis.

Deletion of function words: These revisions involved the deletion of closed class words (e.g., prepositions, determiners) with little or no other alteration to the structure. Most common were those of the form shown in 2 below; others, such as 3, involved some rearrangement of the phrase.

2. A: Each of the fields specifies ...

    B: Each field specifies...

3. A: The size of the units is arbitrary,...

    B: The unit size is arbitrary,...

---

[1] I am not claiming that the original and revised text have the exact same meaning – one can argue that any change to the text affects the meaning, however subtly – only that the change is minimal in this type of editing.

[2] This document was a draft of Bill Mann and Sandra Thompson's paper "Rhetorical Structure Theory: A Theory of Text Organization". The draft was edited by a professional editor, Tom Strini, and then rechecked by both Mann and Thompson, who rejected any changes that altered the intended meaning of the text.

[3] The overlap of instances and variation in the data made it impossibly to partition the instances of changes into types; therefore I did not do any quantitative analyses, such as frequency counts.

Deletion of connective words: While these might be grouped with deletion of function words (above), I felt there were sufficient numbers of them to warrant a separate category. In most cases, the connective was replaced with a semicolon; in others there was a change to two separate sentences. As shown in 4 and 5, the connective which was deleted usually conveyed a stronger relation that was actually present, and the parallel structure of the two connected clauses sufficed to bind them.

4.   A: The term writer refers to the writer of the text being described; <u>similarly</u> *reader* refers to the intended readers(s) of the text...

      B: The term writer refers to the writer of the text being described; *reader* refers to the intended readers(s) of the text...

5.   A: The Enablement provides information designed to increase the reader's ability to perform the action, <u>while</u> Motivation provides information designed to increase the reader's desire to perform the action.

      B: The Enablement provides information designed to increase the reader's ability to perform the action; Motivation provides information designed to increase the reader's desire to perform the action.

Pronominalization: While there were few cases of a full noun phrase changed to a pronoun (e.g., "the text" → "it"), there were several of the form shown below in which a head noun was deleted and the quantifier stood as an indefinite pronoun.

6.   A: The relations Enablement and Motivation form a subgroup since <u>they both</u> involve evoking a reader action...

      B: The relations Enablement and Motivation form a subgroup since <u>both</u> evoke a reader action...

Change in part of speech: In this type, a change in the part of speech of a lexical item both changes what element is the head of the phrase and also allows some functions words to be deleted. The changes cross many different parts of speech; while the most common change was from noun to verb (as in 7 and 8), there were also changes from adjective to adverb (as in 9), from verb to noun (as in 10), and from adjective to verb (as in 11).

7.   A: Hoey thus <u>makes a distinction</u> between ....

      B: Hoey thus <u>distinguishes</u> between ....

8.   A: People <u>are frequently in strong agreement</u> ....

      B: People <u>often strongly agree</u> ....

9.   A: This section defines the terminology of RST <u>in a way that is independent</u> of the particular languages and text types to which <u>it has been applied.</u>

      B: This section defines the terminology of RST <u>independently</u> of the particular languages and text types to which it has been applied.

10.   A: None of these people necessarily agrees with <u>the way we have interpreted</u> their advice.

      B: None of these people necessarily agrees with <u>our interpretation</u> of their advice.

11.   A: The goals <u>are different</u> from ....

      B: The goals <u>differ</u> from ....

Elimination of semantic redundancy: This was one of the most common types of change (it is also one dwelled on in most writing textbooks). In many of these examples, some lexical item semantically entails the information expressed in another part of the phrase, thus licensing its deletion. In example 12, "developing" is a process, so to explicitly say "the process of" is redundant; in example 13, the definition of "audience" is "who the writer is writing for", so it also does not need to be explicitly stated; and in example 14, it is clear that the number refers to the total.

12.   A: We have been <u>in the process of developing</u> RST...

      B: We have been <u>developing</u> RST...

13.   A: *reader* refers to the intended readers(s) of the text, the audience <u>for whom the writer is writing.</u>

      B: *reader* refers to the intended reader(s) of the text, the audience.

14.   A: The connected BARRNet campuses currently have about 5,000 active IP hosts <u>in total.</u>

      B: The connected BARRNet campuses currently have about 5,000 active IP hosts.

Elimination of contextual redundancy: Redundancies also occur when information which is available in the context is made unnecessarily explicit in the text, as in the example 15, where it is clear that the announcement is being used as an example, and in example 16, where it is clear that the sentence refers to the text in the example shown above.

15.   A: **Elaboration** is nicely illustrated by <u>this example, an announcement</u> in the newsletter *Language Sciences.*

B: <u>This announcement</u> from the newsletter *Language Sciences* nicely illustrates **Elaboration.**

16.   A: So, for example, we note that it is the conference, rather than Sweden, that is the element <u>elaborated in the text above.</u>

       B: So, for example, we note that the conference, rather than Sweden, is the element <u>elaborated.</u>

Raising a subordinate clause to matrix position: Most of these changes involved the elimination of a semantically weak matrix, such as the existential "there", as in example 17, and the background information in 18. In many of these examples the weak matrix was a hedge, such as "seem" or "appear", as in 19.

17.   A: <u>There are no doubt other relations which</u> might be reasonable constructs...

       B: <u>Other relations</u> might be reasonable constructs...

18.   A: In our analyses, <u>we have worked with units that</u> are essentially clauses,...

       B: In our analyses, <u>units</u> are essentially clauses,...

19.   A: The text <u>appears to contain</u> a number of non-sequiturs, ...

       B: The text <u>contains</u> a number of non-sequiturs, ...

Movement of an adjunct phrase: There were several examples where an adjunct which syntactically could fit in a variety of places was moved. In example 20, the phrase "for the whole text" is a distraction in its original position and is moved to the end of the sentence. In 21, a separate sentence is moved into an adjunct position in a noun phrase.

20.   A: the analyst is effectively providing an account <u>for the whole text</u> of a plausible reason the writer might have had for including each part.

       B: the analyst effectively provides a plausible reason the writer might have had for including each part <u>of the whole text</u>.

21.   A: <u>A very few texts can be</u> analyzed only if the adjacency constraint is relaxed. These are typically advertisements in which a title line plays a role in the body of the text.

       B: <u>A very few texts, typically advertisements in which a title line plays a role in the body of the text, can be</u> analyzed only if the adjacency constraint is relaxed.

Changes to structural relations: These changes not only involve movement of phrases, but also changes in the relations expressed (or implied) between them. In example 22, there are changes to both the order of the phrases and which is subordinate, which results in a subtle change in causality. In 23, the structural relations are changed by simply changing the connective words rather than actually moving the phrases. The first clause changes from the matrix to a subordinate clause, the second becomes the matrix, and the third, which was originally in a coordinate relation to the first, now becomes subordinate to the second. In 24, a relative clause becomes the matrix clause and the matrix becomes a relative clause.

22.　　A:　The purpose of this paper is to make Rhetorical Structure Theory (RST) more examinable and usable by making it more explicit.

　　　　B:　The purpose of this paper is to make Rhetorical Structure Theory (RST) more explicit and thus more usable and open to examination.

23.　　A:　It is still based on judgments, necessarily, but since it provides a checklist of affirmations it makes it easy to identify the claims underlying a particular analysis.

　　　　B:　Though still based on judgments, necessarily, it provides a checklist of affirmations and thus makes it easy to identify the claims underlying a particular analysis.

24.　　A:　The types of relations Martin considers are similar to those we suggest...

　　　　B:　Martin considers types of relations similar to those we suggest...

Passive to active: Nearly all writing textbooks contain a section on "making your writing more active" which includes both choice of active verbs and use of the active voice. There were many instances in the data of passive voice changed to active (note there were no changes from active to passive). The four strategies employed are listed below:

INTRODUCTION OF AN AGENT. These examples were passives which had no agent expressed. It is interesting to note that the only agent ever introduced was "we". When the implied agent was the reader or the analyst, for example, instead of the writers, some other strategy was used.

25.　　A:　Unit 1 is taken as nuclear.

　　　　B:　We take Unit 1 as nuclear.

CHANGING THE VERB. In these examples, the passive was avoided by choosing a different verb whose required arguments were already present. (Again, the agent was not expressed in the original.)

26.   A: An example of the Evidence relation <u>can be seen in this extract</u> from a letter to the editor of BYTE magazine.

      B: <u>This extract</u> from a letter to the editor of BYTE magazine has an example of the Evidence relation.

METATHESIS. In these cases, the verb and the arguments remained the same, but the relations between them changed so that one of the arguments could act as an agent. Most of them seemed conventional in technical writing style ("examples illustrate", "analysis notes information") rather than metaphorical.

27.   A: <u>The structure is shown in Figure 2.</u>

      B: <u>Figure 2 shows the structure.</u>

SIMPLE PASSIVE TO ACTIVE WITH THE "BY" PHRASE. This final strategy is the one we most often associate with the change from active to passive, but interestingly, it was the least used. For example, in one sample document there were only two instances of the "by" phrase in the fourteen passives changed.

28.   A: <u>Elaboration is nicely illustrated by this example,</u> an announcement in the newsletter *Language Sciences*.

      B: This announcement from the newsletter *Language Sciences* nicely illustrates <u>Elaboration.</u>

Choosing a more precise lexical item: Changes of this type and the next, which adds information to the text, were fewest. This is not surprising, since making the text more specific would require more content changes: remember this is a technical paper being revised by an editor, not one of the authors. (Note in 30 this also shortens the text.)

29.   A: ..., the paper examines <u>several</u> claims and findings of RST: <lists three>

      B: ..., the paper examines <u>three</u> claims and findings of RST: <lists three>

30.   A: knowledge of the context in which the text was <u>put forth,</u>

      B: knowledge of the context in which it was <u>written,</u>

31.   A: The starting point for analyzing a text is to divide it into units.

      B: The first step analyzing a text is dividing it into units.

Making something inferable explicit: These changes seem in direct contrast with many of those discussed above in that they make the text less concise by adding redundancy. In example 32, both the context and the capitalization of Antithesis identify it as a relation, yet the editor decided to strengthen the point by making it explicit. In 33, "agreement" is available from the previous sentence, but there is a great deal of intervening text, so simply saying "this" is potentially ambiguous.

32.   A: ...the definition of Antithesis.

　　 B: ...the definition of the Antithesis relation.

33.   A: <u>This</u> includes responsibility for providing...

　　 B: <u>This agreement</u> includes responsibility for providing...

Changing a function word: While these changes did seem to improve the text, it is very difficult to explain why. For example, in two cases "may" was changed to "might", as shown in 34. There may (might?) be some rule governing which to use, but I don't recall ever being taught it. In three cases, a preposition was changed, as in 35. Prepositions are well known to be slippery: they are a bane to non-native speakers. It is difficult to determine why one might choose the wrong one initially, or how to evaluate that another is better.

34.   A: For some texts, more than one analysis <u>may</u> be appropriate;

　　 B: For some texts, more than one analysis <u>might</u> be appropriate;

35.   A: ...the first two paragraphs from a notice in a UCLA personnel newsletter.

　　 B: ...the first two paragraphs of a notice in a UCLA personnel newsletter.

6.2.2   Categories of Revisions

One of the most obvious uses for analysis of revisions is to look at their function in improving the text. The following were the most common types of improvements:

- MAKING THE TEXT MORE CONCISE: This type constituted over half the total revisions. The changes were for the most part local and many involved only deletions, without any companion additions or reorderings. Types of revisions in this category include use of ellipsis (mainly subject reduction), pronominalization, deletion of function words ("size of the units" → "unit size"), elimination of semantic redundancy ("grouped together" → "grouped"), and change in part of speech ("for the comprehension of the element" → "comprehending the element").

- MAKING THE TEXT MORE EXPLICIT: Changes of this type were the fewest, but this is not surprising, since making the text more specific would require more content changes and this data is revised by an editor rather than the author. There were three major types: choosing a more precise lexical item ("several claims" → "three claims"), making something which is inferable explicit ("This gives rise to ..." → "This view gives rise to ..."), and restoring elided subjects. Note that making the text more explicit is often in direct conflict with making it more concise.

- CHANGING THE EMPHASIS: This category includes those changes in which whole phrases of the text were moved or the structural relations between phrases in the text were changed. Examples include movement of an adjunct phrase and movement of a subordinate clause into main clause position (and vice versa).

- MAKING THE TEXT MORE ACTIVE: This type is one often harped on in writing textbooks. Examples include changing from passive to active voice and eliminating hedge verbs, such as "seem" or "appear".

6.2.3   A Closer Look At Conciseness

One of the most interesting categories (as well as the one with the most instances) is conciseness. Virtually all writing textbooks agree that conciseness is a good thing–and that you must be careful not to to go far:

> Vigorous writing is concise. A sentence should contain no extra words, a paragraph no extra sentences ....This requires not that the writer make all his sentences short, or that he avoid all detail and treat his subjects only in outline, but that every word tell. (Strunk and White, 1979, p.23)

> Almost all writing suffers from wordiness–the tendency to use more words than necessary. When useless words weigh down your prose, the meaning is often lost, confused, hidden .... Beware, however, ...you don't want your prose to become so thin or brief that your meaning disappears completely. Therefore, cut out only the unessential words. (Wyrick, 1984, p.60)

While all agree on the message, none tell you how to decide which words are necessary and which are superfluous. The best they do is provide some examples, such as these from Wyrick (1984), p.61:

> Wordy: She made her decision after giving consideration to his report.

Concise: She decided after considering his report.

Wordy: Each candidate should be evaluated on an individual basis.
Concise: Each candidate should be evaluated individually.

Revisions such as these were quite common in the text I analyzed. Note that the changes do not fall neatly into some single category in the traditional categories of decisions in generation, such as lexical choice, choice of syntactic structure, or organization of the information. They are more easily described in terms of which element is functioning as the head of the phrase, and whether that element is semantically strong (e.g., a content word) or semantically weak (e.g., a function word). In the next section I look more closely at general ways of describing these kinds of decisions.

6.3   GOALS FOR THE ANALYSIS: GENERALITY

Our overall goal is to use the instances of revisions to drive the development of a theory of natural language generation. We therefore want to move from a descriptive analysis to an explanatory analysis. One important issue in such a move is finding what level of generality in which to describe the data will best improve the explanatory power. Generality can be achieved in two ways:

- Within a single example: In a particular pair of original-revised texts the simplest description of the change will be the most general; therefore, if we can postulate a single high level difference which will cause the surface differences to fall out necessarily, it will be more explanatory than simply addressing the surface differences independently.

- Across a body of data: A description that covers the most examples will be the most general and explanatory, and will require us to postulate the least number of generation and revision strategies.

Let's look at particular examples of ranges in these two dimensions of generality.

6.3.1   Levels of Decision Making

A change from one surface form to another can be described at many different points in the generation process. Here we look at how one example can be described at three different levels and what a revision component would have to change if it operated at each of the levels. Consider the example in which the phrase *each of the fields* is made more concise by being changed to *each field*. At the lowest level of description, there are three surface changes: the deletion of two function words ("of" and "the") and a morphological change in the head from plural to singular. A pattern matcher would be necessary to coordinate these changes at the surface level; however, that approach would require a great many independent specialists (for example, to avoid changing "all of the fields" to "all field"). At a more general level, there are two decision points that directly contribute to the surface changes: the change in the determiner (roughly whether the determiner is "the" or "a") and the number of the head. At this level of description, we need not specify the "of", as it is uniquely determined by these two factors: its deletion may be seen as a side effect of the other decisions. While a revision specialist at this level would still have to be particular to each quantifier (to avoid making the mistake on phrases quantified by "all", for example), this would be a more general place to change the determiner policy and the number than at the level of the surface form, since information on the number of the quantifier is also necessary for subject-verb agreement. At a still more general level, these changes can be motivated by a single decision: the perspective chosen to express "field": is it seen as a definite set, "the fields", or as an indefinite element of the set, "a field" (the indefinite determiner is superceded by the quantifier in the example). A single change at this level would account for multiple differences at lower levels. However, a revision specialist making the change must know the relation between the perspective and the resulting degree of conciseness of the text. It must also evaluate whether the change will change the intended meaning of the text: the original choice may have been for a particular emphasis, for example to contrast one subset with another ("which of the photographs on the righthand side ..."). Another example of a single perspective choice that covers a number of surface differences is the decision/decide type of variation (discussed in more detail below). While out of context this change is simply a change in the part of speech, there are many accompanying grammatical changes that must go on within a context. For example, a noun phrase must express number and have a determiner, and a verb phrase must express tense and include obligatory arguments. All of these surface distinctions can be captured by difference between using an *event* perspective or an *object* perspective. We look more closely at this difference in Section 6.4.

6.3.2   Generalities Across The Data

A related dimension of generality is choosing a description that covers the most examples.[4] Such a description allows you to posit fewer strategies for generation

---

[4] While the advantage of general descriptions in developing an explanatory analysis is clear, it is also important not to become too general. The reductio ad absurdum that covers all the data is simply that "something changed". However, this does nothing to help us understand

and revision overall. For example, it is clear that the following examples can be treated uniformly:

1. make a decision → decide

2. make a distinction → distinguish

They can be described as deleting the verb "make", changing the direct object from a noun to a verb, and making it the matrix verb in the clause. This level of description is analogous to the surface level categorized above and would require strategies associated with individual lexical items, such as *make*. A slightly greater level of generality lets you include examples like (3) and (4) in the same group. Rather than describing the change in terms of a single lexical item, "make", we can describe it in terms of a class of lexical items, i.e., weak verbs, including "give" and "be".

3. give a validation of x → validate x

4. is a description of x → describes x

In these examples, the weak verb is deleted and the verb form of its argument moves to matrix verb position. Note that when the noun has an argument, marked by "of" in (3) and (4), the argument remains and becomes the direct object of the verb. The weak verbs in the above examples are idiomatic to the lexical item (decision, distinction, validation) and carry little or no information. The content is carried in the object to the weak verb; in the revised versions, the object moves to the matrix verb position, with an accompanying change in the part of speech. Weak verbs may also be hedges, where the weak verb places the object in a more distant perspective with respect to the reader. These are often in the passive, as in (5), creating a distance from the author as well:

5. are seen to emanate → emanate

6. the text appears to contain → the text contains

Note that in these examples, the argument which moves is already a clause, so our general description of this class need not specify the change in the part of the speech, only that the element moved must be a verb to move into matrix verb position.

An even greater level of generality would allow us to extend our description to other phrase types, including examples of arguments (and adjuncts) becoming the head of phrases such as NPs and adverbial phrases, as in the following:

---

the differences or design generation, evaluation, or revision strategies. The appropriate level of generality must help explain phenomena as well as describe them.

7. the sort of relation → the relation,

8. a way that is independent → independently

The change can now be described as a weak element in head position being displaced by a strong element that was previously in an argument or adjunct position. While the examples differ in the type of phrase being modified and the particulars of the modification (e.g., whether the part of speech changed in the new head), they are all examples of a change in how an element functions in a phrase. This general description allows us to look at one kind of choice (function) in multiple situations.

6.4   ANALYSIS OF THE DATA FOR GENERATION

Analyses such as those above can guide us in determining the intermediate structures and decision points necessary to generate both the original and the revised texts. There are three kinds of information that must be represented in order to capture the generalizations described in the previous section:

1. constituency: many of the examples involved the movement of entire constituents with little or no internal change to the constituent;

2. functional relations (e.g., head, argument, matrix, adjunct);

3. semantic type of the constituent (e.g., event, individual) which reflects the perspective through which the information is being viewed.

In this section we look at how this information can be represented using a notation we have developed for text planning, called the *Text Structure* (Meteer, 1988, 1989). As we see in Figure 6.1, which represents the changes in example 7 (repeated below), the Text Structure notation is particularly useful in capturing these three kinds of information: each node represents a constituent of the utterance, the label in bold signifies the functional relation of the node to its parent, and the second label is a lexical item followed by its semantic type.[5]

---

[5] Since our focus here is to look at examples of revisions, I will only briefly describe the notation itself; the details are described in Meteer (1989). There are essentially two kinds of subtrees in the Text Structure: a composite in which one of the children is the MATRIX and the other children are ADJUNCTS and a kernel, in which the children are ARGUMENTS of their parent. In the diagram, the label in bold signifies the functional relation of the node to its parent; the labels on the roots are either HEAD, signifying a kernel, or COMPOSITE. The second label is the contents of the node. In the text planner, the contents is a first class object representing the information expressed by the constituent; in the diagrams here it is a lexical item followed by its semantic type. Italics are used to abbreviate constituents which are peripheral to the point being illustrated.

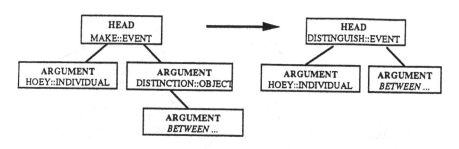

Figure 6.1: Representation of the changes in example 7.

7.   A: Hoey thus <u>makes a distinction</u> between ....

      B: Hoey thus <u>distinguishes</u> between ....

6.4.1 Constituency

Fundamental to most of the revisions in the data is the ability to manipulate entire constituents. A constituent may be as small as a word or as large as a paragraph (though few examples in the data I analyzed manipulated constituents larger than a sentence). In the following example, an adjunct that originally appeared as a separate sentence is moved to a position as an adjunct to an object and is realized in the text as a restrictive relative clause.

1.   A: <u>A very few texts can be</u> analyzed only if the adjacency constraint is relaxed. <u>These are typically advertisements in which a title line plays a role in the body of the text.</u>

      B: <u>A very few texts, typically advertisements in which a title line plays a role in the body of the text, can be</u> analyzed only if the adjacency constraint is relaxed.

As shown in this example (and illustrated in Figure 6.2), one of the primary features of the Text Structure representation is that it transcends the traditional division between structure above the level of the sentence (what is often called "discourse" or "rhetorical" structure) and structure below the level of the sentence (usually described only in syntactic terms).

6.4.2 Functional Relations

In our generalized description of the changes described in Section 6.3.1, what functional role a constituent had in the utterance played a key part. In the

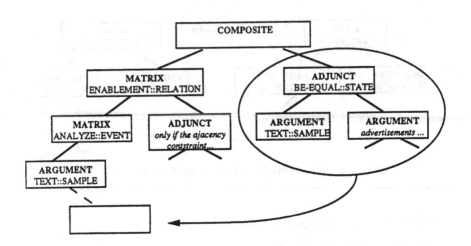

Figure 6.2: Representation of the change in example 21.

example shown below (and illustrated in Figure 6.3), the second argument of the first tree becomes the head of the second tree. Note that the movement does not change the subconstituents of the element that moved.

19.   A: The text appears to contain a number of non-sequiturs, ...

       B: The text contains a number of non-sequiturs, ...

6.4.3   Semantic Types

The Text Structure representation can also capture the conceptual information and perspectives expressed by a particular combination of linguistic resources, where a linguistic resource is more than simply a word, but also syntactic structures, closed class lexical items, inflectional morphology and the like. For example, a single word in an utterance is a composition of the lexeme itself, its part of speech, and grammatical features, such as number. The lexeme carries most of the content. Part of speech can signal perspective, for example the verb *decide* focuses on the process whereas the noun *decision* focuses on the result. (Grimshaw, 1988, presents a more complex discussion of this distinction and its implications). Grammatical features, such as number, also in some sense reflect perspective. The combination of grammatical resources in a phrase can signal perspective on an object, such as indefinite entity *(a dog)*, definite object *(the dog)*, and multiple instances *(dogs)* (Talmy, 1987).

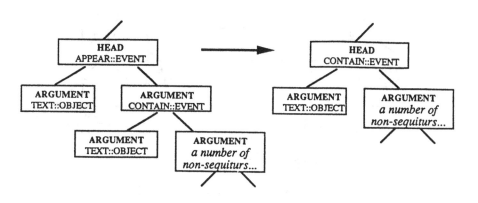

Figure 6.3: Representation of the change in example 19.

In addition to expressing content and perspective, linguistic resources differ in their options for combining with other resources. For example, you can both *decide quickly* or *make a quick decision,* but the result perspective is forced when you need access to the result, as in *make an important decision* (cf. **decide importantly*).[6] The text structure captures this constraint through the semantic types at each node. In the first structure, the RESULT is available and thus can be modified by a PROPERTY (in this case "important"), whereas in the second structure only the EVENT is available, which cannot be modified by a property; therefore the revision in this case is not allowed. (This is illustrated in Figure 6.4.) It would only be possible if there was manner adverb for "important" available as a linguistic resource.

A: Micheal made an important decision.

B: *Micheal decided importantly.

6.5 ANALYSIS FOR GENERATION

A descriptive analysis such as that presented above outlines the range of phenomena under consideration independent of any particular theoretical framework for the process itself. In order to make use of the analysis in the design of a generation system, we must provide such a theoretical framework, one which

---

[6]Following the general convention in linguistics, I use a "*" to mark ungrammatical sentences and a "?" to mark questionable ones.

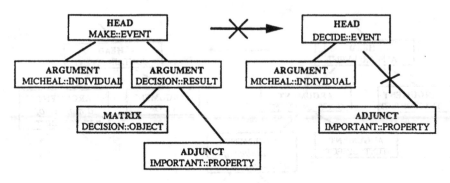

Figure 6.4: A case where revision is not allowed

would allow us to explain the data in terms of the generation process. In this section, I present the considerations by which you arrive at such a framework.

First, let's review the processes we are trying to explain. We can summarize them in terms of three questions:

- How was the original text produced?
- What changes were made to produce the revised text¡?
- How could the need for the changes be noticed?

Our overall goal is to span the distance between the data itself and the answer to these three questions. I begin by proposing a framework based on an efficiency model of generation and then consider the question of why revision is necessary in this framework to produce written quality text.

6.5.1 An Efficiency Model Of Generation

Consider the following examples of revisions which function to make the text more concise:

1. in a way that is independent → independently

2. the way that we interpreted their advice → our interpretation of their advice

These phrases both fall into the class described in Section 6.3.2: they began with a semantically weak head which was modified with the semantically important information. The change makes the semantically important information in the modifying phrase into the head of the whole phrase, with a corresponding change in perspective.

The existence of the two versions, original and revised, presents an interesting problem of how decisions are made during initial generation. In the first example, we can assume that *independently* is a word the author knew when he wrote the original text. Why didn't he use it? Why didn't he make the optimization that would produce the revised text in the original generation pass?

This apparent variance in ability on the part of the speaker can be explained by taking into account the relative familiarity of the situation the speaker is in. In McDonald, Meteer and Pustejovsky (1987), we argue on the grounds of efficiency that there is a direct link between the familiarity of the situation and the ease of generation. When the speaker is in a familiar situation (an extreme case is answering the phone) then fewer decisions need to be made about what to include in the message and how to express it. We can think of "familiar" situations as reified objects with an established mapping to the linguistic resources (lexical items, syntactic structures) for expressing them. New ideas and contexts ("unfamiliar" situations) can be expressed by composing familiar ones (as in descriptions of objects we don't have names for). However, in expressing these composite objects we will have to use general strategies, as we will not have any established already way of expressing them.

There are two other important aspects of this efficiency model: decisions are made locally (and not necessarily simultaneously), and they are made indelibly (there is no backtracking – generation is not search) (McDonald, 1984). A result of these design criteria is that a message (or message element) built compositionally in multiple steps may be functionally equivalent to some "familiar" object, but the speaker cannot necessarily know that in advance and therefore cannot take advantage of the familiar object's established mapping to linguistic resources.

6.5.2   Why Revision: Tension Between Goals

Now let's look at our earlier example in terms of this framework. The larger context in which the example appeared was as follows:

This section defines RST **in a way that is independent [independently]** *of the particular languages and text types to which it has been applied.*

If the speaker had already chosen "independent" to modify the event *(defining RST)*, then an established mapping would have produced the adverb. However, suppose the speaker first decides to modify the manner of the action, but has not yet decided on the particulars of the modification. He can choose a compositional construction which provides a weak head that simply contributes "manner" *(in a way)* and then later add modifications to the head. Notice in the examples below that this construction allows many options for expressing information that cannot be expressed simply as an adverb in English:

> in a way that is dependent on the particular language ...
> in a way that emphasizes ...
> in a particular way ...

This makes the construction more appropriate when the particulars have not yet been chosen, because almost no options have been cut off. One can continue talking, just saying "in a way", without immediately establishing the particulars and still feel relatively confident that any choice will be acceptable.

Figures 6.5 and 6.6 show this incremental production using the Text Structure representation. Again, the object types Event, Property and Manner capture constraints on the composition of the elements. They may be thought of as "conceptual constituents" in Jackendoff's terms (Jackendoff, 1983), and map to syntactic constituents in later stages of the processing. By using abstract linguistic terms such as these to represent the message built by the text planner, we can ensure that the message will be expressible, that is, that there will be linguistic resources available that the parts of the message can map into.

9.   A: This section defines the terminology of RST in a way that is independent of the particular languages and text types to which it has been applied.

      B: This section defines the terminology of RST independently of the particular languages and text types to which it has been applied.

As this example shows, the initial formulation of this model of generation appears to have potential as it helps account for the variance in ability on the part of the writer. Expressing complex notions requires choosing between a number of linguistic resources which will compose into an utterance. Furthermore, written text has greater demands on its form than spoken text since the audience is not present to interact with the speaker when the text is unclear or ambiguous. The need for revision stems from the tension between such multiple goals in the generation process: tension between making choices that make the text clear (e.g., making as much explicit as possible), that make the text concise (e.g., leaving as much implicit as possible to reduce the number of words), and that leave open the most degrees of freedom (e.g., the most possibilities for composing more information into the utterance). As discussed in Section 6.5.1, this tension may already be resolved in familiar situations. When the audience is known, the choice of what to make implicit and what to leave explicit can be made with greater assurance; when the extent of what is to be communicated is known, there is less of a need to leave open more degrees of freedom.

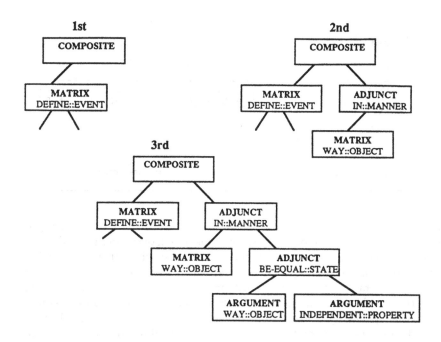

Figure 6.5: Incremental production using Text Structure representation - 1

6.6 CONCLUSION

Revisions of text provide a window into language production[7] in much the same way as speech errors do. Garrett (1975) used classes of exchange errors to posit levels of processing, roughly semantic, syntactic, and phonetic. While the revisions I have focused on in this work are not errors in the same sense as Garrett's speech errors (they are more linguistic variations than deviations), classification of changes suggest initial generation strategies as well as revision strategies. For example, the case of replacing a weak verb and direct object with a strong verb *(make a decision → decide)* reflects both the revision strategy "make the text concise" and initial generation strategies such as realizing a particular perspective (viewing *the decision* as an object in the original rather than as an event) or leaving the most options open (the nominalization is more open to modification: *make an important decision*). Formulating these general strategies can help us to postulate particular decision points and decision criteria.

The early results of this work indicate the importance of text analysis in pro-

---

[7] Following the practice of psycholinguists, I use the term "production" to distinguish what people do from what machines do.

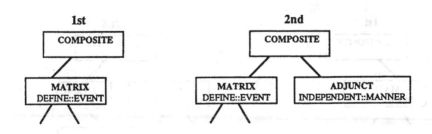

Figure 6.6: Incremental production using Text Structure representation - 2

viding a descriptive account of well written text (in contrast to a prescriptive account, as is found in most writing textbooks). Furthermore, generalizations of the data can guide us in determining the intermediate structures and decisions points necessary to generate variations of texts. Finally, the apparent need for writers to revise and the instances of revisions that I have analyzed support an architecture for generation that favors efficiency and expressibility over initial optimality of expression. If that were not true, i.e., optimality were favored, then the "first draft" text in the data would not occur and revisions would not be necessary. This architecture accounts for variance of ability on the part of writers through the use of general generation strategies when realizing conceptual structures built compositionally. Improvements are made by evaluating the text and then regenerating it to produce more optimal text.

BIBLIOGRAPHY

Garrett, M.F. (1975) 'The Analysis of Sentence Production' *Psychology of Learning and Motivation,* Vol.98 Academic Press, Inc, New York, pp.133-177.

Grimshaw, Jane (1988) 'On the Representation of Two Kinds of Noun' Presented at Theoretical Issues in Computation and Lexical Semantics Workshop, Brandeis University, April 1988.

Jackendoff, Ray (1983) *Semantics and Cognition,* MIT Press, Cambridge, Massachusetts.

Mann, William and Sandra Thompson (1987) 'Rhetorical Structure Theory: Description and Construction of Text Structures', in Kempen (ed) Natural Language Generation, Martinus Nijhoff Publishers, Dordrecht, The Netherlands, p.279-300.

McDonald, David D. (1984) 'Description Directed Control', *Computers and*

Mathematics, 9(1) Reprinted in Grosz, *et al.* (eds.) *Readings in Natural Language Processing*, Morgan Kaufmann Publishers, California, 1986, pp.519-538.

McDonald, David D., Marie W. Meteer (Vaughan), and James D. Pustejovsky (1987) 'Factors Contributing to Efficiency in Natural Language Generation', in Kempen (ed.) *Natural Language Generation*, Martinus Nijhoff Publishers, Dordrecht, The Netherlands, p. 159-182.

Meteer, Marie W. (1988) 'Defining a Vocabulary for Text Planning' *Proceedings of the AAAI-88 Workshop on Text Planning and Generation*, St. Paul, Minnesota, August 25, 1988.

Meteer, Marie W. (1989) *The SPOKESMAN Natural Language Generation System*, BBN Technical Report 7090.

Strunk and White (1979) The Elements of Style, 3rd edition, MacMillan Publishing Co. New York, NY.

Talmy, Leonard (1987) 'The Relation of Grammar to Cognition' (ed) B. Rudzka-Ostyn, *Topics in Cognitive Linguistics*, John Benjamins.

Wyrick, Jean (1984) *Steps to Writing Well: A concise guide to composition*, Holt, Rinehart, and Winston, New York, NY.

Chapter 7

POPEL – A Parallel and Incremental Natural Language Generation System

Norbert Reithinger

Abstract: This contribution presents an overview of POPEL, a natural language generation system that is part of the XTRA dialog system. POPEL's main features are: bidirectional interaction between the "what-to-say" and the "how-to-say" components, incremental selection and realization of the utterance, and the generation of pointing gestures adapted to the user. The "what-to-say" component consists of a selector which determines the conceptual content, an activator which passes the conceptual units to the realizer, a request handler for requests resulting from the verbalization process, and a context handler which handles the choice of descriptions. The decisions made by these components are based heavily on contextual knowledge. The "how-to-say" component is especially designed for the requirements of POPEL. Using intermediate linguistic based descriptions, it translates the non-linguistically oriented representation of the content into natural language. The gesture generator ZORA determines and visualizes pointing gestures based on domain dependent rules. POPEL is realized on a (simulated) parallel processor.

7.1   INTRODUCTION

The starting point for the generator presented here was the development of a dialog system requiring natural language output. Therefore, the entire generation module had to be designed.

A major constraint was that the generator has to be fully integrated in the overall system and has to use the knowledge base of the entire dialog system.

Thus, the natural language generation (NLG) system POPEL[1] — the generator in XTRA[2] — has been designed as a generator which pays special attention to discourse phenomena and integration in the overall system.

XTRA, a natural language access system to expert systems (3), is briefly described in the following section. Section 7.3 gives a short survey on context-specific knowledge that is to be used in an NLG system designed for discourse processing. Section 7.4 outlines the principles behind POPEL's architecture. The following three sections present the three components of POPEL.

7.2   THE NATURAL LANGUAGE ACCESS SYSTEM XTRA

XTRA allows for natural language communication (in German) with a connected expert system. From user input, it extracts data relevant to the expert system, answers terminology related inquiries and provides verbalizations of results and explanations given by the expert system that are tailored to the user. In addition to natural language, pointing gestures to a graphic presented on a terminal screen can be used to refer to information concerning the domain that is presented visually. The first (and current) domain is an expert system which assists a user in filling out a German annual tax withholding adjustment form.

The fact that POPEL is a part of a dialog system — and not a stand-alone system — poses various restrictions on its internal structure. For example, because POPEL is integrated in the XTRA system, it has to use the knowledge base of that system. Both the user's input and the system's reaction must be processed by means of the same representations in order to enable mutual access to the contributions of the dialog partner.

The basic knowledge representation formalism of XTRA is SB-ONE (14; 22), a representation language similar to KL-ONE. Two different knowledge sources within the system are defined using this language. One is the *functional-semantic structure* (FSS), which represents, on its terminological level, linguistically well-formed predicate/argument structures of German sentences where

---

[1] POPEL is an acronym for "Production Of {Perhaps, Possibly, P...} Eloquent Language".
[2] XTRA is an acronym for " eXpert TRAnslator"

concepts serve as semantic predicates and links represent functional roles between concepts. During generation or analysis, individualizations of FSS structures are generated.

The other SB-ONE based knowledge source is the *conceptual knowledge base* (CKB), which is non-linguistically oriented. The structure of the terminological level of the CKB depends on the domain and is designed to be well suited for interactions with the connected expert system and the inference component internal to XTRA. For instance, it is possible (and quite usual) that a role in the CKB has to be expressed linguistically as a predicate.

An interface enables communication between the CKB and the expert system and supplies the expert system with information. It also connects the CKB with the declarative knowledge of the expert system, thus making possible a uniform view of both knowledge sources by means of SB-ONE access functions.

7.3 CONTEXTUAL KNOWLEDGE FOR DISCOURSE PROCESSING

A discourse processing system relies heavily on contextual knowledge. In order to provide an impression of the contextual knowledge that is used in the XTRA system, a short overview is given. Again, the knowledge sources are used and updated both by the analysis and the generation components.

7.3.1 User Model

If an NLG system is to produce dialog contributions that will fit the user's needs and wants, a user model must exist, which contains assumptions about the user's state of knowledge – for a general discussion on user models see (15). The generation of descriptions (13) or the generation of explanations (12), among other things, presuppose such a model.

The user modeling component of XTRA, which models the knowledge states of both the user and the system — the indexbeliefbelief, goal and plan maintenance system BGP-MS — partitions the conceptual knowledge source into different contexts. For example, the partition MB (mutual beliefs) contains those chunks of knowledge that are known by both dialog partners. BPG-MS provides functions to determine for each part of the CKB whether it is known by the user, whether the user believes that the system knows it, and so on. There is also an inheritance hierarchy between the different partitions. For instance, SB (system beliefs) inherits the contents of MB.

Since the wants of the system with respect to the user are also represented by BGP-MS, the results of the reasoning process of XTRA — or the connected expert system — which are to be communicated to the user are stored in a separate partition, labeled SWMB (system wants a mutual belief to exist). It contains the (factual) knowledge the system wants to be known by both dialog partners after a dialog contribution has been generated by POPEL. This is the partition from which the generator starts when invoked.

7.3.2 Discourse Structure

Another important contextual knowledge source for an NLG system is a discourse structure model. This model stores the structure of the previous discourse and the underlying intentions.

Theories of discourse and its structure exist – e.g., (9), (23), (16), (21). Based on these theories, we are currently developing a discourse model which is part of UNSIN (24). It is structured according to the suggestions presented in (9) and consists of the *linguistic dialog memory* (LDM) that stores the *attentional structure* of the previous dialog and the *intentional structure*.

The intentional structure represents the purpose of the whole dialog and the purposes of the dialog segments. Given task-oriented dialogs like those which processes XTRA, this structure is determined both by the structure of the expert system's task and actions like 'request for clarification' which are unrelated to the task. Although XTRA currently has no genuine discourse processing component which has control over this structure, we (partially) simulate this structure to exploit its effects for the other components of XTRA.

As one of these components, the linguistic dialog memory which represents the attentional state requires such a structure. The LDM consists of three parts

- referential objects

- the dialog sequence memory

- the dialog context memory

Each object introduced into the dialog — whether an element of the visual context or an object introduced verbally — is represented as a *referential object*. It consists of links to other knowledge sources of the system. One link is to the conceptual representation of the object in the CKB. The other components are pairs of pointers. One pointer refers to a functional semantic structure for this object, while the other refers to the dialog sequence memory, marking the position in the dialog at which this linguistic description for the conceptual entity was used. Therefore, a referential object contains the information as to which object was introduced in the dialog at which time and how it was subsequently referred to in different thematic contexts.

The *dialog sequence memory* represents the sequence of dialog contributions of both the system and the user. Apart from the representation of the sequence, each element also stores a focus value and links the corresponding referential object of the contribution to the representation of the attentional state, the *dialog context memory*.

The dialog is structured by this memory according to the dialog segment purposes. A *context space*, which is the basic structure of the dialog context memory, contains pointers to the elements in the sequence memory which contribute to a certain discourse segment purpose.

Each context space has a certain *state*. For example, the currently active space is *active*. If the intentional structure has changed and a segment that is not part of the current context space's purpose is analysed or generated, a *context-move* is generated. Depending on the type of the context-move, the former *active* space gets a new state (e.g., *closed*) and a new context space is created. If a connection exists between the segment purpose of the new context space and the segment purpose of an already existing one, a link is created between them, annotated with the type of the relation (e.g., a *return* to a context space which has been interrupted).

With this structure, the LDM represents the structure of the dialog with respect to the various discourse segment purposes and their mutual dependencies. It combines the theories of Grosz and Sidner on the one hand, and Reichman's on the other. A dominance hierarchy, representing discourse segment purposes and a kind of 'focus' stack, is represented by the connections between the context spaces. But a description of the interrelationships between differentdiscourse segments, like the one provided by Reichman's theory, is given as well.

7.4 THE ARCHITECTURE OF POPEL

7.4.1 A Classification of Generation Systems

Today, most generation systems distinguish between a "what-to-say" part, where the content of the utterance is determined, and a "how-to-say" part, where the linguistic realization takes place. According to the nature of the data flow between these two parts there are three different architectural models of NLG systems:

- sequential models: a unidirectional data flow exists from the "what-to-say" to the "how-to-say" part (e.g., MUMBLE (17)).

- models with feedback: bidirectional communication between the two parts is possible (e.g., PAULINE (10)).

- integrated models: no distinction is made between the two parts (e.g., KAMP (Appelt, 1985)).

Each model has its advantages and disadvantages. Advantages of the models are, amongst others: the adaptability of a "how-to-say" component to different systems in the *sequential model*, a clear separation of knowledge sources in the *feedback model*, which, however, allows necessary interactions between them, and a uniform approach to generation in the *integrated model*.

But each model also has its disadvantages. In the *sequential model*, a "what-to-say" component has either to plan without linguistic restrictions or has to contain additional linguistic knowledge itself. In the *feedback model*, any part of the generator is difficult to port. And in the *integrated model*, control knowledge is spread throughout the knowledge sources.

7.4.2   POPEL – a Model with Feedback

It was mentioned above that the conceptual knowledge of XTRA — the level where POPEL begins — is encoded non-linguistically. Consequently, a "what-to-say" component in a sequential model must contain additional linguistic information in order to select a message that can be rendered as text. An integrated model would cause major problems, since the common use of knowledge sources by both the analysis and generation components does not allow generation-specific planning knowledge to be spread throughout the knowledge sources.

POPEL's architecture (see Figure 7.1) follows the second model: it is realized as a system with feedback. The "what-to-say" component, called *POPEL-WHAT*, has to decide — for a given discourse-independent content — which CKB structures should be included or excluded in a dialog contribution and in which order to utter them. The selection decisions are based on the contextual information discussed in section 7.3 and on linguistic restrictions from the realization component, called *POPEL-HOW*. POPEL-HOW maps the conceptual description onto a domain-independent semantic description, builds a syntactic description of the utterance, inflects the words, and finally, prints them on the screen. During the generation process, POPEL-WHAT also decides whether the reference to a conceptual entity can and should be accompanied with a pointing gesture. If this is possible, it passes the information to the gesture generation component ZORA which selects and visualizes an appropriate gesture on the terminal screen.

Feedback between the modules will take place in the following cases:

- *linguistic requirements regarding the content of the utterance*: due to the domain-dependent encoding of the CKB, linguistic restrictions may arise during the realization of the utterance that are not accounted for in the selected conceptual representation. For example, if a conceptual entity is mapped onto a verb, another conceptual entity has to be selected that can be realized as the verb's subject. However, if this piece of knowledge is

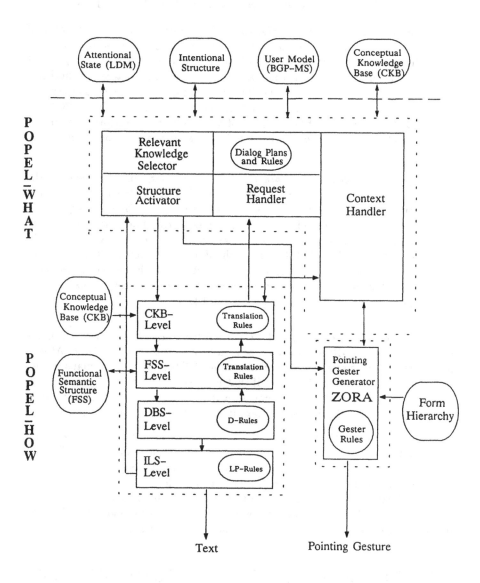

Figure 7.1: The architecture of POPEL

already known by the user, it may not be considered as something that has to be selected by POPEL-WHAT at first. POPEL-WHAT will consider the possible inclusion only if a request is made by POPEL-HOW.

- *selection of descriptions*: POPEL-WHAT does not know what part of the conceptual representation is to be verbalized as a verb or a noun phrase. POPEL-HOW, on the other side, doesn't know anything about the discourse context in which a description is to be uttered. Whether a noun phrase or a pronominal will be generated, and which words to choose can only be determined if both parts interact. Additionally, if POPEL-HOW decides to verbalize a part of the CKB as a description, POPEL-WHAT can determine whether a pointing gesture should be generated by ZORA.

- *sequence of selections within a sentence*: in German, the order of the phrases which are arguments of the verb is largely dependent upon the focus value of the facts expressed by these phrases. Facts already known are uttered immediately after the inflected verb while new or important ones are placed near the end of the sentence or before the verb. POPEL-HOW tells POPEL-WHAT about the dynamic structure of the sentence just generated so that the latter can determine the selection sequence of CKB structures according to an importance value computed from the current focus information stored in the LDM.

Interactions are only useful if POPEL-WHAT does not pass a complete message to POPEL-HOW. Instead, selection proceeds *incrementally*. After a part of the CKB is selected for verbalization, POPEL-HOW first maps it onto a semantic description and then — if that is successful — onto a syntactic one. During these processes, the aforementioned information feedback takes place and influences the selection of the next items to be selected from the CKB.

This requires that the parts of the generator have to run parallel and not sequentially. While POPEL-WHAT selects the next parts out of the CKB for verbalization, POPEL-HOW can go on with the verbalization of the previously selected parts and ZORA generates a gesture parallel to this. But also within POPEL-HOW, the processing of an utterance represented in the various levels proceeds in parallel. Since we do not have a parallel processor available, the implementation of POPEL is based on a simulation system.

7.5   THE STRUCTURE OF POPEL-WHAT

In contrast to TEXT (McKeown, 1985) which first determines the entire relevant knowledge pool and then selects from this pool, POPEL-WHAT starts from a core representation — the content of SWMB. This core can be expanded if additional requirements during the generation process occur. Additionally,

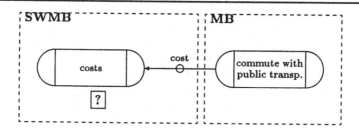

Figure 7.2: An example for the content of SWMB.

the intentional structure contains a goal which the system wants to achieve with the utterance to be generated.[3]

An example for the content of SWMB is given in Figure 7.2. The corresponding intentional goal is

(SWMB (REQUEST H *costs cost*))

The goal expresses that the system wants to know the costs of daily commuting. It may be verbalized as

Was kostet die Fahrt?
(How much is the trip?)

if the conceptual content which is expressed by "the trip" has already been mentioned during the discourse.

7.5.1 The Relevant Knowledge Selector

The relevant knowledge selector is responsible for the selection of the conceptual content that has to be included in the system's output in order to achieve the intentional goal and communicate the items stored in the partition SWMB. It also has to ensure that the sequence of the item's selection guarantees a coherent dialog. The goals can be simple ones like in the example above which can be directly achieved by simply saying the items. But they can also be complex one's like the request for the explanation of a CKB concept, e.g.,

(SMWB (KNOW H *tax-action*)).

---

[3]The two representations express partially the same wants of the system by different representations.

Therefore, a flexible framework is needed that handles both extremes presented with the examples, and that covers the range of phenomena that lie in between. We think that *Rhetorical Structure Theory* (16) (RST) provides such a framework. The relevant knowledge selector uses a modified version of the RST operationalisation as presented in (20) or (19) (both in this volume).[4]

The relevant knowledge consists of a top-down planner[5] that uses dialog plans. Each plan consists of the intended effect, a constraint, a nucleus and satellites. The conditions in the constraint slot of a plan consist of calls to the ASK interface of SB-ONE (1) and to the contextual knowledge sources. The latter enables a declarative encoding of contextual influences from the user model and the discourse structure on the plan selection process.

The plan which is used for the example in Figure 7.2 looks like

effect: (SWMB (REQUEST H ?range-iconcept ?irole))
constraints: ((IROLE ?irole ?domain-iconcept ?range-iconcept))
nucleus: (REQUEST S H ?range-iconcept ?irole ?domain-iconcept)
satellites: nil

During the instantiation the individualized concept *commute with public transp.* which was not in the SWMB partition is bound to the variable *?domain-iconcept*. The nucleus is a primitive speech act, which is then passed to the structure activator.

7.5.2   The Structure Activator

The structure activator receives the speech act and is the interface to POPEL-HOW and ZORA.

First, it passes the type of the speech act to POPEL-HOW. Then, it computes an importance value for each element of the SB-ONE expression. The assignment of the importance value is based on various criteria. For example, if there was a change in the dialog segment purpose, the topic bearing element gets the highest value. Elements which already have been mentioned get one that is computed via focus values of the LDM[6].

As mentioned in section 7.4.2, the linear precedence of nonverbal phrases in German sentences depends heavily on the importance of the fact expressed by the phrase. For example, in declarative sentences, the phrase which expresses the most important fact is placed in front of the finite verb, i.e., it must be

---

[4] The two articles also elaborate the use of RST for explanations and the use of contextual knowledge for the text planning process.

[5] Thanks to C. Paris and ISI who made it possible to use their planner as the starting point.

[6] The basic assignment rules are adapted from (23).

activated first. After the finite verb, however, the dynamic changes: given information is placed near the finite verb, while new or emphasized information is placed near the end of the sentence. If an NLG system for German has no information available for the computation of the importance of an item, it can fall back on default linearization rules. However, the output produced this way sounds unnatural or is boring at the very least.

In order to select the CKB objects with respect to the dynamic structure of the clause currently generated, POPEL-HOW sets a flag for POPEL-WHAT, which changes during the generation of a clause. If the value of the flag is *decreasing*, the elements to be verbalized are activated in decreasing importance value order. If it is *increasing*, the CKB objects with the lowest importance value are selected first and passed to POPEL-HOW. The sequence of the selection should be respected by POPEL-HOW, i.e., a reordering is allowed only if the verbalization of the given sequence would violate syntactic restrictions.

Before the activator passes an element to POPEL-HOW, it also checks whether there is a corresponding element in the graphic which can be pointed at. If this is true, it checks the feasibility of the gesture. For example, a pointing gesture is not created if the object has been introduced recently in the discourse and has still a high focus value. Gestures are used preferably for references to newly introduced, not focused objects (26).

In the above example the activator first passes the individualized concept *costs* to POPEL-HOW. It is marked with $\boxed{?}$ in the SWMB partition, which means that this is the item the system wants to request from the user. Therefore, it is the most important item to be verbalized.

7.5.3   The Request Handler

Parallel to the activation process, POPEL-WHAT handles the requests from POPEL-HOW concerning additionally needed CKB objects.

If POPEL-HOW requests an additional element of the CKB, its importance value is checked. If the value is zero, the request will not be fulfilled. POPEL-HOW must be able to handle such situations and generate the appropriate elliptical expressions.

If the importance value does not equal zero, the CKB object which is requested is activated and passed to POPEL-HOW.

7.5.4   The Context Handler

During the generation of descriptions, both parts of POPEL interact to generate an appropriate surface form. The *context handler* is the module of POPEL-WHAT which handles problems concerning descriptions.

If POPEL-HOW knows that a certain part of the CKB will be realized as a description, it asks the context handler whether this piece of knowledge is already known. If it is not in the SBUB[7] partition of BGP-MS, POPEL-HOW gets the message 'new'. It must compute the linguistic structure and the words for this description from scratch and use an indefinite article. If the CKB item is in SBUB but not in the LDM, it is in the (assumed) implicit knowledge of the user. POPEL-HOW gets an 'implicitly known' message from the context handler. The consequences will be the same as in the case of 'new' except that a definite article can be used.

If the LDM contains a referential object for the CKB item, the context handler will apply reference rules which are adapted from (23). For example, the rule for pronominalization states that only elements in high focus in a currently active context space may be referred to pronominally.

If the rules allow the generation of a pronoun, POPEL-WHAT additionally asks POPEL-HOW whether the already realized part of the sentence also allows the generation of a pronoun – see e.g., (25). For instance, in German, it is hardly possible to generate a pronominal NP if a lexical NP or PP after the finite verb exists, and a pronominal NP is to follow this phrase (6). If the tests are positive, a pronoun can be generated.

In all other cases, a definite description has to be generated. The selection of the attributes is determined in part by the reference rules and the descriptions already used for the same object. They are accessible through the referential object for the CKB object.

For the above example, the referential expression "the trip" is generated because the individualized CKB concept *commute with public transp.* has been introduced earlier, e.g., with the sentence

> Ich fahre täglich von hier mit einem Bus nach Völklingen.
> (I commute daily from here to Völklingen by bus.)

If the reference is to an element which was mentioned for the last time in a context-space not connected to the current *active* one, the context handler can add metacommunicative or text deictic statements, e.g., the dialog purpose of the context-space which contains the last reference

> ...the insurance company *that was mentioned in the section deductibles* ...

---

[7]System believes that user believes

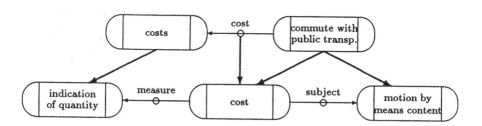

Figure 7.3: The mapping from the CKB level to the FSS level.

7.6   THE STRUCTURE OF POPEL-HOW

7.6.1   The Four Levels of POPEL-HOW

Starting with the CKB, there are four different processing levels in POPEL-HOW (8) which must be passed through before the generated text is printed on the screen. Beginning at the conceptual level, a semantic description of the utterance is created in the FSS level. The next two levels are related to the syntactic structure of the utterance. The *dependency based structure* (DBS) contains the syntactic dominance representation of the utterance's phrases, while in the *inflection and linearization* level (ILS level), the linear precedence is determined. This is also the level where the words are inflected with the package MORPHIX (7).

The transition between the CKB level and FSS level is governed by transformation rules which are attached to the concepts of the source knowledge structure. Each rule contains a possible translation for the source concept and its roles into the target knowledge base, and conditions which must be fulfilled by the attribute descriptions of the source structure for the rule to apply.

Between the FSS level and the DBS level, a given concept on the general level of the FSS contains rules with possible mappings from individualizations to syntactic phrases and from semantic roles to syntactic relations.

Figure 7.3 shows the mapping from the CKB level to the FSS level for the example. The individualized concept *costs* is mapped to *indication of quantity* on the FSS level. For the individualized concept *commute with public transp.* three different rules are applicable. One rule maps the concept to *motion by means content* on the FSS level, another maps the role *cost* to an object representing the concept *cost*. These mappings are shown in the figure. The third rule maps the CKB individualization to an object representing *motion by means*. Since

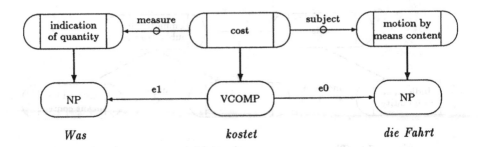

Figure 7.4: The mapping from the FSS level to the DBS level.

this object finds no connection to the other objects on the FSS level, it cannot apply rules to map itself into the DBS level.

For the example, Figure 7.4 shows the mapping from the FSS level to the DBS level and the resulting sentence. The labels *e0* and *e1* stand for the syntactic relation between the verb and the noun phrases. e0 means subject, e1 direct object (see also 7.6.3).

It is assumed that the mapping of an utterance's representation from one level to another is made up of the mapping of its components. The incremental processing with feedback in the first three levels is based on this composition-ality.

If the representation structure of an utterance's part is created within a processing level, it is tested whether a rule that will create or augment a structure in the target level is applicable. The transformation rule may apply to an atomic structure in one level, but may also require the existence of attribute structures. If a rule is applicable, processing proceeds in the target level as well as in the processing level.

If no rule is applicable, it is tested as to which precondition of a rule must be satisfied, i.e., it is checked which attribute must be added so that a rule can be applied. This missing attribute is translated back to the level 'above' as a request with respect to the already existing structure in that level. If a level receives a request which cannot be satisfied, it will map it to the next level. A request in the CKB level is finally passed to POPEL-WHAT which will consider this linguistically motivated request in further planning.

The selection of words is performed in two steps. While CKB structures are translated into FSS structures, the *content words* — e.g., verbs and nouns — are selected. In the first realization of POPEL-HOW, discrimination networks are used for this task. The selection of *function words* that depends on the selected semantic or syntactic structure of the utterance — e.g., prepositions which depend on the meaning of the verb — is performed during the mapping between the FSS level and the DBS level.

7.6.2 Parallel Verbalization in POPEL-HOW

If a piece of knowledge is inserted in a processing level of POPEL-HOW, an independent *active object* which — in the ideal case — has its own processor is created. The connections between the units of the knowledge representation formalism correspond to links between the active objects and are used for message passing. Each object knows only about its local connections. In the levels which are based on SB-ONE, an individualization is such an active object and the roles correspond to the links. In the DBS level, the active objects correspond to the nodes of the dependency-based tree and the links correspond to the syntactic relations between them.

Therefore, each level — except the ILS level, which is a single process — is a distributed system of independently running active objects. The topology of the network corresponds to the structure of the underlying representation.

As outlined before, POPEL-WHAT activates the parts of the utterance in a piecemeal fashion. The consequence for POPEL-HOW is that the active objects for an utterance are not created all at once. Rather, processing proceeds in a cascade fashion.

7.6.3 Syntactic Knowledge

There are good reasons to separate knowledge concerning dominance relations and linear precedence, especially in incremental NLG systems (5) (this volume). Also, for a language with a relatively free word order like German, this separation facilitates syntactic processing. POPEL-GRAM, the grammar of the generator, follows this approach.

Its linguistic background is *dependency*, an approach continental linguists are quite familiar with (c.f. (27), (6)). The fundamental relation in this formalism is the dominance relation between a head and its modifiers. For instance, the head of a sentence is the *verb*, with the *noun phrases* being determined by the valency of the verb as its modifiers. A dependency-based representation of a sentence also supports incremental generation: a phrase which is to be added is simply attached to its head.

Processing in the DBS level differs from that within the CKB level and the FSS level. The task is not to apply rules which map a given structure onto another. Rather, while the dependency-based tree is built up, the feature exchange has to be executed. If a node in the tree has received all relevant information necessary for inflection, its description is passed to the ILS level.

Since a dependency tree contains words in both the nodes and the leaves, it does not explicitly represent the linear order of the sentence. There must be a separate component which linearizes the tree. The linearization takes place in POPEL-HOW in the ILS level.

POPEL-GRAM is formulated in the PATR-II formalism (28). The basic data structure of PATR-II is a directed acyclic graph (DAG) — the basic operation is unification on these graphs. The original interpretation of the PATR-II formalism does not allow for the definition of grammars which separate the dominance relation from the linear precedence. Therefore, the interpretation of the rules has been modified. There are two different sets of grammar rules which are processed in different levels of POPEL-HOW. In the DBS level, the context free part of the rules is interpreted as the dominance part which builds up the syntactical structure (D-Rules), while in the ILS level, the rules are used as constraints for the syntactically correct order of phrases (LP-Rules).

For example, the DAG for the interrogative pronoun *was* on the DBS level is

```
[O: [CAT: E1
     FSET: [ANAPHER: +
            HEAD: [STEM: "was"]
            SYNTAX: [ARTICLE: WITHOUT
                     CASE: AKK
                     GENDER: FEM
                     NUMBER: SG
                     PERSON: 3
                     VOICE: ACTIVE]
            SYNCHRONIZE: [DOWN: [CASE: <O FSET SYNTAX CASE>]
                         UP: [VOICE: ACTIVE]]
            SURFACE:
            [NP: [NP-ENG:
                  [INTERROGATIVPRONOMEN:
                         [STEM: <O FSET HEAD STEM>
                          SYNTAX: <O FSET SYNTAX>]]]]]
     PROCESS: [ALLOWED-TO-SEND-P: +
               COMPLETE-P: +
               INDEX: 1
               SUBDAG-CHANGED-P: -]]
 1: [CAT: NP
     FSET: [SYNCHRONIZE: [DOWN: [ARTICLE: <O FSET SYNTAX ARTICLE>
                                CASE: <O FSET SYNTAX CASE>
                                GENDER: <O FSET SYNTAX GENDER>
                                NUMBER: <O FSET SYNTAX NUMBER>
                                PERSON: <O FSET SYNTAX PERSON>]]
            ANAPHER: <O FSET ANAPHER>
            HEAD: <O FSET HEAD>
            SYNTAX: <O FSET SYNTAX>
            SURFACE: <O FSET SURFACE NP>]]
     ARITY: 1]
```

7.6.4   Syntactical Processing in a Distributed System

In the SB-ONE based levels each active object directly corresponds to a unit of the representation language. Such a direct correspondence does not exist in the the DBS level.

The representation in the DBS level is divided up into two parts. The topology of the active object's network represents the dependency-based tree. Additionally, each object has an internal structure consisting of the syntactic description of this phrase by means of DAGs.

Besides the basic operations of active objects, the objects in the DBS level use methods in order to process DAGs. For example, two connected objects must exchange syntactic features. Therefore, their DAGs are unified, which is performed by a search algorithm using the rules of POPEL-GRAM.

Since a conceptual unit may have alternative readings, it is possible that the DBS level contains competing active objects which express these readings. Therefore, methods for the active objects were defined to cope with this problem, for example methods to synchronize competing objects.

The PROCESS feature in the example DAG is used to collect process related information. The SYNCHRONIZE feature contains all features of a local DAG which might be changed, if the context of the object is changed by a competing object.

7.7   THE GESTURE GENERATOR ZORA

Communication between the user and XTRA is not only possible by means of natural language, but also by the use of pointing gestures to a graphic object which is presented on the terminal screen. Within XTRA, the processing of pointing gestures is based on the *simulation approach* which simulates natural pointing gestures. In contrast, the *performance approach* achieves the functionality of natural pointing gestures with functional equivalents, e.g., framing the object. For a further discussion on the conditions of the use of pointing gestures during generation see (26).

From the viewpoint of an NL dialog system, pointing actions are descriptions which are accompanied by a pointing gesture. They focus the user's visual attention and can therefore localize visual objects. As mentioned above, if the structure activator notes during the generation of an element of the CKB that there is a link to an item on the graphic, it may activate ZORA, the pointing gesture generator.

ZORA (11) provides a flexible, rule-based framework for the selection and visualisation of gestures. It is based on rules which classify the item on the graphic according to geometric patterns, determine its form-specific type, link the type to a gesture and define the gestures by means of atomic actions e.g., *move left, move right, draw circle.*

The algorithm consists of four steps. The first is the preprocessing phase which computes geometric features of the object to point at. Next comes the classification phase which determines the object's type and a set of suitable gestures. In the selection phase the best fitting gesture is computed, using an anticipation feedback loop. In this loop, the possible gestures are processed by the analysis component TACTILUS-II (2) to simulate the user's understanding of the gesture. The anticipation of the user's understanding allows for a correction of the gesture, if the intended item on the graphic was not recognized by TACTILUS-II which indicates that the reference might fail. In the final phase, ZORA visualises the gesture by displaying an icon on the graphic, e.g., a hand holding a pencil.

7.8   CONCLUSION AND FUTURE WORK

In this paper, an outline of the design principles and the architecture of POPEL is presented. The most important features of POPEL are

- division into a "what-to-say", a "how-to-say" and a gesture generation component,
- interaction between the components in a limited and controlled way, both backwards and forwards,
- incremental generation,
- extensive use of context-related knowledge — i.e., knowledge about discourse structure and a user model,
- generation from a non-linguistically coded knowledge source,
- generation of multimodal output,
- parallel generation of language.

A prototype of POPEL exists and runs on a Symbolics 36xx lisp machine — including the simulation of the parallel processor which is based on the process facilities of the lisp machine. In order to demonstrate the validity of POPEL's approach to parallel verbalization, no special simulation environment was implemented. Rather, the scheduler of the lisp machine is used without intervention by POPEL.

While the development of ZORA is finished, the main emphasis of the future work will be on the extension of POPEL-HOW and the further implementation of POPEL-WHAT. The planner will be integrated and more plans have to be written. Also, the context handler will be rebuilt according to the presented specifications.

ACKNOWLEDGMENTS

The author thanks to Wolfgang Finkler, Günter Neumann, Jürgen Jung, Axel Kresse, Ralph Schäfer, Cécile Paris, and the anonymous reviewers. The work presented here is being supported by the German Science Foundation (DFG) in its Special Collaborative Program on AI and Knowledge-Based Systems (SFB 314), project N1 (XTRA).

BIBLIOGRAPHY

[1] J. Allgayer. $\mathcal{L}_{SB-ONE^+}$: *Die Zugangssprache zu* **SB-ONE$^+$**. Memo, Univ. des Saarlandes, 1989.

[2] J. Allgayer. Eine Graphikkomponente zur Integration von Zeigehandlungen in natürlichsprachliche KI-Systeme. In *Proceedings der 16. GI-Jahrestagung*, pages 284–298, Springer, Berlin, 1986.

[3] J. Allgayer, R. Jansen-Winkeln, C. Reddig, and N. Reithinger. Bidirectional use of knowledge in the multi-modal NL access system XTRA. In *11. IJCAI*, Morgan Kaufmann, Los Angeles, CA., 1989.

[4] D. Appelt. *Planning English Sentences*. Cambridge University Press, Cambridge, 1985.

[5] K. DeSmedt and G. Kempen. The representation of grammatical knowledge in a model for incremental sentence generation. In *Natural Language Generation in Artificial Intelligence and Computational Linguistics*, (this volume). Paris, Swartout, Mann (Eds). Kluwer Academic Publishers, Norwell, MA, 1990.

[6] U. Engel. *Deutsche Grammatik*. Julius Groos, Heidelberg, 1988.

[7] W. Finkler and G. Neumann. MORPHIX — a fast realization of a classification-based approach to morphology. In Harald Trost, editor, *4. Österreichische Artificial-Intelligence-Tagung, Wiener Workshop Wissensbasierte Sprachverarbeitung*, pages 11–19, Springer, Berlin, 1988.

[8] W. Finkler and G. Neumann. POPEL-HOW – a distributed parallel model for incremental natural language production with feedback. In *11. IJCAI*, Morgan Kaufmann, Los Angeles, CA., 1989.

[9] B.J. Grosz and C.L. Sidner. Attention, intentions, and the structure of discourse. *Computational Linguistics*, 12(3):175–204, July–September 1986.

[10] E. Hovy. *Generating Natural Language Under Pragmatic Constraints*. PhD thesis, Yale University, 1987.

[11] J. Jung, A. Kresse, N. Reithinger, and R. Schäfer. Das System ZORA – Wissensbasierte Generierung von Zeigegesten. In D. Metzing, editor, *GWAI-89*, Springer, Berlin, 1989.

[12] R. Kass and T. Finin. *The need for user models in generating expert system explanations*. Technical Report MS-CIS-87-86, Department of Computer and Information Science, University of Philadelphia, 1987.

[13] A. Kobsa. *Benutzermodellierung in Dialogsystemen*. Springer, Berlin, 1985.

[14] A. Kobsa. The SB-ONE representation workbench. In *Workshop on formal aspects of semantic networks*, Santa Catalina Island, CA., 1989.

[15] A. Kobsa and W. Wahlster, editors. *User Models in Dialog Systems. Symbolic Computation Series*, Springer, Berlin, 1988.

[16] W.C. Mann and S.A. Thompson. *Rhetorical Structure Theory: A Theory of Text Organisation*. Technical Report ISI/RS-87-190, USC/ISI, Marina del Rey, CA., 1987.

[17] D.D. McDonald. Surface generation for a variety of applications. In *National Computer Conference*, pages 105–110, 1985.

[18] K.R. McKeown. *Text generation*. Cambridge University Press, Cambridge, 1985.

[19] J.D. Moore and W.R. Swartout. A reactive approach to explanation: Taking the user's feedback into account. In *Natural Language Generation in Artificial Intelligence and Computational Linguistics*, (this volume). Paris, Swartout, Mann (Eds). Kluwer Academic Publishers, Norwell, MA, 1990.

[20] C.L. Paris. Generation and explanation: building an explanation facility for the explainable expert systems framework. In *Natural Language Generation in Artificial Intelligence and Computational Linguistics*, (this volume). Paris, Swartout, Mann (Eds). Kluwer Academic Publishers, Norwell, MA, 1990.

[21] L. Polanyi. *The Linguistic Discourse Model: Towards a Formal Theory of Discourse Structure*. Technical Report 6409, BBN Laboratories, Cambridge, MA., 1986.

[22] H.-J. Profitlich. *SB-ONE: Ein Wissensrepräsentationssystem basierend auf KL-ONE*. Master's thesis, Universität des Saarlandes, Saarbrücken, 1989.

[23] R. Reichman. *Getting Computers to Talk Like You and Me*. MIT Press, Cambridge, MA., 1985.

[24] N. Reithinger. *Dialogstrukturen in XTRA*. Memo, Universität des Saarlandes, Saarbrücken, 1989. To appear.

[25] N. Reithinger. Generating referring expressions and pointing gestures. In Gerard Kempen, editor, *Natural Language Generation*, pages 71–81, Martinus Nijhoff, Dordrecht, 1987.

[26] D. Schmauks and N. Reithinger. Generating multimodal output — conditions, advantages and problems. In *12th COLING*, pages 584–588, Budapest, 1988.

[27] P. Sgall, E. Hajičová, and J. Panevová. *The Meaning of the Sentence in its Semantic and Pragmatic Aspects*. Reidel, Dordrecht, 1987.

[28] S.M. Shieber, H. Uszkoreit, F.C.N Pereira, J.J. Robinson, and M. Tyson. The formalism and implementation of PATR-II. In *Research on interactive acquisition and use of knowledge*, pages 39–79, SRI International, Menlo Park, CA, 1983.

Chapter 8

Tailoring output to the user: What does user modelling in generation mean?

Karen Sparck Jones

Abstract: This paper examines the implications, for linguistic output generation tailored to the interactive system user, of earlier analyses of the components of user modelling and of the constraints realism imposes on modelling. Using a range of detailed examples it argues that tailoring based only on the actual dialogue and on the decision model required for the system task is quite adequate, and that more ambitious modelling is both dangerous and unnecessary.

8.1   INTRODUCTION

There is a general presumption that natural language output generated by interactive systems should be tailored to the user. Thus in question answering or dialogue, outputs should not only be linguistically fitting, e.g., be anaphorically coherent, and appropriate in content, e.g., give answers to questions; they should provide cooperative responses, e.g., by volunteering information, based on the inferred beliefs, goals etc of the user (Webber, 1986). Tailoring output to the user, in other words, assumes a model of the user (Kobsa and Wahlster, 1989).

But what does this imply? Does having an individual user model mean that the system should always be looking for, and address, the person behind the user's inputs, forming hypotheses about the person that influence both the content and form of outputs, whether these convey information to, or seek further information from, the user? Or is the user no more than his inputs, so generation should just fit these? In much work on interactive systems there is a tacit assumption that the more tailoring the better, which is taken to imply that the more intensive and extensive the modelling the better. This seems natural for the advisory or consultation paradigm within which many application systems fall; and it seems plausible by analogy with interaction between humans given the aim of making human-machine interaction as much like human-human interaction as possible (as tacitly assumed in e.g., Grosz and Sidner, 1986).

I have argued in earlier papers that user modelling as a whole has many elements, and that this complex notion needs unpacking for a proper approach to modelling in any particular case. I have also argued that the difficulty of obtaining robust enough information means that modelling should be very conservative. In this paper I shall look specifically at what this means for generation. The conclusion is that, in a fundamental sense, the user is indeed his inputs. I am not claiming this as an original conclusion. My aim is rather to explore and make clear, using my previous analysis, what this interpretation of user modelling implies for output tailoring. The argument is thus that we should be doing what we are doing, but not for the reasons commonly taken for granted; and if the grounds for model-based generation are not those usually assumed, what constitute rational aims for the future are not those usually assumed either. My concerns are therefore with the basis for generation, and not with the specific mechanisms of generation.

Section 8.2 1 recapitulates my previous analysis: this somewhat lengthy preamble is needed to provide an adequate framework for the subsequent discussion. In Section 8.3, I consider some (hypothetical) example systems designed to illustrate alternative approaches to tailoring output. In Section 8.4, I look at the implications of these examples for the characterisation of user models. Section 8.5 then considers what follows from this for generation, with a further example. Section 8.6 summarises the argument and conclusions. I shall try to flesh out the distinction between modelling the user in a strong sense as an autonomous human individual with characteristics which are not relevant to the functional task for which the system is designed, and modelling in a more restricted sense limited to those characteristics that are relevant to the system's task, and examine what follows from this distinction for output generation with natural language interfaces. In practice hitherto there has been no call for this distinction, mainly because our system tasks and modelling capabilities have been limited, but also because maintaining dialogue is deemed a system task. Maintaining dialogue is, however, an essentially subordinate task: it is possible to separate a system's primary decision task - diagnosing a disease, determining a flight booking - from dependent support tasks, like gathering information and communicating decisions. In modelling, therefore, the main question about how the user is viewed is in relation to the system's primary decision task. However any need to communicate a system decision depends on some view of the user which may presuppose some characteristics not needed for primary decision purposes, and modelling beyond decision data is to that extent justified. Indeed interacting comprehensibly and cooperatively in natural language may require a rather more substantial view, in his role as discourse participant, of the user. But these considerations still only imply a generically based and restricted approach to modelling, and hence a moderate approach to output tailoring.

8.2   BACKGROUND

In previous papers (Sparck Jones, 1984, 1989) I considered user modelling in a wide variety of contexts, to provide a general framework within which particular systems with specific tasks and domains, and modelling conditions, could be placed. My aim was to supply the base for a proper analysis in approaching modelling in any particular case. I identified both several classes of modelling factor and a range of system functions, implying a complex set of possibilities for modelling to serve functional requirements.

Thus modelling has to take into account the user's role in relation to the system: there are two possible roles, patient, referring to the subject of the system's primary decision making, and agent, referring to the system's driver. There may be systems with only one human role, as patient or as agent, or systems with both roles, which may be filled by the same or distinct people: the last in particular may imply a rich modelling situation.[1] Modelling has also to take the status of the user's properties into account: they may be decision properties for the system's primary task, or other, non-decision properties. The nature of the user's properties is relevant as well: they may be broadly

---

[1] I shall use "user" generically where the point applies to either patient or agent, and whether or not distinct human beings are involved: where any of these distinctions apply, and they are not made explicitly, they should be clear from the context.

categorised as objective (and hence relatively accessible and uncontroversial), or subjective (as in beliefs and goals, which are generally less accessible). and also categorised as static (unchanging through a session with the system) or dynamic (changing over the session). These category distinctions cut across one another, and also across the decision/non-decision distinction, and may of course hold in quite different ways when there are distinct people as patient and agent.

At the same time, because modelling is done for a purpose, it is necessary to consider the different functions it can serve. The obvious one is effectiveness, the system's ability to reach a 'correct' decision. But it is also possible to address efficiency, the system's ability to reach a decision economically, and acceptability, the way what the system does and how it does it looks to the user. Acceptability is a complex notion, referring both to the intrinsic decision making of the system and to how this is presented to the user. In general, information about any property of a user in either role can be exploited to serve every function, with the exceptions that agents do not have decision properties and that effectiveness depends directly only on the patient's decision properties.

Thus in the social security illustration of (Sparck Jones, 1984, 1989) for example, the system used information about non-decision properties of the elderly patient, like her honesty and her ignorance of social security benefits, to control the acquisition of information about her income and to provide explanations making its announced decision more comprehensible and hence more acceptable to her, as well as information about her decision properties - age, disability, and so forth - to calculate the benefits themselves; and it used its agent model of the mediating clerk both to seek information using technical language and to bypass his supposed chauvinism. This and the other (hypothetical) systems considered in (Sparck Jones, 1984) show that though differences in the domain and task specifications cut very different ways on the distinctions made, these distinctions are always relevant, and modelling recognising them can influence system behaviour and performance. The examples showed in particular that the non-decision properties of patient and agent could in principle be significant, and that they should therefore be noted, checked, and used. These included, in the social security example for instance, the patient's honesty (not in itself a decision property for benefit calculations), and the agent's chauvinism.

Within the general framework of factors and functions, individual systems with different tasks and modes of use can impose quite different constraints on, or offer quite different opportunities for, modelling. Where there is a human patient, decision property modelling is of course required, but beyond that it has been tacitly assumed that modelling is always useful and hence desirable. Information about the user is obviously and also most naturally acquired for the patient role, and about decision properties (especially objective ones), to support modelling for effectiveness. But there are many difficulties in obtaining relevant and reliable information even here, and the value of modelling is much more problematic in relation to other user characteristics or system contexts.

This is clearly seen where the user's implicit beliefs and plans are important as they are patient decision properties, but is also the case in situations where other roles and property categories are relevant.

I therefore suggested in (Sparck Jones, 1989) that, for the kinds of system with very limited power we can currently envisage, where the evidence for modelling hypotheses is likely to be poor in quantity and quality, it is necessary to be conservative in modelling both in relation to the system's primary decision making, as in an expert system, and in relation to the system's conduct of its interaction with the user. The system should not be quick to make assumptions about the user, whether in seeking or providing information, and should be slow in abandoning general for specific grounds either in interpreting the user's inputs or in determining the form and content of its own outputs. Thus it is generally safer to avoid tailoring outputs on the basis of selective but poorly supported hypotheses about the user, and to seek more information from the user if this would not be oppressive or to proffer information on a neutral basis, and perhaps somewhat beyond the bare minimum. This applies both to the use of decision properties, especially where it is not necessary to attempt exhaustive data gathering before offering a candidate decision, and more importantly, to the use of non- decision properties. Thus with a notional travel advice system, it is not necessary to hypothesise from an inquiry about trains that the user is motivated by economy (price being a decision property and assuming trains are cheap), or alternatively by fear of flying (a non-decision property), to provide a perfectly adequate response, even if in principle adopting either of these specific hypotheses might lead to a more targeted one; in practice, with a poorly supported hypothesis about miserliness or fear (which would be only too likely), a targeted response could be very inappropriate, and it would be much safer to give straightforward train information. But even with a conservative approach it is important to recognise the various aspects of modelling I distinguished, for example that users can have different roles even where they are not different people, and that it may be feasible as well as useful to exploit modelling to serve several functions, as in output designed to promote both efficiency and effectiveness.

These discussions used expert (alias knowledge based) systems as examples, but with a wide definition, and were, moreover, intended to apply to a very broad range of situations involving computational systems and their human users, including those where the system's primary task is user independent, or where the human involved is more a subject than a user in the ordinary sense, or where interaction is slight, as well as those, like teaching systems, where the system exists for the sake of its user, and where it operates highly interactively. But even in cases where the user is more conspicuous there can be great variations, for example in the type of task, in the source of initiative in interaction and of direction in problem solving, and so forth.

In general, however, it was assumed that, within the framework of the system's global specification, referring to its task (e.g., diagnosis, dissemination),

domain (machines, law) and user class(es) (children, technicians), modelling
could in principle apply as much in less obvious cases, like process control, as
in the more obvious ones like consultation or instruction; it was further evident
not only that all the system's functions could involve modelling, but that to
support both the system's internal effectiveness and efficiency functions[2] and
its external acceptability function, the system's interaction with the user could
exploit all of the kinds of model data and hypotheses. Modelling may therefore, as the illustrative examples in (Sparck Jones, 1984, 1989) showed, be very
complex even if in practice, playing for safety implies radical simplification.

These discussions did not presuppose communication in language, and especially natural language, though natural language is a particularly powerful
means of communication and in general provides more support for modelling
than other means. However even where natural language is used for communication it may not always be required for both input to and output from
the system, though modelling can apply to either;[3] modelling may also apply
whether inputs or outputs occur independently, i.e., are not paired in any material sense, are essentially paired as in 'one-shot' exchanges, or form elements
of a more extensive dialogue; further, modelling may be relevant, especially for
the system's output, whether the output content is an end in itself, as in announcing a system decision, or is a means to an end, as in seeking more data.
Finally, modelling can be related to the form as well as the content both of the
system's output and its input. In this paper I shall consider only communication in free natural language, taking it for granted that it will be required both
for system input and system output, for a variety of specific purposes, whether
or not it is also the sole means of communication.

What my previous analysis implied, therefore, was that within a general
context presupposing cooperative behaviour on the system's part for those operations that are connected with its user(s),[4] the system's outputs can and
should be tailored to the user(s), i.e., in a given session to the one or more
individual users (agents and/or patients) involved. This applies whether information is being supplied or sought and whatever function is being served.
Of course the extent to which an output is motivated by the user will depend
on the system task, on its global and local state, and on the communicative
purpose of the output (reply versus signal) as well as on such features of the
user as their role; but it is commonly assumed that output should be tailored
to the user as an actual and not just representative individual. However as I
suggested in (Sparck Jones, 1989), the fact that modelling is notionally feasible
as well as apparently desirable is offset by the fact that it is difficult to get reliable modelling information, so caution is required in forming hypotheses and

---

[2] If effectiveness is in decisions about the user, outwardness is derived or secondary.

[3] For input I am considering here only modelling derived from interpretation and not
modelling required to achieve interpretation, though in general the points referring to the
former also refer to the latter; but for output I am of course considering modelling influencing
generation.

[4] An industrial plant controller, for instance, will have other concerns as well.

applying them to internal processes and external interaction.

Thus given the general framework outlined, I shall now consider the specific issue of tailoring output in more detail: what could tailoring output in principle, and what should it in practice, look like?

I shall try to answer these questions, and especially the second, through examples. The examples in the next section are designed to compare outputs pushing user modelling with alternatives adopting the more cautious approach advocated in (Sparck Jones, 1989), at particular points in a notional interaction. I have given a number of examples in order to show how the comparisons work across different contexts in terms of system tasks and user roles. The later and more elaborate illustration of Section 8.5 looks in more detail at the implications of realism for generating tailored output in successive system responses in an extended dialogue.

8.3 SYSTEM EXAMPLES

In many actual or planned systems, there are simplifications either because the number of factors affecting modelling is reduced or because the factors present are so only in a limited form. For example in the common advice case, patient and agent are identical, all the recognisable user properties are decision properties, and the system's task is to react to the user's inputs ad hoc; for example with a train inquiry system there may be no global system goal to achieve in the form of designing a whole trip to meet the user's requirements; the system may have to do no more than respond to user-set 'local' goals by supplying individual pieces of information like a train time. The same applies to systems like UC (Wilensky *et al.*, 1988). However even here we can have a mix of objective and subjective user properties, or of static and dynamic ones. We can also, even within this restricted consultative paradigm which has been a common base for work on user modelling, have more complex situations since we can distinguish, somewhat schematically, the cases where the user is talking about himself from those where he is talking about something else. In the first he is seeking advice about and for himself, for example about books which would suit him; in the second about something else, but (directly) for himself, for example about a failed engine. The contrast between the user talking about himself and about something 'out there' affects modelling because in the first case the user's attitudes are the paramount factor, and in the second case they are not so, though for some task systems they may be very important, for example in choosing college courses. In instruction systems the user talking as himself is the dominating factor. Expert systems with a single user can be designed to occupy very different positions along the line from patient dominance to agent subservience.

My examples are designed to cover differences of task, user role, executive dominance, i.e., whether the task execution is system or user driven (it may be a mixture of both), communicative direction, i.e., whether communication is system or user initiated (or a mix), and interactive mode, i.e., whether we have independent, one-shot or dialogue interaction. The examples are primarily of consultation situations as these are obvious ones for user modelling, but of varying kinds, and I have included some non-consultation cases as well, to emphasise the wider relevance of the points being made. But I have deliberately, in spite of the importance of user modelling for instruction, excluded instruction examples because they may often involve non-linguistic inputs (for instance worked sums) or need more space than is convenient here. The points made nevertheless apply to them too. In referring to advisory and consultation systems, on the other hand, I am referring to more than what Morik (1989) calls 'information-seeking' as opposed to 'action- achieving' systems. A travel system that only recommended holidays would be an information-seeking system for Morik, one that made bookings as well would be an action-achieving system. But an action-achieving system can allow for consultation by the user, as in the preliminaries to booking, so the points made apply to advice-seeking interaction in general. Consultation or inquiry may also of course be an allowed form of interaction with a system primarily intended for independent action as in, say, a police traffic controller or as illustrated in a more limited way by XCALIBUR, for example (Carbonell *et al.*, 1983).

To simplify I shall consider only the effectiveness and acceptability functions. Effectiveness is an internal system function determined by the system's task though, depending on the nature of this task, it may have more or less outward manifestation for the user: more as in instruction, less as in plant monitoring. Acceptability is an external function with a wholly outward manifestation. Note here that giving individuals what they like, say in an advisory context driven by personal preferences (as in choosing dresses), is still a matter of effectiveness because the system's decisions are based on the user's wants; acceptability has to do with the way things are presented to the user. However whether a particular feature of the system output in the advisory case is motivated by effectiveness, i.e., giving the system's decision, or by acceptability, giving it in one way rather than another, is a complex matter and one with no simple relationship to the user's decision or non-decision properties. While in an advisory situation communicating the system's decisions might be deemed a necessary component of effectiveness, communication raises many presentational issues and it is hard to adhere to any 'neutral' notion of communication which might be taken as associated with the decision taking itself. I shall nevertheless assume that 'neutral' information exists and has to be conveyed as the decision advice through the system's output. (I shall return to this point in Section 8.5.)

It may also be noted that even in preferentially-based advisory situations, if the system's decision making is complex, or the relation between the way the user couches his preferences and the way the system characterises the objects it deals with (as in choosing library books), whether the system's specific decisions in themselves are acceptable may itself be a concern for the user, as in other types of application. Presenting decisions comprehensibly merges gradually into justifying them convincingly. I shall assume here that confidence in the system as such, and therefore its acceptability as a whole as a device for carrying out its generic task, is not in question, so acceptability is primarily a presentational matter relating to individual decisions.[5] This clearly includes not merely the 'outward trappings' of response, but rendering the system's decisions explicable in terms of its knowledge resources. Whether or not in an advisory situation the system's decisions are in fact accepted is a separate question: with the travel advisor for instance, the user may recognise that the recommended trip is wholly reasonable, i.e., is well-founded and the best on offer, but still not take the advice.

The examples below are all of hypothetical systems, with idealised language processing capabilities. Note that the pieces of discourse given are not necessarily opening ones for the session, and that the system could already have some model information, derived from the current or a previous session. In these examples U represents user inputs, S system outputs. System outputs marked with a *, as in *S3, are key ones to be discussed; the immediately following outputs, for example S3a, are alternatives to these. These key outputs and their alternatives represent different ways and degrees of tailoring to the user.

Example 1

This is an equipment repair advisor, so with only a human agent. Imagine we have the following portion of dialogue.

```
    U1  :  The freezer seems to be on all the time, making a lot
           of noise, and its only got a pound of coffee beans
           in it.
    S1  :  How old is it?
    U2  :  About two years.
    S2  :  Have you checked the controller?
    U3  :  Seems to be OK: the thermostat is OK.
*   S3  :  But did you look at the thermometer?
    S3a :  What is the state of the thermometer?
```

I am assuming here that the controller relating thermostat and thermometer is designed so the state of the thermometer shows whether the thermostat is working without any independent indicator on the thermostat itself, i.e., that it is the state of the thermometer rather than that of the thermostat which shows whether the thermostat is working. Then U3 is ambiguous because it could indicate either that the user does understand the mechanism and having looked correctly at the thermometer is indicating his conclusion about the thermostat,

---

[5] This is quite compatible with having a limited system as long as the user is aware of the limitations.

or that he doesn't understand and is looking at the wrong thing. *S3 would be a natural system response to the second hypothesis.

But it is not necessary to be so user-oriented. The system could combine its knowledge of the structure of the controller with the amount of information explicitly supplied by the user, without bothering about the user as the man behind U1, U2 and U3 and about the reasons for his inputs, to decide on the alternative output S3a.[6] S3a, without being tailored to the user as someone with beliefs etc, i.e., as being more than his inputs, is formulated in a manner which would make it acceptable to the user even if he had looked at the thermometer: i.e., it is not couched to imply he is incompetent.

Example 2

This is a horticultural designer where because, as in the travel agent case, the system is designed to work from the user's attitudes, we have a human patient, who we will suppose is also the agent. (As noted earlier, if there is an actual garden involved, the extent to which its characteristics are treated as (objective) properties of the user or as defining a non-human task subject is determined by the global system task specification, i.e., whether it is to assist or determine; clearly there are complex borderline cases, especially with systems with a range of behaviour options.)

Suppose, then, we have:[7]

```
U1    :   The soil is rather heavy, so what's good for that? I
          believe roses are OK but I don't like them.
S1    :   Well there's peonies and ranunculas.
U2    :   Do they need a lot of watering?
* S2  :   Only occasionally when its very dry.
S2a   :   Not over the year.
S2b   :   They never need a lot at once.
S2c   :   They will only need watering if it is very dry, which
          does not often happen in Western Scotland, and even
          then will need only a modest sprinkle each day.
```

U2 could suggest various hypotheses about the user: that he doesn't like watering, that he can't afford to buy water, or that he can't carry heavy cans. *S2 is essentially motivated by the first hypothesis and so is tailored to this view of the user; the alternative S2a is motivated by by the second, and S2b by the third. But it is surely adequate and indeed preferable, as each of these replies though natural in form is not wholly unambiguous, to generate the straight and full response of S2c, i.e., a response to the simple question U2 amplified using system domain knowledge about different aspects of watering relevant to

---

[6] If the user had already input information about the thermometer as well as about the thermostat, the situation would of course be quite different.

[7] I am assuming the system already knows the user's garden is in Western Scotland.

gardening. Carefully generating an unambiguous response for each hypothesis, e.g., 'Even in a dry season they never need much water each day' instead of S2b would, after all, lead to nearly as much, and as slightly plonking, an output as S2c, with the added danger of missing the point. In fact, in this case as in the previous one, the system needs generic task knowledge as well as domain knowledge: it depends, implicitly if not explicitly, on some notion of the kind of task for which it is designed, here advising, as well as on knowledge about the topic on which advice is sought and being offered. The task and domain knowledge together constitute the system's generic application model, which is instantiated in a specific session as a particular application model. (Note that the assumption in the example is that while the user's attitudes to flowers are part of the system's decision model, his attitudes to watering are not; however information about the watering needs of plants is part of the domain knowledge base used for decisions.)

Example 3

Here we assume a libel advisor operated by a lawyer with a client who wishes to sue. The publicity typically associated with libel suits means that the patient's attitudes are important; but as the separate agent has to interpret the system's advice, his properties may also be significant. Such a legal advice system could be a full decision maker or merely responsive to queries: here I assume the latter.

```
  S1   :   Your client wants to sue Megajunk News about an
           article calling him a bigamist?
  U1   :   Yes.
  S2   :   And is he?
  U2   :   He says not.
* S3   :   How resilient do you think he is? Megajunk aren't
           exactly scrupulous.
  S3a  :   Ask him if he believes he could withstand a relentless
           and unscrupulous newspaper campaign with harrying
           reporters and numerous damaging stories about him.
```

In *S3 the system is seeking to exploit a model of the lawyer (which we will assume is in fact a personal one already built up, and not just a type one) as an experienced judge of the real qualities of clients. But if the system has to rely for its client assessment on a model of the lawyer which is more than a stereotype this implies that it should have a high quality model which would be very difficult to establish because it would depend, in cases like the present, on some means of evaluating the accuracy of the lawyer's judgments of his client. But even then, it is not clear that this would be superior to using the agent merely as a (deemed reliable) transmitter, and using the previous dialogue plus task and domain information to obtain the information required about the client via the alternative system output S3a.

Example 4

Just to emphasise that these considerations also apply to cases where the
user is not seeking advice, and where the system takes independent, perhaps
concurrent, actions, imagine an automated warehouse shipping system translating messages into truck loads and journey instructions.

U1	:	Four hundred of B700s to Smiths at Reading.
S1	:	OK.
U2	:	They'll need some P20s to go with them.
S2	:	Two hundred? It would need two trucks.
U3	:	No, three hundred.
* S3	:	There's one P20 per pair of B700s, so you don't need that many P20s.
S3a	:	You said four hundred B700s.
S3b	:	That's a P20 for each pair of B700s plus 100 P20s.

The system's *S3 response is natural for the hypothesis derived from U3 that
the user does not know what the precise relation between B700s and P20s is,
i.e., that it is two for one. S3a is motivated by the alternative that the user
has forgotten by now, or incorrectly remembers, how many B700s he said. But
S3b, which is simply descriptive, is a better all-round response because it is
informative but neutral in tone.

Example 5

Finally, I shall consider situations where there is no immediate dialogue
context for the system to use, i.e., where the user's input or system's output are
not part of an interactive sequence. Quite apart from the beginning of ordinary
dialogue, these situations may occur naturally with some task systems, even if
the task is complex and follow-up dialogue is possible; they need not however
imply that the system has no previously acquired information about the user.
They also occur with more restricted tasks like conventional database query,
where current front ends, apart from question recording to deal with ellipsis or
more efficient searching, and possibly ad hoc sub-dialogue to handle question
defects like syntax errors, operate on a one-shot exchange basis and cannot treat
input sequences as groups and recognise the user goals or plans motivating them.
But this is a somewhat artificial limitation, as it would be preferable in at least
some applications to have a more powerful consultation front end exploiting the
database management system as a tuple getter. Operational plant control is a
more natural example since there will be occasions where, even with a powerful
front end, simple exchanges or unidirectional messages will be appropriate, and
where the user is not necessarily seeking advice. For present purposes the
assumption is that the system has some available modelling information, say
obtained through earlier interaction, so it is not modelling the user solely on
the basis of the specific current input.

Now consider:

```
U1  : The packing machine seems to be producing unusually
      slowly.
* S1  : How much more slowly than normal?
S1a : How often are the boxes coming off?
```

*S1 could be motivated by a user model that has established the user as a thoroughly experienced observer, i.e., it is not just assuming any operator is experienced (this is easier than in the libel case because the system has an independent task to provide an evaluation context). But while it may be flattering to the agent to be treated as a good judge, from the system's point of view the alternative response S1a, which is not motivated by anything but its domain model, is as good, if not better as capable of getting more precise information. The same would apply to an autonomous system output message, so S1a below is as good in real terms as *S1:

```
* S1  : Shut down the feed valve if the flow's abnormally lumpy.
S1a : Shut down the feed valve if any lumps are larger than
      your hand or the gaps between bursts of feed last
      longer than three seconds.
```

It may be that the former would give a finer plant control, but it is, I maintain, somewhat riskily dependent on the system's capacity to evaluate its human operators. This risk might be reduced by administering explicit 'examinations', but these could hardly be expected, for a complex plant, to be exhaustive. Of course in this last single output case, the system has no preceding linguistic input to exploit as well as its internal knowledge, so S1a would be based on its application model alone.

8.4   EXAMPLE IMPLICATIONS

My argument in all these examples has been that while it would in principle be possible for the system to exploit a user model based on more than the data supplied by the user's language inputs plus the application task and domain knowledge it has for its decision making, it can serve its various functions, in this discussion acceptability as well as effectiveness, perfectly well with just the input data and application information. (Whether or not the life of such a user model is extended beyond the session will depend on the application.) This applies even in the advisory case, where the need for as full a user model as possible appears to be strongest, as well as in systems or interactions where consultation is not the primary activity.

But what exactly does this imply for the notion of user model and for the part it should play in generation?

In general, in those cases where there is a human patient, the important point about the application model to which the patient's decision properties are related is that this is a coherent, or at least connected, whole; i.e., it is generally, if not always, possible to make inferences explaining given patient data or to relate given data to other possible properties of the patient. The importance of the connectivity supplied by the application model is clearly seen in the instruction case. If the pupil is providing the wrong answers to the set mathematics problems, and this is not deemed attributable to frivolity, boredom, fatigue, mistyping or 'simple error', the system has to be able to postulate explanatory processes which are couched in terms appropriate to the domain, e.g., that the pupil has carried out an inappropriate operation, but one of a number-manipulating kind: the notion of 'mal-rules' presupposes this kind of domain- relevant systematicity.

But the same point applies in other contexts, and specifically in relation to situations where the user's dynamic mental properties are in question: these are presumed to be motivated by beliefs, goals and so forth that the system has to identify to produce appropriate responses. The user may indeed have ulterior goals and plans which are outside the scope of the application model, for example the putative train traveller wants to visit a loved one, so there is a top-level unexplained user property "wants to know (for ulterior reason)". But otherwise, seeking to identify the user's beliefs, desires, goals, intentions or plans implies identifying those that would be within the scope of the application model, i.e., beliefs, goals etc that are explicable even if false or mistaken (e.g., Pollack, 1987). For example in a train inquiry system, that if an inquiry is about trains from X to Y, a possible user goal is to go by train from X to Y. Similarly, with something like UC (Wilensky *et al.*, 1988), if the user asks about deleting files, their goal may be one of the things that can be achieved, within Unix, by file deletion, including removing this specific file, making space, deleting old versions etc. (Of course characterising removing a file in terms of these is the hard part of writing the application model.) Moreover, as the application model covers the nature of the task as well as the domain, so that for an inquiry system the generic requirement for the user is to get information and the generic purpose of the system is to supply it, if the user offers information, this is interpreted as a means to this end.

Thus for systems with a human patient, the user's specific given or inferred decision properties constitute the user model required whether the system has a global task (e.g., diagnosis) or is simply responding to whatever local require-ment the user's input sets, and which may be exploited to serve acceptability and efficiency as well as effectiveness. The user's inputs are clearly the prime source of information for this decision model. The role of the system's generic application model is in explaining and filling out the user's inputs through the connectivity the domain element supplies and the motivational base the system's task specification offers. But this connectivity is very valuable: the problem in any attempt to use non-decision properties for modelling is that –

as illustrated in (Sparck Jones, 1989) – it may be hard to pick up potentially useful properties because there is no recognisable relation between them and others.

A patient model can thus be an individual model since in building a decision model it is legitimate for the system to hypothesise an individual. How far a human patient model should be described as a model of a person is partly a matter of the nature of the decision property descriptions the system allows, and partly a philosophical issue. But the important point is that the system can model on the basis that it is dealing with a single autonomous entity because decision properties are supposed to connect in individuals. (With several patients things are more more complicated, but the basic point holds.) At the same time the system can motivate its specific model, and establish connections between patient properties, through its application (i.e., domain and task) knowledge. This provides the reasons for observed or hypothesised property cooccurrence. The application connectivity can in particular allow, to the extent that this is appropriate for the system context, for the patient's subjective or mental states and attitudes. These points apply whether the patient model is used for its primary purpose, namely effectiveness, or for other purposes like efficiency and acceptability.

They also apply even if the system exploits stereotypes as starting points for decision modelling as considered in Rich (1989), for example. The notion of stereotype has been rather variously interpreted, and stereotypes have been used in different ways. I shall use 'stereotype' here more narrowly than Rich, to refer to fixed user characterisations which are not open to individuation through property value choices or through combination, and so are likely to be of a crude sort covering large classes of individual user individual user. Stereotypes in this sense can still refer to decision or non-decision properties, and so to patient or agent, and can be partial or complete characterisations of the user. Stereotypical properties when combined with user input providing an individual characterisation on other properties can provide an overall individual model, as in (Morik, 1989) or (Chin, 1989), but the effect where stereotype properties impinge may still be rather crude because the stereotypes themselves are crude. However in the present context the important point is that while using stereotypes in the broader sense of Rich is really just one strategy for constructing individual user models, stereotypes in my sense are built into the system specification and individuation is on other bases. (This does not of course imply that these stereotypes cannot be helpful, only that rather different assumptions about user modelling are being made from those in question here.)

My argument is thus that with patients the system can engage in serious modelling even though the specific information it gets about the user is through his linguistic inputs. The user's inputs are primary, and the system can only work from these. But assuming the system has a coherent application model, it can then go further in building the patient's decision-property model. This support is not necessarily provided in a similar way for non-decision properties.

Giving primacy to the user's inputs, because the system is dependent on them, suggests that it is not going too far to say the user is his inputs, and in the present context his linguistic inputs: what he says and how he says it. But what does this imply for the elements of user inputs that do not bear on the patient's decision properties; and what happens to the agent role, whether the agent is the same as the patient or is independent, or where there is no human patient?

The most straightforward view of linguistic inputs is that they are just linguistic inputs; so where they do not say anything (directly or indirectly) about decision properties they are not saying anything material about the user as a person. The non-decision properties of linguistic inputs are thus just properties of a participant in the interaction as such, and have no more personal individuality, as opposed to discourse individuality, than this.[8]

Thus as far as non-decision information is concerned, the user has no more personality than that given by the discourse itself. But this in turn has implications for agents. Where there is only an agent, and a non-human patient, the agent is simply the discourse participant, with no properties beyond his linguistic inputs apart from the decision information they convey. Where there is a human patient and the agent is the patient, the distinction between patient and agent roles beyond the patient's decision properties is submerged in the characteristics of the discourse participant. Where there is a distinct agent, the only viable position is that the properties of the discourse, unless they are explicitly signalled as the patient's, are all the agent's, so the patient has nothing but decision properties.

These conclusions do not necessarily imply that the linguistic inputs cannot convey factual or substantive information about the non-decision, and even objective as well as subjective, properties of the user. They may do this. The point is rather that where this information is not manifestly referable to the patient, it must be assumed to be about the agent; and that in either case while it may be exploited by the system, it need not be, and as it is non-decision information it can should only be exploited with caution because it is not ordinarily connected in a well-founded way with other non-decision, or indeed decision, information.

In practice, whatever the patient/agent relationship (since this could apply even where patient and agent are the same), it may be useful to build in an agent type model or stereotype or, if the application makes it appropriate, to allow for several types, perhaps with explicit checking for the relevant type at the beginning of the session. Agent typing of this sort would be used in a uniform way, for example to justify an assumed level of domain knowledge, with individuation only as called for by the linguistic input. (As noted in previous papers, an agent model of this kind may be important for system efficiency

---

[8] Though this does not imply the discourse model is the user model; see also Sparck Jones (1988) and other papers in that issue of Computational Linguistics.

as well as effectiveness.) Thus though there is an independent agent model, it is strictly limited in relation to the modelling aims and assumptions with which I started, and so does not materially undermine the proposition that user modelling can be based on decision properties plus the user's inputs, and indeed should be, to avoid error. Indeed managing an agent type model of this kind could be regarded simply as part of the system's task specification. Certainly it is hard to imagine a system without some default assumptions about the agent built in, for example (in systems of the kind illustrated) that he knows English, is an adult, is not playing games. But the effect on interaction is uniform and is not particular to the individual user.

More specifically, as realism suggests one cannot generally look for any underlying non-decision characterisation of the agent, the agent can be no more than what his linguistic inputs - in their syntactic, semantic and pragmatic form and content - add up to; and he is an individual only to the extent that specific discourse is individual. The agent model is what the linguistic discourse is above any information, and especially decision information, attributable to the patient, or what can be inferred from this discourse on general grounds, e.g., about any human, or via a task stereotype. These general bases for characterising discourse participants indeed allow for all the broader pragmatic information associated with speech acts and communicative intentions and so, for example, for the use of metaplanning knowledge in the style of Litman (1985). So when these generic properties of language use are exploited in conjunction with the specific information supplied by the content and form of the discourse, it may be possible to build a relatively rich, discourse-motivated model of the agent (e.g., deriving information about the lawyer from "The stupid fellow says ..."). But we can only consider, even in principle, information about the agent beyond this if it is given explicitly, since the system cannot be expected to have more general knowledge to support inferences on additional information; and even then it may be impossible to make any use of this explicit non-decision information about the user (e.g., the lawyer saying "As a bachelor I think ..."), because it cannot be related to any of the system's functions. The fact that non-decision information about the agent may rarely figure in inputs in practice is a separate matter. The conclusion, therefore, is that because it is difficult to get a hook on any user properties other than decision ones and those that are expressed as the linguistic discourse properties of user inputs, a user model subsumes, where this is appropriate, a patient model defined by decision properties, and an agent model defined by the discourse properties of the system's linguistic inputs. Overall, modelling the user means modelling the user as, and only as, a user of the system, and considering only those of his properties that are relevant to this. Restricting modelling in this way still allows for the user's subjective properties, and especially his dynamic mental ones, i.e., for treating the user as a thinking and purposive agent; but the scope of the user's activities as an agent in this general sense of "reasoning agent" is defined by the system. This means not only that his specific beliefs, goals etc are limited to ones relevant to the system, but that the notion of belief, goal and so forth are being given a rather shallow, behaviouristically- oriented interpretation in terms of the way users use systems, and specifically a linguistically-oriented interpretation in terms of their expression in the user's inputs. The system's inferences about what lies behind the user's input, where they are not exploiting his previous inputs, are based on the system's application knowledge and are constrained by the limits of this knowledge and by the practical limits on its ability to test and extend its model through interaction with the user. In an important sense the user is his inputs.

But what does all this imply for generation?

8.5   GENERATION

As the user model is what the user says and how he says it, insofar as generation should exploit a user model, this is what it has to exploit. Where there is no human patient, the content and form of a generated output may not be determined solely by the need to respond to the user, in this case the agent; and even where there is a human patient, a spontaneous output, though motivated by a user model, need not be a response to a prompting user input. But where the system is generating output in response to a user input, in a single shot or dialogue, all it really has for the specific user is the linguistic input representing the user as agent, plus any patient model for the application.[9]

Of course if the patient and agent are identical, the system has a richer model to support its interaction with the user in his agent role. A system may have independent agent stereotypes which can influence output as in Cohen and Jones (1989), where explanations about the patient's educational performance are tailored to types of agent. (In Paris (1989) the choice of explanation is rather different as it can be viewed as a system decision for the patient user who is also the agent.) A system like Cohen and Jones' can treat agents as very important - they perhaps verge on being patients - but they are still treated primarily through the dialogue linguistic evidence, and the system has little independent basis for modelling them as individuals. Agent stereotypes are part of the built-in system task specification, and however valuable, do not affect my general arguments for realism in constructing and using individual user models; more generally, while there may be very good reasons for providing for more sophisticated, independent agent models through a connectible property set, without this explicit provision allowing an agent analogue of decision- property operations on the patient, the default for agents has to be that the system has no information about them beyond what comes directly from their behaviour as discourse participants.

But it is clear that many of the constraints on an output generated as a response to an input are motivated by principles governing discourse, whether

---

[9] I am assuming that if the system obtains any non- decision information about the patient only, this will be incidental in every sense.

more narrowly as in adherence to structural rules, for example constraining topicalisation, or in adherence to Gricean principles which in this case would be primarily based on the system's view of the user, for example of the state of his knowledge of the problem domain, as this has been derived from his previous inputs. Thus it would be the session data, which includes the system's own previous output, and the view of the user's state extracted from this, which would determine what constituted unnecessary repetition, for example. Aspects of the generated output not motivated by application needs are therefore determined by the linguistic characteristics of inputs, but these bear on discourse coherence at the textual level, and on cooperative behaviour of the Gricean sort between dialogue participants, i.e., rest on generic considerations applied to the specific discourse and not on anything to do with the originator of the linguistic inputs as persons in their own right.

Generation as a whole is determined by the system's application need to know decision information, and the system's discourse need to maintain communicative interaction. What is an appropriate system output to generate at any point thus depends on, i.e., is the result of the interaction between, the system's application state, i.e., its decision-making state in relation to its global or local task model, and its linguistic discourse state, the significant point being that while the former, with a human patient, may in a real sense represent a person, the latter should not be seen as representing any more than what the linguistic properties of the discourse themselves express, i.e., as representing a discourse participant and not an individual person. Generation, in relation to users, is driven by a mix of person model for patients and a (session) participant model for agents.

All of this leads to generation as illustrated in the following example.

Example 6

The (notional) system here is designed to help someone wanting scientific literature by formulating a proper characterisation of what they want, which will then be submitted to a search service. The patient and agent are therefore one. The example is also for more than a straightforward advisory case or simple action- achieving situation in Morik's sense, since the system has to engage in complex decision-making in its own right, exploiting technical knowledge the user cannot be expected to possess, to follow up the user's needs with literature-searching actions; and I am assuming the system makes use of a range of domain and task knowledge sources relevant to different aspects of this type of literature search situation (Belkin, Seeger and Wersig, 1983; Brooks, 1986; Daniels, 1987).[10] The system outputs in the dialogue which follows are annotated to indicate, summarily, the respective contributions made to them by the application model and by linguistic discourse mechanisms assumed to cover

---

[10]Note that these authors interpret "user model" more narrowly than I am doing. Daniels' user model characterises static, essentially objective, decision properties of the patient providing a context for his actual literature need

broader pragmatic aspects of a Gricean sort as well as narrower matters of
expression, both within and between sentences. The application contributions
to the system output can be either seeking or supplying application information. In the annotations A = indicates application contributions, L = linguistic
contributions.

```
U1 :  I'm looking for literature on prefabricated housing.
S1 :  What are you looking for it for?
 A :  intended use of literature
 L :  question form including anaphors and word ''looking''
U2 :  I'm doing a project for my geography course.
S2 :  So you're a student?
 A :  appropriate literature level
 L :  question form
U3 :  Yes. I've looked at a couple of books Dr Smith
      recommended.
S3 :  What were they? Did you find them helpful?
 A :  literature coverage; topic specification
 L :  question forms; anaphors
U4 :  I found Robin's 'Housing for all' very interesting.
S4 :  Why?
 A :  topic specification
 L :  question form
U5 :  It showed all kinds of houses I'd never thought of as
      prefabricated are really, like Zambian huts made with
      regular poles and ordinary market grass mats which
      come in standard sizes.
S5 :  So you don't just want stuff on Western factory made
      units, but on any kinds of houses made anywhere out
      of existing elements bigger than bricks?
 A :  topic specification
 L :  sentence structure, lexical choice etc.
```

Imagining now a later stage in this dialogue, the system outputs which follow
show how the patient model built up over the session may be applied, in a
manner which is also natural from a linguistic point of view in relation to the
dialogue history, and how the system's application knowledge can be exploited
for cooperative response to avoid possible misunderstanding by the user.[11]

```
S21  :  Do you want weekly trade magazines?
```

---

[11] As Steve Draper has pointed out to me, I have not concerned myself in this example, or
the previous ones, with the manner of the user's adaptation to the system, though adaptation
is clearly if informally assumed in the putatively natural dialogue. The extent to which a
user's conscious adaptation can itself assist the system's modelling is a matter for further
investigation.

U21	:	Why should I?
S22	:	Their technical specification sections ads give a lot of detail. But perhaps that would be more than you want.
A	:	refer to purpose (mentioned far back)
U22	:	Are there a lot of them?
S23	:	I don't think so, but the system's coverage could be poor.
A	:	give domain knowledge
L	:	cooperativity

The illustrations in (Sparck Jones, 1984, 1989) showed how the system's outputs could be motivated by modelling serving the different functions mentioned, for example to acquire more information in order to promote effectiveness, and to express the request in a particular way, to promote acceptability. During a dialogue the system could produce outputs exploiting modelling designed both the serve functions directly themselves and to obtain new information supporting the development and future application of its models. The illustrative dialogues also showed how a single output could serve several functions at once. The more restricted person and participant models for patient and agent respectively considered in this paper may also be exploited to serve the different system functions, effectiveness, efficiency, and acceptability, in the varied ways illustrated in (Sparck Jones, 1984, 1989). So, for example, even the restricted agent model may be exploited for efficiency, or acceptability to patient or agent, the restricted patient model for acceptability to the patient as well as effectiveness.

These functional distinctions are moreover important even in generation in advisory situations (especially where patient and agent are one) they appear difficult to maintain or apply: thus if we subsume communicating the system's decision under effectiveness for the consultation case, what constitutes proper communication? The advice to be given is the system's decision, but it may be hard to separate the advice given from the way it is given, though presentation appears to be an acceptability issue and not a decision matter. For example, deciding what information to select for output from a relevant pool can be viewed as a decision choice or a presentation choice. But it depends on the criterion used to select, which is determined by what the system task specification is in relation to what constitutes advice, which suggests there is still a real distinction between taking a decision and expressing it for the user for any particular system, or in any particular case.

On the other hand, if communicating a decision implies communicating it properly, i.e., effectively, it is more difficult to draw the line clearly, and while preempting false inferences (Joshi *et al.*, 1984), or overanswering (Morik, 1989), may appear to have to do with effectiveness, where choices of speech act (Morik, 1989) or of lexical item may seem to be matters of acceptability, these cannot be general rules, so each instance would have to be categorised independently.

It could on the other hand be claimed that if preempting or overanswering are motivated by Gricean principle, as in Joshi *et al.* and Morik, this follows from the generic system task specification and not from the specific decision, and so has more to do with effectiveness in a global sense than in the sense relating to particular decision making in which I have defined it. All of this is a tricky issue which needs further analysis; but I shall assume here that it is reasonable and possible to make a working distinction between effectiveness and acceptability in generating output, even in communications about or of system decisions. However in the advisory context, unlike other expert system ones, decisions may be final or intermediate, and definite or provisional; and effectiveness is of course also a motive for system outputs designed to gather information as well as to provide it. This all makes the functional status of system outputs very complex.

Considering now the use just of application and linguistic resources as illustrated in the Example 6 literature search dialogue, it is clear that the system outputs can serve various functions, and also for example that application knowledge can serve different functions. If communicating a decision at least in some neutral, information-giving sense is subsumed under effectiveness, then linguistic knowledge can contribute to more than just making the system's behaviour acceptable. This would fit the idea of explanation generation, for instance as illustrated in (Paris, 1989), as a seamless web with subject content and linguistic form all stemming from the system's decision about what explanation to give. But in other cases linguistic knowledge is deployed in a tactical manner which may be more reasonably described as serving acceptable dialogue behaviour. It could also serve efficiency through economical and accurate information gathering.

Thus in Example 6 (but as before concentrating only on effectiveness and acceptability and disregarding efficiency), the system output S5 - about the user not wanting only Western prefabrication - while it is essentially motivated by a concern with effectiveness both in communicating a local decision and gathering information for an ultimate one, can also be seen to be using application knowledge to promote acceptability by showing the user the kinds of distinctions and subject specifications the system is capable of considering in relation to the particular consultation topic.[12] S22 - about the technical advertisement detail - shows a similar combined concern using application knowledge for acceptability as well as effectiveness through the explanatory information associated with the reference to the search purpose. S23, on the other hand, on the system's coverage, is simply an acceptability-oriented explanation.

The linguistic contributions on the other hand are equally dual purpose in many cases since they are partly serving effectiveness, as communications about decision information, and partly acceptability: maintaining discourse coherence works both ways, for example. The linguistic form of S3 - asking the user about the books read - is designed both to extend the existing model information,

---

[12] It might also be taken as seeking to promote confidence in the system as a whole.

i.e., is effectiveness motivated, and also to promote acceptability, through its careful form. Similarly S5, on the building types, by opening with "So", is exhibiting the system's consequential response both as a matter of content and of conversational linking.

8.6   CONCLUSION

This discussion has been a reaction to what I believe is the assumed, if not stated, long-term goal in natural language interface design, which has been encouraged by a concern with advisory systems, namely that the aim is personalisation. My conclusion is that the elements of modelling are those I identified before: it is necessary to distinguish user roles, user property types, and modelling functions; but also, reiterating my conclusion in (Sparck Jones, 1989), that modelling itself should be approached simply, partly because information about the user is not available but also, more importantly, because fancy modelling chasing the real person is unnecessary. My view is that personalisation in a strong sense is a misconceived aim. Seeking to tailor the system's generated output ever more tightly to an ever more refined characterisation of the individual, and especially to one going beyond what is required for decision effectiveness, is a mistake, for two reasons. The first is that in human interaction many socially relevant properties of those involved are recognised as important and are exploited, notably supposed class, status, authority and nous; but where these are not decision properties, systems are unlikely to be able to perceive them. At the same time, many ordinary human interactions, as in shops, do not bother about properties of the user as an individual behind what he says (and does) and what it is necessary to know for the specific task in hand, and at most take note in addition of stereotypical properties like sex.

Thus, for example, if sex is a decision property it has to be and can normally be obtained; and it may then be exploited for non-decision functions like acceptability; if it happens, though not a decision-property, to be known, it may be usefully exploited; but if it is not known, general politeness in generated output will be an adequate substitute.

In other words, there are too many constraints on man-machine interaction which are not just those imposed by our current system-building limitations, for it to be rational to seek model- based generation beyond what in fact suffices for many ordinary human situations. Thus what we are actually doing now, which is modelling confined to decision properties and discourse information, which is sometimes seen as an inferior substitute for the real thing, should instead be seen as an appropriate strategy in its own right, and not as a way station to something better. Though this of course is not implying that model-based generation, even if limited to decision information and discourse pragmatics, is easy.

BIBLIOGRAPHY

Belkin, N.J., Seeger, T. and Wersig, G. 'Distributed expert problem treatment as a model for information system analysis and design', Journal of Information Science 5, 1983, 153-167.

Brooks, H.M. An intelligent interface for document retrieval systems: developing the problem description and retrieval strategy components, PhD Thesis, City University, London, 1986.

Carbonell, J. *et al.* 'The XCALIBUR project: a natural language interface to expert systems', Proceedings of the Eighth International Joint Conference on Artificial Intelligence, 1983, 653-656.

Chin, D.M. 'KNOME: modelling what the user knows in UC', in Kobsa and Wahlster (1989).

Cohen, R. and Jones, M. 'Incorporating user models into expert systems for educational diagnosis', in Kobsa and Wahlster (1989).

Daniels, P.J. Developing the user modelling function of an intelligent interface to document retrieval systems, PhD Thesis, City University, London, 1987.

Grosz, B.J. and Sidner, C.L. 'Assertions, intentions, and the structure of discourse', Computational Linguistics 12, 1986, 175-204.

Joshi, A., Webber, B. and Weischedel, R. 'Preventing false inferences', Proceedings of COLING84, 1984, 134-138.

Kobsa, A. and Wahlster, W. (eds) User models in dialogue systems, Berlin: Springer, 1989.

Litman, D.J. Plan recognition and discourse analysis: an integrated approach to understanding dialogues, PhD Thesis, TR 170, Department of Computer Science, University of Rochester, 1985.

Morik, K. 'User models and conversational settings: modelling the user's wants', in Kobsa and Wahlster (1989).

Paris, C.L. 'Tailoring object descriptions to a user's level of expertise', in Kobsa and Wahlster (1989).

Pollack, M.E. Inferring domain plans in question answering, Technical Note 403, SRI International, Menlo Park, 1986.

Rich, E. 'Stereotypes and user modelling', in Kobsa and Wahlster (1989).

Sparck Jones, K. User models and expert systems, Technical Report 61, Computer Laboratory, University of Cambridge, 1984.

Sparck Jones, K. 'User models, discourse models, and some others', Computational Linguistics 14, 1988, 98-100.

Sparck Jones, K. 'Realism about user modelling', in Kobsa and Wahlster (1989); also Technical Report 111, Computer Laboratory, University of Cambridge, 1987

Webber, B.L. 'Questions, answers and responses: interacting with knowledge base systems', in On knowledge base systems (ed Brodie and Mylopoulos), Berlin: Springer, 1986.

Wilensky, R. *et al.* 'The Berkeley UNIX Consultant project', Computational Linguistics 14, 1988, 35-84.

Part II

LEXICAL CHOICE

Chapter 9

On the Place of Words In the Generation Process

David D. McDonald

Abstract: This paper describes preliminary research on "lexical choice" in generation: the relationships between words and the representations employed by the speaker for reasoning and modeling the situation. We hold that the bulk of the variance that we see at the surface level in language has its origins very deep in the conceptual system. Consequently, most of the burden of lexical choice must be taken on by this internal representation, and not by the generator proper as is customary today.

This work is exploratory rather than comprehensive. It studies the design consequences of three examples of lexical choice, introducing the devices "lexical clusters" and "action chains" as part of the representational system that organizes the selection process. In the first example the choice follows directly from the speaker's categorial judgements. The next describes how the very same information can receive two substantially different lexical realizations depending on the speaker's attitude toward it. In the last a choice usually ascribed to the generator is reanalyzed as conceptual, leading to a simpler processing architecture. These studies lend support to the conclusion that the selection of key lexical items is the first step in generation, with the choice criteria taken almost exclusively from the conceptual model and intentional attitudes of the speaker.

9.1   INTRODUCTION

With only a few exceptions, generation researchers have paid little attention to the nature of words. Cumming's 1986 review of generation lexicons identifies many more open problems than it does accepted solutions. Marcus in Tinlap-III (1987) chides us for systematically trivializing the problem of lexical selection in the way we focus our research.

There have been good reasons for this inattention. A generator can do no better than the material it has to work with. This material is supplied by the application program that underlies and directs the generation process, i.e., the program that provides the motivations for the utterances the generator produces and grounds its processing in an actual situation addressing a specific interlocutor. As a consequence, the representation and model that the "underlying program" uses have an enormous impact on what the generator is able to do.

For the most part, the applications programs that have been used to date to drive generators have all employed the same representational style, a style where the conceptual model is built from a large number of very specific primitives which invariably have ready correspondences to individual English words or fixed phrases. For all intents and purposes these programs are already "thinking in words". There is very little for their generators to do in the way of lexical selection beyond reading out and artfully composing what has already been fixed within the underlying application program.[1]

Today, however, the linguistic competence of our generators is quickly exceeding the modeling and reasoning ability of our client underlying programs. We can begin to see rationales for complex texts but cannot find legitimate sources or motivations for these rationales in the programs we have to work with. If we are to make progress in generation we must find or develop programs with deeper conceptions of what they know and how they reason with it, conceptions that lead these programs to take on more complex perspectives and intentional states. This increase in complexity would remove application

---

[1] On the other side of the coin are programs with representations based on a very small number of primitives, most notably Conceptual Dependency Theory (CD). Historically these have fostered a great deal of work on lexical selection in generation (Goldman, 1974; Wilensky, 1978; McGuire, 1980; Hovy, 1988). Since it is impossible to map directly to surface vocabulary when you are working with only, e.g., 13 primitive action terms, CD-based generation systems have always employed discrimination techniques capable of appreciating the context in which a term occurs and from that identifying the most precise word to use; the most thorough discussion of this style of lexical selection is in Goldman's 1974 thesis. Technically it is a simple matter to extend the discrimination process beyond simply looking at the semantic type of an action's arguments to considering rhetorical factors such as the speaker's point of view (Wilensky, 1978) or affective goals (Hovy, 1988). We will have nothing more to say about this kind of lexical choice procedure: applications with this style of representation are increasingly in the minority (having been displaced by designs where the comparable generalizations are captured in class hierarchies or taxonomic lattices), and they are not part of any of the systems we are dealing with.

programs from the realm of "capital letter semantics", with its trivialization of lexical choice, and into designs where terms in the programs no longer map one to one onto the entries of an English lexicon but instead prompt substantial judgements about how they should be realized. A significant part of the research to develop these deeper conceptions will come down to exploring the nature of words.[2]

This paper presents a few steps towards a model of the place of words with respect to underlying conceptual representations and of the process of lexical choice. This model is emerging from a body of ongoing research done in collaboration with Marie Meteer (BBN) and James Pustejovsky (Brandeis University). The paper will attempt to establish that lexical choice is primarily a matter of the model and attitudes held by the speaker at the time of speech, i.e., that the primary resolution of of options in decisions involving lexical choice occurs within the underlying program or directly reflects its categorizations and perspectives.

This in effect places words just outside of the generator proper—a possibly self-contradictory statement that requires some clarification. In generation research we talk about words in terms of "lexical selection" because we are focusing on the decision-making processes involved: why is one word chosen rather and another; what are the computational and contextual circumstances that define or constrain the available options; what is the character of the deliberations involved in making the choice; how is this choice represented once it is made. By saying that lexical choice directly reflects the categorizations and attitudes of the underlying program we are saying that no decisions of much consequence remain for the generator as the identity of the words is fixed by considerations that properly belong to the reasoning and modeling capacities of the underlying program rather than the linguistic capacities of the generator, e.g., inferential consequence, perceptual categorization, perspective, relative salience.

The generator does, of course, establish what words are available;[3] but since the mapping of information into words is based on criteria outside of the generator's scope, then its work with words will be largely confined to accommodating to the constraints the lexical choices carry with them.[4] Similarly, the gener-

---

[2] We are ultimately not just concerned with the selection of individual words, but with a broad set of non-compositional information-bearing linguistic devices: collocations, polywords, idioms, productive phrases, marked syntactic constructions, productive morphology, etc.—a set that may be collectively termed linguistic resources to emphasize their role as units the text planner can draw on in assembling an utterance. This is in keeping with the general presumption of generation researchers that "lexical" information includes far more than simply lists of words and their properties – see for example Hovy (1987) or Jacobs (1988). Differences emerge in how this range of resources is encoded and deployed, some making the "lexicon" primary to the point of subsuming the grammar, and others doing the reverse. As my present goal is only to broaden the readers conception of where and how lexical choice might be done and not to present a detailed architecture, I will have nothing to say about such design alternatives.

[3] Gaps in this competence pose important and methodologically useful problems for text planning in generation. These will not be considered here; but see Meteer (1988).

[4] Note, this discussion only applies to open-class, content words and information-bearing

ator is where the actual "act" of lexical selection takes place since the use of words is not relevant to the underlying program's activities. The generator provides the impetus, but the decision criteria are primarily within the underlying application program.

9.2 THE RELATIONSHIP BETWEEN WORDS AND CONCEPTUAL STRUCTURES: FEATURE MATCHING OR DIRECT LOOKUP?

A proper place to start in a discussion of lexical choice is with some examples of what people actually do. Of course since we do not have direct knowledge of the generation processes people use, some judgement is required when interpreting the texts we collect when doing an empirical study; however I think even shallow observations are very telling.

Consider the two excerpts below from a transcribed description by a person of the layout of her apartment. This data comes from a preliminary study done in collaboration with Alison Huettner and Penelope Sibun. A report on its background and methodology appears in (Sibun, Huettner and McDonald, 1988). The first excerpt is typical of these monologues overall: things and locations are described by simple NPs built on familiar common nouns; spatial relationships are given by clauses built on a regular pattern that the speaker fell into almost immediately when asked to do the task.

> "then, in the kitchen there's a large window which faces the back-yard, with two smaller windows flanking it. And if we're facing towards the backyard now, on the righthand side is a sliding glass door, and a few feet from that is a smaller window, towards the living room."

The second excerpt comes at a point when the speaker has had to name a place in the apartment that we suspect she has never needed to name before. It is not a conventional place-type in a house: neither quite a room nor a hallway but a mixture of both, and not a place that the people in the household ever did anything in—just a spot that they passed through on their way elsewhere. This speaker, like virtually every other speaker in our corpus for this house, hesitates, then composes a characterization of the place using very general vocabulary and specializing phrases.

closed-class words ('above', 'after'). Function words such as 'to' or 'the' we take to be introduced late in the generation process as the realization of grammatical relations and grammaticised semantic categories (such as definite/indefinite).

> "Then in the righthand doorway, we have like a um we have a hall–
> large hallway that leads into the kitchen. ... and we walk down that
> wide hallway, which is almost a room in itself. There's a closet, on
> the lefthand wall, in the lefthand wall lets say of that hallway."

The issue I wish to illustrate with these excerpts concerns the character of the work that is done each time a lexical choice is made: is it a calculation or a memory lookup? We start from the hopefully uncontroversial premise that naming is primarily a matter of characterization. The speaker called her kitchen a 'kitchen' because it fell into that category of room-types by warrant of its appliances, furniture, primary use, etc.[5] Her hesitation over what to call the room/hallway in the second excerpt reflects her uncertainty as to what kind of thing it is. (Others used phrases like 'the L-shaped room'.)

How did the speaker decide what she was going to use as descriptions of the rooms? She surely did not have to deliberate over how to classify her kitchen; rather she simply recalled the long standing association between that specific room and the name 'kitchen' that goes with that room-type. By the same token, when a category was not immediately available in the case of the odd room/hallway, the speaker was forced to think about what room-name best fit the space's properties before she could give a satisfactory description. (Notice her restarts and use of the hedge 'like'.) Once the categorization was established, however, she is at least in part drawing on her memory of what she said before, since she uses the subsequent reference forms 'that' and the dropping of modifiers. (Notice though, that the modifier has changed from 'large' to 'wide'. Whether this reflects a reclassification or the adoption of a collocation particular to hallways is difficult to determine.)

I take observations like these as evidence that one of the prevalent themes in research on lexical choice is misguided. This is the idea that lexical choice is a "feature matching process" (see for example Levelt and Schriffers, 1987; Nirenburg and Nirenburg, 1988). In such a process, the items that serve as the conceptual sources of the individuals and relations to be expressed are characterized for the generator as a vector of abstract features and values. (Whether this property vector is also used internally by the reasoning system is seldom clear. If it were, it would strengthen the case for this kind of design.) The generation lexicon is taken to consist of a set of lexical entries that are characterized in this same currency of features and values, and the lexical choice

---

[5] The utility of characterizing a room as, e.g., a kitchen is of course socially mediated. She calls the room a kitchen in no small part because her fellow interlocutors understand her when she does so. She might be less successful with, say, 'breakfast nook' unless that was a socially effective characterization in her household. An additional consideration is the extension of basic descriptions to provide discriminating information. A large house might have an 'upstairs kitchen' and a 'downstairs kitchen' for example. The choice of modifiers in a case like this has less to do with categorization than with what attributes the speaker can expect to be salient to her audience. For a discussion of the range of issues in noun phrase descriptions see (Appelt, 1985).

process is a matter of looking for a "best match"—finding the lexical entry whose property vector values are closest by some metric to those of the item to be expressed (Nirenburg and Nirenburg, 1988).

The feature matching model of lexical choice has a number of potential technical problems that must be settled satisfactorily before it can be adopted: is the entire lexicon being searched every time, or just a subset? On what basis do we determine which properties are relevant in a given case? Does the processing initiative come from the conceptual objects or the lexicon? What communications bandwidth and processor architecture is being assumed? Can one be sure that the algorithms will run in comparable time for all normal cases?

But even ignoring these technical problems, there is an a-priori matter that, to my mind, makes the entire enterprise very dubious. It is one thing to say that some sort of comparison of properties and prototypes takes place the very first time that we take notice of an object or have occasion to reify it or refer to it—such a process is needed to do categorial perception. It is another thing entirely to claim that after we have arrived at a categorization we proceed to forget what we have learned and to redo our calculations each and every time the object is used. More likely, we cache the calculations in memory, associating the mental object with the linguistic resources that we selected for it. On subsequent occasions, rather than go through the best match calculation again, we draw on this direct link that we have saved, and make our "choice" on the basis of table lookup rather than judgements from first principles.

In all of this, the crucial question is how we design and optimize our architecture for lexical selection. Should it be for best match calculations, which if I am correct are only needed the first time an object is considered, or should it instead be for the retrieval of long-established associations? I personally opt for the later alternative, and thus prefer direct mapping, "dictionary" based architectures (McDonald, 1983; McKeown, 1985), where the objects that are referenced by the text planner or the underlying program are already tied to a specific entry or class of entries in the lexicon, either as individuals or because of their conceptual class. In this kind of architecture, lexical choice is not a matter for the generator, since in normal speech the choice that goes on is at a conceptual, rather than a linguistic, level.

This is not to say that feature matching should be ignored. Like language learning, it is a capacity that will have to be included in any complete language system. Furthermore, it may well be used frequently in some domains, for instance diplomatic announcements or stock market reports (Kukich, 1988). In domains like these there may be relatively few recurring individuals but a great deal of global summarization via a small set of conventional phrases. A phrase like 'trading was moderate' reflects a context-sensitive judgement that summarizes a great deal of numerical information using a sublanguage that its intended audience is very sensitive to.

In summary, the point of this section has been to argue that the typical means by which an item's lexical realization is determined is just a simple memory lookup. Proponents of lexical selection strictly by feature matching must explain why prior decisions cannot be stored and recalled but must be recalculated each time—this will not be an easy task. Given that some kind of search through a feature space does, of course, occasionally occur (as the example of the previously unnamed room illustrated), then the next question is whether this is a standard enough operation to imagine that provisions have been made for it within the core generation process, or whether, as I expect, it will turn out that these new phrases are formed by an off-line calculation that draws on central, non- linguistic mental resources and is not part of the generation "linguistic module" in the sense of Fodor (1983).

9.3 "LEXICAL CLUSTERS" TO REALIZE "SUBLEXICAL" CONCEPTUAL UNITS

Nearly all generation research has been done for application/reasoning programs that were built by others and designed without regard for the needs of the generator. As a result, there are almost no proposals, let alone answers, as to how words and other linguistic phenomena might be deeply integrated with the internal representations that support reasoning.[6] That such an integration is possible, even preferable to facilitate reasoning, is an attractive possibility to many people, since they are drawn to the Sapir-Whorf hypothesis that the conceptual structures of one's language and one's thoughts are intimately linked. If the two are indeed linked, then generation becomes largely a problem of realization rather than translation, and a great many potentially insurmountable problems go away.

In this section, I will briefly lay out a design for lexical selection based on an underlying program that is being built from the ground up with the needs of generation firmly in mind. James Pustejovsky and I are building a reasoning system, called JEEVES , that will act as an appointment secretary able to monitor one's everyday activities and look for conflicts. Our point is not to develop a competent time manager for its own sake (though that would certainly be nice), but to use the program as a laboratory for studying how deeply one can sensibly embed words within a computational model used for commonsense

---

[6]There is of course the trivial relationship between words and internal representation that is all too common in today's programs, namely identity: applications programmers have a proclivity for using ordinary English words for the symbol names in their systems, and with a little artful programming these symbols can be substituted for variables in canned print statements to produce quite realistic output texts. The shallowness of the conceptual model behind these symbols, however, makes these systems quite brittle: if the utterance is made outside of the very specific context that the programmer had in mind when the print statement was written, it is almost inevitable that the words will not be used with their correct senses or connotations.

reasoning. We selected the domain of planning everyday activities because we will be making use of Pustejovsky's *Theory of Aspect Calculus* (1988), and that domain has a heavy concentration of action verbs and temporal expressions.

Pustejovsky and I are concentrating our study on nearly synonymous utterances such as these:

> You can only stay until 4.
> You have to leave by 4.

The "synonymy" of this pair of texts is due to the fact that they communicate largely the same information—each entails the other. At the same time they have a difference in perspective or connotation that one can begin to see by exploring specific scenarios where they could be used. As an example, imagine that you are spending the day at DEC consulting. You would usually leave when everyone else does at 5:30, but today you want to run an errand to pick up some film that you've left for developing at the Coop (a Cambridge department store). When you give this change in plans to JEEVES, it proceeds to work through the implications, letting you know if there are going to be any problems. In this particular case, given the distance to be covered, the closing time of the store, and the uncertainties of rush hour traffic, JEEVES might conclude that if you're going to get to the Coop before it closes that you're going to have to leave by 4:00. If (like just now) the attention is on the errand, it feels most natural to us that JEEVES express this using the 'leave' phrasing; if, alternatively, attention were on the ongoing activity (say JEEVES already knows about the errand and you tell it you want to attend a lecture at 3:00), the 'stay' phrasing feels better.[7]

9.3.1 "Sublexical" Conceptual Sources For Words

In exploring these two alternative phrasings as a problem in lexical selection, we first considered what their source within the reasoning program (JEEVES) could reasonably be. Given our goal of experimenting with the Sapir-Whorf hypothesis, we wanted in particular to see how close to the surface wording the source concept(s) could be while still being an effective and general part of JEEVES' mental repertoire. In this case, as in almost all of the others we have analyzed, we were drawn to the early conclusion that the object best identified as the source was in fact sublexical. This is to say that it encodes less information than is required to specify a word or other atomic surface-level linguistic resource—to map it directly to a word would amount to committing

---

[7] We believe that it is not especially important whether we are correct in the particular connotations that we ascribe, so long as there is consensus that such subtle differences do exist. In any event our approach to such analyses is always to ground them in concrete and plausible scenarios such as this one. As a result, we expect that these connotations, while possibly very bound to their contexts, should nevertheless be realistic.

to more specificity than the object warrants in isolation from its situation of use. Only when taken in conjunction with other information in the program's state is it possible to determine which real natural language word or other linguistic resource to use.

To make this clear we must first look in more detail at JEEVES' operation in this scenario. JEEVES' reasoning is based on a set of highly schematized specialists each able to reason about a different class of activity. The specialists communicate via a model of the user's schedule that serves as a shared blackboard, and are organized in a specialization hierarchy. The specialist for 'picking up photographs at the Coop' is, for example, a specialization of 'running an errand at a department store', which is in turn a composition of 'errand' and 'activity at a department store', which are themselves ultimately specializations of "activity."

When you inform JEEVES of your intention to pick up the photographs today, the agent for this errand is instantiated, its parameters are bound (e.g., prior location is DEC Marlboro, default time is 'end of the work day'), and the calculations are done to determine the implications of the errand for other, already scheduled, activities. When this is finished, the agent posts itself on the schedule blackboard. Part of the posting is an object— the source of our example utterance—that embodies the conclusion of the agent that is most important to the other scheduled activities, namely the time at which the errand activity has to start if it is to succeed. For convenience we can call this object `transition-at-4pm`.

`Transition-at-4pm` contains information that identifies the time, 4 pm, as the value of an object of type "necessary moment of transition". The object has its parameter values set to suit this instance, e.g., the transition is between the two specific activities: the consulting day and the errand, and it is "necessary" because otherwise there won't be time to complete the errand. Being a constraint, it will activate a sentinel (Rosenberg, 1978) associated with the pending consulting activity, which in turn will note that that doing the errand implies ending your day at DEC prematurely. Depending on where we set JEEVES' thresholds, this sentinel's activation could be enough to raise the significance of the object above the level needed for JEEVES to bring it to your attention. A inline call would then evoke the generator with the instruction to express the information packaged in the object.

Tacitly this amounts to an indirect speech act since it will have the impact of making you consider whether you really want to run the errand today or wait for another time. It would invite responses such as giving JEEVES an adjustment to your plans, asking *'why?'*, or starting an exploration of variations on the parts of plans that you knew had been assumed (e.g., *'but suppose I took route 2 instead of the turnpike?'*). Any proper treatment of the utterance as a speech act should include this kind of knowledge about its impact on subsequent discourse.[8]

---

[8] At the moment, however, Pustejovsky and I do not anticipate doing any research on this

To get the most utility out of `transition-at-4pm`, the object is designed to not just be the statement of a constraint between the two activities, but also the representation of their respective start and end times. (Under this design, rather than the start-time slot of the errand having the value 4 pm, a object of type clock-time, it has as its value `transition-at-4pm`, an object of type necessary-moment-of-transition. The object is effectively a variable—revised calculations may give it different values without changing its identity—and it has the value 4 pm.[9]) Since in this case the transition between them involves a physical change of location, the categorization of 4 pm as a start/end time can be specialized (subsumed) by a categorization in terms of stay and leave, which is what makes our target utterances relevant. It is this multiple categorization that is largely what is responsible for my speaking of the object as being sublexical: if an object can have multiple realizations depending on how it is classified (which in turn depends upon how it is being used at that moment), then none of those realizations can be justified outside of a classifying context.

9.3.2   The Mechanics of Selection From a Lexical Cluster

The act of making the lexical selections that realize `transition-at-4pm` takes place within the generator after JEEVES has passed it the object. The selection is essentially the first thing that the generator does, since we see the identity of the selected wording as the chief linguistic constraint on the rest of decisions that the generator will make. By making this most constraining decision very early, we are able to insure that the process overall can be done indelibly since the implications of the decision will be available to direct or modulate all later decisions.

I will focus here just on the lexical selection mechanism we are proposing. Our design for the early stages of the generation process overall—what is generally termed "text planning"—is otherwise in flux. What had been a simple matter under earlier, dictionary-based, designs is now very intricate. A short description of some of what we have been doing in text planning can be found in (McDonald and Meteer, 1988) and (Meteer, 1988, 1989).

The object `transition-at-4pm` is a reification of a body of relationships among other objects in JEEVES' representation of the user's schedule and its own background knowledge. It was formed by successive layering of information (functional composition) in the course of the errand agent's calculations. Since

---

sort of discourse control problem, and will just have a specific call to the generator as part of JEEVES' hardwired code. When we do take up this problem again it will likely be along the lines sketched in (McDonald *et al.*, 1986) and be done in collaboration with Philip Werner.

[9] A data structure with such a multifaceted "personality" obviously does not have a simple implementation. This paper is not the place to go into any depth on the design. Suffice it to say that we are using a design where objects like our example are first class entities in the representation (meaning that they can be linked to other such objects by explicit functions/relations) and are composed out of other such objects which occupy named "slots" as in a conventional frame-based notation.

it is a composite object, its realization by the generator will be compositional, and in this case will deliberately mimic the composition of the two target utterances. The two utterances, 'you have to leave by 4' and 'you can only stay until 4' are both statements of actions by the user ('you'), are both marked as necessary ('have to', 'can only'), and are both grounded on an action verb-preposition pair ('stay until', 'leave by'), which takes one argument ('4 pm'). We will look here just at the process of choosing the verb-preposition pair, since this is the part of the utterance that involves a lexical cluster.

Given this compositionality, the precise source for the verb-preposition element of the utterance is not the object transition-at-4pm as a whole but a sub-object in one of its fields. For convenience, we can refer to this object as StayTill/LeaveBy. Following our design rule that the association between a object and its realization is a direct link rather than a matching process (recall Section 9.2), there will be a long term link from StayTill/LeaveBy to an entity we are tentatively calling a "lexical cluster". StayTill/LeaveBy is a permanent part of JEEVES' knowledge base, used in many rules and rule schemas; the instance object specific to this particular session with the user is transition-at-4pm. Transition-at-4pm could not have a permanent link to a lexical cluster (or any other kind of generation structure) since it only came into existence during this session. Its realization is controlled by links to its class rather than to it as an individual.

The process of lexical choice goes as follows. The generator looks up and activates the lexical cluster for StayTill/LeaveBy: The cluster examines the context (see below), establishes what it is about this context that will dictate its choice, and makes its decision, returning a specific lexical element that the generator incorporates into the appropriate place in its growing linguistic plan for the utterance.

The lexical cluster that StayTill/LeaveBy is linked to is specific to the pair 'stay until/leave by', returning whichever of these two fits the current context. There would be a comparable cluster for every permanent object in JEEVES that denotes a sublexical body of information: 'go/come', 'buy/sell', 'send to/receive from', etc.

As a point of contrast, the kind of decision made by a lexical cluster is very different, as we see it, from that needed to choose between, say, 'you have to leave by 4 or you won't have time to do your errand' and just 'you have to leave by 4'; or to choose between 'you have to leave by 4' and 'you have to leave in 10 minutes' (spoken at 3:50) or 'you have to leave soon'. Presumably, these other classes of decisions are amenable to general, structural accounts like the one are making for these lexical clusters; we have yet to study them in any detail.

Functionally the decision procedure of a lexical cluster is a discrimination net that tests JEEVES' state. Our goal in designing the tests is of course to capture as much generality as possible, and to this end we are employing an analysis of 'stay until' and 'leave by' that is based on Pustejovsky's *Theory of Aspect Calculus* (1988). Briefly this theory postulates an algebra of events and process types for temporal aspect akin to Vendler's. Unit events combine into X-bar like trees, where position in a tree carries general entailments and presuppositions that follow from the shape of the tree rather than the specific events it organizes.

In an aspect calculus analysis, the verb 'stay' corresponds to a tree whose root is a node of type process whose daughters are some unspecified sequence of simple events. The phrase 'stay until' corresponds to a larger tree built on top of the tree for 'stay' that is rooted in an accomplishment and whose daughters are the tree for the 'stay' process followed by an event that is anchored to the moment in time that is the argument of 'stay until'. Similarly the analysis of 'leave' by is a tree whose first level constituents are an event anchored to the moment in time when you must leave followed by a tree for a process. In our present example, these two time- anchored events correspond to the very same object, `transition-at-4pm`, and the flanking processes correspond to the consulting activity (for 'stay') and the errand activity (for 'leave').

To make its discriminating tests, the lexical cluster must first establish the just-mentioned correspondences, which it does by following out the links from StayTill/LeaveBy via transition-at-4pm to the two activities (recall that transition-at-4pm is simultaneously the end point of the consulting activity and the starting point of the errand). Making the choice now comes down to determining which of these two activities is more salient given the point in JEEVES' code from which the generator was called on this occasion. For instance if the motive for informing you of `transition-at-4pm` came from the errand agent announcing a new thing that you now had to do, the errand would be more salient (this comes down to it being the activity in control at the moment of speech) and the utterance would come out as: 'you have to leave by 4'. Alternatively if the motive had come from the sentinel posted by the consulting activity, perhaps because its rules say that upon reflection you might not want to leave earlier than usual, then the utterance would come out as: 'you can only stay until 4'.

To summarize this section, our approach has been to work backwards from an instance of a lexical perspective pair in a concrete scenario, in this case 'stay until/leave by'. We developed a model in our scheduling domain that relates the difference in perspective to differences in the state of the scheduling program. Lexical choice is done by following a permanent link from a "sublexical" internal object to a "lexical cluster", which is an organization of alternative lexical choices into a discrimination net that tests the state of the underlying program to determine what is most salient and therefore which lexical choice should be made.

9.4 CHOICES MADE IN THE UNDERLY-ING PROGRAM RATHER THAN THE GENERATOR

In a conventionally organized generator, lexical and syntactic choices are made independently by different modules that are not active simultaneously. In these generators, a quandary arises from the possibility of close interaction and dependency between the two kinds of linguistic resources: Choices involving the two kinds of resources may be difficult to serialize consistently or may sometimes lead to backtracking–a markedly more complex control structure than one would like – See discussion in (Danlos, 1984). To my mind part of this quandary has been an artificial limitation of the discussion. Lexical and syntactic alternatives are taken to be adjudicated only within the generator; we seldom consider the possibility that the solution could lie in the choice being made in the underlying program before the generator runs.

An instance of this limitation occurred in a recent workshop.[10] It comes in an argument made by Sergei Nirenburg in favor of a highly distributed model of the generation process as an alternative to the conventional design. He used as examples the two phrases below, both expressing the idea that at some time in the past the speaker had an intention "to go" but it didn't come to pass.

'I planned to go ... '
'I would have gone ... '

Nirenburg regards this as a case where the same conceptual unit may be realized either by lexical means ('planned') or by syntactic means ('would have'). He then draws on a principle that is common to most theories of generation (indeed, to most theories of deliberate action of any kind), namely that for two different outcomes to be treated as equal alternatives in a decision process, they must be formally accessible at the same time within a single choice point – See the recent discussion of this issue in (Bateman, 1988).

If we provisionally accept Nirenburg's claim that the two alternative realizations are indeed properly characterized as involving lexical and syntactic resources respectively, then this data, plus the principle of simultaneously available alternatives, leads to the architectural claim that lexical and syntactic decision making must intermingle freely in a common phase of processing. Such a claim would mandate markedly more freedom ininterleaving lexical and grammatical decision making than some researchers (such as myself) would allow. Yet without this relatively free mixing of the two kinds of decisions, a realization component would not be able to present both realizations simultaneously

---

[10]The 1987 Natural Language Planning Workshop sponsored by the Northeast Artificial Intelligence Consortium at Minnowbrook Conference Center, Blue Mountain Lake, N.Y. Proceedings available from NAIC c/o the Department of Computer Science, Syracuse University.

as alternatives for the text planner to choose between. Drawing on the support of this argument, Nirenburg (1988, 1989) proposes a highly distributed model for language generation where such interleaving is facilitated.

9.4.1 Two Objects, Two Realizations

While it is true that these two phrases are "synonymous" in that they do communicate the same information, they are of the same type semantically: one is a possession ('I had a plan to go'), the other a state ('I might have gone but I didn't'). This is problematic, since it is hard to imagine that any general (i.e., non-idiosyncratic) linguistic class of alternatives could be motivated that would include both a possession and a state on equal terms, regardless of the generator's architecture.

This difficulty and others suggest that we look for other ways of analyzing the two phrases. I believe that rather than give up the otherwise successful premise that lexical choices precede syntactic ones,[11] we should look closely at the presumption that the two phrases should be seen as having exactly the same source in an underlying program. If the case can be made that the actual difference between the two is not the choice of linguistic realizations but rather a matter best appreciated before realization is begun, then the argument evaporates: There would no longer one object with two realizations, but two objects each with its own independent realization. (Note that it does not particularly matter what may be the case with the objects in an application program that we could take off the shelf today. This paper started with the assertion that we should treat the modelling and representational techniques of today's programs as suspect—too shallow in their treatments to support the delicacy and precision that we see in how people use language. New techniques are needed, and the demands imposed by sophisticated generation systems will play a significant role in their development.)

Certainly there is no reason to take it for granted that a reasoning system will always represent ostensibly synonymous texts with the same internal expression. It is true that early parsing systems would collapse "unimportant" text variations to the same "canonical form" (e.g., passive- with-by-phrase clauses

---

[11]More precisely, the premise is that for the unit of information encompassed by an elementary surface structure tree in a Tree Adjoining Grammar (Joshi, 1985) the first and most influential choice is the lexical realization of the phrase's head. This selection determines the family of trees that can be employed (what in Mumble-86 is known as a "realization class", see Meteer *et al.*, 1987), and with it the possibilities for expressing arguments, temporal information, existential status, multiplicity, etc. Note that this premise does not, however, carry with it any presumptions about the relative timing of realization decisions involving sets of these units severally or collectively (e.g., within complex sentences or paragraphs), nor any about the timing of the realization of information units syntactically embedded within an elementary tree (e.g., NPs embedded in clauses or some kinds of modifiers inside NPs—for instance the fact that some subunit will be expressed as a pronoun might well be known prior to realization of the unit as a whole).

collapsing to the same internal expression as active clauses). But the reasoning performed by these parsers' backend applications was anything but sophisticated. Today we appreciate that the nuances texts can convey cannot be reasoned with unless they are reflected in the reasoner's representation. If it means something slightly different to the reasoner 'to have had a plan to do something but not been able to carry it out' than 'to have not done something', then there must be two different expressions in the underlying program. No doubt the expressions would be closely related and might literally share common parts, but some difference in categorization or internal makeup must be present if the difference in information content is to be consequential.

9.4.2 "Canonical Action Chains" To Carry Shared Inferences

Assuming for the sake of argument that the 'planned to go/would have' gone texts do correspond to different internal expressions and that the choice between them is a matter of promotion/selection rather than realization, a new question arises. How does the speaker/reasoner know that the texts are synonymous, i.e., that they can lead to the same inferences when communicated to a suitable audience? It is important to know this in order to carry on a fluent discourse: The response to what one says may be couched in a different way that one's audience assumed was an available alternative, yet it must still be recognized as cohesive. For instance suppose that one said 'I would have gone on vacation, but there was just too much work to do' and got back the reply 'Oh, where had you been planning to go?'. The reply must be recognized as referring to what had just been said, which means that the close relationship between the two different surface events must be represented somehow.

One way to do this is to posit cognitive structures incorporating both alternatives that are mutually known by speaker and audience as a matter of common sense and shared experience. These structures would relate the two internal objects corresponding to these texts, as well as related ones, all as instances of a general structure. Upon hearing one of the texts the audience would recognize and bring to mind the structure it was part of and thereby have access to any of the information that they would have gotten had they heard an alternative instead. Since the speaker knows that this will happen (through presumed mutual belief), he is free to use any particular item within the structure that he chooses, and can thereby communicate the nuances that come from deliberately holding a specific perspective.

As a candidate for the cognitive structure that would be needed in this case, I propose that our mental models include what might be called "canonical action chains", script-like structures that represent customary sequences of mental states and actions. In this case the chain might be: The chain would be parameterized by the specific action and actor involved, and should include

[1] 'wanting <to go>' →
  [2] 'planning how <to go>' →
    [3] 'intending <to go>' →
      [4] 'doing <to go>' →
        [5] 'having done <to go>'.

provisions for action failures or unforeseen contingencies as overlays to the default chain of events. In this example we had indeed 'planned to go' (stage 2), and if nothing had intervened 'would have gone' (stage 5).

The idea is that given any step in the chain, an audience will automatically infer the whole chain. Armed with this inference rule, a speaker can choose most any step of the chain as the basis of the utterance and expect to have an equivalent effect on the hearer. We would then look to other aspects of the speaker's intentional state to find the motivation behind the choice in a given case; for example this could be the relative salience of the steps to the internal agent that prompted the speech, as in the previous section.

There is obviously much more to be developed before a notion like canonical action chains could be accepted as coherent or useful (let alone psychologically plausible): more examples must be worked out, the particulars formalized and implemented, and evidence accumulated that the behaviors we would expect such a mental structure to facilitate in fact occur. Consequently my point here is not to convince anyone that some or another conceptual representation belongs in every application program, but simply to illustrate that we have many more options open to us as analysts than we tend to consider. We should not automatically assume that the difficulties we meet in doing our generation research should be solved within the generation process: a great deal of the variance that we see at the surface level in language may have its origins very deep in the conceptual system.

9.5   CONCLUDING REMARKS

The title of this paper asks what is the place of words in the generation process. As a field we have put off asking this question for a long time, probably for excusable reasons, but if we are to make further progress, particularly in the area of text planning, then we cannot put it off any longer. My answer to the question, at least for the moment, is that while the words per se are presumably linguistic elements and as such part of the generator, the criteria governing their use are dictated by the underlying program (mind) that drives and motivates the generator. This applies, furthermore, not simply to words but to linguistic resources of all kinds: collocations, idioms, marked syntactic constructions, etc., to the extent that these are not grammatically conditioned—which is only to say that there are other kinds of atomic linguistic packagings for meaning besides words.

This paper has argued for this view by example, showing that in the cases considered, the simpler and most direct designs all involved dependence on information from the underlying program's model and intentional state, rather than the linguistic state of the generator. This is in keeping with the idea that lexical choice is the first thing that the generator does, i.e., before it has established any substantial linguistic state.

For overlearned, highly familiar items like kitchens and keyboards, we argued that there was really no "choice" at all, the decision being implicit in the categorization. For the case where there appeared to be a linguistic decision required between syntactic and lexical alternatives, we argued that a natural conceptual representation, the "action chain", permitted a more motivated decision, again at a conceptual rather than a linguistic level. In the most elaborate example, we argued that the internal object whose information was being expressed was intrinsically "sublexical", and so could not receive a realization without also incorporating information about the speaker's attitude toward the object.

All of this of course only scratches the surface of the problems presented by lexical choice: There has been no discussion of the impact of prose style, or of the issue of what level of categorization to use (e.g., 'Mac-II' vs. 'computer'), to mention just two things. But I hope that an overall message has come through: for too long we have tended to focus our research on linguistic issues and not on mental models, and so have neglected the possibility that the input our generators receive may be conceptually far more refined and richly structured than what they are getting presently. This means we have missed opportunities for more elegant and extensible solutions where the underlying program's attitudes and models carry as much weight or more as the actions within the generator, thereby permitting many decisions to be motivated by general principles taking into account the system as a whole, rather than simply stipulated within the generator alone. Unless we collectively spread our focus to take in these models, we will not arrive at any satisfactory computational theories of lexical choice.

BIBLIOGRAPHY

Appelt, Doug (1985) "Some Pragmatic Issues in the Planning of Definite and Indefinite Noun Phrases", in *Proceedings of the 23rd Annual Meeting of the Association of Computational Linguistics*, July 8-12, Univ. of Chicago, 198-203.

Bateman, John A. (1988) 'Aspects of clause politeness in Japanese: an extended inquiry semantics treatment'. *Proceedings of the 26th International Conference on Computational Linguistics*, Buffalo, New York, pp147-154.

Cumming, Susanna (1986) "The Lexicon in Text Generation", Workshop on Automating the Lexicon, Pisa, Italy; available at a Technical Report from Information Sciences Institute, Marina Del Rey, California.

Danlos, Laurence (1984) "Conceptual and linguistic decisions in generation", in *Proceedings of COLING-84*, Stanford University, July 2-6, 501- 504.

Goldman, Neal (1975) "Conceptual Generation", in Schank (ed.) Conceptual Information Processing, Elsevier.

Hovy, Eduard (1987) Generating Natural Language under Pragmatic Constraints, Ph.D. Dissertation, Yale University.

Hovy, Eduard (1988) "Generating Language with a Phrasal Lexicon", in *Natural Language Generation Systems*, McDonald and Bolc (eds.), Springer Verlag, 1988, 353-384.

Jacobs, Paul (1988) "Phred: a Generator for Natural Language Interfaces", in *Natural Language Generation Systems*, McDonald and Bolc (eds.), Springer Verlag, 1988, 312-354.

Kempen, Gerard (1987) editor, *Natural Language Generation: Recent Advances in Artificial Intelligence, Psychology, and Linguistics*, Kluwer Academic Publishers, Dordrecht, The Netherlands.

Kukich, Karen (1988) "Fluency in Natural Language Reports", in *Natural Language Generation Systems*, McDonald and Bolc (eds.), Springer Verlag, 1988, 280-312.

Levelt, Willem J.M. and Herbert Schriffers (1987) "Stages of Lexical Access" in *Natural Language Generation: Recent Advances in Artificial Intelligence, Psychology, and Linguistics*, Kluwer Academic Publishers, Kempen (ed.) 1987, 395-404.

Marcus, Mitchell (1987) "Generation Systems Should Choose Their Words", Proceedings of TINLAP-3, New Mexico State University, January 7-9, 211-214.

McDonald, David (1983) "Natural Language Generation as a Computational Problem: an introduction", in Brady and Berwick (eds.) *Computational Models of Discourse*, MIT Press, 1983, pp. 209-266.

McDonald, David, JoAnn Brooks, Beverly Woolf and Philip Werner, Transition Networks for Discourse Management, Technical Report #86-34, Dept. Computer and Information Science, UMass., April 1986.

McDonald, David and Marie Meteer (1988) "From Water to Wine: generating natural language text from today's application programs", in *Proceedings of the 2nd Conference on Applied Natural Language Processing* (ACL), Austin, February 9-12, 41-48.

McGuire, Rod (1980) "Political Primaries and Words of Pain", manuscript, Dept. of Computer Science, Yale; see also section 6 in Lehnert *et al.* "Boris– An Experiment in In-Depth Understanding of Narratives", Artificial Intelligence 20 (1983) 15-62.

McKeown, Kathleen (1985) *Text Generation*, Cambridge University Press.

Meteer, Marie (1988) "Defining a Vocabulary for Text Planning", in *Proceedings of the Workshop on Text Planning and Realization*, AAAI-88, St Paul, Minnesota, August 25, 115-112.

Meteer, Marie (1989) "The Spokesman Natural Language Generation System", Technical Report 7090, Bolt, Beranek, and Newman Inc., Cambridge, MA.

Meteer, Marie, David McDonald Scott Anderson, David Forster, Linda Gay, Alison Huettner and Penelope Sibun (1987) "Mumble-86: Design and Implementation", TR #87-87 Dept. Computer & Information Science, UMass., September 1987, 174 pgs.

Nirenburg, Sergei, Victor Lesser and Eric Nyberg (1989) "Controlling a Language Generation Planner", in *Proceedings of IJCAI-89*, Detroit, August 21-25.

Nirenburg, Sergei and Irene Nirenburg (1988) "A Framework for Lexical Selection in Natural Language Generation", in *Proceedings of COLING-88*, Budapest, August 22-27, 471-475.

Pustejovsky, James and Sergei Nirenburg (1987) "Lexical Selection in the Process of Language Generation", *Proceedings of the 25th Annual Meeting of the Association for Computational Linguistics*, Stanford, July 6-9, 201- 206.

Pustejovsky, James and Sergei Nirenburg (1988) "Event Semantic Structure", Technical Report, Brandeis University.

Rosenberg, Steve (1978) "Understanding in Incomplete Worlds", AIM #475, Artificial Intelligence Lab, MIT.

Wilensky, Robert (1976) "Using Plans to Understand Natural Language", in *Proceedings of the annual meeting of the Association for Computing Machinery*, Houston.

Chapter 10

Lexico(Grammatical) choice in text generation

Christian Matthiessen

Abstract: This paper discusses the problem of lexical choice in text generation, suggesting that it has to be viewed as part of the problem of lexicogrammatical choice instead of being isolated. First, the importance of the problem and the need for a general survey are noted. Next, in order to interpret the contributions these approaches have made and to identify the full spectrum of factors that have to be considered, an abstract model of lexis within lexicogrammar is presented. Then, existing approaches are discussed and located in relation to the abstract model. This paper is a shorter version of a longer treatment that also goes into the abstract model presented here in more detail.

10.1   THE PROBLEM: LEXICAL CHOICE IN TEXT GENERATION

In a contribution to a panel discussion on text generation, Marcus (1987) observes about natural language generation systems:

> Such systems operate by incrementally specifying fragments of linguistic structure in a top-down fashion, typically inserting specific lexical items only when the frontier of the structure is encountered. In some important sense, these systems have no real knowledge of lexical semantics and only rarely make lexical choices. ... The alternative, which we must face up to sooner or later, is to attack the closely related problems of lexical semantics and lexical choice directly.

The basic issue identified by Marcus is the problem of dealing with *lexical choice*. We may disagree with his characterization of the state of work on lexical selection in text generation in details or more generally: for instance, the typical approach to lexical selection is arguably not the one of Marcus' characterization; rather, lexical choice often precedes the process of grammatical expression in text generation systems. However, Marcus does point to a central problem or rather cluster of problems that have come into focus in work on text generation but have not been discussed in a general way.

Certain subproblems have received attention – for example, the relationship to the knowledge base, e.g., (Matthiessen, 1981; McDonald, 1981), lexical repetition (Granville, 1983), some type of 'idioms' (Jacobs, 1985), and audience considerations (Hovy, 1987a,b): see the appendix for a partial list of work on lexis in generation. What we need to do now is to take stock of the various approaches that have been developed and to relate them to an abstract general characterization of lexical choice and lexical resources. Such a characterization can then serve to guide us in further work on lexical choice and lexical organization in text generation.[1] This paper is offered as a step in that direction; it is intended as a complement to Cumming's (1986) survey of the lexicon in text generation and the various lexical phenomena that have to be taken into account in full-fledged general generation systems and also Pustejovsky's and Nirenburg's (1987) discussion of "lexical selection in the process of language generation".

---

[1] Although I will present the discussion in terms of text generation, I don't mean to suggest that the lexical resources are different from those used in text understanding and parsing. Kasper (e.g., 1988) has developed a parser version of the systemic Nigel grammar, based on Martin Kay's Functional Unification Grammar, and he has shown that systemic grammar and Functional Unification Grammar are intertranslatable. There is thus every reason to believe that the kind of systemic lexis I will sketch here for generation can be represented for parsing purposes; Martin Kay (p.c., 1981) has indicated the general compatibility of Halliday's thesaurus-like model of lexis with Functional Unification Grammar.

I'll begin by asking four related questions:

(i) how lexical choice is related to other processes in generation (i.e., the external aspect of the organization of lexical choice), in particular to grammatical choice and expression;

(ii) how the process of lexical choice is organized internally;

(iii) what functions are achieved in lexical choice. And, since there are several functions, how to integrate and reconcile the various functions so that a unique choice can be made;

(iv) what contextual factors influence lexical choice.

I have asked these questions in terms of processes; but we also need to ask the corresponding resource questions: how are the lexical resources related to other resources in a generator; what is the internal organization of lexis; what are the functions of lexis; and how are the lexical resources differentiated according to contextual factors?

It is important to emphasize that the relationship between the answers to the two sets of questions raised above will depend on the extent to which the lexical resources are organized to guide the processes. For instance, an ordinary dictionary provides no guidance for the choice of lexical items so all the guidance has to be built into the process of lexical choice; in contrast, the thesaurus model of lexical organization to be discussed below provides a good deal of guidance for the process of lexical choice. Because of their potential for guiding lexical choice, I will devote a good deal of attention to the organization of lexical resources.

The three issues identified above are the central ones; there are also a number of related subproblems, such as:

(v) how to handle lexical choices that are collocationally conditioned (say, the conditioning between *regret + deeply* and *turn + sour*);

(vi) how to handle lexical items above word rank and 'idioms' of various types (*she is X if she is a day; turn over a new leaf; the eye of the storm*; etc.).

We can address issues such as those I've just identified in the context of a particular generation task or cluster of generation tasks such as those provided by a particular expert system. The value of doing this is that we can then develop a very detailed and explicit model since we can simplify or set aside a number of the factors that have to be taken into consideration when we build lexical models. The problem is that the model will only be as general as the questions we are asking. We need more than one level of abstraction in the development of lexical models.[2] As a complement to this kind of detailed and explicit model we can explore an abstract one, which is what I will do in this paper. It can make up for a certain lack in detail and explicitness by providing a very general overview that will be relevant to the generation of casual conversation as well as to the generation of economic reports or of advertisements. The danger we have to avoid is to develop superficially general models that are only responsive to a small set of issues that come up in the currently still fairly restricted text generation tasks. Instead, we have to provide for a dialogue between general abstract models and particular concrete implementations.

Before I start, let me make one terminological observation. I will use the term **lexis** for the resources of vocabulary. It covers both the static organization of vocabulary and the process of lexical choice. It is important not to invoke the lexicon as a model of lexical organization from the outset, as often happens: as we will see, the lexicon is only one possible model of vocabulary, although this has often been overlooked precisely because the lexicon is taken as the starting point.[3]

10.2   AN ABSTRACT SYSTEMIC-FUNCTIONAL MODEL OF LEXIS FOR TEXT GENERATION

I will now sketch an abstract model for text generation which contrasts with a good deal of the past work in text generation and thus can serve to identify issues for future work. I will show how it provides approaches to the questions raised above in Sections 10.3 through 10.6. I will then relate the model to past work in text generation in Section 10.7. The model is abstract in that it does not constitute a concrete implementation; there are various ways of implementing it. Since it is abstract, it can be more general and cover more ground than any given implemented model can afford to do: implemented models are simplified according to the particular generation task or set of task they have been been developed for. At the very least, I hope the abstract model may be useful as a 'checklist'.

The abstract model used here is a systemic-functional one; it derives from a functional-rhetorical approach to language rather than a formal-logical one. In general, it assumes that the boundary between the strategic and tactical parts

---

[2] Another approach is to explore the representation of one lexical item or a small number of related items: cf. McDonald's contribution to this volume. It is important to do this against the background of the systems of which it is a part, as European structuralist linguistic work on lexical fields has shown, from (Trier, 1931) onwards.

[3] The use of the term *lexicon* is quite variable in any case; cf. Cumming (1986) for some discussion of this point. For instance, as I will note in Section 10.3, the lexicon of one model may include information that is part of the grammar of transitivity of another model.

of a generator does not fall in such a way that grammar and lexis are merely tactical: strategic considerations are embodied in grammatical and lexical choices and 'tactics' is a matter of the realization of these choices.

Let me characterize the model very briefly in systemic terms first and then 'unpack' this characterization.[4]

Lexis is the most delicate part of the metafunctionally diverse resource of lexicogrammatical, which is organized as a set of inter-related choices available to the speaker, realizing semantic choices made under the influence of contextual factors.

This characterization uses the 'dimensions' of systemic theory – delicacy, stratification, metafunctional diversification – to locate lexis in the overall model;[5] diagrammatically shown in Figure 10.1. So I'll now 'unpack' the brief characterization and its diagrammatic equivalent.

Resource: Lexis is a resource for expressing meanings of various kinds; as a resource, it is organized as a set of inter-related lexical choices. This organization of lexis or any other linguistic resource as a set of inter-related options is called paradigmatic organization and is represented by means of the *indexsystem networksystem network* of systemic theory. One lexical choice or a combination of choices may be realized (expressed, coded) by a particular lexical item. (The diagram does not show the distinction between the organization of lexis as inter-related options and their realizations by means of lexical items.)

Delicacy: Lexis and grammar together constitute one unified resource, called *lexicogrammar* in systemic linguistics. Lexis is thus one part of lexicogrammar; more specifically, if we model lexicogrammar as a large network of inter-related grammatical and lexical choices, these choices are ordered taxonomically from very general ones to more specific ones and lexical choices are more specific than grammatical ones. (Thus lexis and grammar are not related in terms of constituency but in terms of specificity. This way of relating lexis and grammar is different from approaches based on structure rather than choice; the two ways of approaching the relationship between lexis and grammar have to be kept separate or terminological and conceptual confusions are likely to arise.) The taxonomic ordering is called delicacy and lexical choices are thus more delicate than grammatical ones. Grammatical choices are realized grammatically by means of specifications of grammatical structure; lexical choices are realized lexically by means of lexical items; together structure and

---

[4] Discussions of systemic linguistics in the context of computational linguistics have concentrated on systemic grammar; see e.g., (Winograd, 1983). But for present purposes we also need to take account of systemic lexical theory – see in particular (Halliday, 1961, 1966; Hasan, 1987) and the systemic notions of context and register, e.g., (Halliday, 1978; Halliday and Hasan, 1985). For a discussion that relates systemic semantic theory to the latter two notions, see (Patten, 1988) and (Bateman and Paris, 1989).

[5] Delicacy and stratification (organization into levels) are discussed in (Halliday, 1961), which also contains the first systemic observations about lexis. Metafunctional diversification is a later addition; cf. for example (Halliday, 1967/8).

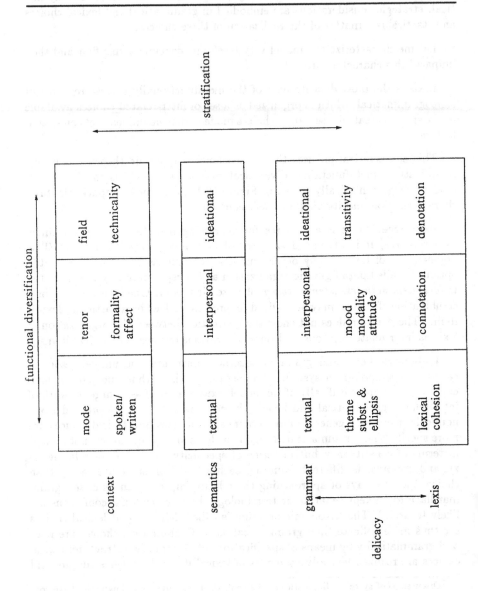

Figure 10.1: Abstract model of lexical organization and choice

items form wordings.[6] In the diagram, I have labelled some of the most important clause grammar systems and glossed the lexical areas; they are diversified
according to metafunction, as we will see below.

Stratification: The linguistic system is organized into a three levels or
strata of abstraction – phonology, lexicogrammar (sometimes simply called
linguistic form), and semantics.[7] Each pair is directly related by realization;
phonology realizes lexicogrammar, which in turn realizes semantics. (Phonology
is not shown in the diagram in Figure 10.1; it would appear below lexicogrammar.) This organization into strata is known as **stratification**.

All of lexicogrammar is covered by a uniform semantic interface to the context of the linguistic system. Just as lexicogrammar consists of lexis as well as
grammar, the semantic interface comprises lexical semantics as well grammatical semantics. This interface may take the form of the chooser and inquiry interface developed for systemic generation grammars within the Penman project
(Mann, 1983; Matthiessen, 1988) or it may take some other form such as a
semantic system network (Halliday, 1973) developed for and implemented in a
text generation system by Patten (1988). The distinction between lexicogrammatical and semantic considerations is a matter of stratification. I will focus on
lexis as part of lexicogrammar rather than on the topics commonly discussed
under the heading of lexical semantics (such as different types of opposition;
cf. for example, (Lyons, 1977; Evens *et al.*, 1980) and (Cruse, 1986) and I
have not elaborated the semantic stratum in the diagram: I want to discuss the
organization of the vocabulary resources in terms of which lexical choices are
made.

The **context** of the linguistic system is the context of its use – all the various
situations in which we draw upon the resources of language. Different situation
types constitute *different ways of using language* and these differences influence lexical organization and lexical choice. For instance, one use may require
the re-lexicalization of the domain of discourse; in particular, the scientific interpretation of a domain and the concomitant lexicalization of it may be quite
different from the vernacular or folk interpretation and lexicalization of it. More
generally, the linguistic system is differentiated according to the spectrum of
situation types in which it is used. For any situation type, we can recognize a

---

[6]This is not meant to suggest that there is a sharp boundary between lexis and grammar; on the contrary, delicacy is a scale. Lexical items occur in grammatical environments
and grammatical choices may be realized by grammatical items, so-called function words,
that form closed systems such as the system of determiners in English. Similarly, particular
grammatical structures (such as the transitivity structures Actor [*Peter*] Process [*handed*]
Recipient [*me*] Goal [*the wrench*] and Attribuend [*he*] Process [*was*] Attribute [*a dependency
grammarian*]) often imply particular sets of lexical items and any given lexical item will have
certain grammatical implications.

[7]We might call phonology, lexicogrammar, and semantics components or modules as is
often done in overviews of non-systemic models. The problem here is that the componential or
modular breakdown of a model typically fails to clarify what the nature of the modularization
is: is it stratification, metafunctional diversification (to be discussed below), or rank (levels
in a hierarchy, as with syntax and morphology)?

particular variety of the language; such a variety is called a functional variety
or **register**. It is of importance for present purposes since lexical items may
be register-specific and this differentiation has to be controlled (e.g., *once* vs.
once upon a time [indicating story]).

Metafunctional diversification: The linguistic system, more specifically lexicogrammar and semantics, is multifunctional. It reflects three simultaneous
metafunctions, viz. the ideational, interpersonal, and textual metafunctions.
The ideational metafunction is concerned with the interpretation and representation of experience. The interpersonal metafunction provides for the resources for interaction between speaker and listener: for assigning speech roles
to speaker and listener, for providing or eliciting comments, and so on. The textual metafunction is concerned with the presentation of ideational and interpersonal information as contextualized text. For instance, a clause selects simultaneously for transitivity (ideational), mood (interpersonal), and theme (textual).
In other words, the linguistic system and the texts it produces are **metafunctionally diverse**. Summary characterizations of the three metafunctions are
tabulated in Figure 10.2 together with indications of related distinctions and
the three metafunctional perspectives on the grammatical structure of *Tomor-
row we'll fix it won't we?* Any lexical choice will potentially reflect all three
metafunctions. Ideationally, it represents some phenomenon by classifying it
in relation to a lexical taxonomy. Interpersonally, it is a positioning in terms
of formality, attitude, and so on. Textually, it relates to previous discourse by
repeating, varying, generalizing, or summarizing a previous lexical item.

The metafunctional diversification just sketched is a property of the linguistic system, but we also find a functional kind of **diversification in context**.
Context consists of three functionally differentiated aspects: **field, tenor**, and
mode. These three aspects are categories of context as an organization of
higher-level cultural meaning – "they are a conceptual framework for representing the social context as the semiotic environment in which people exchange
meanings" (Halliday, 1978: 110);[8] they can be characterized briefly as follows
(from Halliday, op cit.: 142-3):

> **field**: "that which is 'going on', and has recognizable meaning in the
> social system; typically a complex of acts in some ordered config-
> uration, and in which the text is playing some part, and including
> 'subject-matter' as one special aspect". An example of a field is
> news reporting, involving both the different stages in reporting (ob-
> serving, interviewing, drafting, editing, and so on) and the 'subject
> matters' that are salient enough to be reported on. – Field is thus
> more specifically "a field of significant social action".

---

[8] Semiotics or the general approach to symbolic systems for creating and expressing meaning has not really entered work within AI and computational linguistics yet. It is important
in the longterm perspective, as a complement to another inter-disciplinary approach, viz.
cognitive science.

	characterization	related typologies	major resources
ideational	ideation -- interpretation and representation of the world in and around us.	semantic representational denotative propositional content cognitive	transitivity (process + participants + circumstances)
interpersonal	interaction between speaker and listener; assignments of speech roles and modal-attitudinal comments	conative-expressive (pragmatic)	mood & modality key
textual	presentation of ideational & interpersonal information as text in context; control of texual statuses and conjunctive development of text	pragmatic discourse functional sentence perspective	theme; information; conjunction

Figure 10.2: The three metafunctions of language

tenor: "the cluster of socially meaningful participant relationships, both permanent attributes of the participants and role relationships that are specific to the situation, including the speech roles, those that come into being through the exchange of verbal meanings". An example of tenor is the relationship between journalist and his/her readers, as 'objective' expert committed to the 'truth' to readers seeking information, but also as producer and consumer of a commodity (news). – Tenor is thus more specifically "a tenor of role relationships".

mode: "the particular status that is assigned to the text within the situation; its function in relation to the social action and the role structure, including the channel or medium, and the rhetorical mode". An example of mode is role news articles play as written, monologic discourse, intended to inform. – Mode is thus more specifically "a mode of symbolic organization".

(Field is comparable to the notion of **domain** in NLP, except that fields can be construed more abstractly than domains typically are. For instance, one field is that of exploring the world and learning and it spans many particular domains. That is why it is important to include the social process – learning/ instructing, reporting, entertaining, and so on – as well as the 'subject matter'.)

We can now return to the three questions concerning lexis in generation discussed in the Section 10.1 and characterize the answers to them in terms of the abstract systemic model sketched above. I will start with the internal organization of lexis and then discuss how lexis is related to other resources.

10.3   INTERNAL ORGANIZATION OF LEXIS

In systemic theory, lexis as a resource (i.e., its paradigmatic organization) is represented by means of networks of systems: lexical system networks.[9] A

---

[9] The terms of lexical systems are essentially like components in *componential analysis*. Feature terms in systems correspond to componential values. For instance, the component ± male can be represented as the system +male / –male (or male / female). It is important to note, however, that all lexical systems are automatically located in a system network, as reflected in their entry conditions. In other words, the system network embodies what is sometimes represented by means of redundancy rules in other frameworks. It is also important to emphasize that lexical items do not *consist* of lexical features; rather, they realize lexical features. The purpose of lexical features is to show how lexical items are related to one another. Given this interpretation of lexical features, the term component is thus potentially misleading. (There is a general tendency in linguistics to foreground structure at the expense of paradigmatic organization; this leads to interpretations that are unnecessarily concrete such as those that treat specific lexical items as *composed of* more general lexical items, as in generative semantics – lexical decomposition. But this is a reflection of the theoretical framework rather than lexis, the phenomenon described.)

lexical system network shows what lexical options are available to the speaker – what he or she can do lexically. The overall organization of the network reflects the taxonomic organization of vocabulary (more specifically, ideational vocabulary: interpersonal and textual lexis are largely organized in terms of the ideational taxonomic organization; see Section 10.5 below). This taxonomic organization of vocabulary is the principle behind Roget's (1852) thesaurus. The properties of this organization – taxonomic 'depth', favoured and basic levels of lexicalization, and so on – are quite interesting; they have been studied particularly in anthropological linguistics – see e.g., (Berlin *et al.*, 1973); cf. also the work by Eleanor Rosch).

Figure 10.3 gives an example from the nominal group to illustrate the system network organization of lexis. The example is adapted from (Leech, 1974: 121):[10]

Hasan (1987) presents a more complex example of a lexical system network; other examples can be found in (Fawcett, 1980; Berry, 1977; Matthiessen,1989). (A lexical system network like this raises a number of representational questions, such as the representation of a choice of a general term such as *creature*, but it would take to long to discuss these questions here; they are explored in the longer version of the paper.)

As already noted, lexis is basically organized on the model of a thesaurus, but there are three important revisions of the thesaurus model.

(i) Roget's thesaurus is organized as a strict taxonomy or discrimination network; systemic lexis is organized as a *system network* rather than a discrimination network. We thus find simultaneous systems (such as the systems 'male / female', 'human / animal', and 'adult / nonadult' in Figure 10.3) and complex entry conditions (such as the conjunction of 'count' and 'concrete' in the entry condition to the system 'animate / inanimate').

(ii) Roget's thesaurus is organized according to fields of experience (such as organic matter and the intellect). In systemic lexis, fields like these are organized in terms of the categories of the grammar (see Section 10.4) – categories such as material, mental, verbal, and relational processes.

(iii) The taxonomic organization of the thesaurus reflects the ideational organization of lexis; systemic lexis also takes the interpersonal and textual metafunctions into consideration (see Section 10.5).

Once we have established the taxonomic organization of the lexical resources, we can reason about it with respect to lexical choice. Lexical choice can be guided by the taxonomic organization: Goldman's (1974) use of lexical

---

[10]I have left out one system and increased the delicacy of the entry conditions of male / female and adult / nonadult from animate to creature.

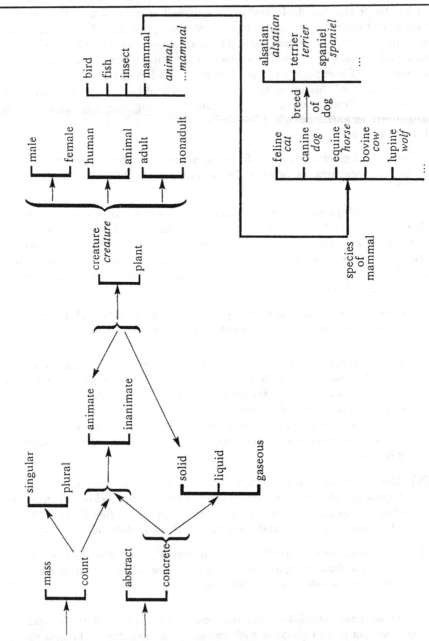

Figure 10.3: Lexical organization as system network

discrimination networks (illustrated below) showed the value of this. Lexical choice can proceed by gradual approximation identifying potential lexical *sets*, which may be relevant later on in the discourse, as well as the final choice of a unique lexical item.

For instance, in one of R.K. Narayan's short stories one of the two main characters is an old blind man. The lexical choices in all (non-pronominal) references to him are the same to the feature 'human' in the system network in Figure 10.3; within that category there is a more delicately differentiated set, giving a lexical spread to the naming of the man throughout the story − *beggar, old man, blind man, master* and *tyrant*. All of them are potential lexical candidates throughout the story, as they all describe the man; the selections from the set correlate with different stages in the story.

In general, lexical choice is not a matter of starting by choosing among individual lexical items − that is too concrete, low-level a view; rather, it is choice according to the parameters that make up the lexical organization. (Alternatively, if a particular lexical item is given, for instance because it has already figured in the discourse and should be repeated, the system network can be used as a set of redundancy rules by means of back-chaining.)

Having identified the taxonomic organization, we can also reason about different levels in the taxonomy. It turns out that certain levels are favoured in lexical choice; it is possible to identify a 'basic' taxonomic level which is selected much more frequently than subordinate and superordinate levels: see (Downing, 1981) for evidence from stories; it seems quite clear that registers vary in the favoured level of specificity.

10.4 LEXIS IN RELATION TO OTHER RE- SOURCES

Let's now turn to the question of how lexis relates to other resources in the overall model. I'll begin by discussing its relation to grammar. Once it has been related to grammar (Section 10.4.1 below), its relation to other higher-level system follows automatically (Section 10.4.2 below).

10.4.1 Lexis in Relation to Grammar: Lexicogrammar

Lexis and grammar form one unified resource − lexicogrammar. How they are related will depend on how they are modelled. For instance, they may both be represented by means of the functional descriptions of Kay's (1979) Functional Unification Grammar, in which case lexical and grammatical representations can simply be unified − cf. for example (McKeown, 1982) and her contribution in this volume. Now, if we represent lexis systemically and the grammar is also represented systemically, we can explore the hypothesis that lexis *is most delicate grammar*; that lexis and grammar are related along the dimension of delicacy as specific to general.[11] Halliday (1961) called this possibility the *grammarian's dream*; in a sense, it is the inverse of the lexicographer's dream that grammar is most general lexis. Halliday (1978: 43) states the position as follows.

> The lexical system is not something that is fitted in afterwards to a set of slots defined by the grammar. The lexicon – if I may go back to a definition I used many years ago – is simply the most delicate grammar. In other words, there is only one network of lexicogrammatical options. And as these become more and more specific, they tend more and more to be realized by the choice of a lexical item rather than by the choice of a grammatical structure. But it is all part of a single grammatical system.

Trier's (1931) work highlights the organization of lexis into fields and the thesaurus illustrates this clustering into fields. The unification of lexis and grammar implies that grammar is also organized into fields represented by system networks; the difference is only one of degree: *'grammatical fields'* are more general than *'lexical fields'*. For instance, the general process types identified by Halliday (e.g., 1985) in the grammar of transitivity constitute general grammatical fields – the fields of doing, sensing, saying, and being and having, whereas culinary metamorphosis constitutes a lexical one – the field of boiling, baking, and frying.

Hasan (1987) demonstrates the feasibility of the grammarian's dream for the lexical field of disposal – processes of gathering, collecting, scattering, dividing, and so on; she focuses on *gather, collect, accumulate, scatter, divide, distribute, strew, spill,* and *share*. She writes in her conclusion:

> Lack of space does not permit a detailed discussion of the implications of turning the whole of linguistic form into grammar, but if the account of the nine lexical items presented above has appeared valid, then it certainly upholds the systemic functional view of an uninterrupted continuity between grammar and lexis. It rejects the approach wherein the bricks of lexis are joined together by the mortar of grammar. The notion of the lexicon as an inventory of items, each having its own meaning in itself, stands refuted, and the insights of Saussure (1916), Firth (1935), Hjelmslev (1961), Whorf (1956) and Halliday (1961) are confirmed.

---

[11] This hypothesis will only make sense if the fundamental organizing principle of both lexis and grammar is paradigmatic rather than syntagmatic; it's hard to make sense of it in terms of most current formal grammars, since they focus on structure.

The conclusion, then, is that lexical choice is not disembodied from grammatical choice; it is part of the same process. And it does not proceed on an item by item basis, but in terms of fields of related items. In text generation, Goldman's (1974) discrimination network of processes of ingesting is an example of the taxonomic organization of one lexical field. It can be related to the grammatical fields of doing, saying, and so on identified in Halliday's analysis of transitivity. Ingesting (as conceived of in Goldman's discrimination network) is one type of doing. Like other doings, processes of ingesting involve an Actor and a Goal, as in

```
He      drank   the hot coffee in a great hurry
Actor   Proc    Goal           Manner
```

```
What    he      did with  the coffee was drink  it
        Actor   Proc      Goal          Process Goal

        in a great hurry
        Manner
```

The patterns involving Actor and Goal and other elements illustrated above follow automatically if the lexical system network of ingesting is integrated with the grammatical systemic network of transitivity, as I have done in the diagram below (Figure 10.4), based on Goldman's discrimination network.

There are a number of immediate subtypes of dispositive doing – motions, alterations, operations, and so on. This area of the grammar has to be worked out in more detail; for present purposes, we can just assume that processes of ingesting are a subtype of operations, with a number of intermediate steps in delicacy. They share with all types of doing the possibility of having a Goal as well as an Actor; but unlike processes of transfer (giving, donating, sending, and so on) they cannot have a Recipient.

To summarize, the systemic-functional model relates lexis to grammar as specific to general; lexis and grammar constitute one unified resource – *lexicogrammar* – and lexis is merely the most specific or delicate end of it but not necessarily the smallest; lexical items may be clauses and groups as well as words – idioms of various kinds.

10.4.2 Lexis in Relation to Higher Levels of Organization

If we treat lexis as an extension of grammar, the methods for relating it to higher levels of organization – for instance, the knowledge base and the addressee model

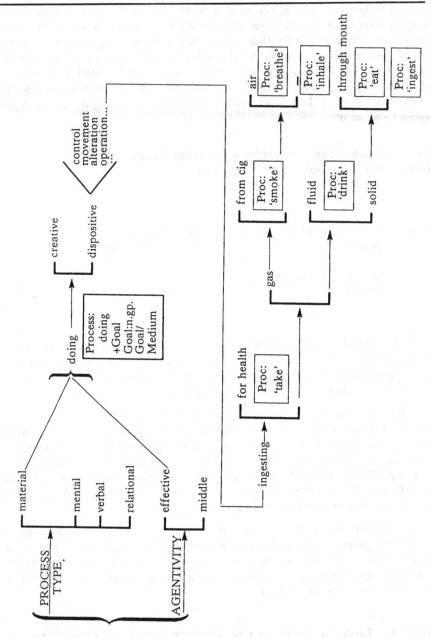

Figure 10.4: Processes of ingesting integrated with transitivity

of a generation system – follow automatically: no additional mechanisms are needed. This includes lexical choice: lexical and grammatical choice proceed according to the same principles.

There are two basic approaches in systemic work on text generation used for relating systemic grammar to higher levels of organization, viz. (i) chooser and inquiry semantics and (ii) semantic networks; both of them are equally applicable to the extended lexicogrammar.

(i) **Chooser and inquiry semantics.** One is the chooser and inquiry semantics developed within the context of the Penman project for the Nigel grammar – e.g., (Mann, 1983; Matthiessen, 1988) – and also used for the grammars of Japanese developed at Kyoto University – e.g., (Bateman *et al.*, 1987). The basic principle is to associate a semantic expert with each system in the lexicogrammatical system network. This expert will present inquiries to knowledge sources such as the knowledge base and will choose according to the responses that are computed.[12] The lexicogrammatical system network is traversed from left to right (cf. the network in Figure 10.3), i.e., by the method of forward-chaining.

(ii) **Semantic system networks.** The other approach has been developed by Patten (1988) for his SLANG system; it is based on Halliday's (1973, 1978) work on semantic system networks for specific communicative situations such as the semantic strategies for controlling somebody's behaviour. The semantic system network is organized independently of the lexicogrammatical one, but choices in the semantic network determine choices in the lexicogrammatical one by means of preselection of lexicogrammatical features. The situation-specific semantic system network is traversed left to right but the lexicogrammatical system network is traversed by means of backward-chaining from the preselected features. For some discussion of this approach to the semantic interface and its strengths, see Patten's contribution to this volume.

10.5 FUNCTIONALITY

So far I have focussed on the ideational metafunction, but the systemic model is *multifunctional*; lexis is textual and interpersonal as well as ideational. As

---

[12]For instance, an inquiry response may be computed by consulting the conceptual taxonomy in the knowledge base; see (Nebel and Sondheimer, 1986) for a discussion of the implementation of inquiries. In general, there is a boundary between the chooser and inquiry interface and other higher-level resources; this boundary makes it possible to maintain modularity in the overall generation system and allows for various alternative ways of representing information in the knowledge base and other resources that may support responses to inquiries. Since Nebel and Sondheimer (op cit.), a special 'interface language' has been developed for recording responses to inquiries. It simplifies the task of interfacing the grammar and its inquiry semantic interface with different knowledge bases and other external knowledge sources.

within the grammatical part of lexicogrammar, each metafunction makes a specific contribution:

(i) From an **ideational** point of view, lexis is concerned with 'denotation' and it is organized as taxonomies of things, events, and so on; that is, it is a taxonomic interpretation and representation of our experience of the world.

(ii) From an **interpersonal** point of view, lexis is concerned with 'connotation' – with meanings concerned with the relationship between speaker and listener and the speaker's intrusion into the speech situation; these meanings include formality and politeness as well as affect.

(iii) From a **textual** point of view, lexis is concerned with the creation of text – with continuity in text, textual boundaries, and so on.

I'll start by focusing on what interpersonal lexis and textual lexis have in common and will then turn to them individually.

10.5.1   Interpersonal and Textual Lexis

Interpersonal and textual lexis may either (i) make independent contributions or (ii) combine with ideational lexis. In the former case specific lexical systems are either interpersonal or textual; in the latter the interpersonal and lexical systems work in terms of the ideational systems and the lexical items chosen reflect ideational features as well as interpersonal and/or textual ones. Examples of the two cases are tabulated in Figure 10.5:

(The example of the right bottom corner of the table shows how a general noun, *bloke*, can be used cohesively – see (Halliday and Hasan, 1976: Section 6.1), alternating in this case with personal pronouns.)

The formal representation of independent interpersonal and textual lexical organization is quite straightforward. However, the representation of interpersonal and textual lexis in combination with ideational lexis raises a number of issues. I discuss them in the longer version of this paper, but I won't go into them here. I'll just briefly exemplify the way in which interpersonal and textual lexis combine with ideational lexis.

10.5.2   Interpersonal Lexis Combined with Ideational Lexis

Interpersonal considerations have traditionally been discussed under the heading of **connotation**; they cover a number of factors having to do with the

	interpersonal	textual
(i) Independent	**modal lexis (modality, polarity, attitude, etc.)** But surely, my dear Mrs. Warren, you know the reason.	**phoric lexis (reference, substitution, conjunction)** But surely, my dear Mrs. Warren, you know the reason. Anyway I suggested Ian tried to stay with him and he did.
(ii) in combination with ideational lexis	**'connotation': affect formality** Anyway I suggested Ian tried to stay with him and he did and I meanwhile I'd told Ian all about how daft this bloke was so Ian goes and stays with him and then he goes and tells him all about it.	**lexical cohesion: repetition, etc.** Anyway I suggested Ian tried to stay with him and he did and I meanwhile I'd told Ian all about how daft this bloke was so Ian goes and stays with him and then he goes and tells him all about it.

Figure 10.5: Interpersonal and textual lexis

relationship between speaker and listener. They have usually not been considered in generation systems, but Hovy and Schank (1984) and Hovy (1987a,b) are exceptions. Hovy built a system, PAULINE, for generating news items. It is sensitive to the reader's sympathies and interests and these factors are taken into consideration in lexical selection (as well as other aspects of the generation process). For instance, the following two excerpts are taken from texts written for an IRA terrorist and a neutral American, respectively (Hovy and Schank, op cit.: 190-1):

> "An Austin car was used by two freedom-fighters to escape from Belfast Football Stadium yesterday."
>
> "An Austin car was used by two terrorists to escape from Belfast Football Stadium yesterday."

In general, the interpersonal factors fall into two broad categories, distance between interactants and affect, the "degree of emotional charge" (Halliday, 1978: 33). For example:

(i) Distance between interactants:

> "...but our grant of sixteen thousand quid terminates at the end of seventy-six" (CEC, 791)

(ii) Affect:

> "(answers telephone) Excuse me (speaks for some time on telephone) *Stupid bastard* (continues speaking on telephone) Isn't it *bloody extraordinary*. Make me sick, some of these *bloody people* that come on, you know. It's just sort of one word every about ten seconds coming out." (CEC, 785).
>
> ...but the *unfortunate* thing is that Mrs. Morton is away this week so I'll have to look it up myself" (CEC, 787)

The distance between the interactants includes both hierarchic distance (how far apart are they socially?) – relative power or status – and distance in familiarity (how involved are they with one another?); it includes the traditional notion of formality.

10.5.3   Textual Lexis Combined with Ideational Lexis

Textual considerations have to do with **lexical cohesion** (Halliday and Hasan, 1976: Ch. 6; cf. also Martin, 1990: Ch. 5). For example, one lexical cohesive strategy is to move from a specific lexical item in one mention to a more general one in a subsequent mention, as is illustrated in the following excerpt.

> "One of the very largest <u>dinosaurs</u> was Brontosaurus (bron-toe-SAWR-us). This <u>giant</u> was about 70 feet and probably weighed as much as 30 tons." (Dinosaurs)

Here the choice of the general term *giant* serves to summarize the information given about the dinosaur: 'creature + large size'. In general, lexical cohesive strategies operate in terms of the ideational taxonomy of lexis; they use it by moving up and down it, for example, as a text proceeds with successive lexical choices. Additional examples include:
maintain: repetition

> "*Pebbles* in the stomach probably ground up the plant material so that it could be digested easily. *These pebbles* were very numerous and ground smooth from the active motion within the stomach." (100 Dinosaurs)

maintain: synonym

> "There were large numbers of cone-shaped, bony *studs* arranged in rows along the back. They were extremely hard and would have damaged the teeth of the strongest predator.There is an interesting arrangement of *these projections* just behind the head, where they form groups of three." (100 Dinosaurs)

generalize: superordinate

> "*Apatosaurus* was a sauropod and belonged to the diplodocids. As far as we know, *these dinosaurs* were the longest ever to live on the Earth." (100 Dinosaurs)

generalize: general item

> "Antarctosaurus was one of the group of sauropods, or "lizard feet." *The creatures* probably fed on plants which they stripped off using their teeth." (100 Dinosaurs)

Textual choices are very clearly choices in context. The choice in context can be illustrated from the following three paragraphs from the entry on Antarctosaurus.

> **Antarctosaurus** was one of the group of sauropods, or "lizard feet." *The creatures* probably fed on plants which *they* stripped off using *their* teeth. With such long necks *they* could reach up high to pick at the best vegetation which many other creatures were unable to reach. [...]
> The head was very small for the body, measuring only 24 inches (60

centimeters) in length. No complete skeletons of **Antarctosaurus** have been found. Much of the information we have about *the creature* is guesswork based on the bones and parts of the skeleton discovered.

Antarctosaurus means "not northern lizard." *This animal* belonged to the titanosaurids and was probably one of the largest dinosaurs. One thighbone was about 7.6 feet (2.3 meters) in length." (100 Dinosaurs)

As the extract illustrates, the choice to generalize and to use a general term depends on whether the mention is 'paragraph' initial or not: initial mention favours the specific term (*Antarctosaurus*), whereas second mention favours the move to a general term (*creature, animal*).

As with interpersonal lexis, hardly any attention has been paid to this in text generation. Granville's (1983) generator Paul, which was developed at IBM and makes use of Heidorn's (1972) Natural Language Processor work, is an exception. He presents a system for lexical substitution in text generation based on Halliday and Hasan's (1976) work. When a referent has been mentioned, the generator can choose among strategies involving pronominal reference, repetition, a superordinate term, a general noun, and a synonym. These strategies are ranked according to their ability to be used to identify a referent unambiguously; for example, pronouns are weaker in this ranking than repetition together with the definite article. The tasks in which anaphoric reference to an antecedent is needed are also ranked depending on e.g., the distance to the antecedent and on topicality (called focus by Granville). The ranked referring strategies are then matched against this ranking of referring task and a referring strategy is picked according to the match. This method is quite similar to Givón's approach to cohesion in terms of topic continuity (Givón, 1983). As Granville points out, the generator is insensitive to many important considerations such as text organization and paragraph boundaries – cf. (Hinds, 1977), but the work is important in that it illustrates how one aspect of lexical cohesion can be approached in text generation.

10.6   CONTEXTUAL FACTORS

So far I have discussed the resource of lexis itself, but let's now briefly consider context. How does the context of use influence lexical organization and lexical choice? This question has been set aside in much work on text generation since it has dealt with single uses. However, portability and multiple uses of text generation systems are becoming increasingly important and we need to map out the ways in which the context of use influences lexis.

Contextual influences can be broken down into the three aspects of context mentioned above, viz. field, tenor, and mode. These three contextual components influence the organization of lexis and lexical choice within the three metafunctions in the following way – cf. (Halliday, 1978; Halliday and Hasan, 1985; Martin, 1990: Ch. 7):

field – ideational: for instance, the technicality of the field influences the organization of ideational taxonomies and different fields vary with respect to the use and specificity of taxonomies – cf. (Wignell *et al.*, 1987; Martin *et al.*, 1988),

tenor – interpersonal: the tenor of the relationship between speaker and listener – affect, formality, expertise, etc. influences the interpersonal meaning of the choice of formal and attitudinal items – see e.g., (Poynton, 1984, 1985). Examples of how the tenor of the relationship influences the choice of lexis in the area of personal pronouns and terms of address have illustrated in detail in (Brown and Gilman, 1960; Ervin-Tripp, 1969.); and

mode – textual: the mode distinction between spoken and written influences the degree of lexical specificity and the 'density' of lexical items per unit of running text, a question of how information is distributed across units in text – see e.g., (Halliday, 1978: 224; 1985b; Ure, 1971).

That is to say, the field tends to determine ideational meanings, the tenor interpersonal ones, and the mode textual ones. For instance, the significant social action is reflected in the ideational resources of transitivity, whereas the tenor of the relations between speaker and listener is reflected in selections of mood and modality. These influences can be seen in lexis as well as in grammar.

Different fields imply different lexical subsystems, which is behind the notion of lexical fields already discussed above such as the field of cuisine (cf. Lehrer, 1967); but in addition fields may differ lexically in various respects. For instance, the field of music theory is lexicalized by a largely Italian vocabulary. Fields may be related to tenor, e.g., by being sacred, profane, or taboo, and this will have influence on lexical choice. But the most important consideration for present purposes is probably the degree of technicality of the field. Often the same field may be construed in common every day terms as well as in technical terms. The technicality of the construal of the field functions as selector of lexical taxonomies. For instance, Wignell *et al.* (1987) exemplify three different taxonomies of birds of prey. One is an 'uninformed' folk taxonomy, the second is a birdwatchers' folk taxonomy, and the third is the scientific taxonomy.

If the lexical systems of the system network are equipped with semantic choice processes, the choosers of the chooser and inquiry framework mentioned above, they can ascertain the information about conceptual patterns (concepts + roles and role restrictions), intended affect, discourse history, and so on that is needed to make multifunctionally appropriate lexical selections.

10.7   THE SYSTEMIC MODEL IN RELATION TO OTHER APPROACHES TO THE ISSUES

Let's now consider how the systemic model sketched above is related to the approaches to the issues identified in Section 10.1 that have been or could be taken in text generation. (This is not intended as a comprehensive overview of the lexicon in text generation; for an overview, see Cumming, 1986, and for a general discussion of the lexicon in natural language processing, see Ingria, 1986.) The table in Figure 10.6 (Figure 10.6) presents a summary of the systemic model and treatments of lexis in text generation that are similar to it. These treatments have already been mentioned in the preceding sections and I will now focus points of alternation.

10.7.1   The Internal Organization of Lexis

First, let's deal with the internal organization of lexis itself. There are essentially two approaches to the internal organization of lexis, both of which derive from traditional lexicographic models – see e.g., (McArthur, 1986) who calls the two approaches alphabetic lexicography and thematic lexicography):[13]

(i) the dictionary: a collection of lexical entries; the lexicon component of generative models and many NLP systems.

(ii) the thesaurus: semantically oriented taxonomy of lexical items; this is a rough model of systemic lexis.

(i) The dictionary. The dictionary treats lexis as a collection of *lexical entries*, usually listed alphabetically. It developed originally not in response to the writer's needs to express himself or herself but as bilingual glossaries and lists of "hard" or foreign words.

The dictionary is better known, more widely understood, and more widely used than the thesaurus and it is the model that has been incorporated into various generative theories of language as the 'lexicon'. When the dictionary is taken as the model for semantic memory, as Quillian (e.g., 1967) did when he developed the semantic net, and the organization of the dictionary is made explicit by associative links, each lexical entry is still the hub of organization. There is no taxonomic root from which a tree grows, as there is in the thesaurus, and it took a while in the work on knowledge representation before the taxonomic relation was given special significance, as it is e.g., in (Brachman, 1978).

---

[13] The thesaurus is a development of the thematic tradition.

			Systemic model	Example of generation system
(i) internal organization of lexis	dictionary (item-based)			Goldman's (1974) BABEL
	thesaurus (system-based; independent lexical org.)		✓	
(ii) lexis in relation to grammar	independent components			
	one unified resource	grammatical	✓	
		lexical		
(iii) metfunctional diversification	unifunctional: ideational (denotation)			
	multifunctional: ideational interpersonal textual		✓	Hovy's (87) PAULINE Granville's (83) P.
(iv) contextual factors determining registrial variation	not part of the model			
	part of the moel (field, tenor mode)		✓	cf. Hovy (87)

Figure 10.6: Systemic model and treatments of lexis in text generation

In the modern dictionary, there is a good deal of organization beyond the alphabetical listing, of course, but it remains implicit in e.g., the vocabulary used in dictionary definitions (see e.g., Amsler (1981) who has analysed the organization of the Merriam-Webster pocket dictionary). Theoretical lexicons make a lot of organization explicit, but they are still essentially item-based: the entry into the dictionary organization is the lexical entry. Each lexical entry is a 'hub' from which other entries can be accessed.

The most sophisticated and elaborated notion of what constitutes a lexical entry is probably the one developed for the Explanatory Combinatorial Dictionary component of the Meaning-Text Model by Mel'čuk, Zholkovsky, and others – e.g., (Apresyan, Mel'čuk and Zholkovsky, 1970; Mel'čuk, 1982; 1986). A lexical entry in an Explanatory Combinatorial Dictionary consists of three major entries (Mel'čuk, 1986: 57):

> semantic zone;
> syntactic zone; and
> lexical cooccurrence zone

For present purposes, the most interesting aspect of the lexical entry is the lexical cooccurrence zone: it encodes (among other things) information about lexical collocations that will constrain lexical selection. Mel'čuk (op cit., p. 60) notes that it "embodies the major novelty proposed in an [Explanatory Combinatorial Dictionary, CM]: namely, exhaustive and systematic description of restricted lexical cooccurrence of the entry lexeme." Lexical cooccurrencies are represented by means of **lexical** functions, characterized as follows (p. 60):

> A lexical function (henceforth, LF) **f** is, like any mathematical function, a dependency that associates with a given "quantity" - its argument - a variable "quantity" - its value, the latter being controlled by the former. More precisely, an LF **f** associates with a lexical unit **W** (a word or a phrase) a set W_i of (more or less synonymous) lexical units that express - contingent of **W** - a specific idea (such as 'very', 'begin', 'implement') represented by **f**.

For instance, there is a lexical function Magn (roughly 'very'), which, when applied to *grateful* yields *deeply* and when applied to *sophisticated* yields *highly*.

The notion of lexical cooccurrence is not new with the lMeaning-Text Model. It is in many respects similar to Firth's notion of **collocation**. Further, lexical functions are foreshadowed in e.g., Lodwick's (1652) **augmentations** to root words (such as 'Custome' and 'Inchoation') and Wilkins' (1668) use of **transcendental particles**. The transcendental particles are combined with the root words of his taxonomic tables to yield derived words. For instance, corresponding to the lexical function Son (meaning the typical sound produced by what it is applied to), Wilkins has the transcendental particle voice; Son (*dog*) yields *bark* and voice (*lion*) yields *roar*.

However, the most extensive account of how a lexical item may be related to others is undoubtedly the list of lexical functions identified with the Meaning-Text Model. Now, their collection of lexical functions is fairly heterogeneous, I think. This heterogeneity should not be surprising since the lexical entry itself is a way of compiling information that may be dispersed in a system-based account of lexical organization. The lexical functions correspond to different aspects of a systemic lexis. Some of the relations are inherent in the system network itself, while other relations require different treatments.

(ii) **The thesaurus.** In contrast to the lexicon, the thesaurus treats lexis as a resource of related lexical alternatives. It is this model that suggests what systemic ideational lexis is like. Roget's thesaurus is a strict taxonomy but it can nevertheless serve as a rough guide to what a lexical system network might look like. The thesaurus has not usually been incorporated in natural language processing systems, which is not to say that it would not be useful. The thesaurus was explored as a tool in machine translation in Masterman's early machine translation project in Cambridge – cf. for example (Halliday, 1956) and (Sparck-Jones, 1964/86) – and it is important as a model in work on information retrieval – cf. for example (Emblen, 1970); but it has not been used as a model in text generation, with the partial exception of Goldman's (1974) approach to lexical selection.

The dictionary and the thesaurus are not mutually exclusive, but are rather complementary perspectives on lexical organization. The thesaurus is *system-based* while the dictionary is *item-based*. In principle, we should be able to compile a dictionary from a system-based organization of lexis by collecting all the information available for each lexical item. Now, if lexis and grammar constitute one unified resource – lexicogrammar – there should be a grammatical equivalent to the lexical dictionary and it turns out that there is. In parsing, where we can expect the dictionary view of lexis to be helpful, we can compile grammatical tables from the system-based grammar about particular items. For instance, Kasper's (1988) Nigel parser operates with a table – a 'dictionary' – of grammatical functions which lists all the conflations for any given function. It is thus possible to look up the function Subject in this table and find Subject / Agent, / Medium, / Beneficiary, and so on together with the appropriate paradigmatic contexts in which the conflations occur.

If the dictionary and the thesaurus are complementary perspectives on lexis, the question is which is more helpful in text generation. The systemic-functional model incorporates the thesaurus principle and I have already indicated how it can support lexical choice in generation. While the dictionary started as a translation aid and as a glossary for 'difficult' words, the thesaurus started as an *aid in expressing thought*; Roget stated the object of his thesaurus as follows (from the introduction to the original edition of 1852):

> The present Work is intended to supply, with respect to the En-
> glish language, a desideratum hitherto unsupplied in any language;
> namely, a collection peculiar to it, arranged, not in alphabetical or-
> der as they are in a Dictionary, but according to the *ideas* which they
> express. The purpose of an ordinary dictionary is simply to explain
> the meaning of the words; and the problem of which it professes to
> furnish the solution may be stated thus: - The word being given,
> to find its signification, or the idea it is intended to convey. The
> object aimed at in the present undertaking is exactly the converse
> of this: namely, - The idea being given, to find the word, or words,
> by which that idea may be most fitly and aptly expressed. For this
> purpose, the words and phrases of the language are here classed, not
> according to their sound or their orthography, but strictly according
> to their *signification*.

In a sense, then, Roget designed his thesaurus for text generation, while
the dictionary is designed as a supplement to traditional grammar, which is
concerned with the signification and uses of grammatical forms. Equipped with
a traditional grammar and a dictionary, one can parse sentences.

As Roget's remarks quoted above suggest, the thesaurus provides an organization that can serve as a resource in making lexical choice, whereas the
dictionary does not. Although we might expect to see thesauri in most generation systems, we find dictionary (lexicon) components (cf. Cumming, 1986).
Goldman's (1974) BABEL generator is an important exception, in which lexis
is organized in a thesaurus-like fashion by means of discrimination nets and the
process of lexical choice is one of stepping through these discrimination nets (see
Figure 10.4 above; cf. also Pustejovsky and Nirenburg (1987), who suggest the
use of discrimination nets for the selection of open class lexical items).[14] As
Goldman's work shows, the thesaurus can help us organize the lexical resources
and the process of lexical choice.

There is another reason for taking the thesaurus model very seriously. Collocational restrictions can be stated in terms of specific lexical items by
means of lexical functions as was illustrated above. However, it turns out that
these restrictions are often not confined to pairs of individual lexical items.
They apply to *lexical classes* that can be identified in the taxonomic organization of the thesaurus model. For example, we can record a collocation such
as 'fall + temperature'. However, we can also generalize to the lexical classes
of 'process of change' + 'objects measured against a scale': the process can
be *drop, fall* (decrease) or *rise* (increase) in addition to the more general *decrease* vs. *increase*; and the object can be 'temperature', 'pressure', 'weight',
'prices', 'employment' (as an economic indicator), etc. The boundaries may be

---

[14] In generators operating with a dictionary, the taxonomic, thesaurus-like organization of
vocabulary may be reflected in the organization of the 'terminological' component of the
knowledge base of the system or presupposed by the system.

fluid, but the generalization is that there is an underlying **lexical metaphor** for representing change in intensity etc. along a scale – cf. (Whorf, 1956). It treats the scale as if it were the vertical axis in a space in which the object can move up and down. Once the underlying metaphor has been recognized, it can be used creatively, drawing for instance on other members of the lexical class of processes of vertical movement: *prices crept up; the temperature edged up / shot up / took off*. As can be seen from Lakoff and Johnson's (1980) discussion, such metaphors are pervasive and systematic rather than isolated.

10.7.2 Lexical Choice in Relation to Other Generation Processes

Let's now consider the relationship between lexis and lexical choice and grammar and grammatical choice. There are, broadly speaking, two approaches to this relationship:

(i) Lexis and grammar are *independent* components and the processes associated with them are similarly separated and

(ii) lexis and grammar constitute one *unified* resource and there is essentially one process of selection.

(i) Lexis and grammar as independent components

If lexis and grammar are modelled as independent components, either of them can be given priority – (1) lexis or (2) grammar.

(1) Priority given to lexis. One common strategy is to *start by lexical choice* and then to move onto grammatical choice and expression; we find this approach in e.g., Goldman's (1974) BABEL, McDonald's (1980) MUMBLE, and McKeown's (1982) TEXT. Lexical choice is here, more specifically, *ideational lexical choice*; the first step is to select a verb with a case frame, which will then be turned into a clause by subsequent grammatical processing.

In Goldman's BABEL, lexical selection produces word senses of lexical items and case frames, which are then passed off to surface generation, based on an ATN grammar. McDonald divides generation in MUMBLE into two stages; the first deals with lexical selection in the dictionary and the second turns to the grammar.

Similarly, in TEXT, the dictionary is ordered before the tactical component. The dictionary interface produces a 'deep structure' with lexical items. This information is represented in terms of functional unification grammar descriptions and these descriptions are the input to the tactical component, which uses a functional unification grammar. In this second stage, the lexical information is unified with grammatical descriptions.

This approach to lexical selection in relation to 'syntactic' generation is also very much along the lines of Dik's (1978, 1987) Functional Grammar: predicate frames are selected from the lexicon, they are instantiated and expanded and are then passed on to the syntactic and pragmatic components.

(2) Priority given to grammar. The other alternative is to create grammatical structure first and then to fill it in lexically from the lexical component of the model, as implied by early phrase structure grammars. It is perhaps worth emphasizing in this connection that the relationship between grammar and lexis is not a compositional one; it is not a relationship of size, as the frequent use of the term word instead of lexical item implies. Halliday (1961) notes that lexical items are not just morphemes or words and he observes; a lexical item is variable in size: "the theoretical place of the move from grammar to lexis is therefore not a feature of rank but one of delicacy".

(ii) Lexis and grammar as one unified resource

The common approach just sketched can be contrasted with one where lexis and grammar constitute one unified resource. For instance, the information encoded in the lexicon corresponds to ideational lexis and partly also to ideational grammar in the systemic-functional model and the syntactic component ordered after the lexicon corresponds largely to textual and interpersonal grammar, as shown in the diagram in Figure 10.7.[15]

The diagram also indicates concomitant differences in the modelling of metafunctions. I will return to the metafunctional aspects of the difference between the two approaches diagrammed above; see Section 10.7.3.

There are several reasons why the unified model of the systemic alternative is worth exploring in text generation. I'll just mention three here: (a) a number or lexical properties are interpretable in terms of the grammar; (b) lexis and grammar interact; and (c) textual grammar is not a matter of post-production after lexical choice.

(a) One reason for exploring the systemic alternative is that a number of properties of ideational lexis only make sense in terms of the **categories of ideational grammar.** For instance, a lexical collocation such as *spread + news* (as in *the news spread rapidly that an agreement had been reached* or *the delegates spread the news ...*) is an instance of a general class (cf. *spread + word / rumour / lie*) recognizable in the grammar of processes of 'saying' (verbal processes). It may be selected as an impersonal version of *people + say* and the difference between the two alternatives is lexicogrammatical, i.e. it shows

---

[15] Both lexical and grammatical information may, however, be encoded using the same kind of representation. For instance, lexical information in McKeown's (1982) TEXT system can be unified with grammatical information thanks to the use of the functional unification-based form of representation. Whenever this happens, there is good reason to ask whether the old lexicon and grammar model is still the best way of conceiving of the design.

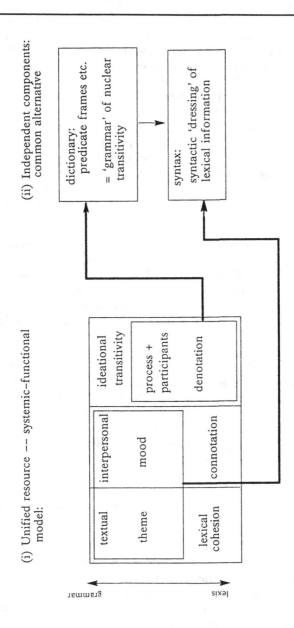

Figure 10.7: Systemic functional lexicogrammar and alternative

up both in structure (the difference in structure between e.g. *people said (to us) that an agreement had been reached and the news spread that an agreement had been reached* and in vocabulary (the collocation of e.g., *spread + news*, reflecting the lexicosemantic metaphor of information as a substance that can be distributed). In general, lexical choice does not necessarily proceed on an item by item basis but collocational combinations may be chosen together. These collocations are identifiable in terms of certain combinations of grammatical functions – in particular Process + Medium (e.g, *fall + temperature*), Process + Range (e.g., *scale + mountain*), Process + Manner: degree (e.g., *regret + deeply*); Facet + Thing (e.g., *gaggle + geese*), and Thing + Epithet: degree (e.g., *deep + regret*) – see (Halliday, 1985) for these terms. These combinations constitute lexicogrammatical 'nuclei' and can be located on a scale from one single lexical item to two items chosen independently of one another: the more nuclear a combination is, the more likely it is to enter into a collocation such as *fall + temperature*.

(b) Another reason has to do with the **interaction between lexis and grammar** in determining both the availability of grammatical choices and the organization of lexical ones in the lexical taxonomy. Combinations of Process + Medium[16] in the transitivity organization of the clause are a case in point. Grammatically, it is possible to add an Agent to indicate an external cause bringing about the occurrence of the combination of Process + Medium. Thus, if we have the combination *open + door*, there is the potential for specifying an Agent – *Henry + open + door*, as in *Henry opened the squeaky door very cautiously*, alongside *The squeaky door opened*. But the possibility of specifying or not specifying the Agent in any given instance depends on the nature of the Medium as well as on the nature of the Process. For instance, the agentive option is the only possibility if the Medium is *bank account* instead of door; we get *Henry opened a new bank account* but *A new bank account opened today* is less likely. However, with a different type of Process, such as *empty*, both options would appear to be possible: *Henry's bank account has emptied again* and *Henry has emptied his bank account again*. Combinations with run illustrate the same point; for example, alongside *the door opened* and *they opened the door*, we can get *Henry ran out of town* as well as *They ran Henry out of town;* but only *Henry's nose is running* and not normally *Henry is running his nose*.

Lexically, verbs considered in isolation may be hard to locate hierarchically in a taxonomy, but if we widen the scope to take into account the grammatical nucleus of Process + Medium, the picture is much clearer. For instance, the taxonomy of processes of motion depends on the nature of the mover – see (Cruse, 1986: 151-2) for discussion of examples.

---

[16]Medium is the participant most closely related to the process; it is a participant function in the ergative interpretation of the clause – see e.g., (Halliday, 1985: Section 5.8). For instance, the Process + Medium combination *break + glass* is common to both *The glass broke* and *He broke the glass.*

(c) A third reason is that ideational lexical and grammatical choices may in fact be made to **accommodate textual needs** so it does not always make sense to treat the textual metafunction as a matter of 'post-production'. For instance (to cite the traditional examples), while pairs such as *buy / sell* and *give / receive* certainly differ ideationally, they also accommodate different unmarked textual structures, as in (Themes underlined): *he bought his new car from Cal : Cal sold him his new car* with 'he' and 'Cal' as unmarked Theme/ Subject, respectively. Similarly, metaphorical alternative wordings such as *July sees the arrival of large numbers of Swedish tourists* for *Large numbers of Swedish tourists arrive in July* have different textual effects (in this case making the temporal locative the unmarked Theme of the clause and grouping the process and the Medium together in the unmarked position for new information).

These, then, are some of the reasons for exploring a unified lexicogrammatical model. If we operate with a unified lexicogrammar, there are two complementary perspectives on this resource: (1) viewing this resource from lexis; or (2) viewing it from grammar.

(1) Lexical approach. We can look at lexicogrammar from the lexical end and treat most everything as lexis,[17] as e.g., Hovy (1987a) does for generation and, in another context, Sinclair and co-workers in the Birmingham group do in their work on lexical analysis – e.g., (Sinclair, 1987; 1988) – following up systemic work on lexis started in the 1960s, cf. (Halliday, 1966; Sinclair, 1966).

In computational linguistics, the lexical perspective was inspired by Becker's notion of the phrasal lexicon – a lexicon with a large number of "lexical phrases" of various types.[18] This is how Becker (1975: 62) suggests that it might be used in language production.

> We start with the information that we wish to convey and the attitudes toward that information that we wish to express or evoke, and haul out of our phrasal lexicon some patterns that can provide the major elements of this expression. Then the major problem is to stitch these phrases together into something roughly grammatical, to fill in the blanks with the particulars of the case at hand, to modify the phrases if need be, and if all else fails to generate phrases from scratch to smooth over the transitions or fill in any remaining conceptual holes.

My guess is that phrase-adaption and generative gap-filling are very

---

[17] The metaphor is often that everything is 'in the lexicon'. However, I think the picture is clearer if we see this as approaching lexicogrammar from the lexical end.

[18] Becker (1975) identifies six major categories: (i) polywords (e.g., *blow up* 'explode'), (ii) phrasal constraints (e.g., *by pure coincidence*), (iii) deictic locutions (e.g., *for that matter* 'I just thought of a better way of making my point'), (iv) sentence builders (e.g., *[A] gave [B] a (long) song and dance about [C]* 'A tried to convince B of something, and was cynical and perhaps less than truthful about what he said'), (v) situational utterances (e.g, *How can I ever repay you?*), and (vi) verbatim texts (e.g., *Better late than never*).

roughly equally important in language production as measured in processing time spent on each, or in constituents arising from each.

Following these ideas, Hovy (1987a) suggests that the lexicon contains specific phrases as well as more general patterns:

> Taking this view seriously, I believe that all formative aspects of language should be treated as phrasal. Multi-predicate phrases, formative rules of grammar, and words with idiosyncratic formative requirements – all entities that deal with the ordering of words and syntactic environments – should be contained in the lexicon as frozen, semi-frozen, and very general phrases. The lexicon should be the sole repository of the patterns that make up language – some very specific, some very general.

"Taking this view seriously" leads to the inclusion of "multi-predicate phrases" such as

```
[not only [SENTENCE (verb relocated, with ''do'')], but [SENTENCE]]
```

as well as one-word lexical entries. If this means recording the 'inversion' of Subject and Finite (realized by *do* or another auxiliary) in a number of different lexical entries, there is, of course, a good deal of repetition and we miss the general grammatical principle that thematic negative (clause) polarity always leads to the sequence Finite ˆ Subject (this is related to the bonding between polarity and finiteness in English; the sequence Finite ˆ Subject means that the Finite follows the thematic realization of negative polarity).

There is a more serious consideration concerning Becker's proposal. He speaks of hauling "out of our phrasal lexicon some patterns that can provide the major elements of this expression". The question is how this hauling out is to be achieved and how, once hauled out, the patterns are to be "stitched together" grammatically. This question is, of course, not a problem in the systemic model.

There is yet another consideration. In text generation, the approach from the lexical end is likely to be useful if we are faced with a specific, fairly restricted generation task such as generating stock-market reports: cf. Kukich's (1983) use of a phrasal lexicon, inspired by Becker's notion of the phrasal lexicon, in her Ana generator. However, building a generator for a specific, restricted register is very different from building a general-purpose generator. In particular, the task of building the latter type of generator brings the general resources of grammar into focus.

(2) Grammatical approach. The considerations just discussed above suggest that the grammatical approach is worth exploring as an alternative to the lexical one. We can look at lexicogrammar from the grammatical end and view lexis as

the more specific part of lexicogrammar, which has been suggested in systemic linguistics (Halliday, 1961), as noted in Section 10.2. If this approach is followed, it becomes clear that lexical patterns that might at first sight look as if they were unique to particular lexical items and would be recorded in their lexical entries in fact apply to lexicogrammatical classes, not just to individual items. It was noted above that they apply to lexical classes, but the classes may in fact also be grammatically identifiable and are thus lexicogrammatical. For instance, we might record *deeply* as they item to use for intensifying *love*; but it turns out to be applicable to a more general grammatical class of processes of mental reaction (including *admire, respect, distrust,* and *be grateful, sorry*); and it alternates with e.g., *profoundly.* Further cases are discussed in the longer version of this paper.

10.7.3 Metafunctional Organization of Lexis

The discussion in the previous section focuses on the issue of the recognition and representation of the taxonomic organization of lexis, but that reflects only the ideational aspect of lexical organization and choice. We can in fact distinguish two broadly different approaches to the functions lexical resources serve, the first of which focuses only on the ideational metafunction:

(i) unifunctional– the focus is on one type of function, viz. the ideational one; and

(ii) multifunctional – several functions are in focus, in principle all three general functions: ideational, interpersonal, and textual.

(i) **Unifunctional: ideational.** Past work on text generation has almost exclusively been unifunctional. More specifically, it has paid attention to the ideational metafunction, which means to denotation and the taxonomic organization of vocabulary when we are dealing with lexis: there is typically some kind of mapping between a terminological concept in the knowledge base of the system and a lexical item, as in (McDonald, 1981; Matthiessen, 1981; McKeown, 1982, and Jacobs, 1985).

(ii) **Multifunctional:** ideational and beyond. In contrast, a multifunctional approach goes beyond the ideational metafunction and takes into account other functions as well, viz. the textual and interpersonal metafunctions, as shown in Figure 10.8:

It is quite clear that in a general account of lexical organization and lexical choice all three metafunctions have to be taken into account. With a few exceptions mentioned in Section 10.5 such Hovy's (1987a,b) work lexical choice and 'affect' and Granville's (1983) work one type of lexical cohesion (repetition) – cf. also (Kukich, 1983) – the multifunctional approach has not yet come into focus in work on text generation.

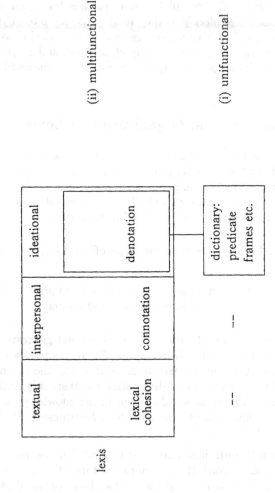

Figure 10.8: Unifunctional vs. multifunctional lexis

10.8 CONCLUSION

The suggestion that we need to deal with the full functional spectrum of lexis concludes my discussion of lexis in text generation. As with any linguistic system, we can discus lexis at a variety of different levels – contextual and linguistic; and within linguistic, semantics and 'form' (or indeed, phonology, noting sound symbolism and sound imitation). I've focussed mainly on linguistic 'form', i.e., lexicogrammar or the resources for 'wording' meanings: the relationship between lexis and grammar, the internal organization of lexis, and the multifunctionality of lexis. I have also said a little bit about contextual factors influencing lexical organization and lexical choice – the way in which they organize different alternative lexical taxonomies and so on. We could also focus on the level of semantics, on lexical semantics and its relationship to grammatical semantics. The obvious question is: "This looks quite extravagant; do we really need all these levels and metafunctions to account for lexis and lexical choice?" The answer is quite unequivocally "yes, we do!", although it would, needless to say, take volumes to explore and demonstrate it; but the answer has to be followed up: as always, any particular model will depend on the function it has to serve. Halliday's (1964) observation that the form of syntax depends on the consumer is equally applicable in the area of lexis: any specific model of lexis will reflect the purpose for which it was created and it may be constrained in a number of functionally motivated ways. For instance, if our task is to generate weather forecasts we can make a number of simplifying assumptions about lexis as well as grammar: this reflects the notion of sublanguage or register (functional variety of language) in systemic linguistics. At the same time, since we have fewer variables to control, we can afford to – indeed we have to, given the generation task – make the model fully explicit and programmable. In contrast, the model I've sketched is intended to be general across registers. A general model should have the advantage that it can attempt to cover the full lexical spectrum; but there is an obvious price to be paid: at present, we cannot build fully explicit and detailed general lexical models; they have to be sketches. The middle path is to 'shunt' between general and specific models. Moreover, there are clearly various ways of implementing the kind of general model sketched here. For instance, it would be possible to elaborate the kind of model presented in (McDonald, 1981) and (Matthiessen, 1981), where lexical organization is stated in terms of the knowledge base, by adding interpersonal information to differentiate among lexical items associated with particular concepts, by allowing for textual moves in the search for lexical items, and so on.

One problem here is the reductionist lexical model in linguistics that looks like a general one: it comes from the Chomskyan type of formal approaches to the interpretation of language. They tend to take over the traditional dictionary model rather unquestioningly and then elaborate and formalize it (just as other traditional accounts were taken over and formalized, such as the traditional Subject + Predicate analysis of the clause). It may come to look quite different from what we'd normally mean by 'dictionary' or 'lexicon'; but the

basic conception of lexis as dictionary is never really questioned, even if the
division of labour between the syntactic component and the lexical one changes
quite dramatically. If our concern is text generation, it is important to recognize that these models are special-case models just as much as a model of lexis
in say an economic report generator: the difference is that their special-case
status is meta-registerial – they are created in the context of the specific set
of questions about language that derives from the Chomskyan paradigm and
these questions exclude text generation as well as text analysis.

The 'shunting' between specific and general models of lexis in the context of
text generation is, I think, an opportunity for building general models of lexis
that grounded in the task of generating text and it is important to build these
models rather than just adapting those created for other purposes.

In conclusion, let me mention one consideration that I haven't focussed
on, since I think it will be a few years before the the kinds of text we can
generate are sufficiently long and sophisticated to bring it out: this is the issue
of **instantial lexical systems** and the introduction and development of lexical
items in the unfolding of a text. Given a general lexical system, any text
may create lexical relations that are given significance within that particular
text – instantial lexical relations – see (Halliday and Hasan, 1985) and (Fries,
1982); also, different strategies for introducing and defining lexical items may
be adopted – cf. (Martin, 1989).

ACKNOWLEDGEMENTS

The paper has benefited from the work by the members of the Penman project
at USC/ISI. I have drawn on discussions with Lynn Poulton and with Susanna
Cumming. I am also grateful to Robert Albano, John Bateman, Ed Hovy,
Bill Mann, and Cécile Paris for comments on earlier presentations of the paper
and to participants in the Fourth International Language Generation Workshop.
Lexis in generation was a topic that received a good deal of attention: this paper
takes into account a number of relevant points emerging from the workshop.

BIBLIOGRAPHY

Amsler, R. 1981. A Taxonomy for English Nouns and Verbs. In Proceedings of
the 19th Annual Meeting of the Association for Computational Linguistics.

Apresyan, Y. I. Mel'čuk, A. Zholkovsky. 1970. Semantics and lexicography,
toward a new type of unilingual dictionary. In F. Kiefer (ed.), Studies in Syntax
and Semantics. Dordrecht: Reidel.

Bateman, J., Gen-ichirou, and Atsuchi Tabuchi. 1987. Designing a computational systemic grammar for text generation: a progress report. Department of Electrical Engineering, Kyoto University.

Bateman, J. and C. Paris. 1989. Constraining the development of lexicogrammatical resources during text generation: towards a computational instantiation of register theory. Paper presented at ISC 16. Forthcoming.

Bazell, C., I. Catford and M.A.K. Halliday (eds). 1966. In Memory of J.R. Firth. London: Longman.

Becker, J. 1975. The Phrasal Lexicon. In Schank, R. and B. Webber (eds.), Theoretical Issues in Natural Language Processing. Cambridge: .

Benson, J., M. Cummings and W. Greaves (eds). 1988. Linguistics in a systemic perspective. Amsterdam: Benjamins.

Berlin, B., D. Breedlove, and P. Raven. 1973. General Principles of Classification and Nomenclature in Folk Biology. American Anthropologist, 75: 214-42.

Berry, M. 1977. Introduction to Systemic Linguistics II: levels and links. London: Batsford.

Brachman, R. 1978. A Structural Paradigm for Representing Knowledge. BBN Report No. 3605, Bolt Beranek and Newman, Inc. Cambridge, MA.

Brown, R. and A. Gilman. 1960. The pronouns of power and solidarity. In T. Sebeok (ed), Style in language. Cambridge, Mass: MIT Press.

CEC = A Corpus of English Conversation, ed. by R. Quirk and J. Svartvik. 1980. Lund: C W K Gleerup.

Cruse, D. 1986. Lexical Semantics. Cambridge: Cambridge University Press.

Cumming, S. 1986. The Lexicon in Text Generation. USC/Information Sciences Institute, ISI/RR-86-168.

Cumming, S., R. Albano, and N. Sondheimer. 1988. [Paper presented at lex. semantics workshop]

Danlos, L. 1984. Conceptual and linguistic decisions in generation. In Proceedings of Coling 84, Stanford University. Association for Computational Linguistics.

Dik, S. 1978. Functional Grammar. Amsterdam: North-Holland.

Dik, S. 1987. Generating answers from a linguistically coded knowledge base. In Kempen (ed.). Natural Language Generation. Dordrecht: Martinus Nijhoff Publishers.

Dinosaurs = Zallinger, P. 1977. Dinosaurs. New York: Random House.

100 Dinosaurs = Wilson, R. 100 Dinosaurs from A to Z. New York: Grosset and Dunlap.

Downing, P. 1981. [Lexical choice paper in Pear Stories Volume] In W. Chafe (ed), The Pear Stories. Norwood, NJ: Ablex.

Emblen, D. 1970. Peter Mark Roget. The word and the man. New York: Crowell.

Ervin-Tripp, S. 1969. Sociolinguistics. Advances in Experimental Social Psychology 4.

Evens, M., B. Litowitz, J. Markowitz, R. Smith, and O. Werner. 1980. Lexical-Semantic Relations: A Comparative Survey. Edmonton: Linguistic Research, Inc.

Fawcett, R. 1980. Cognitive Linguistics and Social Interaction: Towards an Integrated Model of a Systemic Functional Grammar and the other Components of a Communicating Mind. Heidelberg: Julius Groos Verlag, and Exeter: University of Exeter.

Fries, P. 1982. On Repetition and Interpretation. Forum Linguisticum 7(1): 50-64.

Givn, T. (ed.). 1983. Topic Continuity in Language. Amsterdam: Benjamins.

Goldman, N. 1974. Computer Generation of Natural-Language from a Deep Conceptual Base. Yale University Dissertation.

Granville, R. 1983. Cohesion in Computer Text Generation: Lexical Substitution. MIT/LCS/TR-310.

Halliday, M.A.K. 1956. The linguistic basis of a mechanical thesaurus. Mechanical Translation 3.3: 81-8.

Halliday, M.A.K. 1961. Scales and categories of the theory of grammar. Word 17.3, 241-92.

Halliday, M.A.K. 1964. Syntax and the consumer. Monograph Series in Languages and Linguistics 17: pp. 14-23. Washington, DC: Georgetown University Press.

Halliday, M.A.K. 1966. Lexis as a linguistic level. In Bazell et al.

Halliday, M.A.K. 1967/8. Notes on transitivity and theme in English. Journal of Linguistics. V. 3.1, 3.2, and 4.2.

Halliday, M.A.K. 1973. Explorations in the functions of language. London: Edward Arnold.

Halliday, M.A.K. 1978. Language as social semiotic. The social interpretation of language and meaning. London: Edward Arnold.

Halliday, M.A.K. 1985. Introduction to Functional Grammar. London: Edward Arnold.

Halliday, M.A.K. 1985b. Spoken and written language. Geelong, Vic: Deakin University Press. (Republished in 1988 by Oxford University Press.)

Halliday, M.A.K. and R. Hasan. 1976. Cohesion in English. London: Longman.

Halliday, M.A.K. and R. Hasan. 1985. Language, context, and text: Aspects of language in a social-semiotic perspective. Deakin University Press.

Hasan, R. 1987. The grammarian's dream. In M.A.K. Halliday and R. Fawcett (eds). New Developments in Systemic Linguistics. London: Frances Pinter.

Hinds, J. 1977. Paragraph Structure and Pronominalization. Papers in Linguistics 10: 77-99.

Hovy, E. 1987a. Generating Language with a Phrasal Lexicon. In McDonald, D. and Bolc. (eds.). Papers in Natural Language Generation. New York: Springer-Verlag.

Hovy, E. 1987b. Generating Natural Language under Pragmatic Constraints. YALEU/CSD/RR#521. Yale University, Ph.D. Dissertation.

Hovy, E. and R. Schank. 1984. Language Generation. In Bara and Guida (eds.), Computational Models of Natural Language Processing. Amsterdam: North-Holland.

Ingria, R. 1986. [ACL Tutorial]

Jacobs, P. 1985. PHRED: A Generator for Natural Language Interfaces. Computational Linguistics. Volume 11, 4.

Jacobs, P. 1987. KING: A knowledge-intensive natural language generator. In Kempen (ed).

Kasper, R. 1988. Systemic Grammar and Functional Uvnification Grammar. In Benson, J. and W. Greaves (eds), Systemic Functional Approaches to Discourse: Selected Papers from the 12th International Systemic Workshop. Norwood, NJ: Ablex.

Kay, M. 1979. Functional Grammar. In Proceedings of the Fifth Annual Meeting of the Berkeley Linguistic Society.

Kempen, G. (ed.). 1987. Natural Language Generation. Dordrecht: Martinus Nijhoff.

Kittredge, R. and I. Mel'čuk. 1983. Towards a computable model of meaning-text relations within a natural sublanguage. IJCAI.

Kukich, K. 1983. Design of a Knowledge-Based Report Generator. Proceedings of the 21st Annual Meeting of the ACL.

Lakoff, G. and M. Johnson. 1980. Metaphors we live by. Chicago: Chicago University Press.

Leech, G. 1974. Semantics. Harmondsworth: Penguin Books.

Lehrer, A. 1967. Semantic Cuisine. Journal of Linguistics.

Lodwick, F. 1652. The Ground-Work, or foundation laid (or so intended) for the Framing of a New Perfect Language: And an Universall or Common Writing.

Lyne, A. 1988. Systemic syntax from a lexical point of view. In Benson et al.

Lyons, J. 1977. Semantics. Cambridge: Cambridge University Press.

McArthur, T. 1986. Worlds of Reference. Cambridge: Cambridge University Press.

McDonald, D. 1980. Language Production as a Process of Decision-making under Constraints. MIT Ph.D. Dissertation, 1980. MIT Report.

McDonald, D. 1981. Language Production: the Source of the Dictionary. In Proceedings of the 19th Annual Meeting of the Association for Computational Linguistics.

McKeown, K. 1982. Generating Natural Language Text in Response to Questions about Database Structure. Ph.D. Dissertation, University of Pennsylvania.

Mann, W. 1983. Inquiry semantics: a functional semantics of natural language. In Proceedings of the First Annual Conference of the Association for Computational Linguistics, European Chapter. Pisa.

Marcus, M. 1987. Generation Systems Should Choose Their Words. In Y. Wilks (ed.), TINLAP-3. Theoretical Issues in Natural Language Processing-3. Memoranda in Computer and Cognitive Science. New Mexico State University.

Martin, J.R. 1989. Life as a noun. Arresting the universe. Paper presented at ISC 16, 1989. Forthcoming.

Martin, J.R. 1990. English Text:system and structure. Benjamins.

Martin, J.R., P. Wignell, S. Eggins and J. Rothery. 1988. Secret English: Discourse Technology in a Junior Secondary School. In L. Gerot, J. Oldenburg, T. Van Leeuwen (eds), Language and socialisation: home and school. Proceedings from the Working Conference on Language in Education. Macquarie University, 1988.

Matthiessen, C. 1981. A Grammar and a Lexicon for a Text-Production System. In Proceedings of the 19th Annual Meeting of the Association for Computational Linguistics.

Matthiessen, C. 1988. A systemic semantics: the chooser and inquiry framework. In Benson, Cummings and Greaves (eds.). Also as ISI/RS-87-189.

Matthiessen, C. 1989. Lexicogrammatical cartography: English systems. Department of Linguistics, Sydney University. MS.

Mel'čuk, I. 1982. Lexical Functions in Lexicographic Description. In Proceedings of the Eighth Annual Meeting of the Berkeley Linguistic Society.

Mel'čuk, I. 1986. Semantic Bases of Linguistic Description (Meaning-Text Linguistic Theory). In M. Marino and L. Prez (eds.). The Twelfth Lacus Forum, 1985. Lake Bluff: LACUS.

Nebel, B. and N. Sondheimer. 1986. A Logical-Form and Knowledge-Based Design for Natural Language Generation. In Proceedings of AAAI-86, Vol. 1.

Patten, T. 1988. Systemic text generation as problem solving. Cambridge: Cambridge University Press.

Poynton, C. 1984. Names as vocatives: forms and functions. Nottingham Linguistic Circular 13 (Special Issue on Systemic Linguistics).

Poynton, C. 1985. Language and gender: making the difference. Geelong, Vic.: Deakin University Press. (Republished by London: Oxford University Press, 1988.)

Pustejovsky, J. and S. Nirenburg. 1987. Lexical Selection in the Process of Language Generation. In Proceedings of the 25th Annual Meeting of the Association for Computational Linguistics.

Quillian, R. 1967. Word Concepts: A Theory and Simulation of Some Basic Semantic Capabilities. Behavioral Science 12: 410-30. Reprinted in Brachman and Levesque (eds.).

Roget, M. 1852. A Thesaurus of English Words and Phrases, Classified and Arranged so as to facilitate the Expression of Ideas and assist in Literary Composition. Many editions.

Sigurd, B. 1987. Meta-comments in text-generation. In Kempen (ed.).

Sinclair, J. 1966. Beginning the study of lexis. In Bazell et al.

Sinclair, J. 1987. Collocation: a progress report. In R. Steele and T. Threadgold (eds), Language Topics. Amsterdam: Benjamins.

Sinclair, J. 1988. Sense and structure in lexis. In Benson et al.

Sparck-Jones, K. 1964. Synonymy and Semantic Classification. University of Cambridge Ph.D. thesis. Printed in 1986, Edinburgh: Edinburgh University Press.

Trier, J. 1931. Der deutsche Wortschatz im Sinnbezirk des Verstandes. Heidelberg: Carl Winter.

Ure, J. 1971. Lexical density and register differentiation. In G.E. Perren and J.L.M Tim (eds), Applications of linguistics: selected papers of the 2nd International Congress of Applied Linguistics, Cambridge 1969. Cambridge: Cambridge University Press.

Whorf, B.L. 1956. Language Thought and Reality. Selected Writing of Benjamin Lee Whorf, edited by J. Carroll. Cambridge: The MIT Press.

Wignell, P., J. R. Martin and S. Eggins. 1987. The discourse of geography: ordering and explaining the experiential world. In Suzanne Eggins, James R. Martin and Peter Wignell (eds), Writing Project Report 1987. Sydney: University of Sydney Linguistics Department (Working Papers in Linguistics, 5: 25-65)

Wilkins, J. 1668. An Essay Towards a Real Character and a Philosophical Language. London.

Winograd, T. 1983. Language as a cognitive process. Syntax. Menlo Park: Addison-Wesley.

Chapter 11

Lexical Selection and Paraphrase in a Meaning-Text Generation Model

Lidija Iordanskaja,
Richard Kittredge and
Alain Polguère

Abstract: We introduce a computationally tractable model for language generation based on the Meaning-Text Theory of Mel'čuk *et al.*, in which the lexicon plays a central role. To illustrate the descriptive scope and paraphrase capabilities of the model, we show how the lexicon influences the set of choices at four different points during the multi-stage realization process: (1) semantic net simplification, (2) determination of root lexical node for the deep syntactic dependency tree, (3) possible application of deep paraphrase rules using lexical functions, and (4) surface syntactic realization. We also show some of the ways in which the theme/rheme specifications within the semantic net influence lexical and syntactic choices during realization. Examples are taken primarily from an implemented system which generates paragraph-length reports about the usage of operating systems.

11.1 INTRODUCTION

As the goals of language generation work have become more diverse and ambitious, the necessity of having a powerful and complete linguistic model has become more evident. One measure of the power and completeness of a language model is its ability to represent all the possible ways that a human speaker could choose to "say the same thing" by using linguistic knowledge (as opposed to world knowledge).

The ability of a generation model to provide paraphrase alternatives is not just a measure of its grammatical and lexical coverage. It is an integral part of its ability to produce compact, unambiguous and stylistically satisfying text. Texts in typically complex domains must meet a large number of constraints or optimize over a large set of preference functions. A linguistically rich model can provide a basis for "paraphrasing around" problems which arise when the most direct lexical and syntactic realization path runs into conflicting constraints, or scores poorly on the aggregate preference rating.

In the following section we introduce a language generation model for English based on Meaning-Text Theory (MTT) first described by Mel'čuk and Zholkovsky in (Mel'čuk, 1974, 1981; Mel'čuk and Zholkovsky, 1970). One major attraction of this model lies exactly in its clear and direct representation of the lexical, semantic and syntactic means of paraphrase. We feel that such a Meaning-Text Model (MTM) can offer both the descriptive power and the directness of implementation that generation goals now require.

In the latter sections of this paper we will illustrate some of the ability of an MTM to provide linguistic paraphrase alternatives during the generation process. In particular, we focus on four sources of paraphrase due to lexical choice and to syntactic ways of playing on the chosen lexical items. As we will see, the large amount of information associated with each lexeme in an MTM lexicon allows much better usage of lexeme-specific information than is the case in most language models.

11.2 SOME FEATURES OF AN MTM

MTT describes a set of possible models (MTMs) for relating texts to their meaning representations. An MTM describes the (bidirectional) mapping between linguistic meanings and texts which carry those meanings in a given language. In principle, seven levels of description are used:

1. semantic representations (SemR)

2. deep syntactic representations (DSyntR)

3. surface syntactic representations (SSyntR)

4. deep morphological representations (DMorphR)

5. surface morphological representations (SMorphR)

6. deep phonetic representations (DPhonR)

7. surface phonetic representations (SPhonR)

This rather extreme stratification of linguistic phenomena allows each stage of the mapping to be stated simply while permitting the inclusion of a much wider range of phenomena in a wider variety of languages than is typically covered by a grammatical model. (This motivation of simplicity may be similar to that which seems to underly the stratification of choice systems in systemic grammar, cf. (Matthiessen, 1983).

For languages such as English the "interesting" representation levels are really three: semantic nets (SemR), deep syntactic trees (DSyntR), and surface syntactic trees (SSyntR).[1] The two syntactic levels use dependency trees, with explicitly labeled grammatical relations on the arcs, and lexemes (roughly, dictionary words) or grammatical words on the nodes.

The use of dependency trees for syntactic representations highlights the central role that MTMs give to the lexicon: subtle and idiosyncratic lexical co-occurrences and dependencies can be stated more simply in such trees than in phrase structure trees. The sheer diversity of the lexicon (including a wide range of idiomatic expressions), which has been thoroughly documented by Gross *et al.* (1975) does not overpower such a model. An MTM takes lexical complexity as the primary fact of life and orders itself accordingly (see below). Whereas other generation systems are putting increased emphasis on the lexicon – cf. (Cumming, 1985) and (Nirenburg, 1988) –, the models on which these systems are based do not yet appear to provide for the same range of phenomena (such as paraphrase) as is provided by MTMs.

A further important feature of MTMs is the inclusion of theme/rheme information at each level of sentence description. The *theme* of a sentence (or clause) corresponds, on each level of the sentence's representation, to the focus of attention of the speaker. The *rheme* is the value of some parameter of interest with respect to the theme. Our notion of theme and rheme – see (Iordanskaja, 1989) is a further development of these notions as used by the Prague functionalist school – cf. (Sgall, Hajičová and Panevová, 1986).

The specification of theme/rheme structure allows sentences to be generated which obey important principles of textual development in multi-sentential text. This structure helps to constrain the lexical and syntactic choices on the "interesting" levels (Iordanskaja and Polguère, 1988). Although some other workers

---

[1] This does not imply that the remaining levels are trivial. However, for our generation of written English texts, we have dispensed with the two phonetic levels. Also, it has been sufficient to use a single unified morphological level (MorphR) between SSyntR and the output word string.

in generation include thematic structuring (cf. McKeown's current focus (McKeown, 1985), its use is not as fully integrated with lexical and syntactic decisions as is the case in an MTM (see below).

A generation-oriented MTM does not incorporate text planning beyond the sentence boundary. (Broader text planning is more than just a linguistic problem.) An MTM takes as input a sequence of sentence-sized semantic nets, the sequencing having already been determined by the text planner. Each net is processed separately through the MTM generator. However the planner has also provided information that results in marking each sentence network for theme and rheme. This explicit marking of the semantic net with theme/rheme constraints ensures the proper linking of new information to old information within each sentence and between succeeding sentences. Each sentence is generated using the marked theme and rheme constraints. MTM rules influence clause ordering, pronominalization, the choice of predicate lexeme and other features on the basis of these constraints.

Our computational implementation of an MTM (Iordanskaja *et al.*, 1988) is the first (to our knowledge) for the purposes of text generation. We have been obliged not only to create a good deal of lexical description for the purposes of the domain, but also to fill in gaps in MTM theory. Furthermore, we have faced the relatively unfamiliar problem of computing efficient net-to-tree and tree-to-tree transduction for dependency trees. The theoretical and practical solutions to these problems constitute a separate subject matter which is beyond the scope of this paper – see (Iordanskaja and Polguère, 1988). Suffice it to say that much remains to be done in optimizing the transduction process and in evaluating the feedback to MTM theory from heuristic discoveries.

Our current work focuses on the problem of generating paragraph-length summaries on the usage of operating systems, within the context of computer security. Where possible, examples are from this domain. Technical domains do not, however, provide the richest source of examples for all features of the MTM paraphrase system.

11.3   THE MTM'S LEXICON

11.3.1   Lexical Entries in the Explanatory Combinatorial Dictionary

Lexical information in the MTM is presented in an "Explanatory Combinatorial Dictionary" (ECD) which aims to cover *all* possible *linguistic* knowledge (as opposed to world knowledge) governing the usage of words in texts (Mel'čuk *et al.*, 1984). A unique feature of the ECD is the inclusion of lexical functions (Mel'čuk, 1982), i.e., pointers to other words which are semantically or collocationally related to the entry word.

Lexical entries are divided into zones – cf. (Mel'čuk and Polguère, 1987). The **semantic zone** specifies a semantic network which defines the meaning of the lexical entry in terms of the next simpler word meaning elements (called "semantemes"). This network is a formalization of the human intuition to paraphrase the meaning of a word through a minimally complex locution using words which are one step simpler in their meanings. As we will see below, this property allows large semantic networks to be reduced incrementally, by substituting single-node complex meanings for subnetworks which define them with simpler meanings. And since the whole network system is based on human intuitions about word meaning, the nets can usually be informally "verbalized" by reading the meanings as if they were words.

The **syntactic zone** of an entry specifies (1) the entry's syntactic class, (2) the syntactic features used to identify special constructions which accept the lexeme, and (3) government patterns which show how the semantic actants (cases) of the lexical entry are manifested on the two syntactic levels.

A third zone, the **lexical combinatorics zone**, specifies semantically related lexemes as the values of "lexical functions". MTT has identified approximately 60 simple lexical functions which may be defined for lexemes of languages. Some lexical functions are "paradigmatic" (e.g., the functions which compute synonyms, superordinate terms and converse terms), in that they identify semantically related words of the same syntactic class. Other lexical functions are "syntagmatic" (e.g., the *Magn* function which computes the augmentative adjective or adverb which can modify the entry word). Syntagmatic lexical functions calculate the values of collocational words co-occurring in the same sentence in specified (deep) syntactic relationship with the entry word. Composition of functions may also be defined for certain functions and lexemes.

The abstractness of lexical functions allows very general statement of "deep structure paraphrasing rules" (see section 4.3 below). These rules allow dependency structures corresponding to sentences like:

(1a) *Paul used Emacs frequently Friday.*

to be recast as structures directly corresponding to:

(1b) *Paul made frequent use of Emacs Friday.*

or even (in the case of appropriate theme/rheme constraints):

(1c) *Friday saw Paul making frequent use of Emacs.*

In general, the lexical function paraphrase rules can be formulated in a way valid for large classes of languages – see (Mel'čuk, 1974) for Russian examples, and (Mel'čuk, 1988) for French.

11.3.2 Points of Lexicalization

In an MTM generation model there are three important "sources" of lexical items:

- Most open class items (nouns, verbs and adjectives) are chosen during the mapping from SemR to DSyntR in a process known as "lexicalization". In addition to major class words, certain "semantically full" prepositions and adverbs take on a lexicalized form at this point as well.

- Most closed class items, including grammatically determined words (e.g., most prepositions and articles), are determined during the passage from DSyntR into SSyntR.

- Open class items which are introduced as values of lexical functions in the course of deep-structure paraphrasing rules (see section 4.3 below) are not computed until the passage into SSyntR.

11.4 SOURCES OF PARAPHRASE

The ECD lexicon, interacting with grammar rules and theme/rheme constraints, makes possible at least four major sources of paraphrase during the generation process:

1. network reductions from relatively primitive lexeme meanings to semantically more complex lexeme meanings, either of which may be verbalized directly;

2. lexicalization choices made during the passage from SemR nets to DSyntR dependency trees (under constraints of theme/rheme structure);

3. deep syntactic paraphrasing using general rules which utilise lexical functions;

4. various alternative renderings of the DSyntR trees as SSyntR trees; (there may also be a secondary usage of lexical functions, which we will not go into in this paper, as a means of circumventing blockages which may occur when contradictory sets of constraints arise).

These sources of paraphrase will be discussed, each in turn, in the following sections.

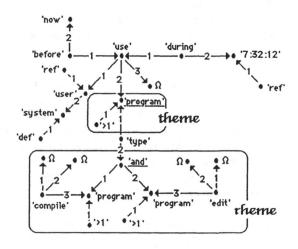

Figure 11.1: SemR for sentences (2a) and (2b)

11.4.1   Incremental Reductions (Simplifications) in the Semantic Net

An MTM for English models the generation of English sentences beginning with semantic nets, which represent the sentence's literal meaning. These networks can generally be "verbalized" directly, since the semantic elements on the network nodes are for the most part meanings of simple lexemes of English. Typically, however, the direct verbalization of an input network would make a sentence which is much longer than necessary. A semantic networks can be recursively reduced or simplified. First, one finds a subnetwork which is the meaning definition of a semantically more complex term. The subnetwork is then replaced by a simple node which represents the semantically complex meaning. This process may then be repeated. In each case the defining network for each lexeme's meaning is found in the lexeme's ECD dictionary definition. The reduced networks, because they also use lexeme meanings, can also be verbalized (as shorter sentences). At some point, this reduction must terminate, but each step in the net reduction generally gives a paraphrase when realized as a sentence by the most direct route.

An Example

As an example of net reduction, consider the network of Figure 11.1. In the form given, this can be verbalized (roughly) as follows:

> (2a) *The referred-to user(s) of the system used (before now), during the referred-to period of 7 hours, 32 minutes and 12 seconds, more than one program of a type such that someone compiles something with these programs and some edits something with these programs.*

One network reduction replaces the left-hand subnetwork shown in the rheme box, (verbalized by) *programs such that someone compiles something with these programs*, by *compilers*. A similar reduction replaces the right-hand subnetwork in the same box by *editors*. The temporal relation predication (verbalized by) *before now* on the main proposition is obligatorily replaced by a 'grammeme' which will become the simple past tense on the verb when the network is mapped to a deep syntactic tree. At this point the reduced network can be (roughly) verbalized as:

> (2b) *The aforementioned users of the system used programs of compiler type and of editor type during the referred-to period of 7 hours, 32 minutes and 12 seconds.*

A further specialized reduction involving the *type* lexeme gives something like:

> (2c) *The aforementioned users of the system used compilers and editors during ...*

Although there may be preference rules which dictate reducing the network as much as possible before lexicalization in DSyntR, the unreduced networks still can give grammatical resultant sentences which carry the same information, although usually in a clumsier way. Under some stylistic conditions, however, some of the longer paraphrase variants may be even favored (to give parallel structures with surrounding sentences, create euphony, etc.).

Alternative Maximal Reductions in the Semantic Net

Another source of paraphrase alternatives arises when there is more than one way to simplify a large network to get two distinct networks, both maximally reduced. This can lead to paraphrastic variant sentences which exhibit quite different lexicalizations. Something like this may occur, for example, when a verb can incorporate part but not all of the meaning of its manner modifier. Thus there may be two alternative verbal predicate reductions, leaving part of the manner modification to be encoded separately. This would be illustrated in English by:

> (3a) *Fred limped across the road quickly.*

and

(3b) *Fred hurried across the road with a limp.*

The semantic networks from which these sentences are lexicalized are presumably both equally reduced, although derivable from the same unreduced network. But since they have distributed the same semantic material differently, they give rise to different direct lexicalizations.[2]

It is interesting to note that in French, neither the manner of locomotion modifier nor the rate adverbial can be merged with the motion verb meaning in such sentences. The only net reduction (from a similar unreduced French source network) available from the ECD of French would be something akin to English:

(3c) *Fred crossed the road, limping quickly.*

Substitution of collocationally bound lexemes

One special case of network "reduction" involves the substitution of a more specialized lexeme meaning for a general one, in a specific network context. This does not involve a change in the size of the network, but merely in the linguistic meanings on nodes. For example, the semantic predicate 'use' can be replaced in the networks corresponding to sentences (2a),(2b) and (2c) by the predicate 'run', giving a different network, which could be directly verbalized as:

(4) *The aforementioned users of the system ran compilers and editors during*
...

Alternatively, this sort of substitution might also be carried out during the lexicalization process described below.

11.4.2 Passage from semantic net to deep syntactic tree

One of the most important points at which paraphrastic choices can be made during generation with an MTM occurs when (reduced or unreduced) semantic nets are mapped to deep syntactic trees. For example the semantic network in Figure 11.2 can be mapped either to the deep syntactic representation (DSyntR) indicated in Figure 11.3 or the DSyntR in Figure 11.4. The structure in Figure 11.3 will give rise to output sentences such as:

(5a) *The user who ran editors is called Martin.*

The alternative DSyntR in Figure 11.4 gives output sentences such as:

(5b) *The name of the user who ran editors is Martin.*

---

[2]It can be argued that (3a,b,c) are not perfect paraphrases and differ precisely with respect to the location of the manner information in the communicative structure.

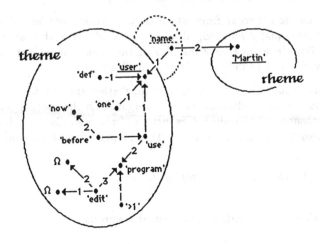

Figure 11.2: SemR for sentences (5a) and (5b)

The two sentences (5a) and (5b) are good paraphrases of each other. They not only have equivalent meanings, but also both preserve the theme and rheme structure of the initial semantic net of Figure 11.2. Sentences with equivalent meanings except for inverted theme/rheme structure would include (5c):

(5c) *Martin is the name of the user who ran editors.*

Determination of Lexical Root Node

The first and most important step in determining the DSyntR which corresponds to a given SemR is to choose the *entry node* of the semantic net. An entry node in the net will correspond to the root verbal lexeme of the DSyntR. A semantic node can be an entry node if it is a predicate node and either (i) is the dominant node of the theme or rheme, or (ii) directly governs the dominant node of the theme, or (iii) connects the dominant nodes of the theme and the rheme. In Figure 11.1, the entry node could be the predicate node 'use', using condition (ii), in which case the DSyntR would have root lexeme *use* and give rise to sentences such as:

(6a) *System users ran compilers and editors during this time.*

However, a second candidate entry node would be the predicate node 'type', which connects the dominant nodes of both the theme and the rheme (condition iii). The choice of a non-verbal predicate forces the introduction of the copula

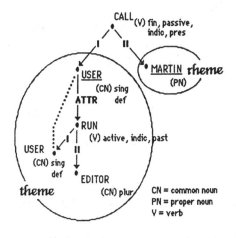

Figure 11.3: DSyntR for sentence (5a)

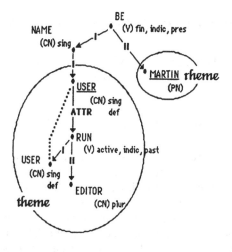

Figure 11.4: DSyntR for sentence (5b)

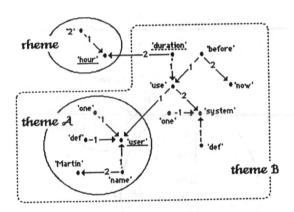

Figure 11.5: SemR with alternative Themes A and B corresponding to sentences
(7a) and (7b) respectively.

verb *be* as root verbal lexeme in DSyntR. This would give rise to sentences such
as:

(6b) *The types of programs that users ran during this time were compilers
and editors*

If 'type' is not chosen as entry node, it may be eliminated later by a special
rule which simplifies generic constructions.

Influence of Communicative Structure On Lexical Selection

The communicative structure specified in the initial semantic net gives separate
theme and rheme regions of the net, such as those indicated in Figure 11.1. During the search for candidate lexicalizations of the net, the semantic definitions of
lexemes are matched against subnetworks. When two competing lexemes, such
as the conversive terms *send/receive*, both match a subnet, the communicative
structure imposes a way of choosing between them. The preferred lexicalization
will be the one whose first actant is in the theme region of the net.

A second case where theme/rheme structure influences lexicalization is ex-
emplified by nets such as those of Figure 11.5, which contain a new time duration specification (unlike the net in Figure 11.1, which is referentially linked
to earlier text by the 'ref' node). The semantic predicate 'duration' typically
gives rise to lexicalization using *for*, provided the 'duration' node is not the

dominant node of the theme (cf. Figure 11.5, with "Theme A" as theme). This leads to sentences such as:

(7a) *Martin used the system for two hours.*

which have DSyntR as given in Figure 11.6.

However, if 'duration' IS the dominant node of the theme (cf. Figure 11.5 with "Theme B" as theme), this will give a different lexicalization, using the word *duration* (cf. DSyntR as in Figure 11.7):

(7b) *The duration of Martin's use of the system was two hours.*

In fact the case illustrated by sentences (7a) and (7b) might be explained by a more general principle governing theme/rheme constraints. It appears that there are general rules dictating that words from certain lexical classes cannot be theme in DSyntR. For example, conjunctions and prepositions are excluded from this role. Furthermore certain words (e.g., *always*) cannot be rheme. Therefore, if a lexicalization rule would cause a word or lexical class item to appear in the prohibited part of the theme/rheme structure which the DSyntR inherits from the SemR, this lexicalization rule is blocked.

11.4.3 DSyntR Paraphrasing Rules Using Lexical Functions (LFs)

As mentioned above during discussion of the ECD lexicon, each lexical item is associated with a number of semantically related items by means of a standard set of lexical functions (LFs). These functional expressions are particularly convenient for representing structural correspondences between paraphrases such as those between (8a) and (8b), and between (9a) and (9b):

(8a) *Martin used Emacs a lot.*
(8b) *Martin made heavy use of Emacs.*

(9a) *Martin edited a large text file.*
(9b) *Martin did some editing of a large text file.*

In both (8a) and (9a) the simple verb form (*use, edit*) is paraphrasable by a complex verb phrase which introduces a new "empty" verb (*make, do*), with the nominalization of the simple verb as its object. The syntactic change in the verb phrase of (8a) to (8b) also carries with it a change in the degree adverbial. Both sentence pairs illustrate the use of the lexical function $Oper_1$. The DSyntR forms of (8b) and (9b) are derived from the forms for (8a) and (9a) respectively by the application of the paraphrasing rule (10):

(10) $X_{(verb)} ==> Oper_1(X) - -II - - > S_0(X).$

The rule states that a verb node in DSyntR is replaceable by the two-node dependency tree specified in the right-hand part of the rule. The second deep syntactic argument of the new verb is the action nominal (S_0) of the old

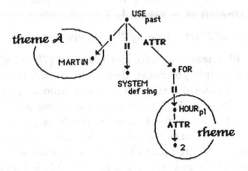

Figure 11.6: DSyntR for SemR of fig 5 with Theme A.

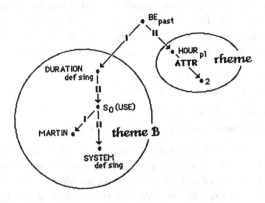

Figure 11.7: DSyntR for SemR of fig 5 with Theme B.

verb (X). Notice that this rule is independent of the particular lexical item or even the particular language. The particular lexical values of the items $Oper_1(X)$ and $S_0(X)$ are found in the lexical entry of X in the ECD of the particular application language or sublanguage. For examples (9a,b) we have $Oper_1(use) = make, S_0(use) = use$.

In the case of (8a,b), the degree modifiers (*a lot, heavy*) are lexicalized differently, even though the meaning contribution of the two modifiers is quite the same. This constant meaning contribution is represented by the lexical function signifying intensification, *Magn*.

In the DSyntR corresponding to example (8a) the locution *a lot* is represented only as the node labeled "Magn". It is a dependent node hanging from the X node, which means that it applies to this parent node, giving *a lot* as lexical value if realized directly in SSyntR. Under the deep structure paraphrasing rule, all dependents of the X node are carried over as dependents of the node $S_0(X)$. This means that Magn now hangs from that node and applies to its lexical value. The noun *use* has as its lexical entry for Magn the word *heavy*. Thus the paraphrasing operation takes place on an abstract structure. The lexical consequences of the operation are sorted out by the computation of lexical functions, after consulting the ECD, on the level of SSyntR.

In many cases, the application of a deep-syntactic paraphrasing rule using LFs is an optional operation which gives one more way of realizing the initial DSyntR. However, it may turn out that such an operation gives the only viable output. Consider, for example, sentences (11a) and (11b):

(11a) *A would-be penetrator attacked the system full-scale-ly(??).*
(11b) *A would-be penetrator mounted a full-scale attack on the system.*

The realization of sentence (11a) using *attack* as a verb, requires that there be a value for the lexical function *Magn* applied to the verb *attack*. However, no suitable adverb or even adverbial locution, seems to be available in this domain for *Magn(attack)* when *attack* is a verb. The existence of this "lexical hole" makes it necessary for the generation system to resort to the deep structure paraphrasing rule (10) to produce the acceptable output of (11b). In this domain, Magn is defined on the **noun** *attack*: Magn(*attack*) = *full scale*. Thus, even though a default generation strategy might avoid application of DSyntR paraphrasing rules, these rules may be called upon when direct-path lexical realization is blocked for lack of lexical stock.

11.4.4 Surface Syntactic Realization

The last major point at which paraphrastic alternatives are determined is during the passage from DSyntR to SSyntR. The noun phrases given in (12a) and (12b) are derived from the surface syntactic structures given in Figures 11.9 and 11.10 respectively.

(12a) *the users who used the system ...*
(12b) *the users using the system ...*

These forms are equivalent (at least in past-tense sentence contexts) and are both derivable from the same DSyntR, given as Figure 11.8.

One of the major choices available during the passage from DSyntR to SSyntR is in the particular surface realization of the deep syntactic government pattern. For example, when a verb has two complements, there may be some freedom in the order of surface manifestation of these complements (cf. "dative movement" phenomena, etc.). Needless to say, the communicative structure of the DSyntR will strongly influence the choice of surface order.

A third choice in mapping DSyntR to SSyntR may occur if a lexical function expressed in DSyntR has two or more possible values. Since we have $Oper_1(login) = do, perform$, we may generate either *Max did several logins at tty02* or *Max performed several logins at tty02* by choosing a particular value at this point. Of course, global stylistic constraints may give preference to a particular form.

11.5   IMPLEMENTATION CONTEXT

Our implementation of an MTM for language generation deals specifically with production of written text beginning with semantic net representations of text sentences. The semantic nets are calculated by a translation procedure from "conceptual communicative representations" (CCRs) that are output by a simple planning component which does not constitute part of the MTM. The CCRs, like the semantic nets, contain theme/rheme specifications. But unlike the nets, which use language-dependent elements of linguistic meaning, the CCRs are formulated in conceptual terms appropriate for domain reasoning. These CCRs are therefore considered language-independent (Iordanskaja and Polguère, 1988). In the case of technical domains such as operating systems, however, we expect the semantic nets to use meanings which are a closer reflection of the conceptual elements than is the case in non-technical domains.

Our specific implementation resides in a system we have called GOSSiP (Generation of Operating System Summaries in Prolog). All of the MTM linguistic rules (which map SemRs down to word strings) and the ECD dictionary entries are written in Prolog. GOSSiP runs on a Sun 3 workstation and has been provided with an appropriate linguistic development environment geared to MTMs. Figure 11.11 shows the Sun screen displaying windows for the SemR, DSyntR, SSyntR and MorphR for the sentence *Martin used the system for 2:34:10.* On the semantic and syntactic levels the region included in the sentence theme is indicated by the blackened semantic or lexical nodes (e.g., 'martin' and its dependent nodes). Rheme is indicated by the gray (hatched) nodes (e.g., 'duration', *for* and their dependents). On the level of MorphR,

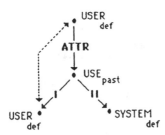

Figure 11.8: DSyntR for sentence fragments (12a) and (12b).

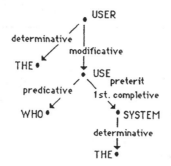

Figure 11.9: SSyntR for (12a)

theme and rheme are indicated among the relevant features displayed for individual words.

11.6 SUMMARY

We have argued that the ability of a linguistic model to provide paraphrastic alternatives during the generation process is a measure of its adequacy for producing text under multiple constraints or preferences. Meaning–Text Models provide ways of representing the semantic, syntactic and lexical sources of paraphrase in a framework specifically geared to language generation.

The lexicon of an MTM (its ECD) gives semantic network definitions of lexical meanings, allowing for the recursive reduction of an input semantic net with many possible resultants, each a candidate for separate mapping through the representation levels to give a possible output sentence. Alternative syntactic

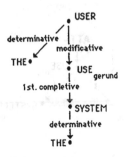

Figure 11.10: SSyntR for (12b)

renderings on the level of DSyntR, and then again on the level of SSyntR, combine with optional usage of lexical function paraphrasing rules within DSyntR to give a proliferation of possible output sentences for a given input meaning representation (SemR).

Clearly, the introduction of greater paraphrase possibilities in a linguistic model also increases the potential for non-determinism during the generation process. This potential problem is greatly reduced by the use of MTM's supplementary communicative structure, which specifies the theme and rheme of a sentence on each of its linguistic representation levels. Only a subset of possible paraphrases on any representation level of a sentence preserve the communicative structure specified in the input semantic network.

In the GOSSiP system as implemented thus far, the communicative structure provides the primary means of controlling choice among the (otherwise) paraphrastic possibilities for lexicalization and choice of grammatical structure. As more of MTM's paraphrase mechanisms and lexical resources become implemented in GOSSiP, we anticipate the need to explore ways of adding general stylistic constraints over the full text in order to help choose the optimal final form for each sentence.

ACKNOWLEDGEMENTS

This work was supported by the U.S. Air Force, Rome Air Development Center, under contract F30602-86-C-0115.

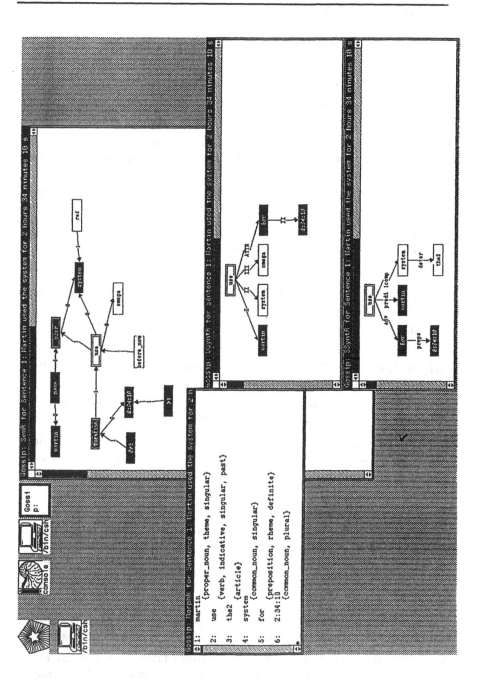

Figure 11.11: MTM development environment showing SemR, DSyntR, SyntR and MorphR for sentence *Martin used the system for 2:34:10.*

BIBLIOGRAPHY

Cumming, Susanna (1985) *The Lexicon in Text Generation*, technical report, USC-ISI.

Gross, Maurice (1975) *Méthodes en syntaxe*. Hermann.

Iordanskaja, Lidija (1989) *Communicative Structure and its Use During Text Generation*, Technical report TR 15-10, Odyssey Research Associates.

Iordanskaja, Lidija, Kittredge, Richard and Polguère, Alain (1988) "Implementing the Meaning-Text Model for Language Generation", paper presented at *COLING-88*.

Iordanskaja, Lidija and Polguère, Alain (1988) "Semantic Processing for Text Generation", *Proc. of the ICSC Conference*, Hong Kong.

Matthiessen, Christian M.I.M. (1983) *How to Make Grammatical Choices in Text Generation*. ISI Reprint Series, ISI/RS-83-120.

McKeown, Kathleen (1985) *Text Generation*. Cambridge University Press.

Mel'čuk, Igor (1974) *Towards a Theory of Linguistic Models of the Meaning–Text Type*. [in Russian] Nauka, Moscow.

Mel'čuk, Igor (1981) "Meaning–Text Models", *Annual Review of Anthropology*, vol.10,pp.27-62.

Mel'čuk, Igor (1982) "Lexical Functions in Lexicographic Description", *Proc. of the 8th Annual Meeting of the Berkeley Linguistic Society*.

Mel'čuk, Igor (1988) "Paraphrase et lexique dans la théorie linguistique Sens-Texte" *Cahiers de lexicologie*, vol.52, no.1 (pp.5–50), no.2 (pp.5–53).

Mel'čuk, Igor and Polguère, Alain (1987) "A Formal Lexicon in the Meaning-Text Theory", *Computational Linguistics*, vol.13, nos.3-4 [Special Issue on the Lexicon], pp.261-275.

Mel'čuk, Igor and Zholkovsky, Alexander (1970) "Towards a functioning meaning-text model of language", *Linguistics*, vol.57, pp.10-47.

Mel'čuk, Igor *et al.* (1984) *Dictionnaire explicatif et combinatoire du français contemporain*. Presses de l'Université de Montréal.

Nirenburg, Sergei (1987) "A Natural Language Generation System that Emphasizes Lexical Selection", *Proc. Natural Language Planning Workshop*, Blue Mountain Lake.

Nirenburg, Sergei and Nirenburg, Irene (1988) "A Framework for Lexical Selection in Natural Language Generation", *Proc. of COLING-88*, Budapest.

Sgall, Petr, Hajičová, Eva and Panevová, Jarmila (1986) *The Meaning of the Sentence inits Semantic and Pragmatic Aspects*, Academia Publishers, Prague.

Ward, Nigel (1988) "Issues in Word Choice", *Proc. of COLING-88*, Budapest.

Part III

GRAMMATICAL RESOURCES

Chapter 12

Referent Grammar In Text Generation

Bengt Sigurd

Abstract: A text may be seen as the result of input from the external world and human internal aspects on it. The paper shows how the same event - a submarine following a trawler - may give rise to different types (genres) of text, e.g., a report on the facts, an evaluation of the facts, a summary of the most important features against the background of previous events, or a mixture of some or all of these.

As is well known, it is difficult to teach a computer how to generate interesting and varying text including more abstract, evaluative and summarizing comments. The paper shows how different predicates, e.g., be, go, sail, follow, attack give information of varying interest and how the computer may calculate the news value of an event on the basis of the amount of interest of the predicates and the objects involved. The bulk of the paper demonstrates how Referent Grammar (RG) - a generalized phrase structure grammar with built-in referents - offers a convenient way of keeping track of both the sentence and the discourse referents.

12.1   FROM SCENES AND FACTS TO STORY AND HEADLINE

Text generating systems may start from different kinds of input: a scene, a logical data base, grammatically analyzed sentences transferred from another language (as in automatic translation), or from another text (for a survey, see Kempen, 1986). The input may be more or less close to the output: the text to be generated. Figure 12.1 below illustrates the fact that, generally, a text is not only a simple verbal rendering of a series of pictures. The text goes beyond the pictures and refers to abstract objects, which are not directly visible in the pictures. Computer generated text becomes boring, if it does not move between different levels of abstraction, taking different perspectives, generalizing, etc.

The first scene shows a trawler (fishing-boat) - although not exactly as it may appear on a radar screen. One may try to store this in predicate logic as the simple fact: exist(trawl, time1, loc1), where time1 and loc1 denote the time and place of the event. Similarly, the later existence (appearance) of a submarine may be denoted by: exist(sub, time2, loc2). Scene 3 shows how the submarine follows the trawler, and scene 4 shows that this goes on at a later time, and another location. Scene 5 shows the trawler in the harbour, which may simply be rendered in predicate logic by: exist(trawl, time5, loc5), where loc5 is the harbour.

Even a brief consideration indicates that the pictures say a lot more than such facts given in predicate logic. It is also clear that we would need an enormous set of such facts in order to approach all that is said by the pictures, e.g., that the trawler has two masts, the ships head in the same direction, there is no submarine close to the harbour at time5, etc. But, we will neither discuss suitable formalisms for that purpose nor possible ways of organizing a data base with inference rules now. Instead we will examine the structure of the related newspaper story to be found under the heading: "UNIDENTIFIED SUB FOLLOWS TRAWLER".

Our main problem may be stated: How does one generate such a text on the basis of the events indicated by the scenes and facts? In order to discuss this problem we will:

- identify the main discourse referents in the text and state what is said about them (produce a referent dynamic analysis of the text);

- present Referent Grammar, a Generalized Phrase Structure Grammar which takes discourse referents into account;

- present functional analyses of the sentences of the text according to a Referent Grammar (module) of English;

- show how Referent Grammar can be used in the generation of a text, if there is an interface which determines "what to say" and offers a functional representation and information about focus as input to the grammatical module;

- discuss how such an interface can be constructed for the sample text taking the status of the referents and the semantic weights of differents predicates into account.

12.2   A REFERENT DYNAMIC ANALYSIS OF THE TEXT

Five main discourse referents (see Karttunen, 1976, Webber, 1983, Sigurd, 1987) can be identifed in our text: the trawler (R1), the submarine (R2), the hunt (R3), Karlskrona, a Swedish port (R4), and the whole incident (R5). We may also distinguish five main propositions (P1-P5) as shown in the table below.

Proposition No		Referent:				
		Sub R1	Trawler R2	Hunt=P1 R3	Karlskr R4	Incident = P1-P4 R5
P1:	R1 follows R2 outside R4	⊗	⊗		⊗	
P2:	R3 lasts 1 hour			⊗		
P3:	R2 heads for R4		⊗		⊗	
P4:	R1 disappears near R4	⊗			⊗	
P5:	R5 is third incident					⊗

The table shows the referential skeleton of the text. We note that the submarine and the trawler are referred to twice, while the port is referred to three times and the hunt and the incident only once. We also note that the submarine, the trawler and the harbour are the only referents which can be identified with physical objects and thus clearly seen in the pictures. The hunt is a more abstract referent, which may be identified with the first proposition (P1: the hunting of the trawler by the submarine). Hunting is, in fact, here a pattern of movements which can only be identified indirectly by noting that the ships move in the same direction, that the submarine is fairly close to the trawler. Even more abstract is the referent R5. The appearance of the submarine and its chasing of the trawler is seen as a cognitive whole by this referent and the word 'incident' indicates that the situation is evaluated as 'unfortunate'. The facts of the last sentence can only be derived by looking into a data base for similar events - this is standard procedure, when accidents are reported by news media. The referent labeled 'incident' (R5) may be identified with all the propositions (above all P1) as indicated.

We think the creation of discourse referents is a fundamental process in text generation and that the structure of natural language reflects this in its great potentials for encoding referents by simple and complex noun phrases. Furthermore, we think that a grammar should take this into account, e.g., as is done in Referent Grammar (RG; Sigurd, 1987, 1988a, 1988b). After a brief introduction, we will now show how the text can analyzed by Referent Grammar.

12.3 REFERENT GRAMMAR

Referent Grammar is a kind of generalized phrase structure grammar and thus without (overt) transformations (for a presentation of GPSG, see Gazdar *et al.*, 1985). The following are some characteristics of Referent Grammar:

- Built-in referent numbers (variables) in the functional representations, which make it possible, e.g., to solve the coreference (antecedent) problem in noun phrases with relative clauses and keep track of discourse referents;

- Normalized functional representations (f-representations) in addition to categorial representations;

- Labeled defective categories, e.g., 'odpp' = object defective prepositional phrase, 'sdsent'= subject defective sentence (equivalent to the usual GPSG slash categories);

- No null (zero, empty) categories;

- Grammatical rules which take mode and focused constituents into account;

- Prolog implementation in Definite Clause Grammar (DCG) which makes it possible to use the rules both in parsing (analysis) and generation (synthesis).

A (simplified) functional RG representation of "The trawler which the submarine followed fled" would look as follows, where the numbers denote the two referents involved:

```
s (subj (np (R1:trawler,
          s (subj (R2:submarine), pred (followed), obj (R1)))),
    pred (fled))
```

Note how the relative clause occurs beside 'trawler', the head of the noun phrase and how the object of the relative clause is coreferential with (has the same referent number (R1) as) the head.

The following related (simplified) DCG rules illustrate how the defective categories and the functional representations (to the left of the arrow) are used:

```
np (R1:X,F) → np(X), [which], odsent(R1,F).
```

```
odsent (R1, s(subj(Y), pred(Z), obj (R1)) → np (Y), vtrans (Z).
```

The first rule states that an np is assigned the referent number R1 and the functional representation: X, F if we find an X which is an np (such as 'the trawler') followed by the (object) relative pronoun 'which' followed by an object defective sentence (odsent), whose functional representation is F. The second rule shows the functional representation of an object defective sentence (in the second slot to the left of the arrow) if we find a Y which is an np (such as 'the submarine') followed by a verb Z which is transitive (such as 'followed'). The rules will make sure that the object of the relative clause gets the same referent number (R1) as the head (and the whole np). If we read the rule generatively, it states that an np may include an (object) relative pronoun followed by an object defective sentence (clause), in which case the functional representation of the np includes the functional representation of the relative clause.

Referent Grammar has been used in the automatic translation project SWE-TRA (Swedish Computer Translation Research; Sigurd 1988a, b) and substantial fragments of Swedish, English and Russian grammars have been implemented. The translation from Swedish into English is carried out by having the Swedish grammar module parse the source sentence and deliver a functional representation (with the word meaning coded in a special semantic representation). This representation is then given to the English grammar module with the goal of finding an equivalent English sentence. Given a functional representation as input the Referent Grammar module will arrange the words in proper order (preposing constituents if indicated by the focusing variable), assigning agreement and other inflections (as for the potential of RG in translation, see Sigurd and Gawronska-Werngren, 1989).

Referent Grammars can be used both for parsing and generation of sentences and text, as we will demonstrate below using both English and Swedish examples.

12.4 REFERENT GRAMMAR IN TEXT ANALYSIS

We will now demonstrate the functional representations suiting our sample text.

The sentence "An unidentified submarine followed a trawler outside Karl-skrona today" would have the following (simplified) functional representation, where R1, R2, etc. are as in the table above:

```
s (subj (np (R1:submarine, sg, indef, unidentified)),
   pred (follow, past),
   obj (np (R2:trawler, sg, indef)),
   advl (pp (outside, np (R4:  Karlskrona))),
   advl (today))
```

This functional representation with semi-English semantic coding of the word meanings would also be used in the analysis of the equivalent Swedish sentence, which is: "En oidentifierad ubåt (för)följde en trålare utanför Karl-skrona idag."

The sentence "The hunt went on for an hour, while the trawler headed for Karlskrona" would get the following simplified functional representation, where "pp" denotes prepositional phrase and "cp" denotes conjunctional phrase (clause):

```
s (subj (np (R3:hunt, sg, def)),
   padv (on),
   pred (go, past)
   advl (pp (for, np (hour, sg))),
   advl (cp (while, s (subj (np (R2:trawler, sg, def)),
                       pred (head, past),
                       advl (pp (for, np (R4:Karlskrona)))))))
```

The corresponding Swedish would be: "Jakten pågick under en timme, medan trålaren stävade mot Karlskrona." Note that the phrase 'went on' is analyzed as a verb plus a particle in English, but this combination of 'go' and 'on' has to be rendered by one verb ('pågick'; infinitive:'pågå'), where the equivalent of 'on' is prefixed in Swedish. The referent numbers have been inserted according to the referent dynamic analyses above.

The sentence: "The submarine disappeared near Karlskrona" is analyzed as:

```
s (subj (np (R1:submarine, def))),
   pred (disappear, past),
   advl (pp (near, np (R4:Karlskrona)))
```

The Swedish equivalent is: "Ubåten försvann nära Karlskrona". The last sentence: "This is the third incident during this month" may be analyzed as:

```
s (subj (np (R5:this)),
   pred (be, pr),
   predicative (np (R5:incident, third, sg, def)),
   advl (pp (during, np (R6:month, def, this))))).
```

The Swedish equivalent is: "Detta är den tredje incidenten under denna månaden".

There is a problem in determining how many referents there are in the little text, which we so far have avoided by talking only about the main five referents. It is clear that 'this month' also includes a referent (R6), which was not mentioned above. We have assigned R5 to 'this' (and to the phrase "the third incident").

All these functional representations can be derived by running the sample sentences through the SWETRA programs, but the special procedures needed to assign the referent numbers as required during the analysis have only been implemented partly. These procedures should assign R1 to the first (indefinite) noun phrase (e.g., by using the built-in predicate gensym, which gives numbered items). Similarly, the second indefinite noun phrase should get the referent number R2. The next noun phrase 'the hunt' should be assigned referent (R3). If we have stored the sentences (propositions) R3 may be identified with the first proposition, as 'hunt' and 'follow' are semantically related. The definite article of 'the hunt' indicates that this referent should, in fact, be known. The second mention of 'the trawler', 'the submarine' and 'Karlskrona' should easily be assigned the same referent numbers. The noun phrases 'This' and 'the third incident' get a new referent number (R5), but discourse analysis should also be able to identify R5 with the previously mentioned sentences (propositions).

Referent identification is difficult to simulate perfectly by computer. It is, however, necessary when translating from a language without definite and indefinite articles such as Russian into a language with articles such as English. For a discussion of these problems and a presentation of an experimental RG implementation, see Gawronska-Werngren (1989).

12.5 REFERENT GRAMMAR IN TEXT GENERATION

Referent Grammar needs an input in a special functional representation format, accepting only the following main functional roles: 'subj', 'obj', 'dobj'= dative object, 'sadvl"= sentence adverbial, 'advl' = adverbial. The contents of an np should include a referent variable and the "meaning" of the head noun and the whole np as shown above. The functional representations are expected to include information about definiteness and pronominalization. In addition information about the mode of the sentence (declarative, question, imperative) and the focused constituent (generally preposed in English and Swedish) is needed. Most of this is readily available, when we use Referent Grammar in automatic translation (although not definiteness, when translating from e.g., Russian, as mentioned above).

If we are to use Referent Grammar in a text generating system taking e.g., a series of scenes as input or a data base, we need a very sophisticated kind of interface between the (real) physical and mental world and the Referent Grammar. This interface should be able to select the appropriate subjects, predicates, objects and adverbials on the basis of data (coordinate values) from the scenes and the thoughts evoked. How this can be done has been discussed in Badler (1975) and Davey (1978). Sigurd (1982), Fornell (1983) and Nilsson *et al.* (1988) describe how the text generating program Commentator, which exists in several implementations works. Commentator comments (in writing or speech) on a scene where objects, e.g., persons or ships move around. We will have that system in mind in the following discussion.

It is clear that many statements are true of such scenes as those shown in Figure 12.1, but most of them should not be mentioned, as they are trivial, have been mentioned before, are irrelevant etc. It is also true that scenes can be commented on from different perspectives. The comments on the marine scene above are typical of a newspaper and we will discuss ways of arriving at such commentary texts.

12.6   RANKING REFERENTS ACCORDING TO INTEREST

Initially, our text stays on the concrete level, referring to moving objects. The choice of comments on this level can partly be made on the basis of priority measures. We assign a priority (status) figure (status:1-10) to all objects of the scene, which will control the chances to become subject in a comment, e.g., the submarine 9, the trawler 5, Karlskrona 2. These figures are meant to reflect the intuition that a submarine is generally more interesting than a trawler, which in turn is more interesting than a port. We also assign priority figures to different predicates according to their interest, news value or semantic weight, e.g.. attack 9, follow 7, appear 6, turn 5, disappear 4, head (towards) 3, be (situated at) 1. These figures should reflect the intuition that it is more interesting to hear that a ship attacks than that it follows something, which in turn is more interesting than the appearance of something, etc. These figures, of course, are somewhat arbitrary and depend on the situation. One could therefore imagine "dynamic" (rolling) priority lists, where the values vary according to the situation, but we will not try to elaborate on this now. It is clear that the evaluation of objects and predicates has to be based on a kind of user model. In this case, we assume that the user is interested in national security and therefore curious about submarines, particularly if they threaten other ships.

12.7 RANKING PREDICATES ACCORDING TO INCLUSIVENESS

We note that certain predicates could be said to include or imply others. Thus, if a ship follows another, they are both heading in the same direction (and they both exist). One could also say that certain predicates give more information than others. This is indicated by the following table, where the verbs to the right in the list include more information that the words to the left. The column indicates the type of information that is added as we move to the right along the row of predicates.

Components	Predicates:						
	be	sit	go	sail	head for	follow	attack
"transitive"					(+)	+	+
means, etc				+			+
movement			+	+	+	(+)	
posture		+	(+)				(+)
state	+	+					
exist	+	+	+	+	+	+	+

Table 1. The semantic components of some predicates. Heavier predicates are further to the right

One may assign movement verbs higher values than state verbs. The last five verbs (go, sail, head for, follow, attack) will then get higher values. Furthermore a verb may be assigned a higher value if it involves another person, object, etc ("transitive"). This will give the last three verbs higher values. A verb which specifies the posture or the means or manner of the state or movement may also get a higher value. This will give 'sit', 'lie', 'stand' higher values than 'be' and 'sail', 'fly' and 'creep' higher values than 'go'. It is not easy to apply this classification, however, as is indicated by the parentheses in the table. Should 'sail' be marked for posture, as sailing-boats generally take an upright position? Given a reasonable analysis of the verbs we would be able to make comments which are as 'telling' as possible. We would then prefer to say that a ship is attacking to saying that it is following, prefer to say that it is sailing to that it is going, etc. Furthermore, the priority figures of the objects (referents) could be added to the priority figures of the predicates to get an overall figure for a sentence. Only sentences with a certain overall priority value (above a certain threshold) should be uttered. This is, in fact, the approach taken by the version of Commentator implemented by Nilsson *et al.* (1988).

12.8 GENERALIZATIONS AND ABSTRACT REFERENTS

As noted above, there are some abstract referents to be found in our sample text: the hunt and the incident. What is the reason for talking about the hunt and not the submarine or the trawler anymore? How should such referents be rated? The utterance "The hunt went on for an hour", illustrates an interesting step, where the abstract hunt becomes the subject and the duration is realized as a finite verb 'go on' instead of as a preposition in an adverbial. It is clearly refreshing to find a more abstract and inclusive referent at this point of the text. A text needs inclusive observations, overview comments and generalizations in order to keep the interest of the listener/reader. Generally, texts produced by Commentator and similar systems only comment on the positions and movements of concrete objects, and that is one of the reasons why such texts soon get monotonous and boring.

A generalization is also illustrated by the last sentence, where it is stated that this incident is the third this month. By this comment the author shows that he has lifted his eyes above the concrete events of the scene and looked in the records.

The heading of the little story selects the semantically heavy sentence: "Unidentified submarine follows trawler outside Karlskrona", with the verb in present tense as is common in headlines. It seems headlines such as "Trawler hunt lasts one hour" or "Third submarine incident this month" would have been too vague and abstract to catch the eye of a reader. But writing headlines is an art, and certainly difficult to simulate by computer. We note that headlines often are noun phrases and thus only utilize the noun phrase rules of the generating grammar. It is important then to have complex noun phrase rules and know how they are related to the full sentence rules of the grammar.

12.9 CONCLUSIONS

There are great differences between describing an event, e.g., the appearance of a submarine, by a series of pictures, sets of facts in a data base and a newspaper text. The problem of "How to say it" can be solved by Referent Grammar, a GPSG grammar which can be implemented directly in Prolog and which permits us to locate discourse referents within the functional representations of sentences and follow the sequence of referents during the discourse. The problem of "What to say" means selecting appropriate referents and predicates creating an interesting text and this is notoriously difficult.

It is clear that a text such as a newspaper story relating to an event must not only state the facts about the positions and movements of the objects. The text must also take a more abstract approach, change perspectives and generalize.

Some ways of selecting the most interesting sentences on the basis of the status of the referents and the semantic weights of the predicates are discussed.

BIBLIOGRAPHY

Badler, N.I. "Temporal scene analysis: conceptual descriptions of object movements." Technical Report No 80. University of Toronto, 1975.

Davey, A. *Discourse production: A computer model of some aspects of a speaker.* Edinburgh University Press, 1978.

Fornell, J. and B. Sigurd, "Commentator - ett mikrodatorbaserat forskningsredskap foer lingvister." Praktisk Lingvistik 8. Dept of Linguistics Lund. 1983.

Gawronska-Werngren, B. "Tracking discourse referents for machine translation from Russian." Paper presented at Nordiske Datalingvistikdage 1989, Reykjavik.

Gazdar, G., Klein, E., Pullum, G. and Sag, I. *Generalized Phrase Structure Grammar.* Oxford (1985: Basil Blackwell).

Karttunen,L. "Discourse referents," In: *Syntax and Semantics*, vol 7. J. McCawley (ed), New York (1976: Academic Press).

Kempen, G. "Language generation systems." In: *Computational linguistics. An International handbook on computer oriented language research and applications.* Batori *et al.* (eds), Berlin/New York (1986:de Gruyter).

Kempen, G. (ed) *Natural Language Generation: New results in Artificial Intelligence, Psychology and Linguistics.* Dortdrecht (1987:Martinus Nijhoff).

Nilsson, M., J.Eriksson, J. Gustafsson and O.Joensson. "Commentator a TurboPascal implementation." (Dept of Linguistics, Lund,1988).

Okada, N. Conceptual taxonomy of Japanese verbs for understanding natural language and picture patterns. In: *Proc. of the eigth International conference on computational linguistics*, Tokyo 1980.

Sigurd, B. (1982) "COMMENTATOR: A Computer Model of Text Generation." Linguistics 20 (1982), 611-632.

Sigurd, B. (1987) "Referent Grammar (RG): A Generalized Phrase Structure Grammar with built-in referents." Studia Linguistica 41:2.

Sigurd, B. (1988a) "SWETRA - a multilingual computer translation system using referent grammar." In: *Proc. of the International Workshop "New Directions in Automatic Translations*, Schubert, C. (ed) Budapest 1988. (Amsterdam:Foris).

Sigurd, B. (1988b) "Using Referent Grammar (RG) in Computer Comprehension, Generation and Translation." Nordic Journal of Linguistics 11 (1988), 129-150.

Sigurd, B. and B. "Gawronska-Werngren, The Potential of Swetra - A Multi-language MT-system." Computers and Translation 3 (1989), 237-250.

Webber, B. So what can we talk about now? In: *Computational models of discoursenew* . Brady, M. and C. Berwick (eds), Cambridge:Mass (1983 MIT Press).

FIG FROM SCENES AND FACTS TO STORY AND HEADLINE

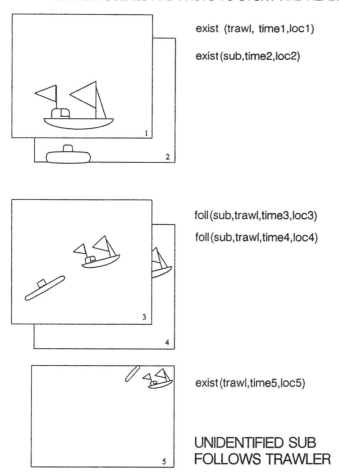

exist (trawl, time1,loc1)

exist(sub,time2,loc2)

foll(sub,trawl,time3,loc3)

foll(sub,trawl,time4,loc4)

exist(trawl,time5,loc5)

UNIDENTIFIED SUB
FOLLOWS TRAWLER

STORY: AN UNIDENTIFIED SUBMARINE FOLLOWED A
TRAWLER OUTSIDE KARLSKRONA TODAY. THE HUNT
WENT ON FOR AN HOUR WHILE THE TRAWLER HEADED
FOR KARLSFRONA. THE SUBMARINE DISAPPEARED
NEAR KARLSKRONA. THIS IS THE THIRD
INCIDENT DURING THIS MONTH.

Figure 12.1: 'Unidentified sub follows trawler'

Chapter 13

Segment Grammar: a Formalism for Incremental Sentence Generation

Koenraad De Smedt
and Gerard Kempen

Abstract: Incremental sentence generation imposes special constraints on the representation of the grammar and the design of the formulator (the module which is responsible for constructing the syntactic and morphological structure). In the model of natural speech production presented here, a formalism called Segment Grammar is used for the representation of linguistic knowledge. We give a definition of this formalism and present a formulator design which relies on it. Next, we present an object- oriented implementation of Segment Grammar. Finally, we compare Segment Grammar with other formalisms.

13.1   INTRODUCTION

Natural speech is often produced in a piecemeal fashion: speakers start to articulate a sentence before the syntactic structure, or even the meaning content of that sentence has been fully determined. Under the assumption that the human language processing apparatus is capable of carrying out different tasks in parallel, the speaker may already utter the first fragments of a sentence while simultaneously processing more content to be incorporated in the sentence. This mode of generation, which we call *incremental* generation, seems to serve a system whose major purpose is to articulate speech without long pauses, even if it is imperfect or incomplete.

Once a speaker has started to utter a sentence, the *formulator* (i.e. the module which is responsible for the syntactic and morphological structure) will try to complete the sentence in a maximally grammatical way and will try to avoid making revisions. However, a speaker who starts a sentence without knowing the entire content in detail forces the formulator to operate with incomplete knowledge. In an incremental mode of production, the formulator will sometimes make a choice which turns out to be incompatible with new conceptual input at a later moment. De Smedt and Kempen (1987) discuss how various conceptual changes may affect the structure of the utterance which is under construction.

We are currently designing a computational model of a formulator which operates under the special constraints imposed by incremental generation. In this paper we discuss some aspects of that formulator and of the grammatical knowledge it uses. In particular, we argue that, regardless of their formal generative properties, not all grammar formalisms are equally suited to support incremental generation. Consider the following requirements put forward by Kempen (1987):

- Three kinds of syntactic incrementation are distinguished: *upward expansion*, *downward expansion*, and *insertion*. A grammar should allow all three varieties (although insertion could be treated as a special case of combined upward and downward expansion).

- Lexical increments can be small, even a single word. Therefore the syntactic tree should be able to grow by individual branches. This implies that all daughters of a node in the tree should not necessarily be generated at once: the formalism should be able to add sister nodes incrementally.

- There is no reason to assume that the chronological order in which branches are attached to the syntactic tree corresponds to their linear precedence in the resulting utterance. Hence the grammar should separate knowledge about immediate dominance from knowledge about linear precedence.

In order to satisfy these requirements, Kempen proposes *Incremental Grammar (IG)*, a new formalism for the representation of grammatical knowledge. It is especially suited to – but not restricted to – incremental generation. In order to clearly distinguish between the grammar formalism and the processing model, we will rename the grammar formalism *Segment Grammar (SG)* and we will refer to the processing model as the *incremental formulator*. After a definition of SG, we discuss how SG representations are used in our incremental formulator. Then we will present an implementation of SG using object-oriented programming techniques, compare it with other formalisms, and point out its main advantages.

13.2   SEGMENT GRAMMAR

Somewhat like a lexical-functional grammar (LFG; Kaplan and Bresnan, 1982), an SG assigns two distinct descriptions to every sentence of the language which it generates. The constituent structure (or *c-structure*) of a sentence is a conventional phrase structure (PS), which is an ordered tree-shaped graph. It indicates the 'surface' grouping and ordering of words and phrases in a sentence. The functional structure (or *f-structure*) provides a more detailed representation of 'functional' relationships between words and phrases, as traditionally expressed by notions like subject, direct object, etc. The representation in f- structures also accounts for phenomena like agreement, and it does so by using features like number, gender, etc. Since SG is used for incremental processing, it assigns representations to partial sentences as well as to full ones.

When an SG is used for generation, semantic and discourse information is mapped into f-structures, which in turn are mapped into c-structures. C-structures are then subjected to morpho-phonological processing, producing phonetic strings which are eventually uttered as speech sounds. This overall process is depicted in Figure 13.1. We will now be concerned with the elements which constitute the grammar.

13.2.1   Formal Definition Of Segment Grammar

A Segment Grammar   G   for a language L_G is a septuple G=(N,T,S,P,F,W,O)   with N a set of non-terminal symbols, T a set of terminal symbols, S a set of segments, P a set of phonetic symbols, F a set of feature symbols, W a set of feature value symbols, and O a set of grammatical function symbols.[1]

For a segment grammar G, f-structures are connected directed acyclic graphs defined by the quintuple (V, E, F_W, F_L, F_O) where V is a set of nodes, E a

---

[1] It is questionable whether grammatical functions are strictly necessary in SG. This will be discussed later.

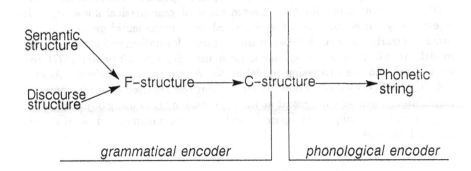

Figure 13.1: Subsequent linguistic descriptions during generation

set of arcs: $E \subseteq V \times V$, F_W a partial function: $F \times V \rightarrow \wp\, W$, F_L a labelling function: $V \rightarrow N \cup T$, and F_O a labelling function $E \rightarrow O^2$.[2] The set of f-structures in G is defined as $\Im_G = S \cup \{ y \mid \exists\, y', y'' \in \Im_G : y \in U(y',y'') \}$ where U is the universal unification function: $\Im_G \times \Im_G \rightarrow \wp\, (\Im_G)$. The unification function is essentially the same as that proposed by Kay (1979).

Each segment $s \in S$ is an f-structure with $V = \{ r,f \}$ and $E = \{ (r,f) \}$ where r is called the root node and f the foot node. The subset of segments $\{ s \in S \mid F_L(f) \in T \}$ is called the set of *lexical segments*.

For a segment grammar G, c-structures (PS trees) consist of a quadruple $(V, F_M, <, F_L)$ where V is a set of nodes, F_M a mother function: $V \rightarrow V \cup \{ \perp \}$, $<$ a well-ordered partial precedence relation: $< \subset V \times V$, and F_L a labelling function: $V \rightarrow N \cup T$. In contrast with LFG and other formalisms where c-structures are derived only by means of a context-free grammar, the c-structures in G are derived from the f-structures in G by means of the destination and linearization processes which are described later.

For a segment grammar G, phonetic strings are structures that are elements of the set P. The phonetic strings in L_G are the sequences of terminal nodes of all possible c-structures in G.

13.2.2   Informal Synopsis of Segment Grammar

Segments are the elementary building blocks of the grammar. They are graphs with two nodes: a root node and a foot node. Isolated segments are conventionally represented in vertical orientation with the root node, labeled with its

---

[2] $\wp$ denotes the powerset.

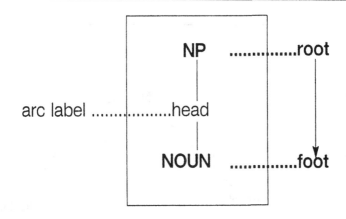

Figure 13.2: A syntactic segment

category, at the top, the foot node, labeled with its category, at the bottom, and an arc, represented as a vertically directed edge labeled with a grammatical function, between the nodes. An example is shown in Figure 13.2. In running text, segments are also written left-to-right (root-to-foot), e.g., S-SUBJECT-NP or NP-HEAD-NOUN.

Syntactic segments are the smallest possible f-structures and may therefore be considered as atomic units. Just like atoms in chemistry combine to form molecules, segments combine to form larger f- structures. These structures are unordered (they are sometimes called mobiles), since word order is assigned at a later stage. F-structures are graphs consisting of nodes labeled with syntactic categories (or with lexical items). C-structures are ordered graphs derived from f-structures by a process described later, and phonetic strings are the sequences of terminal nodes in c-structures.

One basic operation, *unification*, governs the composition of smaller f-structures into larger ones. By unifying two nodes belonging to different f-structures, the nodes may merge into one; thus a graph of interconnected segments is formed. The two basic variants of unification are *concatenation* (vertical composition by unifying a root and a foot) and *furcation* (horizontal composition by unifying two roots). E.g., two segments which are instances of S-SUBJECT-NP and of NP-HEAD-NOUN can be concatenated by unifying their NP nodes; two segments which are instances of NP-DETERMINER-ARTICLE and NP-HEAD-NOUN can be furcated, also by unification of their NP nodes. This is schematically represented in Figure 13.3.

To each node, a set of *features* may be attributed. For example, S nodes have a feature FINITE with '+' or '−' as possible values. If no values are explic-

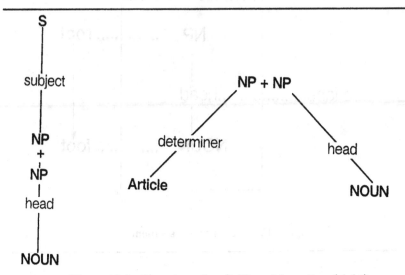

Figure 13.3: Concatenation (left) and furcation (right)

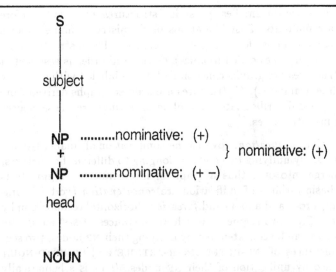

Figure 13.4: Feature unification

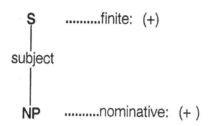

Figure 13.5: Co-occurrence of features in a segment

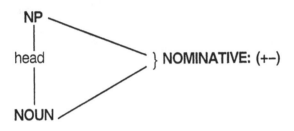

Figure 13.6: Feature sharing

itly specified, then the feature has all possible values by default, in this case the set $(+ -)$.[3] When two nodes are unified (in either concatenation or furcation), their features are also unified. This process, illustrated in Figure 13.4, is essentially the same as feature unification in other unification-based formalisms (Karttunen, 1984). It consists of computing the union of all features in both nodes, and for each feature the intersection of the values in both nodes.

The co-occurrence of feature restrictions on the root of a segment with feature restrictions on the foot may be used to model syntactic constraints. E.g., the constraint that "if the subject of a finite sentence is an NP, it must be nominative" is modeled by specifying a feature FINITE with value '+' on the root of a S-SUBJECT-NP segment, and a feature NOMINATIVE with value '+' on the foot, as depicted in Figure 13.5. In addition, the root and the foot of a segment may *share* certain features. For example, NOMINATIVE is shared in the NP-HEAD-NOUN segment as depicted in Figure 13.6.

The combination of feature sharing and unification amounts to 'feature transport'. By virtue of the sharing relationship in NP-HEAD-NOUN, the con-

---

[3]Sets are represented here in list notation.

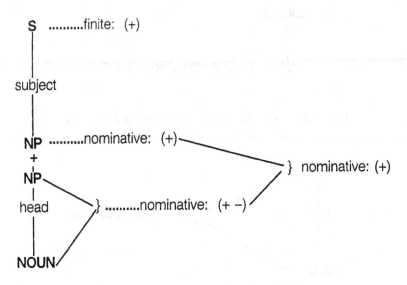

Figure 13.7: Unification of a shared feature

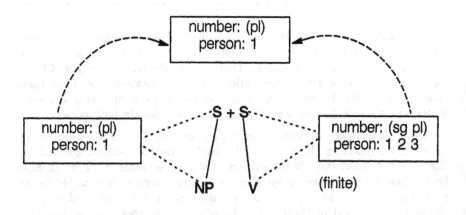

Figure 13.8: Agreement by means of feature sharing

catenation depicted in Figure 13.7 results in a feature change to the foot of the lower segment as well as to its root. Features are in fact not transported, but they are unified. Agreement can easily be modeled by feature sharing in concatenated and furcated segments. For example, the features NUMBER and PERSON are shared in S-SUBJECT-NP as well as in S-HEAD-FINITE-VERB. If such segments are furcated by unifying their S nodes, the shared features in both segments are unified, as depicted in Figure 13.8.

The combination of root and foot in a segment is a declarative representation of a single immediate dominance (ID) relationship. Restrictions on sisterhood are encoded in a procedural way. The addition of function words, e.g., determiners and auxiliaries, is governed by a *functorization* process during formulation, which attaches grammatical combinations of function words to a phrase in a procedure-based way. The addition of non-function-words, i.e., constituents which are in a case relation to the phrase, is driven by the conceptual module and is restricted by valency information in lexical segments. E.g., the possible addition of a direct object in a clause is specified in lexical segments of the type S-HEAD-V.

It is unclear whether there is a need for an explicit specification of additional, more global restrictions on sisterhood, e.g., the restriction that only one direct object may occur in a clause. We assume that conceptual input to the formulator cannot normally give rise to such circumstances, because there will be no contradictory information in case relationships. Hence, these restrictions are seen as emerging properties of the formulation process rather than defining properties of the grammar. If there is evidence that this kind of restrictions must be explicitly defined in the grammar, then it remains possible to specify ad- hoc restrictions on unification based on the grammatical function labels in segments. If not, then the notion of grammatical function is disposable in SG.

Linear precedence (LP) is encoded by assigning to each foot node a POSITIONS feature which contains a list of possible positions that the node may occupy in its destination, i.e., (by default) its mother node in the c-structure. The assignment of left-to-right order in c-structures will be further explained in the next section.

13.3 A LEXICALLY DRIVEN FORMULATOR DESIGN

We now turn to the question of how SG is used in an incremental formulator. The lexical origin of syntactic configurations is present in some form or other in many modern grammar theories. In Government-Binding (GB) theory, for example, the *Projection Principle* states that

> Representations at each syntactic level are projected from the lexicon, in that they observe the subcategorization properties of lexical

items. (Chomsky, 1981)

Conceptual and lexical guidance is also argued for by Kempen and Hoenkamp (1987). Approaches which differ from this principle in that they assume the insertion of lexical material (i.e., content words) into a previously made syntactic structure, as done in early transformational grammar (Chomsky, 1965) but also in some recent psycholinguistic models (e.g., Dell, 1986) are in our opinion unrealistic for purposes of natural language generation.

On the one hand, syntactic tree formation is lexically guided in our theory, because the choice of lexical material clearly puts constraints on syntactic choices. For example, *to see* can take an infinitival object clause whereas *to know* cannot. It follows in our theory that the lexicon is responsible for the choice of any segments to be incorporated into the tree, e.g., the choice between S-OBJECT-INFINITIVAL-S and S-OBJECT-FINITE-S.

On the other hand, the opposite guidance also holds, especially in incremental sentence generation: the choice of lexical material is subject to categorial restrictions imposed by the partial tree which has been constructed so far. For example, *to dedicate* may take a NP as a direct object, but not a S. This categorial restriction will cause a nominal lexical entry to be preferred to a verbal one when the direct object is to be lexicalized.

It will not be surprising that the basic lexico-syntactic building block is modeled as a segment. A *lexical segment* is a segment where the foot is a word. Examples are NP-HEAD-CAKE (a nominal lemma) and S-HEAD-EAT (a verbal lemma). Because these segments always link a word to a phrase, the lexicon is essentially a *phrasal* lexicon. Information which is traditionally assigned to words, such as features and valency, is in our approach assigned to the roots of the lemma segments (the phrases) rather than their feet (the words), as schematically represented in Figure 13.9. Multi-word phrases are part of the lexicon in the form of ready-made furcations of segments, e.g., for *kick the bucket* in Figure 13.10. The lexicon is a set of *lemmas*, which are lexical entries consisting of one or more segments.

The lexical (pre-syntactic) stage in the formulator activates one or more lemmas on the basis of a conceptual fragment. It also assigns features with a non-lexical origin, such as PLURAL or DEFINITENESS, to those lemmas. A case relation gives rise to one or more non-lexical segments, such as S-DIRECT-OBJECT-NP.

The syntactic stage of the formulator tries to attach the lemmas and non-lexical segments to the tree by means of unification, which enforces the categorial and feature restrictions in the existing (partial) tree. F-structures are complete when the head and other obligatory segments (according to the valency information in the phrasal nodes) have been incorporated and when the *functorization* process, which causes the addition of function words such as determiners and auxiliaries, has taken place.

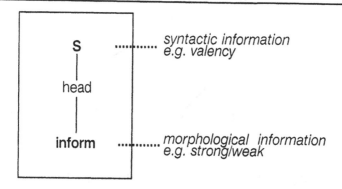

Figure 13.9: Distribution of information in lexical segments

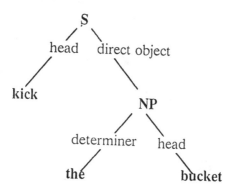

Figure 13.10: A multi-segment lemma

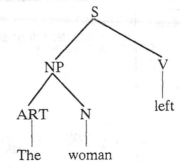

Figure 13.11: C-structure for "The woman left."

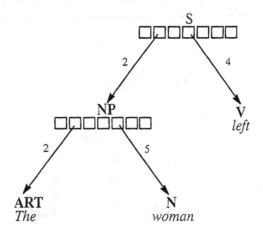

Figure 13.12: Diagram showing the holders for "The woman left."

F-structures, as constructed in this fashion, are unordered. The assignment of left-to-right positions to constituents is not simply an ordering imposed on the existing arcs of an f-structure, because dominance relations in the *c-structure* are not necessarily identical to those in the f-structure (e.g., in the case of discontinuous constituents). Therefore, a completely new, ordered structure – the c-structure, or surface tree – is constructed. The procedure which assigns left-to-right positions is incremental and works in a bottom-up fashion: the foot node of a segment is attached directly under its *destination*, which is normally the root of the segment. However, nodes may go to higher level destinations in situations like *clause union* and *WH-fronting*, which give rise to c-structures which are non-isomorphic to the corresponding f-structures (in particular, they may be flattened). We refer to Kempen and Hoenkamp (1987) for details. Figure 13.11 is an example of a c-structure.

Since f-structures as well as c-structures are constructed in a piecemeal fashion, it is natural to assign word order on a first-come, first-serve basis. For this scheme we use absolute rather than relative positions. With each phrase, a *holder* is associated, which is a vector of slots that can be filled by its constituents. Figure 13.12 shows an example of a constellation of holders and constituents for the c-structure in Figure 13.11.

The foot node of each segment in the grammar has a feature POSITIONS which lists all possible positions that the node can occupy in its destination. E.g., in the grammar for Dutch it is specified that the foot of the S-SUBJECT-NP segment may go to absolute positions 1 or 3. When the foot of such a segment is to be assigned a position in the holder of its destination, it will first attempt to occupy position 1. If position 1 has already been occupied, it will attempt to go to position 3. A schematic overview of such a situation is given in Figure 13.13. If the utterance has proceeded beyond the point where a constituent can be added, a syntactic dead end occurs and a self-correction or restart will be necessary.

13.4   AN OBJECT-ORIENTED IMPLEMENTATION OF SEGMENT GRAMMAR

An object-oriented version of SG has been implemented in CommonORBIT (De Smedt, 1987, 1989). This language (based on Common LISP) stems from the object-oriented and frame-based paradigms. *Objects* are basic computational units which represent physical or abstract entities in the problem domain. The properties of an object as well as the actions it may perform are defined in *aspects (slots)* associated with the object.

SG is implemented by uniformly representing all grammar concepts, such as nodes (phrases, words), features and syntactic segments as *objects*. Segments

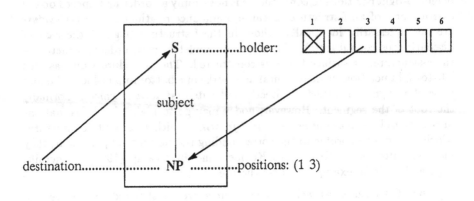

Figure 13.13: Destination and linearization processes: assign NP to the third slot in the holder of its destination

have aspects for the root, foot, arc label, and features which are shared between root and foot. The Commonsc orbit definition of some segments, including a lexical segment, is given below. Also given is a representation of the Dutch word *watermeloen* (watermelon).

```
(defobject np-head-noun
     syntactic-segment              ; delegate to prototypical segment
     (root (a np))
     (arc 'head)
     (foot (a noun))
     (agreement-features '(person plural gender nominative))
     ((foot positions) '(6))         ; word order possibilities
     )

(defobject watermeloen-segment ; a lexical segment
     np-head-noun
     (foot (a watermeloen-noun)))

(defobject watermeloen-noun      ; a word
     compound-noun
     (component-s (list (a water-noun)
                        (a meloen-noun))))
```

Object-oriented and frame-based formalisms typically allow the use of a specialization hierarchy in which specific objects (*clients*) may *delegate* requests for information to other, more general, objects (*proxies*) in order to avoid redundancy. The use of such a hierarchy for linguistic concepts in the grammar as well as the lexicon has been advocated by De Smedt (1984). The prototypical object SYNTACTIC-SEGMENT, which acts as a proxy for specific segments such as NP-HEAD-NOUN, contains general knowledge about segments:

```
(defobject syntactic-segment
    feature-object              ; an object with features
    (root (a syntactic-category))
    (arc)
    (foot (a syntactic-category))
    (agreement-features nil)    ; default = no sharing
    (agree
      :function (self)
      (share-features (root self) (foot self)
                  :features (agreement-features self)))
    (initialize :if-needed #'agree)
    (concatenate-segments
      :function (high low)
      ;; merge the root of. the low one with the foot of
      ;; the high one
      (unify (foot (initialize high)) (root (initialize low))))
    (furcate-segments
      :function (left right)
      ;; merge the roots of both segments
      (unify (root (initialize left)) (root (initialize right))))
))
```

More specific knowledge is distributed among the specific segments. For example, in NP-HEAD-NOUN, categories restricting the root and foot slots are given.

Syntactic categories are also defined as CommonORBIT objects. Phrasal categories, parts of speech and lexical entries are represented in the same delegation hierarchy. Consequently, the grammar and the lexicon are on a continuum: words are merely the most specific objects in the hierarchy of categories. By way of example, some delegation relations between concepts in SG are represented in Figure 13.14.

13.5   DISCUSSION AND RELATION WITH OTHER WORK

The use of segments for the expression of grammatical knowledge is advantageous in an incremental sentence formulator. We will sum up some of these advantages here and at the same time draw comparisons with other work.

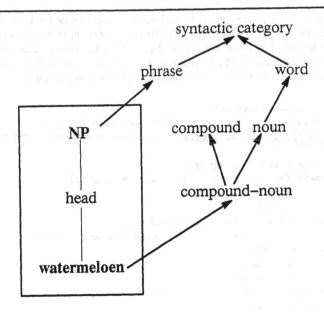

Figure 13.14: Some delegation relations from the nodes in a segment

13.5.1   Phrase Structure Rules and Categorial Grammar

Phrase Structure (PS) rules are string rewriting rules which express immediate dominance (ID, motherhood) relationships *together* with sisterhood (cooccurrence) and linear precedence (LP) relationships. Hence, it is often necessary to express the same dominance relationship more than once, namely for every possible sisterhood and linear precedence relationship. The example below is from Sells (1985).

(1)   a. VP → V NP   kiss the bride
       b. VP → V NP PP   send the message to Kim
       c. VP → V NP S'   tell the class that break is over
       d. VP → V NP VP   expect results to be forthcoming

We must observe that pure PS rules are seldom used. In Government and Binding (GB) theory, which uses PS rules mainly to specify hierarchical structure, order is fixed by other components of the grammar, such as case assignment. Generalized Phrase Structure Grammar (GPSG) (Gazdar, Klein, Pullum and Sag, 1985) uses rules in ID/LP format, where a comma in the right hand side of the rewrite rules indicates that the categories are unordered. These rules are then complemented with separate rules for precedence relations, e.g.:

(2)   a. VP → V, NP   kiss the bride
       b. VP → V, NP, PP   send the message to Kim
       c. VP → V, NP, S'   tell the class that break is over
       d. VP → V, NP, VP   expect results to be forthcoming
       e. V < NP < XP

Notice that, although the linear precedence is now encoded separately, ID relations are still expressed redundantly. SG offers a more economic way of encoding ID by specifying only one relationship between a pair of nodes at a time.

But the real problem in incremental production is that the choice between rules (2a-d) cannot be made deterministically. If daughter constituents are produced one at a time by means of a PS grammar, the system will be forced to choose between rules and backtrack when necessary. By virtue of its orientation toward the representation of separate ID relationships, SG allows the incremental addition of sister nodes and hence avoids backtracking (cf. Kempen and Hoenkamp, 1987).

This problem with PS rules could, in theory, be obviated by redefining the grammar as in (3). But then the PS structures generated by the grammar would not be isomorphic to those generated by grammar (2): the grammars are only weakly equivalent.

(3)   a. VP → V, NP, VPrest

       b. VPrest → Ø

       c. VPrest → PP

       d. VPrest → S'

       e. VPrest → VP

Although classical *categorial grammar* (CG), unlike PS rules, is lexically guided and therefore suited for generation, a similar objection could be raised against it. In classical CG, word order and co-occurrence constraints are encoded as syntactic types on lexical items. Whatever choices there are with respect to either LP or sisterhood will result in alternative syntactic types for the same word. For languages with relatively free word order or many sisterhood alternatives, this may result in a drastic increase of possibilities encoded in the lexicon. By comparison, the opposite is true for SG, which encodes restrictions on sisterhood rather than alternative possibilities. In SG, a relatively word order free language will therefore have a relatively small grammar and lexicon.

13.5.2   Unification

Unification as a general mechanism in language generation as well as in parsing
has been proposed by Kay (1979). In Functional Unification Grammar (FUG),
language processing is seen as the unification of an initial functional description with a grammar which is a very large functional description containing
many alternatives. As shown by Appelt (1985), it is possible to use FUG in
incremental production by letting an initial functional description unify with
the grammar, then unify the result with more input in the form of another
functional description, etc., until a sentence is completed.

However, a drawback of FUG is that the grammar is a complicated, mono-
lithic structure. Our approach is different by virtue of the fact that unification
is a local operation on two nodes. Consequently, the grammar can be represented as a set of segments, which express information at a local level, i.e.
encapsulated in many separate objects rather than in one large structure or
rule base.

The role of features in unification-based grammars (FUG, LFG, PATR-II
and GPSG) is described by Karttunen (1984). Features are often treated as
attribute-value pairs which are grouped in a feature *matrix* which then functions
as the *agreement* of one or more nodes. Our approach is similar but we treat
features as first-class objects in the sense that they may themselves be unified.
This makes unification an even more universal mechanism and obviates the
need for coreference to features by means of variables in the grammar.

13.5.3   TAG

Tree Adjoining Grammar (TAG; Joshi, 1987) is a tree generating system consisting of a finite set of elementary trees and a composition operation (*adjoining*)
which builds derived trees out of elementary trees. Like SG, and opposed to
PS-rules, TAG is tree-based rather than string-based. FTAG, the recent "feature structures based" extension of TAG (Vijay-Shanker and Joshi, 1988) uses
unification of features as a clearer way of specifying restrictions on tree adjoining, and is therefore even more similar to SG. The role of some elementary trees
in TAG is comparable to that of SG segments, while adjoining takes the role
of unification. For example, the auxiliary tree for an adjective (Figure 13.15
(a)) can be said to correspond to the NP-modifier-AP segment (Figure 13.15
(b)), although it must be noted that SG always creates an adjectival phrase
rather than just an adjective. The adjoining operation of the auxiliary tree for
an adjective yields two NP nodes in the resulting structure (Figure 13.16 (a)),
which is redundant, whereas the corresponding composition of SG segments will
result in only one NP node (Figure 13.16 (b)).

Word order and immediate dominance are factored in the TAG formalism,
which provides considerable flexibility in the generation process of a sentence.

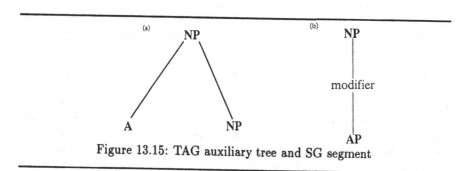

Figure 13.15: TAG auxiliary tree and SG segment

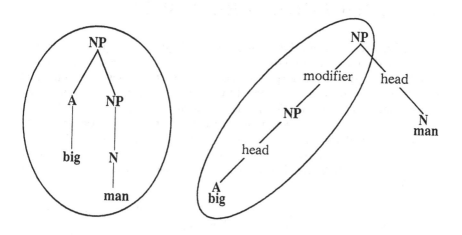

Figure 13.16: Results of TAG adjoining and SG unification

TAG allows incremental generation, but only as defined by the adjoining operation, which means that it does not allow the addition of sister nodes without structural growth in vertical direction. Unlike SG structures, TAG trees always contain all sisters. E.g., there are completely different elementary trees for transitive and intransitive verbs. It does not seem possible to build a transitive tree incrementally by starting with the intransitive tree and expanding it into a transitive one by furcating with a sister node, as SG might allow (if valency permits it).

Also, TAG seems to require, for many lexical items, a number of variants of elementary trees. For example, the transitive verb eat requires separate elementary trees for the constructions *Subj-V-Obj, WH(Obj)-Subj-V, to-V(infinitive)-Obj*, etc. Since, presumably, the speaker has to make a choice between such alternatives at an early stage, this imposes restrictions upon incremental production which are avoided by SG. There, the choice between such constructions can be postponed to a later stage, so that minimal commitments with respect to further incrementation are imposed.

13.6   CONCLUDING REMARKS

SG describes sentences of a language in terms of syntactic segments – atomic units larger than syntactic nodes – and their possible combinations, governed by unification. Because SG specifies ID relations at the level of individual segments, f-structures can be generated by adding daughter, mother, *and* sister nodes incrementally. Because SG specifies LP relations at the level of individual segments, word order can be determined for partial sentences. These properties make SG a particularly flexible formalism for incremental generation. Although other formalisms can in principle be adapted for incremental generation, a lot of bookkeeping would be required to achieve the same effect (e.g., backtracking in PS grammars).

It seems that syntactic segments, as they are proposed here, are elementary structures which are small enough to allow any kind of incrementation, yet large enough to hold information (e.g., features for agreement, valency, LP rules) without having to resort to any additional global knowledge outside the segment definitions. We believe that this approach gives the grammar more modularity because the set of segments for a language is easily extendable and modifiable.

BIBLIOGRAPHY

Appelt, D. 1985. *Planning English Sentences*. Cambridge: Cambridge U.P.

Chomsky, N. 1981. *Lectures on Government and Binding*. Dordrecht: Foris.

Chomsky, N. 1965. *Aspects of the theory of syntax.* Cambridge, MA: MIT Press.

Dell, G.S. 1986. A Spreading-Activation Theory of Retrieval in Sentence Production. *Psychological Review,* 93, 238-321.

De Smedt, K. 1984. Using object-oriented knowledge-representation techniques in morphology and syntax programming. In: O'Shea, T. (ed.) *ECAI-84. Proceedings of the Sixth European Conference on Artificial Intelligence* (pp. 181-184). Amsterdam: Elsevier.

De Smedt, K. and Kempen, G. 1987. Incremental sentence production, self-correction and coordination. In: Kempen, G. (ed.) *Natural language generation: New results in Artificial Intelligence, psychology and linguistics* (pp. 365-376). Dordrecht/Boston: Martinus Nijhoff Publishers (Kluwer Academic Publishers).

De Smedt, K. 1987. Object-oriented programming in Flavors and CommonOR-BIT. In: Hawley, R. (ed.) *Artificial Intelligence Programming Environments* (pp. 157-176). Chichester: Ellis Horwood.

De Smedt, K. 1989. *Object-oriented knowledge representation in CommonOR-BIT.* Internal report 89-NICI-01, Nijmegen Institute for Cognition research and Information Technology, University of Nijmegen.

Gazdar, G., Klein, E., Pullum, G. and Sag, I. 1985. *Generalized Phrase Structure Grammar.* Oxford: Basil Blackwell.

Joshi, A. 1987. The relevance of tree adjoining grammar to generation. In: Kempen, G. (ed.) *Natural language generation: New results in Artificial Intelligence, psychology and linguistics* (pp. 233-252). Dordrecht/Boston: Martinus Nijhoff Publishers (Kluwer Academic Publishers).

Karttunen, L. 1984. Features and values. In: *Proceedings of Coling- 84* (pp. 28-33). Association for Computational Linguistics.

Kay, M. 1979. Functional Grammar. In: *Proceedings of the Fifth Annual Meeting of the Berkeley Linguistic Society* (pp. 142- 158). Berkeley, CA: Berkeley Linguistic Society.

Kempen, G. 1987. A framework for incremental syntactic tree formation. *Proceedings of the tenth IJCAI* (pp. 655-660). Los Altos: Morgan Kaufmann.

Kempen, G. and Hoenkamp, E. 1987. An incremental procedural grammar for sentence formulation. *Cognitive Science,* 11, 201- 258.

Sells, P. 1985. *Lectures on contemporary syntactic theories.* CSLI Lecture notes Nr. 3. Stanford: CSLI.

Vijay-Shanker, K. and Joshi, A. 1988. Feature Structures Based Tree Adjoining Grammars. In: *Coling '88: Proceedings of the 12th International Conference on Computational Linguistics, 22-27 August 1988.* Association for Computational Linguistics.

Chapter 14

A Contrastive Evaluation of Functional Unification Grammar for Surface Language Generation: A Case Study in Choice of Connectives

Kathleen R. McKeown and Michael Elhadad

Abstract: Language generation systems have used a variety of grammatical formalisms for producing syntactic structure and yet, there has been little research evaluating the formalisms for the specifics of the generation task. In our work at Columbia we have primarily used a unification based formalism, a functional Unification Grammar (FUG) and have found it well suited for many of the generation tasks we have addressed. FUG turned out to be better suited for generation than various off-the-shelf parsing formalisms (including an Augmented Transition Network, a Bottom-Up Chart Parser, and a declarative Clause Grammar) that we have also used over the past 5 years. In this paper, we identify the characteristics of FUG that we find useful for generation and focus on *order of decision making* and its impact on *expressions of constraints*. Our claim is that order of decision making in FUG through unification allows for flexible interaction between constraints, which, in turn, allows for a more concise representation of constraints. To illustrate these properties of FUG, we use a subtask of the lexical choice problem, namely the task of selecting a connective (e.g., but, however, nonetheless, since, because, etc.) to conjoin two input propositions.

14.1 INTRODUCTION

Language generation systems have used a variety of grammatical formalisms for
producing syntactic structure and yet, there has been little research evaluating
the formalisms for the specifics of the generation task. In our work at Columbia
we have primarily used a unification based formalism, a Functional Unification
Grammar (FUG) (Kay, 1979) and have found it well suited for many of the
generation tasks we have addressed. Over the course of the past 5 years we
have also explored the use of various off-the-shelf parsing formalisms, including
an Augmented Transition Network (ATN) (Woods, 1970), a Bottom-Up Chart
Parser (BUP) (Finin, 1984), and a Declarative Clause Grammar (DCG) (Pereira
and Warren., 1980). In contrast, we have found that parsing formalisms do not
have the same benefits for the generation task.

In this paper, we identify the characteristics of FUG that we find useful
for generation. Of the following general criteria we have used in evaluating
language generation systems, we focus on *order of decision making* and its
impact on *expression of constraints*:

1. *Input Specification*: Input to a surface language generator should be semantic, or pragmatic, in nature. Ideally, few syntactic details should be
   specified as these should be filled in by the surface generator, which contains the syntactic knowledge for the system. Furthermore, some flexibility should be allowed in what must be provided as input; not all pragmatic
   or semantic features may always be available for each input concept and
   the surface generator should be able to function in their absence. Finally,
   input should be kept simple.

2. *Expression of constraints on decision making:* One main task of a language generator is to make decisions about the syntactic structure and
   vocabulary to use. Such decision making is done under constraints and the
   ability to clearly and concisely represent constraints is important (McK-
   eown and Paris, 1987). If these constraints can be represented declaratively, without duplication, clarity of the system is improved.

3. *Order of decision making*: The order in which decisions must be made
   and the interactions between them has an impact on representation of
   constraints. If decisions must be made in a fixed order, representation
   of constraints on those decisions may become more complex. The order
   of processing, bottom-up, top-down, left to right, or any other variation,
   can significantly influence how constraints interact.

4. *Efficiency*: As in any interactive system, an efficient, speedy response is
   desirable. At this point in time, most grammatical systems can provide a
   response in reasonable real time. In fact, in practice there doesn't appear
   to be significant differences in run time between a deterministic surface

generator such as MUMBLE (McDonald and Pustejovsky, 1985) and unification based processors such as FUG (McKeown and Paris, 1987).

5. *Reversability:* Ultimately, a natural language system that uses only one grammar both for parsing and generation is desirable. Using a reversible grammar means that syntactic knowledge need not be duplicated for the two tasks. In reality, however, a grammatical formalism has usually been developed with one task or the other in mind. Due to the differences in focus between the two tasks, when a formalism is adopted for the other task, the match is often not ideal. For example, when FUG is used for interpretation, an additional, rather complex chart must be supplied (Kay, 1979). On the other hand, when grammars originally developed for interpretation are used for generation, points 1-3 often can not be achieved easily, as we shall attempt to show.

Our claim is that order of decision making in FUG through unification allows for flexibility in interaction between constraints. This, in turn, allows for a more concise representation of constraints. To illustrate these properties of FUG, we use the task of selecting a connective (e.g., but, however, nonetheless, since, because, etc.) to conjoin two input propositions. Connective selection is a subset of the lexical choice problem. Lexical choice has been shown to require complex interaction between constraints (Danlos, 1987; Danlos, 1988), and connective selection in particular contains a number of challenges particular to generation.

Our goal in this paper will be to show the advantages of the following main features of order of decision making in FUG:

- *Not strictly left-to-right:* In FUG, all decisions that can be made at the top-level are made before producing constituents. These decisions can send constraints down to lower levels if necessary. Thus some decisions about later sentence constituents can be made before decisions about prior constituents in the sentence. This is important when a decision made early on in the sentence depends on a decision made later.

- *Bidirectional:* Specifying dependence of a decision on a constraint automatically specifies the inverse because of the use of unification: if the constraint is unspecified on input it will get filled in when the otherwise dependent decision is made.

- *Interaction between different types of constraints is determined dynamically:* How different constraints interact can be determined at run-time depending on the current context of generation. This means the grammar can be modularized by constraints with specific interaction left unspecified. In contrast, the parsing formalisms synchronize in lock-step the influence of different constraints as they proceed through the construction of syntactic structure making their representation difficult.

In the following sections we first give an overview of FUG, showing how decision making is carried out for a simple grammar. We then introduce the problem of connective choice, describing the constraints on choice and the type of decision making required. We show how the basic characteristics of FUG lend themselves to the implementation of connective choice.

Finally, we make comparisons with other formalisms. In particular, we note that control strategies developed for parsing formalisms lack the flexibility FUG provides. Our more general position is that, while reversability of grammatical processors is definitely a worthwhile aim, a syntactic processor that was originally developed for parsing may not be ideal for generation. This results partially from the fact that control of processing is driven in part by the input sentence, or word order, in interpreting language. Emphasis is on using the input to determine which grammatical rules to apply next. In contrast, in generation, there is no need to select words as they appear in a sentence. In fact, many systems determine the verb of the sentence first as this can control the assignment and syntactic structure of the subject and object (e.g., MUMBLE (McDonald and Pustejovsky, 1985)). Part of our goal in identifying the problems in using a parser for generation is to point out some of the characteristics that are useful for generation so that they can be taken into account when future reversible syntactic processors are designed.

Despite our overall preference for FUG, there are certain tasks in selecting connectives that are difficult to represent in FUG, but which can be easily accommodated in other formalisms and we note these in our conclusion.

14.2   OVERVIEW OF FUG

The main characteristic of FUGs (Kay, 1979; Shieber, 1986) is that all information is uniformly described in the same type of structure - the functional description (FD). An FD is a matrix of attribute-value pairs (called features). Both the input and the grammar are represented as FDs. The only mechanism allowed when dealing with FDs is unification. Intuitively, the unification of two FDs consists of building a larger FD that comprises both input FDs and is compatible with both. Crucial features of the process are that it is (1) independent of the order of features in the input FDs, (2) bidirectional, (3) monotonic and (4) completely declarative - a grammar being best viewed as a set of constraints to be added to or checked against an input.

The unification algorithm begins by selecting the syntactic category from the input and unifying the grammar for that category with the input. Unification is controlled by the grammar and basically consists of checking grammar attribute value pairs of this category against the input. If a grammar attribute does not exist in the input, the grammar attribute value pair is added to the input. If the attribute does exist, the grammar and input values for this attribute are unified, and the results added to the input. This stage of unification can be characterized as a breadth first sweep through the top level category adding restrictions governed by this category. Following this stage, each constituent of the resulting FD is in turn unified with the grammar in the same way. Thus at this next stage, unification results in successive refinement of embedded constituents. The constituents that are to be unified are specified by the special attribute CSET (for Constituent Set) and the order in which they occur need not necessarily be the order in which they will occur in the resulting sentence. Again, this means that decision making is top-down but not necessarily left-to-right. A further distinction is that all decisions get made at the top level before moving to embedded constituents.

To see how order of decision making occurs in FUG, consider the unification of a sample grammar (Figures 14.1, 14.2, and 14.3) and input (Figure 14.4).[1] This grammar is a small portion of the clause category of a larger grammar we are currently using (Elhadad, 1988) and is based on the systemic grammar described by Winograd (1983). This portion will generate either action sentences (e.g., "John gives a blue book to Mary.") or attributive sentences (e.g., "This car is expensive."). Note that input to this grammar is specified semantically with the exception that the input must specify the type of phrase we are trying to generate.

The grammar for the clause category is divided into three sections. The first section (Figure 14.1) specifies how syntactic features get added to semantic roles depending on the semantic type of the clause being generated. Thus, in the sample grammar we see that the protagonist role (**prot**) of an action sentence is specified as an np, while the attribute role of an attributive sentence is specified as either adjective or np. The second section (Figure 14.2) identifies the voice-class of the verb and, according to the chosen voice, the grammar determines how the semantic cases are mapped into the syntactic roles, subject, object, and indirect object. Finally, in the third section (Figure 14.3), the syntactic roles are arranged linearly through the use of patterns.

These sections are represented by three large alternatives (**alt**) in the grammar.[2] Output is produced by successively unifying each of these alternatives with the input, thus adding the constraints from each section. This grammar thus implements Kay's (1979) suggestion that the semantic and syntactic grammar be represented separately and unified to produce output.

In unifying input T2, Figure 14.4, with the clause grammar, section 1 which specifies constraints associated with the clause's semantic category, is unified first. Since it consists, itself, of alternatives representing each possible semantic

---

[1] See (Kay, 1979; McKeown, 1985; Appelt, 1985) for more details on FUG.

[2] Alternatives are a special construct of FUGs. They represent a disjunction of possibilities. To unify an FD F with an alternative (**alt** (**fd1 fd2 ... fdn**)), the unifier tries to unify each of the "branches" of the alternative (i.e., the **fdi**s). The result is the disjunction of the successfully unified branches. In our implementation, only the first branch that can be unified with F is returned.

```
;;===================================================================
;; 01 CAT CLAUSE : clause ---------------------------------------
;;===================================================================
((cat clause)
 (alt
  (
   ;; Process-type: action, mental, or relation
   ;; -----------------------------------------

   ;; Process 1: Action --> actions, events, natural phenomena
   ;; inherent cases    --> prot, goal, benef.
   ;; all are optional, but at least one of goal or prot must be
   ;; present. This will be dealt with in the voice alternation.
   ((process-type actions)
    (prot ((cat np) (animate yes)))
    (goal ((cat np)))
    (benef ((cat np)))
    (verb ((process-class actions)
           (lex any))))                          ;there must be a verb given

   ;; Process 3: relation --> equative, attributive
   ;; there need not be a verb, it will be determined by the
   ;; epistemic modality features among the possible copula.
   ((process-type attributive)
    (verb ((process-class attributive)))
    ;; so far all we do if the verb is not given use "be"
    ;; later use modality...
    (opt ((verb ((lex "be")
                 (voice-class non-middle)
                 (transitive-class neutral)))))
    ;; inherent cases    --> carrier, attribute
    ;; both are required.
    (carrier ((cat np) (definite yes)))
    ; attribute can be a property or a class
    ; like in "John is a teacher" or "John is happy".
    (alt
     (((attribute ((cat adj) (lex any))))
      ((attribute ((cat np)  (definite no)))))))))))
```

Figure 14.1: Sample FUG – Section 1

```
;; Voice choice --> operative, receptive, middle.
;; Operative is roughly  active. Receptive, roughly passive.
;; Middle    = sentences with only one participant ("the sun shines")
;; Choice middle/non-middle is based on verb classification
;; Choice receptive/operative is based on focus (using pattern).
;; The voice alternation does the mapping semantic case -> syntactic roles
(alt
   (((voice operative)
     (verb ((voice-class non-middle)
            (voice active)))
     (alt
        (((process-type actions)         ;; The notation (subject (^ prot))
          (subject (^ prot))             ;; is to be read as the equation:
          (object (^ goal))              ;; the value of subject must be the
          (iobject (^ benef)))           ;; same as the value of the path
         ((process-type attributive)     ;; (^ prot).
          (subject (^ carrier))          ;; (^ prot) is a relative path, giving
          (object (^ attribute))         ;; the address of another pair starting
          (iobject none)))))            ;; at the current position. ^ means
     ((voice receptive) <...>)            ;; go up one level (to the embedding
     ((voice middle)    <...>)))          ;; pair).
```

Figure 14.2: Sample FUG – Section 2

clause type (in this grammar, either action or attributive process types), the first step is selecting one of these alternatives. Since the input includes the attribute value pair (process-type action), the first alternative matches. Unification of this alternative results in the addition of the italicized lines in the FD shown in Figure 14.5. At this point the syntactic categories of each semantic role have been determined and some further features added. The unifier now proceeds to the second section based on voice class. At this point, (voice operative) will be selected because no voice is specified in the input and there are no incompatibilities between the (voice operative) alternative and the input. Later on, this choice will be confirmed or rejected by the focus constraint. The result from this unification is the addition of the underlined lines in Figure 14.5 and the FD now contains the mapping of semantic roles to syntactic roles. Finally in unifying the third section of the clause grammar with the input, order of syntactic constituents is determined. This is done in two steps. First the constraint from focus is added (pattern ((* focus) dots)), stating that focus must occur first.[3] In the second step, syntactic constraints on order are added, namely that subject must occur first (Pattern (subject verb dots)). At this point, subject is unified with focus and if they are not the same, the unifier would retract its earlier decision of (voice operative) and select (voice receptive) instead. In this example, subject and focus both refer

---

[3] The * indicates that this element of the pattern must be unified with the element of some other pattern. This feature is not standard in Kay's formalism and was added to increase efficiency.

```
;; General things: arrange syntactic roles together
;; and do the agreements.
;; The patterns are here of course.

; Focus first (change when add modifiers)
(pattern ((* focus) dots))

; Arrange order of complements
(pattern (subject verb dots))
(alt
  ; VERB VOICE ACTIVE
  (((verb ((voice active)))
    (alt
      (((object none)
        (iobject none))
       ; John gave the book
       ((verb ((transitive-class bitransitive)))
        (iobject none)
        (pattern (dots verb object dots)))
       ; John gave Mary the book
       ((verb ((transitive-class bitransitive)
               (dative-prep none)))
        (pattern (dots verb iobject object dots)))
       ((iobject none)
        (pattern (dots verb object dots)))
       ((verb ((dative-prep any)))
        (dative ((cat pp)
                 (prep ((lex (^ ^ ^ verb dative-prep))))
                 (np (^ ^ iobject))))
        (pattern (dots verb object dative dots)))))))))
```

Figure 14.3: Sample FUG – Section 3

```
T2 =

((cat clause)
 (process-type actions)
 (prot ((lex "John")
        (np-type proper)))
 (goal ((lex "book")
        (np-type common)
        (definite no)
        (describer === "blue")))
 (benef ((lex "Mary")
         (np-type proper)))
 (verb ((process-class actions)
        (voice-class non-middle)
        (transitive-class bitransitive)
        (dative-prep "to")
        (lex "give"))))
```

Figure 14.4: Sample Input

to the protagonist and the remaining syntactic details for the active voice are filled into the grammar, specifying the order of the object and indirect object. This results in the addition of the last lines in small caps to the FD in Figure 14.5 and the FD is linearized as "John gives the blue book to Mary.", following unification of its constituents, **prot, goal**, and **benef.**[4]

14.3 CHOICE OF CONNECTIVE: AN EXAMPLE

Choosing a connective (e.g., "but," "although") is a task particular to language generation that requires flexibility in the order that decisions are made and thus, we argue FUG is well suited to represent constraints on connective choice. The need for flexibility arises because the features used to select a connective also have an influence on other aspects of generation. Therefore, there is interaction between the selection of a connective and the generation of the connected propositions. There are two types of interaction that can occur:

- *External:* mutual interaction is necessary between the deep and surface components of the generation, and the order of decision making must be left as flexible as possible between a surface generator and its environment. For example, choice of a connective can influence what can be said

---

[4]Note also that the three patterns in small caps are actually unified by a special pattern unifier to produce the single pattern: (pattern (subject verb object dative dots)) plus the following conflation constraint (focus (^ subject)) derived from the unification of the first two patterns.

T2 after unification with the grammar:

```
((cat clause)
 (process-type actions)
 (prot ((lex 'John')
        (np-type proper)
        (cat np)
        (animate yes)))
 (goal ((lex 'book')
        (np-type common)
        (definite no)
        (describer === 'blue')
        (cat np)))
 (benef ((lex 'Mary')
        (np-type proper)
        (cat np)))
 (verb ((process-class actions)
        (voice-class non-middle)
        (transitive-class bitransitive)
        (dative-prep 'to')
        (lex 'give')
        (voice active)))
 (voice operative)
 (subject (^ prot))
 (object (^ goal))
 (iobject (^ benef))
 (PATTERN ((* FOCUS) DOTS))
 (PATTERN (SUBJECT VERB DOTS))
 (DATIVE ((CAT PP)
        (PREP ((LEX (^ ^ ^ VERB DATIVE-PREP))))
        (NP (^ ^ IOBJECT))))
 (PATTERN (DOTS VERB OBJECT DATIVE DOTS)))
```

Figure 14.5: After unification of the clause level

---

next. Conversely, what must be said next can influence the choice of a connective. Similarly, (Danlos, 1988; Danlos and Namer, 1988) argues that the morphological component of a generation system may have to interact with a deeper component to decide on pronominalization. For example, in French, when deciding whether to pronominalize "Marie" in "Jean aime Marie," the fact that the pronoun "la" would be elided in "Jean l'aime" and therefore loses the distinctive marks of gender, may introduce an ambiguity in the reference. It is therefore necessary to allow the morphological component to interact with other components, dealing with semantic and rhetoric issues.

- *Internal*: there is complex interaction between surface decisions. Therefore order of decision *within* the grammar must be left as flexible as possible. For example, the choice of an adjunct can precede and influence the choice of the verb in a clause, and vice-versa.

In this section, we illustrate interaction between internal decisions of the grammar through an example of lexical choice. In this case, lexical choice in an embedded clause can influence the choice of connective and choice of connective can in turn influence lexical choice of the clause. Thus we have a propagation of constraints from connective down to the clauses it connects and as well, we have a propagation of constraints from the decision made in the clause back up to choice of connective. Constraints between the two constituents are bidirectional and decision making must not be strictly left to right. We illustrate external interaction by showing how different connectives chosen to conjoin the same two clauses allow for different follow-up sentences. To illustrate these two cases, we describe the features that play a role in connective selection, give an example of the two cases of interaction, and describe our implementation of connective selection in FUG through this example.

However, since choosing a connective to link two propositions is a subset of the problem of lexical choice, a problem in language generation that has raised questions about modularization and order of decision making in generation, we first briefly survey previous work on lexical choice.

14.3.1   Previous Work in Lexical Choice

The place of word selection within a complete generation system is a controversial topic. Several options have been put forth in recent work:

During Surface Generation: Many previous systems position the task of lexical choice as part of the component that does surface language generation. One class of such systems (McDonald and Pustejovsky, 1985; McKeown, 1985; Paris, 1987) use a dictionary based on Goldman's (1975) system. The dictionary is keyed by internal concepts for which a word or phrase must be chosen (for Goldman these were conceptual dependency primitives such as *ingest*) and each entry contains a discrimination net which makes tests on various features to determine the word or phrase to use. In MUMBLE (McDonald and Pustejovsky, 1985), the dictionary is accessed from the grammar in the process of building syntactic structure. Thus lexical choice is interleaved with syntactic choice. Since syntactic structure is built by constructing and traversing the syntactic tree in depth-first traversal, words will typically get selected in left-to-right order. There are some exceptions. For example, MUMBLE selects the verb of the sentence first. In other systems – e.g., (McKeown, 1985; Paris, 1987) – all necessary dictionary entries are accessed and lexical choices made before the grammar is invoked.

In NIGEL (Mann and Matthiessen, 1983), the lexicon is only accessed after the grammar has completed its task. Sets of semantic features are used where lexical items would occur and are sufficient for making syntactic choices. Semantic features get added as the grammar systems make choices. After all syntactic choices have been made, the lexicon is accessed to replace each set of features with a lexical item. A lexeme may be preselected (by the deep generator for example) or directly chosen by the grammar (through a `lexify` realization statement). In the latter case, it would provide constraints on other choices. Systemicists term lexical choice as "the most delicate" of decisions as it is represented at the leaves of grammatical systems.

As part of content decisions: Another class of generation systems positions the task of lexical choice as occurring somewhere during the process of deciding what to say, before the surface generator is invoked. This positioning allows lexical choice to influence content and to drive syntactic choice. Danlos (1987) chooses this ordering of decisions for her domain.[5] She makes use of a *discourse grammar* that identifies possible discourse organizations along with the lexical choices that can be used for each organization. Thus lexical choice and order of information are decided simultaneously before other decisions, such as syntactic choice, are made. Systems using phrasal lexicons – e.g., (Kukich, 1983; Jacobs, 1985) – are similar in that they select whole phrases fairly early on in the generation process and the phrases in turn control syntactic choice. In these approaches, emphasis is on idiomatic phrases whose usage is very tightly tied to content in a particular domain. For example, in the stock market domain in which Kukich works, the use of a particular phrase has a very specific meaning and thus choice of a phrase can determine the content conveyed.

Other researchers advocate folding the lexicon into the knowledge representation. In this approach, as soon as a concept is selected for the text, the lexemes associated with it in the knowledge base would automatically be selected as well. One variation on this approach is presented by Matthiessen (1981) who represents the semantic structure of the lexicon as intensional concepts in a KL-ONE (Brachman, 1979) style knowledge base. His approach provides for

---

[5]Note, however, that her analysis of interactions between constraints on lexical choice and other decisions leads her to conclude that no general principles specify interaction between conceptual and surface decisions. For each new domain a new ordering must be developed.

links between the syntactic structure of the lexicon and the semantic structure, showing how, for example, the semantic role of AGENT might function as the syntactic role ACTOR, if the semantic concept for SELL were lexicalized using the verb "to sell."

Specifying Interaction: More recent work aims at specifying the type of interaction that can occur between the two components, rather than merging them. For example, Hovy (1985) specifies five points of interaction between conceptual and linguistic decisions; processing is controlled primarily by the surface generator, with the conceptual component being invoked at predetermined points. Work presented at the Fourth International Workshop on Natural Language Generation (Rubinoff, 1988; Iordanskaja L. and A., 1990; McDonald, 1988) also looks at the types of interaction that must occur.

14.3.2 Constraints on Connective Selection

Before presenting our implementation of connective choice, we first describe the information involved in the decision to use a connective and give an abstract model of the selection procedure. Connectives are functionally defined as the class of words that express a relation between two (or more) utterances or discourse segments. There are many types of relations that can hold between discourse segments, and a given connective can often express more than one relation. In this paper, we look at two relations that connectives can express: a relation between the *argumentative orientation* of the conjoined utterances and the *functional status* of the utterances. We limit our discussion to the connective "but."

Traditional definitions of "but" (Quirk, 1972) indicate that the complex "*p but q*" expresses opposition between *p* and *q* as illustrated in (1) below. However, whatever semantics is given to the concept of *opposition*, it seems unlikely one would maintain that *p* and *q* of (2) can be in opposition, for it is well accepted in our society that beauty deserves a high price. We are likely to agree that the fact that an object is beautiful implies that it is expensive, thus indicating that *p* and *q* of (2) are more in "agreement" than in "opposition."

(1) I want to buy it, but it is expensive.
(2) It is beautiful, but it is expensive.

Although we do maintain that "but" expresses an opposition between the two units it connects, the problem is to determine exactly what is opposed in the two utterances and to define precisely what is meant by "opposition". Ducrot (1983) offers some clues. In *p but q*, *p* is presented as an argument for a certain conclusion *c1* and *q* as an argument for another conclusion *c2*. It is these two conclusions that need to be in opposition.

In our example, the opposition between *p* and *q* is **indirect** and requires the identification of **implicit conclusions**. Such conclusions could be:

A: It's beautiful $\rightarrow$ *I want to buy it*
B: <u>But</u> it's expensive $\rightarrow$ *I don't want to buy it*

We call the set of conclusions compatible with an utterance its **argumentative orientation (AO)**.[6] It is now possible to rephrase the description of 'but' as: 'but' indicates an opposition between the AO of the units it connects. If we consider the conclusions aimed at by utterances as formulae of a first order language,[7] we can define opposition between the conclusions $c1$ and $c2$ each represented by single formula as simply: $oppose(c1,c2) \equiv (c1 \rightarrow \neg c2) \equiv \neg(c1 \wedge c2)$ and between the conclusions $AO1$ and $AO2$ each represented as sets of formula: $oppose(AO1,AO2) \equiv (AO1 \cup AO2)$ *is inconsistent*

In order to rank arguments so that comparisons can be made, we use the notion of **argumentative scale** (Anscombre and Ducrot, 1983). An argumentative scale is simply an ordering between propositions that can be dynamically established during discourse. Naturally, several scales exist in a given situation. To allow comparisons across different scales, Anscombre and Ducrot (1983) use the notion of *topos* originally proposed by Aristotle. *Topoi* can be viewed as conventional argumentative scales underlying communication. They can be represented as gradual inference rules of the form *"the more/less P, the more/less Q"* where P and Q are arbitrary formula along a scale. Using these tools, Q can be determined to provide a better argument than P if it falls higher on the scale. A very similar formal apparatus is described in (Kay, 1987).

Functional status is another feature that we have found plays a role in connective selection. It indicates whether the unit is directive (i.e., makes the primary point of the complex clause) or subordinate. The functional status of individual units is an essential component of the representation of discourse structure as it indicates how units are related. Different connectives constrain the functional status of the units they conjoin in different ways. For example, in "P but Q" Q is the directive act, in "Although P, Q" Q is the directive act, and in "P because Q," P is the directive act.[8] Other features also play a role

---

[6] To say that all utterances have an AO is not a proposal to cast all discourses as argumentative. The AO can be thought of as the set of inferences that can be drawn from a given proposition. For some utterances, the AO can be unconstrained by the linguistic form. The point is that there are certain linguistic devices whose primary function is to constrain the AO of an utterance. Therefore, the notion of AO is necessary to describe the semantic value of these devices. For example, the role of words like 'even' (Fraser, 1971; Anscombre, 1973; Henning, 1983; Kay, 1987), 'almost' (Sadock, 1981), 'only' (Horn, 1969), 'let alone' (Fillmore and O'Connor, 1987) or of many of the connectives we have studied can be described as adding constraints on the AO of the sentences they modify.

[7] Note that conclusions are not utterances or sentences of a natural language. They are part of the meta-language used to describe the meaning of an utterance.

[8] Note that the notion of directive vs. subordinate does not coincide with the more classical notions of coordination vs. subordination (cf. (Quirk, 1972) for a grammatical definition of the gradient coordination/subordination), or to the systemist notion of taxis (Halliday, 1985). For example, the complex "p but q" is grammatically a conjunction and is defined in (Halliday, 1985) as a paratactic relation. But in our analysis, in "p but q," p and q do not have the same functional status. In the structure of the discourse, q is more accessible than p - and

in the selection of a connective, but we do not discuss them here. See (Elhadad and McKeown, 1989) for a full description.

We represent a connective as a *relation between the features of two consecutive utterances*. Therefore, in order to produce a connective, a generator is provided with a set of features for each utterance as input. If these utterance features satisfy a relation, the corresponding connective can be produced. It must be noted that in this model, we go from connectives to relation, and not from relations to connectives: we do not need to establish a classification of possible relations between discourse segments, but consider only those relations that can be realized by certain connectives. Note also that this approach provides a *multi-dimensional* description of the types of relations that can be expressed between discourse segments.

As an example, consider the description of 'but'. It is a set of constraints between the features of two utterances P and Q. For the argumentative and functional status part, it specifies that:

- The argumentative orientations of P and Q must include ordering constraints involving the same scale, and the proposition mentioned in P must have a lesser degree on this scale than the one mentioned in Q. (P_i of σ) $\in$ AO(P) and (Q_j of σ) $\in$ AO(Q) and ($P_i <_\sigma Q_j$) where σ is a scale. If this is not the case, it is difficult to explain why the locutor supports the conclusions of Q. For example, if there is no scale in common between the argumentative orientations of P and Q, the opposition is difficult to understand, as in "John is hungry but he is short." If there is a scale in common, but Q has a lesser degree than P then the preference of the locutor is difficult to directly understand, like in "John is starving but Mary is hungry."[9]

- The topoi used for P and Q must have their right-hand sides of different polarities: if *Topos(P)* = $(..., +\sigma)$ then *Topos(Q)* = $(..., -\sigma)$ and *vice-versa*. This explains the opposition between the argumentative orientations of P and Q. For example, in "this car is nice but it is expensive," one interpretation would use the topoi "*+nice,+desirable*" and "*+expensive,-desirable*".

- P must have a subordinate status and Q a directive status. This constraint accounts for the fact that one must link on Q and not on P after the complex P *but* Q. For example, the combination "this car is nice, but it is expensive. Therefore I will buy it" is (in most situations) not

---

for example, "p but q, therefore c" is only possible if c is argumentatively compatible with q, not with p.

[9]The opposite case "Mary is hungry but John is starving." could be interpreted using a scale along the degree of hunger. The two propositions would be connected using a topos such as "the more X is hungry, the more X has priority for food" and the opposition appears between the two specializations of the right-hand side "John has priority for food" and "Mary has priority for food."

acceptable, because "therefore" links on the argumentative features of P and not on Q.

14.3.3   An Example of Constraint Interaction

An example of interaction between internal constraints occurs in lexical selection. Many adjectives are conventionally associated with argumentative scales (e.g., "small" is associated with the scale of size). Similarly, verbs often 'project' an argumentative aspect on their actants – e.g., "steal" positions its actor on the scale of honesty, as described in (Raccah, 1987). These features of words are described in a lexicon. When a connective is chosen, the values of the argumentative features (AO and Topos) are constrained. As a consequence, the verbs and adjectives chosen in the connected clauses are also constrained.

For example, consider the case where a text generation system wants to convey that a transaction has occurred between two participants, a construction company and the mayor, involving an exchange of money in return for a permit to build. Suppose, furthermore, that the system wants to convey its opinion that the two participants acted dishonestly (i.e., that the transaction was in some way not legal). The propositional content for such an utterance and the AO might be represented as shown in Figure 14.6. If this utterance is to be generated in isolation, the AO must be realized through appropriate lexical choice, for example resulting in the choice of "bribe" for the *exchange* predicate as in sentence (3).

(3) A&C Builders bribed the Mayor with $10,000 to receive a license for the new construction site.

On the other hand, if this utterance is to be conveyed as part of a discourse segment where the AO is attributed to someone other than the system (i.e., someone thinks the participants have acted dishonestly[10]), and is followed by the statement that the transaction is, in fact, legal, then the system can choose to express the AO through the selection of the connective "but". In this case, the lexical choice for *exchange* is no longer constrained to be semantically loaded. The system can choose a more neutral verb to express the exchange such as "buy" as in sentence (4).

(4) A&C Builders bought a license for the new construction site from the Mayor for $10,000, but their intentions were honest.

In this sentence, the inference that the exchange could be considered illegal is triggered by the use of "but" since this connective indicates opposition between the AOs of P and Q.

---

[10] Other features of our definition of "but" account for the fact that the propositional content of P in P *but* Q can be attributed implicitly to someone other than the speaker. See (Elhadad and McKeown, 1988) for details.

Propositional content for (3):

```
(pc ((cat clause)
     (process-type action)
     (concept Exchange)
     (benef/init ((lex 'A&C Builders')
                  (concept A&CB)
                  (np-type proper)))
     (benef/react ((lex 'Mayor')
                   (np-type common)
                   (concept Mayor)
                   (definite homophora)))
     (medium/init ((concept cash)
                   (quantity 10000)
                   (unit $)))
     (medium/react ((head ((lex license)
                           (concept license)
                           (np-type common)))
                    (qualifier ((prep === for)
                                (concept CSite)
                                (head === site)
                                (classifier === construction)
                                (describer ((lex new)
                                            (defining yes)))))))))))
```

Argumentative Orientation for (3):

```
(ao ((scale dishonest)
     (conclusion
      ((process-type attributive)
       (carrier ((concept A&CB)))
       (attribute ((concept dishonest)))))))
```

Figure 14.6: Sample input with argumentative constraint

Lexical choice in P is therefore affected by the decision to use a certain connective. The decision about what verb to use in an embedded clause is determined in part by the decision about a constituent to the right of the verb. Thus decision making must not be purely left to right. Conversely, if it happens that the lexical item "bribe" must be used (e.g., the propositional content of the clause contains the predicate *illegal-exchange* in place of *exchange*), that can in turn have an influence on the decision to generate a complex clause or two single ones. Thus constraints between these two constituents are bidirectional.

Furthermore, constraints made in selection of the connective may in turn place constraints on generation of content by a deep planner. For example, the use of "but" in the previous example allows the generation of different follow-up sentences than would have been the case if "although" had been generated. Since Q is directive in "P but Q", we can use a follow-up sentence such as "We should use them." following (4) above. In contrast, P is directive in "P although Q" and this explains the awkwardness of the sequence "A&C Builders bought a license for the new construction site from the Mayor for $10,000 although their intentions were honest. We should use them." A comprehensive analysis of the interaction between the features we use for connective selection and both deep and surface generation remains to be done. The point is that **a given linguistic device (e.g., a connective) introduces more constraints on a discourse than those that motivated its use.** Thus, in selecting a linguistic device, a surface generator must be able to generate constraints on content that will be fed back to the deep generator.

14.3.4   Implementation

To illustrate how our FUG implementation accounts for this interaction among constraints, we present a simplified version of our full grammar, restricted to 'but' and 'although'. It expects as input an FD of category **discourse-segment**. A discourse segment, following (Roulet, 1985; Sinclair and Coulthard, 1975) is represented as a hierarchical structure, characterized by a directive act and subordinate acts. The directive act is a single utterance, while the subordinate acts recursively form a complex discourse segment. In this paper, for simplicity, we restrict subordinate acts to simple sentences.

The connective grammar is shown in Figures 14.7-14.10. In Figure 14.7, the grammar for discourse segments is shown and it specifies the possible orderings of the clauses and connectives. Whether a connective can be used freely in the initial position (e.g., "although P, Q") is a property of the particular conjunction used. This is represented in the part of the grammar handling conjunctions (Figure 14.8). The feature **position** has a value of **middle** when the conjunction must be in between the two clauses it connects (e.g., 'but') and of **free** otherwise. In the grammar for discourse segments, the feature **connective** is introduced and specified as category **connective**. This category is in turn defined in Figures 14.9 and 14.10. It expects two utterances P and Q as features, and describes the relation that must hold between them when the complex PcQ can be realized. It is at the heart of our selection procedure. The clause section presented in Section 14.2 is used for the generation of each simple clause.

To describe the relation that holds between P and Q, the connective grammar contains a separate alternative (**alt**) for each class of features. Functional Status (FS) forms one class and argumentative orientation (AO) and Topos forms the class, argumentation. The use of alternatives encodes the fact that there is no natural priority in the model between the different features. Furthermore, constraints from one class (e.g., FS) can be stated independently of those from another (e.g., argumentation). Again, the FUG implementation allows us to distinguish between the different types of constraints, and to localize related constraints in the same alt. This separation of constraints of different natures in different regions of the grammar is similar to the distinction we have in the **clause** grammar presented in Section 14.2 between syntactic and semantic features. It allows internal flexible ordering of decision making mentioned on page 361. Constraints from functional status are represented in the first alt (Figure 14.9) and these generate most of the constraints on the ordering of the complex clause (i.e., whether P or Q is the first embedded clause). While the **discourse-segment** section of the grammar expresses all possible orderings, this section selects one based on which clause can be directive as governed by the particular conjunction. Conversely, if constraints on the ordering are generated by the deep planner, they are taken into account by the FS feature constraints. Figure 14.10 presents the part of the grammar handling argumentative features. We represent opposition between two AOs using topoi: two AOs are opposed if their respective scales appear in a topos with opposite signs (the feature **sign-right** of P must be the opposite of **sign-right** of Q).

A sample input to the grammar is shown in Figure 14.11. Note that this input contains an argumentative constraint stating that the clause realizing this proposition must argue for the conclusion that A&C Builders and the Mayor were involved in a dishonest transaction. The rest of this input FD is primarily a description of the propositional content (the value of the feature pc). Note that the lexical specification for the verb is not given, but only specifies that the concept to be expressed is "exchange." Part of the task of the grammar is to choose a verb that will express this concept.

Figure 14.12 shows a fragment of the lexicon that helps map concept to verb. The fragment shows that the verbs "buy," "bribe" and "sell" all can express the concept of "exchange", but "bribe" adds the desired argumentative orientation (i.e., the transaction was dishonest) to the clause. Figure 14.13 shows how the argumentative constraint given in the input can be satisfied by the choice of verb. The first fragment is taken from the grammar for verbs. It shows how the verb's argumentative feature from the lexicon, when there is one, is sent up to the clause using the feature (**justified yes**) in the AO description. The second fragment, taken from the clause grammar, indicates that the AO feature of a clause **must** eventually be justified.

```
;; ============================================================
;; CAT DISCOURSE-SEGMENT ----------------------------------------
;; ============================================================
((cat discourse-segment)
 (directive ((cat utterance) (FS directive)))
 (subordinate ((cat discourse-segment) (FS subordinate)))
 (alt
   (((connective  ((cat connective)
                   (P (^ ^ directive))
                   (Q (^ ^ subordinate))))
     (alt
       (((pattern (directive connective subordinate)))
        ((pattern (connective subordinate directive))
         (c ((position free))))))))
    ((connective ((cat connective)
                  (P (^ ^ subordinate))
                  (Q (^ ^ directive))))
     (alt
       (((pattern (subordinate connective directive)))
        ((pattern (connective directive subordinate))
         (c ((position free)))))))))))
```

Figure 14.7: The CATegory Discourse-segment

When the simple clause C1 is unified with the grammar, the concept "exchange" is first mapped to the verb "buy." But the entry for "buy" contains no AO and the feature justified remains unbound. Thus, this first unification fails, the unifier backtracks and tries the verb "bribe." Since the lexical entry for "bribe" contains an AO, the feature justified is set to yes, and the argumentative constraint of the input is satisfied. The grammar eventually produces the sentence "A&C Builders bribed the Mayor with $10,000 to receive the license for the construction site."

Figure 14.14 now shows the same proposition, with the same argumentative constraint but embedded in a complex clause. This complex input represents a type of concessive move: the locutor concedes that A&C Builders "exchanged" $10,000 for a license and that this exchange can be an argument for dishonesty of A&C, but states a stronger belief that A&C acted honestly in the directive move.

The unification of C2 leads to the generation of "A&C Builders bought a license for the construction site from the Mayor for $10,000, but their intentions were honest." The first step of the unification will go through the discourse-segment category of Figure 14.7 where the pattern SCD will be chosen. Next, the unifier applies the constraints from functional status and argumentation. At the end of this first sweep through the connective category, all the constraints that can be derived from the input on the features have

```
;; ================================================================
;; CAT CONJ -------------------------------------------------------
;; ================================================================
((cat conj)
 (alt
   (((position free)
     (alt
       (((lex 'although'))
        ((lex 'since'))
        ((lex 'because')))))
    ((position middle)
     (lex 'but')))))
```

Figure 14.8: Grammar for CONJunctions

```
;; ================================================================
;; CAT CONNECTIVE -------------------------------------------------
;; ================================================================
((cat connective)
 ;; The parts common to all connectives
 (pattern (c))
 (c ((cat conj)))
 ;; Themes must intersect
 (TEST (FD-intersection @(^ ^ P Th) @(^ ^ Q Th)))

 ;; First alt: Functional Status
 ;; For but: S-D order, all other, D-S order.
 (alt
   (((P ((FS subordinate)))
     (Q ((FS directive)))
     (c ((lex 'but'))))
    ((P ((FS directive)))
     (Q ((FS subordinate)))
     (alt (((c ((lex 'although'))))
           ((c ((lex 'because'))))
           ((c ((lex 'since')))))))))))
```

Figure 14.9: The Connective FUG – Section 1

```
;; Second alt: Argumentation
;; AO has 2 (main) features: conclusion and scale.
;; Topos has 4 (main) features: sign and scale/left and right.
;; For ''although'', Topos(P) must be none,
;; because the opposition between P and Q must be direct,
;; following a pattern (P, P arg -Q) and not through an implicit
;; conclusion reached through a topos in P like in (P arg C, Q arg -C)
;; which is possible with ''but''

(alt
  (((P ((Topos none)))
    (alt
      (((Q ((Topos ((scale-left  (^ ^ ^ Q AO scale))
                    (sign-right -)
                    (scale-right (^ ^ ^ P AO scale)))))))
        (c ((lex 'although'))))
       <...other connectives...>)))
  ((P ((Topos ((scale-left   (^ ^ ^ P AO scale))
               (scale-right (^ ^ ^ Q Topos scale-right)))))))
   (Q ((Topos ((scale-left  (^ ^ ^ Q AO scale))))))
   ;; sign-right of Topos(P) and Topos(Q) must be opposed
   (alt
     (((P ((Topos ((sign-right +)))))
       (Q ((Topos ((sign-right -))))))
      ((P ((Topos ((sign-right -)))))
       (Q ((Topos ((sign-right +)))))))))
;; The AO of P and Q is justified by the use of the connective
(P ((AO ((justified yes)))))
(Q ((AO ((justified yes)))))
```

Figure 14.10: The Connective FUG – Section 2

```
C1 =

((cat discourse-segment)
 (directive
  ((th ~(A&CB License  CSite Mayor $10,000 Exchange))
   (if ((force assert)))
   (ao ((scale dishonest)
        (conclusion ((process-type attributive)
                     (carrier ((concept A&CB)))
                     (attribute ((concept dishonest)))))))))
    (pc ((cat clause)
         (process-type action)
         (concept Exchange)
         (benef/init ((lex 'A&C Builders')
                      (concept A&CB)
                      (np-type proper)))
         (benef/react ((lex 'Mayor')
                       (np-type common)
                       (concept Mayor)
                       (definite homophora)))
         (medium/init ((concept cash)
                       (quantity 10000)
                       (unit $)))
         (medium/react ((head ((lex license)
                               (concept license)
                               (np-type common)))
                        (qualifier ((prep === for)
                                    (concept CSite)
                                    (head === site)
                                    (classifier === construction)
                                    (describer ((lex new)
                                                (defining yes)))))))))))))

((cat discourse-segment)
 (directive
  ((th ~(A&CB Exchange Honest))
   (if ((force assert)))
   (ao ((scale honest)
        (conclusion ((process-type attributive)
                     (carrier ((concept A&CB)))
                     (attribute ((concept honest)))))))))
    (pc ((cat clause)
         (process-type attributive)
         (carrier ((head ((concept intention)))
                   (number plural)
                   (determiner ((possessive yes)
                                (np-type pronoun)
                                (pronoun-type personal)
                                (concept A&CB)
                                (number plural)
                                (person third)))))
         (attribute === honest))))))
```

Figure 14.11: Sample input with argumentative constraint

Lexicon =

```
(alt (((concept Move) ...)
        ...
        ;; Different verbs to express the Concept Exchange
        ;; For each verb, map the concept specific roles to more
        ;; general semantic roles accepted by the grammar.
        ;; Also preselect the governing prepositions if needed.

        ;; to buy: BI buys MR from BR for MI.
        ((concept Exchange)
         (lex 'buy')
         (agent (^ benef/init))
         (medium (^ medium/react))
         (instrument (^ medium/init))
         (benef (^ benef/react))
         (instrument ((prep === for)))
         (benef ((prep === from))))

        ;; to bribe: BI bribes BR with MI in order to possess MR.
        ;; is also marked on its argumentative function
        ((concept Exchange)
         (lex 'bribe')
         (AO ((conclusion
                ((process-type attributive)
                 (carrier (^ ^ ^ ^ pc agent))
                 (attribute dishonest)))
              (scale dishonest)))
         (agent (^ benef/init))
         (medium (^ benef/react))
         (instrument (^ medium/init))
         (purpose ((cat clause)
                   (concept Possess)
                   (agent (^ ^ agent))
                   (medium (^ ^ medium/react))))
         (instrument ((prep === with))))

        ;; to sell: BR sells MR to BI for MI.
        ((concept Exchange)
         (lex 'sell')
         (agent (^ benef/react))
         (medium (^ medium/react))
         (instrument (^ medium/init))
         (benef (^ benef/init))
         (instrument ((prep === for)))
         (benef ((prep === to))))
        ...))
```

Figure 14.12: A fragment from the lexicon

In grammar for verb:

```
((cat verb)
 ...
 (alt (((ao (^ ^ ^ ao))
        (ao ((justified yes))))
       ((ao none)))))
```

The AO of the verb can justify the AO of the clause if the verb is argumentatively loaded.

In grammar for clauses:

```
((cat clause)
 ...
 (ao ((justified any))))
```

The AO of a clause must be justified by one of the linguistic devices realizing the clause.

Figure 14.13: Fragments from the grammars for verbs and clauses

been verified or added to C2 and the modified input will be as shown in Figure 14.15. The unifier then proceeds to the unification of the clauses. The argumentative constraint given in input to the subordinate clause is now satisfied by a constraint coming from the choice of the connective "but." When the lexicon is reached, the default verb "buy" is chosen, and the choice need not be reconsidered, since the input constraint is already satisfied.

This example demonstrates how complex interaction between lexical choice in the clause and connective selection can be implemented by the FUG without requiring the grammar writer to explicitly express the interaction. Similarly, if the deep planner had any constraints on lexical choice, they would be included in the PC feature of the discourse segment. The argumentative constraints implied by the lexical choice would be reflected at the Discourse-segment level by the argumentative part of the category Discourse-segment in the grammar (not presented in the figure). Therefore, if one of the features is "preselected" at any level, the constraint it implies are enforced at the highest possible level immediately.

14.4   COMPARISON WITH OTHER FORMALISMS

In this section we compare order of decision making in FUG with order of decision making in two of the parsing formalisms we have used, the ATN and the DCG. Because there are a number of similarities between the two, we focus on the ATN showing how order of decision making would occur for both the sample syntactic grammar and connective choice. We then point out where processing

```
C2 =

((cat discourse-segment)
 (subordinate
  ((directive
    ((th ~(A&CB License  CSite Mayor $10,000 Exchange))
     (if ((force assert)))
     (ao ((scale dishonest)
          (conclusion ((process-type attributive)
                       (carrier ((concept A&CB)))
                       (attribute ((concept dishonest)))))))
     (pc ((cat clause)
          (process-type action)
          (concept Exchange)
          (benef/init ((lex 'A&C Builders')
                       (concept A&CB)
                       (np-type proper)))
          (benef/react ((lex 'Mayor')
                        (np-type common)
                        (concept Mayor)
                        (definite homophora)))
          (medium/init ((concept cash)
                        (quantity 10000)
                        (unit $)))
          (medium/react ((head ((lex license)
                                (concept license)
                                (np-type common)))
                         (qualifier ((prep === for)
                                     (concept CSite)
                                     (head === site)
                                     (classifier === construction)
                                     (describer ((lex new)
                                                 (defining yes)))))))))))))
  (directive
   ((cat discourse-segment)
    (directive
     ((th ~(A&CB Exchange Honest))
      (if ((force assert)))
      (ao ((scale honest)
           (conclusion ((process-type attributive)
                        (carrier ((concept A&CB)))
                        (attribute ((concept honest)))))))
      (pc ((cat clause)
           (process-type attributive)
           (carrier ((head ((concept intention)))
                     (number plural)
                     (determiner ((possessive yes)
                                  (np-type pronoun)
                                  (pronoun-type personal)
                                  (concept A&CB)
                                  (number plural)
                                  (person third)))))
           (attribute === honest)))))))))
```

Figure 14.14: Sample input for connective

Argumentative features added to C2:

```
((directive
   ((AO ((conclusion ((process-type attributive)
                      (carrier ((concept A&CB)))
                      (attribute ((concept dishonest)))))
         (orientation -)
         (scale dishonesty)))
    (Topos ((scale-left honesty)
            (sign-left +)
            (scale-right dishonesty)
            (sign-right -)))))
 (subordinate
   ((AO ((conclusion ((process-type attributive)
                      (carrier ((concept A&CB)))
                      (attribute ((concept dishonest)))))
         (orientation +)
         (scale dishonesty)))
    (Topos ((scale-left Bribe)
            (sign-left +)
            (scale-right dishonesty)
            (sign-right +)))))))
```

Figure 14.15: Argumentative features added to C2

in the DCG diverges from the ATN, allowing an added degree of flexibility. Both the ATN and the DCG, however, favor a syntagmatic mode of grammar organization, while FUGs allow a paradigmatic organization. Generation is more concerned with choice based on the paradigmatic axis. Therefore, when order of decision making follows the syntactic structure of the utterance being produced, we run into problems both in the degree of flexibility and in the representation of constraints.

Finally, we turn to two formalisms that have been used for generation, the systemic formalism (Mann, 1983; Patten, 1988) and MUMBLE (McDonald and Pustejovsky, 1985).

14.4.1 Using an ATN for Generation

Difficulties arise in using the ATN for language generation given the depth first traversal of the network and the need to synchronize in lock-step the influence of different constraints as syntactic structure is constructed. The traversal algorithm means that production of leftward constituents can not be influenced by decisions made in producing constituents towards the end of the sentence. Furthermore, it can be difficult to allow for complex interaction between constraints since different constraints must be coordinated as the system traverses the network. To show why this is the case, we first describe how generation is done in the ATN and then show through examples of a simple grammar and a grammar for connectives how decision making is constrained.

The ATN generator we use makes the following assumptions:

- Input to the ATN interpreter is a list of case roles, such as *prot*, *goal*, *predicate*, etc. Registers are initially filled with the values for these case roles and can be accessed when traversing the grammar.

- The generator works by traversing the net, producing a word whenever it encounters a cat arc. On traversal of a cat arc, the special register * is set to contain the word produced.

- The same grammar can be used for both interpretation and generation provided:

  1. Rather than building a tree structure from registers at pop arcs, the grammar strings registers together in list form to construct the sentence produced.

  2. The grammar writer provides arbitrary LISP functions associated with each category that access specified registers to determine the word or words to generate for the category at this point in the sentence. A cat arc can be traversed if the associated LISP function can select a word for the given category. For example, the grammar writer might provide functions *produce-adj*, *produce-det*, and *produce-noun* which would access specified input registers when the cat **det**, **adj**, and **noun** arcs are traversed to determine if a word in those categories can be produced.

  3. The grammar writer may choose to add actions to any arcs to manipulate input registers. For example, when attempting to construct the subject of a sentence from the input prot register, one common action would be to send the value of the prot register down to the np network. Similarly, one could send the value of the goal register down to the NP network when constructing the object of the sentence. This allows the NP network to access a single register when constructing a NP whose content varies depending on its context in the sentence.

The ATN interpreter for language generation makes decisions in two ways. Decisions are made about what to produce each time the system has a choice of arc to take next. Constraints on this type of choice can be represented as arbitrary LISP tests on the arc. Alternatively decisions can be made on traversal of a *cat* arc by its associated function. This function may decide whether a word of the specified category may be produced at all, and if so, what word will be produced.

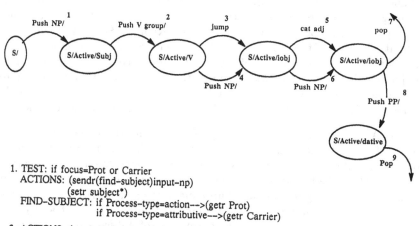

1. TEST: if focus=Prot or Carrier
   ACTIONS: (sendr(find-subject)input-np)
           (setr subject*)
   FIND-SUBJECT: if Process-type=action-->(getr Prot)
                 if Process-type=attributive-->(getr Carrier)

2. ACTIONS: (sendr Process-type) (sendr Verb) (setr Verbgroup *)

4. TEST: if Verb-class=bitransitive and if no Dative-prep in Verb
   ACTIONS:(sendr (find-iobject)input-np) (setr iobject *)
   FIND-IOBJECT: if Process-type=action-->(getr Benef)

5. TEST: if Process-type=attributive ACTIONS: (setr object *)

6. ACTIONS: (sendr (find-object)input-np) (setr-object *)
   FIND-OBJECT: if process-type=action-->(getr Goal)
                if process-type=attributive-->(getr Attributive)

7. RETURN: Subject Verbgroup Object if Transitive
           Subject Verbgroup Iobject Object if Bitranstive

8. TEST: if Dative-prep in Verb
   ACTIONS: (sendr (find-iobject) input-np) (sendr Dative-prep input-prep) (setr Dative *)

9. RETURN: Subject Verbgroup Object Dative

Figure 14.16: Sample network

Simple Syntactic Grammar   To compare order of decision making in an ATN with order of decision making in FUG, consider a sample network shown in Figure 14.16 which is one way to translate the sample FUG of Figure 14.1. Syntactic structure of the constituents of the sentence is built by traversing subnetworks. Order of the constituents is also determined by order of arc traversal and by the **buildq** action on pop arcs.[11] Assignment of semantic roles to syntactic ones is done by complex actions on the arcs.

The important point to note in this grammar is that decisions are made in building the syntactic structure of the sentence, top-down and left-to-right. Mapping of semantic roles to syntactic roles, building of syntactic structure, and ordering of roles all occur simultaneously. For example, using T2, Figure 14.4 as input, traversal of the network would begin with arc 1 since **focus** is on the **prot**. At this point, assignment of the semantic role **prot** to the syntactic role **subject** would be made as part of the **sendr** action. In addition, a decision to produce an active sentence would have been made by the test. This arc would produce the NP for the subject, "John" and place it in the **subject** register.

This ATN grammar is but one way of translating the FUG. There are a variety of other possibilities. Since the ATN is turing machine equivalent, it would be possible to follow the FUG more exactly. One could use 3 stages in the ATN, where the first two stages resulted in the setting of registers used for features corresponding to FUG attributes and in the final stage only, would the sentence actually be produced. This grammar would only use **test** and **jump** arcs and would not correspond to the normal use of ATNs. Most of the work for generation would be done in the LISP functions used as actions or tests on the arcs. Clearly, this is not a desirable solution.

Characterization of Differences   In the ATN version of the FUG that we presented here, the ordering of constituents in the resulting sentence is conflated with the assignment of syntactic structure to constituents while in FUG these tasks were represented in two separate sections of the grammar. The necessity to mix different sorts of information as well as the depth-first traversal algorithm of the ATN results in these primary differences:

Left-to-right Traversal: In the ATN version, decisions about embedded constituents will get made before some top-level decisions. In the example, the subject "John" is fully determined before syntactic ordering decisions such as where the indirect object is placed. In FUG, all decisions that can be made at the top level are made before producing constituents. The ATN's order of decision making will cause problems for the case of connectives where a decision made early on in the sentence depends on a decision further to the right.

---

[11] Actually, a more sophisticated ATN interpreter might construct linear order of constituents in the sentence simply by tracking order of arc traversal thus allowing the user to omit the **buildq** statements.

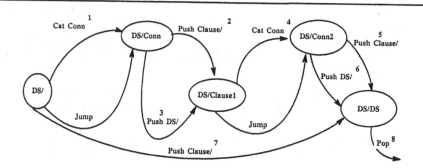

1. (setr Conn*)
2. (sendr Directive input–clause) (setr Clause1*) (setr DirT)
3. (sendr Subordinate input–clause) (setr Clause1 *) (setr Sub T)
4. IF Conn empty, (Setr Conn*) (setr Middle T)
5. IF Sub, (sendr Directive input–clause) (setr Clause2 *)
6. IF Dir, (sendr Subordinate input–clause) (setr Clause2 *)
7. (setr Simple T) (sendr Directive input–clause) (setr Clause1 *)
8. IF simple,. return Clause1, ELSE IF Middle, return Clause1 Conn Clause2,
                    ELSE return Conn Clause1 Clause2

Figure 14.17: Top level Network for Complex clause

Synchronization of different types of constraints: An ATN must synchronize in lock-step the influence of different constraints as it proceeds through
the construction of syntactic structure of the sentence. It can be difficult to
coordinate these different constraints and it means that the grammar writer
must know in advance exactly when these constraints will come into play in
producing the sentence.

Implementation of Connective Choice Since the form of an ATN must
follow the syntagmatic structure of the sentence, the network to perform connective choice is made of roughly four parallel paths corresponding to the orders
ScD, cDS, DcS and cSD. The input to the ATN interpreter is a list of registers,
containing the values of all features present in a discourse-segment. Note
that the input does not have the structured aspect of an FD, as all features, at
all levels, must be put in different registers.

Figure 14.17 shows the top level of an ATN that could be used for connective selection. For an ATN interpreter, the Utterance category is realized as a clause. Therefore, on the arcs **directive** and **subordinate** we push to the **clause** subnetwork, and there is no **utterance** subnetwork. All the actions performed by the category utterance in the FUG implementation must therefore be done on the actions of the arcs.

The most natural way to perform connective selection is to associate a procedure to each connective (e.g., *produce-but*, *produce-although*). The procedure will do all the testing required by the description of the conjunction. This means that the selection procedure must be implemented in Lisp. An alternative approach is to write only one procedure implementing the whole selection procedure.

It is therefore the responsibility of these procedures to behave either as testers or as generators when one of the registers being tested turns out to be empty. If the procedures are to work as generators, the grammar writer must basically rewrite the unification algorithm in each procedure.

The difference between the two approaches is that in the FUG implementation, the part of the grammar handling connective selection does not need to be aware of the source of a constraint on a feature: it just tries to unify the feature with possible values. In contrast, the ATN grammar writer must explicitly describe the types of interaction that can occur: what register can affect the value of each feature, and test for all of them. This complexity is derived from our desire to leave order of decision making unconstrained. If, on the other hand, we accept a specification of priorities between the features involved in the selection, then the ATN implementation can be made much simpler. All the procedures can work as tests only, testing more 'primitive' features first, and assigning values to less 'primitive' values as a result. This is, however, the type of rigid interaction we want to avoid.

14.4.2   DCG

DCGs share with ATNs the characteristic of favoring a syntagmatic mode of grammar organization. Typically, a DCG encodes the structural properties of a language in context free rules having both a left and right hand side. These are augmented by extra conditions on the rules. For generation, these tests would make any context sensitive tests required. For example, a rule stating that OBJ → ADJ might have the test that process-type is attributive since action process-types do not have adjectival objects. In addition, pragmatic information could be tested to determine certain syntactic choices. For example, focus might be tested as part of a rule that determines the active form be used.

Mapping of semantic roles to syntactic roles is achieved through the use of arguments to rules. For example, the DCG we use in one of our generation systems (Derr and McKeown, 1984) contains the rule shown in Figure 14.18. This rule builds syntactic structure for a sentence (nplist followed by vb_phrase) and

```
sentence(clause(Verb,Prot,Goal,Bene,Focus,Advs,Mods)) -->
                [trimcore]
                nplist(Focus,subj),
                vb_phrase(Verb,Prot,Goal,Bene,Focus,Advs),
                mods(Mods).
```

Figure 14.18: Sample DCG Rule

maps the semantic roles provided in input (verb, prot, goal, beneficiary, focus) to syntactic roles such as subject and object by passing them to subconstituents of the sentence (e.g., focus is passed to nplist to be used as the subject of the sentence).

As in the ATN, then, the result is a conflation of different types of constraints into individual rules. Mapping of semantic roles to syntactic roles, building of syntactic structure, and ordering of syntactic roles based on pragmatic constraints are represented as synchronized decisions that occur in lock-step as the sentence is produced. Furthermore, as in the ATN, processing of rules is top-down, left-to-right meaning that a constituent to the left in the sentence will be fully determined before other decisions get made.

Unlike the ATN, the DCG uses unification as the mechanism for processing rules and this results in two types of added flexibility. Through unification of arguments, some constraints can be expressed at a higher level and passed down to lower level constituents. More importantly, constraints are necessarily bidirectional precisely because of the use of unification.

14.4.3 MUMBLE

Order of decision making in MUMBLE (McDonald and Pustejovsky, 1985) is quite different from order of decision making in FUG. First, it is determined by the incoming message and not by the grammar. To produce a sentence the incoming message is traversed, replacing each plan unit of the message with a possibly partial syntactic tree structure, until a full tree is produced. The second main difference is McDonald's commitment to a linear algorithm. All decisions are indelible. As far as we can tell, this means that bidirectional constraints can not be accounted for.

To compare order of decision making more directly, consider how MUM-BLE would generate our example sentence "John gives a blue book to Mary." MUMBLE expects as input a *realization specification* for the text, which is a plan represented in semantic and pragmatic terms. A realization specification

---

```
(transfer-event
(main-event #<transfer John Mary indefinite-book>)
(particulars #<attribute book color blue>))
```

Figure 14.19: Realization Specification for "John gives a blue book to Mary"

---

for this sentence might be as shown in Figure 14.19.[12]

MUMBLE's generation process consists of three subprocess: Attachment, Realization, and Phrase Structure Execution (PSE). While these levels are organized as separate modules, they are not strictly ordered in the overall process. Rather, they are interleaved processes that pass information and partially refined structures between themselves. Flow of control is in part dictated by the input plan and in part by programmed knowledge dictating when to invoke the next component. Attachment is responsible for assigning plan units to positions within the surface structure tree that MUMBLE builds. At any point in the process, the surface structure contains "attachment points" to which new structures can be added. Initially, the first plan unit is assigned to the only available attachment point, the node dominating the first sentence. Attachment is interleaved with PSE. As soon as a partial tree is constructed, PSE takes over and does a depth-first traversal of the tree. PSE invokes procedures indicated by labels of the tree to perform transformations or enforce syntactic constraints. Words undergo morphological analysis and are produced when the leaves of the tree are reached. PSE re-invokes Attachment if it arrives at a node that is an attachment point (e.g., any noun phrase would allow the attachment of qualifying clauses) to check if there are additional plan units that can appear at this point. PSE invokes Realization when it encounters plan units in the surface structure.

Realization is responsible for all choices that have to be made during language generation. It selects an appropriate word or phrase to "realize" a plan unit. There are two types of realization classes: domain dependent classes, which are essentially dictionary entries that list possible word choices for plan elements, and linguistic classes, which identify transformation families for a particular syntactic constituent. For example, McDonald defines a linguistic realization class for transitive verbs that can be nominalized that identifies seven syntactic choices for realizing any verb of this class (e.g., active, passive, gerundive with subject, gerundive passive with subject, etc.). Thus, grammatical decisions are made by two components: by realization classes, which make syntactic choice, and by procedures, which enforce syntactic constraints and are invoked by tree labels encountered by PSE during traversal.

---

[12] we hypothesize about the primitives of this example. Papers on MUMBLE do not specify the primitives for the specification language. We base our choice of primitives on an example from (McDonald and Pustejovsky, 1987).

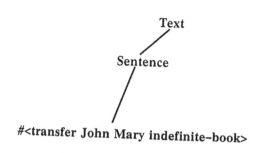

Figure 14.20: Surface Tree after 1st Attachment

In generating from the example input (Figure 14.19), MUMBLE's first step would be to attach the first plan unit (**main-event**) to the node dominating the first sentence in the surface structure (shown in Figure 14.20). PSE would then be invoked to traverse the tree. Almost immediately Realization would be called to realize the main-event. Realization can be done incrementally; its first decision may be to select the verb and construct a new tree under the S node, that includes the verb and its syntactic choice and assigns the remaining plan arguments to syntactic roles (see Figure 14.21). Realization would also denote which of the new nodes were active attachment points (in this case, there would be three, the subject head, the object head, the recipient head and the next clause). PSE continues and when it encounters the attachment point for subject would re-invoke Attachment, only to discover that there were no new plan units that could be incorporated as modifiers or qualifiers of the subject. Realization would be invoked to realize the subject as "John" and this word would be output. Similarly, the verb would next be conjugated and output. On encountering the object, Attachment would be invoked again and this time the plan unit specifying attributes of book would be folded into the surface structure. This new subtree would be traversed and the phrase "the blue book" produced. The recipient label might be responsible for adding the "to" preposition and finally, the phrase "to Mary" would be produced completing the sentence.

As can be seen in this example, order of decision making in MUMBLE has the effect of separating out the representation of different kinds of constraints. Constraints dictating how syntactic structure is built are invoked during PSE and are represented as procedures invoked by node labels. Attachment also plays a role in building syntactic structure and represents constraints on how smaller trees can combine to form larger ones. Constraints on ordering of constituents are represented in linguistic realization classes. They are represented somewhat more declaratively in the class entries, but they still invoke procedures to carry out construction of the tree representing ordering. The mapping

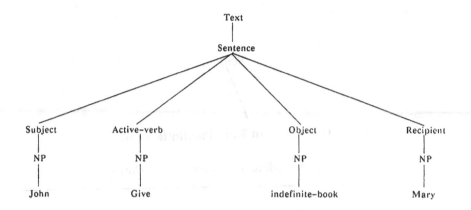

Figure 14.21: Surface Tree after 1st Realization

from semantic input to syntactic roles is done in the domain dependent realization classes. Thus, like FUG, MUMBLE supports a separate representation
of different kinds of constraints. Unlike FUG, however, each type of constraint
is represented differently (e.g., some in procedures, some in realization classes).
Furthermore, the separation of constraints is fixed by the flow of control. In
FUG however, one could decide to add additional classes of constraints in yet
another layer of grammar that is unified with results from earlier layers.

MUMBLE's indelibility constraint is the main significant difference. Decisions get made in a fixed order and this precludes the possibility for constraints
to be bidirectional. As we understand, this means that MUMBLE would not
be able to handle the interaction between selection of connective and the generation of the embedded clause. We can only speculate about how connectives
might be produced, since there is little published material about the generation
of complex sentences – but see (McDonald and Pustejovsky, 1985). We suspect
that there would be separate plan units for the propositional content of the two
clauses to be conjoined. Since MUMBLE proceeds left to right through the
message to generate the first of the clauses (we suspect that the ordering of the
clauses would be governed by the message), Attachment would add the second
clause to the tree only after the first clause is generated.[13] As a result, while

---

[13] The statement "..attachment is interleaved with Phrase Structure Execution so that most
earlier units will have been realized and their text spoken before the last one [plan unit]
is positioned."(McDonald and Pustejovsky, 1985) leads us to believe that this is the case.
However, a second possible interpretation arises from the statement "With the realization of
the first unit, the attachment possibilities for the second can be considered." If "realization"
here refers to the Realization phase and not to the full traversal of the surface structure, it
is possible that all attachments are considered immediately after a tree structure replaces a
plan unit, but before PSE continues. This seems unlikely as this would mean attachment of

decisions made in the production of the clause can influence the connective, the selection of a connective can not influence the clause.

14.4.4 Systemic Formalisms

There have been two recent major implementations of systemic grammar for generation, NIGEL (Mann, 1983) and Patten's system (Patten, 1988), each of which uses a different control strategy for processing. The grammar is represented as an interconnected set of systems, where the lowest levels represent the most delicate decisions (e.g., lexical choice) and the highest level systems the least delicate (e.g., clause type).

NIGEL is part of the PENMAN system, which in addition to the surface grammar, includes a lexicon, an input specification language (called SPL), and the most general part of a knowledge base (called the "upper model"). NIGEL as a surface grammar expects an extremely rich input, represented as a set of features. Within the PENMAN system, the SPL interpreter allows the user to enter specifications in a much simpler way and to only partially specify the features that must be expressed. Figure 14.22 shows a possible SPL specification that might be used as input to generate our example "John gives a blue book to Mary." All the features that are not specified in the SPL input are given a default value. SPL and defaulting are described in (Penman, 1988).

Note that in the SPL input, the values of the slots refer to entities in a knowledge base (the domain model). When needed, NIGEL will query this knowledge base to make a decision through a mechanism using special functions called *inquiry* and *choosers*.

In NIGEL a sentence is produced by "traversing" the grammar systems, starting with the least delicate. In each system, a choice is made by invoking the *chooser* function associated with the system, which in turn invokes one or more primitive *inquiry operators*. These functions will query the domain model of the system for information needed to make the choice. Depending on the results of the choice and the selected system, different systems will be invoked next in the overall process of producing the sentence. Features can be preselected, however. In preselection, a "leaf"[14] feature is input which means that the path from higher level systems to that lower level feature can be avoided in processing.

For example, Figure 14.23 shows the top level systems of the NIGEL grammar. When going through the root system, the grammar will decide the rank of the expression to generate. To make this decision, NIGEL will determine

---

all plan units would be possible before PSE continued and anything was produced. Since this is what McDonald wants to avoid it seems unlikely.

[14] All quoted terms in descriptions of NIGEL are our own terms and may not correspond to the terminology used by the NIGEL group.

```
((GIVE1 / GIVE          ;; GIVE1 is an instance of GIVE in the domain model
   :actor JOHN1
   :destination MARY1
   :object BOOK1
   :tense PRESENT
   :speechact ASSERTION)
 (JOHN1 / PERSON
   :name John)
 (MARY1 / PERSON
   :name Mary)
 (BOOK1 / BOOK
   :determiner A
   :relations  ((C1 / COLORING
                 :domain BOOK1
                 :range BLUE)))
 (BLUE / COLOR))
```

Figure 14.22: Input to NIGEL for "John gives a blue book to Mary"

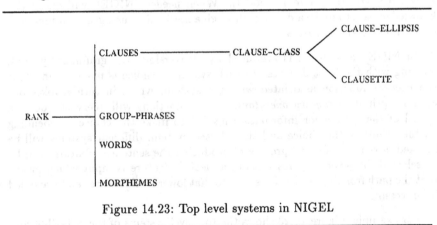

Figure 14.23: Top level systems in NIGEL

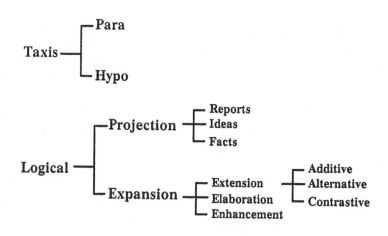

Figure 14.24: Top level systems describing clause connections

whether the input includes a speech act. As our example does contain a speech-act, the next system, CLAUSECLASS is entered. Next, NIGEL needs to determine whether the speech-act has a propositional parameter (that it, if it is applied to a proposition). The answer to this query will determine whether the generated clause will be a full clause or an exclamation or a greeting (which correspond to speech-acts without propositional content). Since our input includes a propositional content, the next system, CLAUSEELLIPSIS, is then selected. NIGEL needs to decide whether the clause is an answer to a question, in which case it can use ellipsis, or not, in which case the clause must be fully expanded. Flow of control continues in the same fashion through all the systems of the grammar, from the most general to the most specific (in what systemists call order of "delicacy").

The selection of connectives in NIGEL follows Halliday's description of clause complexes. Note that the decision to produce a single clause or a clause complex (that is, several clauses, connected in some way) is one of the first decisions made in NIGEL. Figure 14.24 shows the top level systems controlling connective choice.

In order to arrange two clauses to produce a single clause complex, NIGEL determines the type of connections to express in the complex along two dimensions: taxis and logical. The decisions concerning taxis and logical can be made in any order, and are mostly independent of each other.

Taxis determines the syntactic status of each clause within the complex. In a *paratactic* relation, the two clauses have the same syntactic status (this roughly corresponds to the traditional notion of co-ordination); in an *hypotactic* relation, one clause is presented as a modifier of the other, and thus has a lower status (this corresponds to subordination).

The logical system attempts to describe the types of semantic relations between clauses that can be expressed in language. Once the logical and taxis dimensions are determined, NIGEL can choose a connective compatible with the decisions taken. For each combination of features on the taxis and logical systems there correspond one connective. For example, "but" corresponds to the features **paratactic** and **expansion:extension:contrastive**.

The default order of decision making for choosing a connective is therefore: (1) determine the type of connection between the clauses, (2) choose the connective, (3) realize each clause. Note that when the type of connection is determined, all relevant features in each clause get pre-selected. For example, if a hypo-tactic relation is chosen, the feature **dependent** will be selected in the **dependence** system - thus forcing the subordinated clause to be realized in a certain manner. Therefore, the flow of control in NIGEL is usually top-down, with the choice of the connective constraining the realization of each clause, both to the right and to the left of the connective.

In summary, as implemented in NIGEL, decision making is primarily top-down and is not inherently bidirectional. A systemic grammar gives priority to the functional status of language. Since systems are organized around the paradigmatic axis, order of decision making is very different from either of the parsing formalisms discussed so far. For example, top-level decisions will send constraints down to lower level decisions and order of decision making is not governed by left-to-right construction of syntactic constituents. We note that NIGEL is not a finished product, but is continually under development, and order of decision making as currently implemented is not a theoretical claim of its developers.

The mechanism to enforce the bidirectional influence we have mentioned in FUG, where a choice in the clause constrains the choice of the connective, is apparently not implemented in NIGEL. However, Patten's implementation of systemic grammar allows for successive back and forth sweeps through the grammar to deduce all possible choices given a set of preselected features. This control strategy seems to capture the bidirectional constraints for which we have argued in the FUG. Lower level decisions can influence higher level decisions and vice versa. In other respects, decision making is similar to NIGEL as it is guided by functional aspects and not syntactic structure.

14.5   CONCLUSIONS

The strong points of the FUG formalism we have identified for connective selection are the partial specification of the input and flexible order of decision making, both internal and external, that a FUG naturally implements. The

FUG formalism also allows organization of the grammar along the different types of constraints involved. The localization of constraints of the same type in separate regions permits the grammar writer to identify the effect of constraints in an efficient and readable manner. This organization is not enforced by the formalism, but can be used as a guideline to lay out FUGs in a readable way. A side benefit from the type of organization we advocate is that it is easy to detect and remove duplication of constraints across similar cases.

14.5.1   Problems with FUG: Representation and Use of complex constraints

FUG does have problems in representing certain types of constraints. The types of constraints we want to express when implementing the connective selection procedure are: equality of one feature with a constant (e.g., P must have a directive status), equality of two features (e.g., P and Q must have the same utterer), limiting the possible values of a feature (e.g., the thematization of P can be propositional, illocutionary or reinterpretation), and the negation of the previous types. We also need to express set relations: test the intersection of two sets (e.g, Th(P) and Th(Q) are not disjoint), membership (e.g., (P_i as in σ is a member of AO(P)). Other types of constraints can occur (e.g., the right-hand side of the topoi are of opposite signs).

The FUG formalism directly encodes constraints of the first types: equality with a constant is expressed as *(attribute constant)*, equality between two features is expressed as *(attribute1 <path to attribute2>)*. To limit the possible values of a feature, an alternation can be used: *(attribute (alt (val1 ... valn)))*. Negation is not part of the basic unification formalism, but has been added to many unifiers (Shieber, 1986; Karttunen, 1984). It can also be simulated using the special value *none*. More complex constraints can be expressed as composition of the previous types. For example, to express the constraint on the signs of the topoi, the following expression can be used:

```
(alt (((dl-p ((sign-right +)))
       (dl-q ((sign-right -))))
      ((dl-p ((sign-right -)))
       (dl-q ((sign-right +)))))))
```

Constraints on sets are more problematic. It is difficult to express anything about sets using the standard FUG formalism. FDs allow values to be either atomic or FDs. It is possible to write grammars to deal with sets or lists; we actually have written such a grammar to compute the *append* of two lists, test for membership, or compute the intersection of two lists. Such grammars are, however, terribly inefficient and not very readable. It is more productive to acknowledge the limitation of the formalism, and to add facilities to express more complex constraints (Elhadad, 1989).

We have addressed these problems by introducing a special attribute into the formalism, **test**, that has a special unification behavior. This adds to the existing special attributes **pattern, cset,** and **alt**. The value of a **test** attribute can be an arbitrary predicate represented by a Lisp expression, containing, if necessary, references (paths) to other features in the FD being unified. The unification behavior of a **test** feature is to ensure that the predicate is true in the FD resulting from the unification. In practice, the Lisp expression is evaluated at the end of the unification and when it fails, the unifier backtracks.[15] At a more abstract level, a **test** feature enforces a complex constraint on an FD. For example, the following grammar fragment insures that the themes of P and Q are non disjoint:[16]

```
((cat connective)
 ...
 (Test (FD-intersection @(^ ^ P Th) @(^ ^ Q Th))))
```

Partial specifications on values: The **test** feature allows us to achieve an acceptable level of performance for testing complex constraints. Unfortunately, it also has a major drawback: the regular unification algorithm does not make a distinction between testing a constraint and adding a constraint. When testing against a non specified value, the unifier can just add the constraint. The **test** feature, in contrast, does not indicate how the constraint it enforces should be added. In other words, **test** is not bidirectional.

14.5.2   Summary

We argue in this paper that the FUG formalism is a natural choice for the task of text generation. As the scope of text generation extends to include more decisions, of different nature, using different information, the problem of order of decision making becomes more acute. We have distinguished two aspects of this problem: internal - how decisions interact within the surface realization component - and external - how decisions in the surface realization component interact with its environment. Because language imposes arbitrarily complex constraints on any decision, these interactions can be quite complex. They cannot be handled by a module that is not be aware of the linguistic intricacies. Since constraints cannot always be strictly ordered, it is natural to let the linguistic component deal with interactions in the most flexible way.

We have illustrated how FUGs allow for that flexibility by examining the task of connective selection. FUGs allow for flexible internal order of decision

---

[15] A more efficient strategy to choose the moment when the constraint must be evaluated is being implemented.
[16] The symbol ʻ indicates that the following expression is a path referring to a value in the FD.

making, and provide tools for organizing the grammar without duplicating constraints, and allow a clear grouping of similar constraints to increase readability. They allow for flexible external order of decision because unification is bidirectional, and the constraints expressed in the grammar can both generate and test values.

BIBLIOGRAPHY

(Anscombre and Ducrot, 1983) J.C. Anscombre and O. Ducrot. *L'argumentation dans la langue.* Philosophie et langage. Pierre Mardaga, Bruxelles, 1983.

(Anscombre, 1973) J.C. Anscombre. Même le roi de France est sage. un essai de description sémantique. *Communications*, 20:40–82, 1973.

(Appelt, 1985) D.E. Appelt. *Planning English Sentences.* Cambridge University Press, Cambridge, England, 1985.

(Brachman, 1979) R. Brachman. On the epsitemological status of semantic networks. In N. Findler, editor, *Associative networks: representation and use of knowledge by computers.* Academic Press, NY, 1979.

(Danlos and Namer, 1988) L. Danlos and F. Namer. Morphology and cross dependencies in the synthesis of personal pronouns in romance languages. In *Proceedings of COLING-88*, Budapest, 1988.

(Danlos, 1987) L. Danlos. *The Linguistic Basis of Text Generation.* Cambridge University Press, Cambridge, England, 1987.

(Danlos, 1988) L. Danlos. Interaction of decisions in text generation: Some pronominalization issues. Unpubslihed report, 1988.

(Derr and McKeown, 1984) M. Derr and K. McKeown. Using focus to generate complex and simple sentences. In *Coling84*, Stanford, California, July 1984. COLING.

(Ducrot, 1983) O. Ducrot. *Le dire et le dit.* Le sens commun. Les editions de Minuit, Paris, 1983.

(Elhadad and McKeown, 1988) M. Elhadad and K.R. McKeown. What do you need to produce a 'but'. Technical Report CUCS-334-88, Columbia University, January 1988.

(Elhadad and McKeown, 1989) M. Elhadad and K.R. McKeown. A procedure for the selection of connectives in text, generation: How deep is the surface? Technical Report CUCS-419-89, Columbia University, 1989.

(Elhadad, 1988) M. Elhadad. The FUF functional unifier: User's manual. Technical Report CUCS-408-88, Columbia University, June 1988.

(Elhadad, 1989) M. Elhadad. Extended functional unification programmars. Technical Report CUCS-420-89, Columbia University, 1989.

(Fillmore and O'Connor, 1987) Paul Kay Fillmore, C.J. and M.C. O'Connor. Regularity and idiomacity in grammatical constructions: The case of *let alone*. Technical Report 48, Berkeley: UCB Cognitive Science Program, 1987.

(Finin, 1984) T. Finin. Documentation for the bottom-up parser (bup). Unpubslihed report, 1984.

(Fraser, 1971) Bruce Fraser. An analysis of *even* in english. In C.J. Fillmore and D.T. Langendoen, editors, *Studies in linguistics semantics*, pages 151–178. Holt, Rinehart and Winston, New York, 1971.

(Goldman, 1975) N.M. Goldman. Conceptual generation. In R.C. Schank, editor, *Conceptual Information Processing*. North Holland, Amsterdam, 1975.

(Penman, 1988) The Penman Natural Language Generation Group. *The Penman User Guide*. USC-ISI, 4676 Admiralty Way, Marina Del Rey, CA 90292, December 1988. Draft.

(Halliday, 1985) M.A.K Halliday. *An Introduction to Functional Grammar*. Edward Arnold, London, 1985.

(Henning, 1983) Nolke Henning. *Les adverbes paradigmatisants: Fonction et analyse*. Etudes Romanes de l'Université de Copenhague. Universite de Copenhague, 1983. Revue Romane, special issue 23.

(Horn, 1969) L. Horn. A presuppositional analysis of @iOnly and *even*. In *Papers from the Fifth Regional Meeting*, pages 98–107. Chicago Linguistics Society, 1969.

(Hovy, 1985) E.H. Hovy. Integrating text planning and production in generation. In *Proceedings of the 9th IJCAI*, pages 848–851. IJCAI, 1985.

(Iordanskaja L. and A., 1990) Kittredge R. Iordanskaja L. and Polguere A. Lexical selection and paraphrase in a meaning-text generation model. In *Natural Language Generation in Artificial Intelligence and Computational Linguistics*, (this volume). Paris, Swartout, Mann (Eds). Kluwer Academic Publishers, Norwell, MA.

(Jacobs, 1985) P. S. Jacobs. *A knowledge-based approach to language production*. PhD thesis, Univ. of California, Berkeley, 1985.

(Karttunen, 1984) L. Karttunen. Features and values. In *Coling84*, pages 28–33, Stanford, California, July 1984. COLING.

(Kay, 1979) M. Kay. Functional grammar. In *Proceedings of the 5th meeting of the Berkeley Linguistics Society*. Berkeley Linguistics Society, 1979.

(Kay, 1987) Paul Kay. Even. University of California, Berkeley, July 1987.

(Kukich, 1983) K. Kukich. Design of a knowldege based text generator. In *Proceedings of the 21st ACL Conference*. ACL, 1983.

(Mann and Matthiessen, 1983) W.C. Mann and C. Matthiessen. Nigel: a systemic grammar for text generation. Technical Report ISI/RR-83-105, USC/ISI, 1983.

(Mann, 1983) W.C. Mann. An Overview of the Nigel Text Generation Grammar. Technical Report ISI/RR-83-113, USC/ISI, April 1983.

(Matthiessen, 1981) C.M.I.M. Matthiessen. A grammar and a lexicon for a text production system. In *Proceedings of the 19th Conference of the ACL*, pages 49–53. Association for Computational Linguistics, 1981.

(McDonald and Pustejovsky, 1985) D.D. McDonald and J.D. Pustejovsky. Description-directed natural language generation. In *Proceedings of the 9th IJCAI*, pages 799–805. IJCAI, 1985.

(McDonald and Pustejovsky, 1987) D.D. McDonald and J.D. Pustejovsky. Tags as a grammatical formalism for generation. In *Proceedings of the European ACL*, pages 94–103. ACL, 1987.

(McDonald, 1988) D.D McDonald. *On the place of words in the generation process*. In *Natural Language Generation in Artificial Intelligence and Computational Linguistics*, (this volume). Paris, Swartout, Mann (Eds). Kluwer Academic Publishers, Norwell, MA.

(McKeown and Paris, 1987) K.R. McKeown and C.L. Paris. Functional unification grammar revisited. In *Proceedings of the ACL conference*, pages 97–103. ACL, July 1987.

(McKeown, 1985) K.R. McKeown. *Text Generation: Using Discourse Strategies and Focus Constraints to Generate Natural Language Text*. Cambridge University Press, Cambridge, England, 1985.

(Paris, 1987) C.L. Paris. *The Use of Explicit User models in Text Generation: Tailoring to a User's level of expertise*. PhD thesis, Columbia University, 1987. To be published by Frances Pinter Publishers in the "Communication in Artificial intelligence" series, Steiner and Fawcett (Eds)

(Patten, 1988) T. Patten. *A systemic bridge*. Presented at the Workshop on Natural Language Generation, Catalina Island, 1988.

(Pereira and Warren., 1980) F.C.N. Pereira and Warren D.H.D. Definite clause grammars for language analysis - a survey of the formalism and a comparison with augmented transition networks. *Artificial Intelligence*, 13:231–278, 1980.

(Quirk, 1972) R. Quirk *et al.* *A Grammar of Contemporary English*. Longman, 1972.

(Raccah, 1987) P.Y. Raccah. Modelling argumentation and modelling <u>with</u> argumentation. *Argumentation*, 1987.

(Roulet, 1985) E. Roulet *et al* *L'articulation du discours en francais contemporain*. Berne, Lang, 1985.

(Rubinoff, 1988) R. Rubinoff. A cooperative model of strategy and tactics in generation. Presented at the Workshop on Natural Language Generation, Catalina Island, 1988.

(Sadock, 1981) J.M. Sadock. Almost. In P. Cole, editor, *Radical Pragmatics*, pages 257–271. Academic Press, New York, 1981.

(Shieber, 1986) S. Shieber. *An introduction to Unification-Based Approaches to Grammar*, volume 4 of *CSLI Lecture Notes*. University of Chicago Press, Chicago, Il, 1986.

(Sinclair and Coulthard, 1975) Sinclair and Coulthard. *Towards an Analysis of Discourse*. Oxford University Press, Oxford, England, 1975.

(Winograd, 1983) T. Winograd. *Language as a Cognitive Process*. Addison-Wesley, Reading, Ma., 1983.

(Woods, 1970) W.A. Woods. Transition network grammars for natural language analysis. *Communications of the ACM*, 13:591–606, 1970.

Index